The Movement for Black Lives

The Movement for Black Lives

Philosophical Perspectives

Edited by
BRANDON HOGAN, MICHAEL CHOLBI,
ALEX MADVA, AND BENJAMIN S. YOST

OXFORD
UNIVERSITY PRESS

Oxford University Press is a department of the University of Oxford. It furthers
the University's objective of excellence in research, scholarship, and education
by publishing worldwide. Oxford is a registered trade mark of Oxford University
Press in the UK and certain other countries.

Published in the United States of America by Oxford University Press
198 Madison Avenue, New York, NY 10016, United States of America.

© Oxford University Press 2021

All rights reserved. No part of this publication may be reproduced, stored in
a retrieval system, or transmitted, in any form or by any means, without the
prior permission in writing of Oxford University Press, or as expressly permitted
by law, by license, or under terms agreed with the appropriate reproduction
rights organization. Inquiries concerning reproduction outside the scope of the
above should be sent to the Rights Department, Oxford University Press, at the
address above.

You must not circulate this work in any other form
and you must impose this same condition on any acquirer.

Library of Congress Cataloging-in-Publication Data
Names: Hogan, Brandon, editor. | Cholbi, Michael, editor. | Madva, Alex, editor. |
Yost, Benjamin S. (Benjamin Schertz), editor.
Title: The movement for Black lives : philosophical perspectives / eds.,
Brandon Hogan, Michael Cholbi, Alex Madva, and Benjamin S. Yost.
Description: New York, NY : Oxford University Press, [2021] |
Includes bibliographical references and index.
Identifiers: LCCN 2021011724 (print) | LCCN 2021011725 (ebook) |
ISBN 9780197507780 (paperback) | ISBN 9780197507773 (hb) |
ISBN 9780197507803 (epub)
Subjects: LCSH: Black lives matter movement—Philosophy. |
Black power—United States—History. |
Civil rights movements—United States—History—21st century.
Classification: LCC E185.615 .M684 2021 (print) | LCC E185.615 (ebook) |
DDC 323.1196/073001—dc23
LC record available at https://lccn.loc.gov/2021011724
LC ebook record available at https://lccn.loc.gov/2021011725

DOI: 10.1093/oso/9780197507773.001.0001

Contents

Contributors   vii

Introduction   1

PART I: THE VALUE OF BLACK LIVES

1. What "Black Lives Matter" *Should* Mean   15
   Brandon Hogan

2. "And He Ate Jim Crow": Racist Ideology as False Consciousness   35
   Vanessa Wills

3. He Never Mattered: Poor Black Males and the Dark Logic of Intersectional Invisibility   59
   Tommy J. Curry

PART II: THEORIZING RACIAL JUSTICE

4. Reconsidering Reparations: The Movement for Black Lives and Self-Determination   93
   Olúfẹ́mi O. Táíwò

5. The Movement for Black Lives and Transitional Justice   116
   Colleen Murphy

PART III: THE LANGUAGE OF THE M4BL

6. Positive Propaganda and the Pragmatics of Protest   139
   Michael Randall Barnes

7. Value-Based Protest Slogans: An Argument for Reorientation   160
   Myisha Cherry

8. The Movement for Black Lives and the Language of Liberation   176
   Ian Olasov

PART IV: THE M4BL, ANTI-BLACK RACISM, AND PUNISHMENT

9. Can Capital Punishment Survive If Black Lives Matter? 199
   Michael Cholbi and Alex Madva

10. Sentencing Leniency for Black Offenders 218
    Benjamin S. Yost

PART V: STRATEGY AND SOLIDARITY

11. The Violence of Leadership in Black Lives Matter 243
    Dana Francisco Miranda

12. Speaking for, Speaking with, and Shutting up: Models of Solidarity and the Pragmatics of Truth Telling 263
    Mark Norris Lance

13. Sky's the Limit: A Case Study in Envisioning Real Anti-Racist Utopias 280
    Keyvan Shafiei

Index 301

Contributors

Michael Randall Barnes completed his PhD in the philosophy department at Georgetown University, writing his dissertation on how speech maintains oppression. He is currently a postdoctoral fellow at the Rotman Institute of Philosophy at Western University.

Myisha Cherry is Assistant Professor of Philosophy at the University of California, Riverside. Her research interests include the intersection of moral psychology and social and political philosophy. Cherry's work has appeared in scholarly journals such as *Hypatia* and *Critical Philosophy of Race*. She has also written for the *Los Angeles Times, Boston Review, Huffington Post, Salon*, and *New Philosopher Magazine*. Her books include *The Case for Rage* (Oxford, 2020), *The Moral Psychology of Anger* (coedited with Owen Flanagan), and *UnMuted: Conversations on Prejudice, Oppression, and Social Justice* (Oxford, 2019). She is also the host of the UnMute Podcast, where she interviews philosophers about the social and political issues of our day.

Michael Cholbi is Chair in Philosophy at the University of Edinburgh. He has published widely in ethical theory, practical ethics, and the philosophy of death and dying. His books include *Suicide: The Philosophical Dimensions* (Broadview, 2011), *Understanding Kant's Ethics* (Cambridge, 2016), and *Grief: A Philosophical Guide* (Princeton, forthcoming). He is the editor of several scholarly collections, including *Immortality and the Philosophy of Death* (Rowman and Littlefield, 2015); *Procreation, Parenthood, and Educational Rights* (Routledge, 2017); and *The Future of Work, Technology, and Basic Income* (Routledge, 2019). He is the coeditor of the textbook *Exploring the Philosophy of Death and Dying: Classic and Contemporary Perspectives* (Routledge, forthcoming). His work has also appeared in a number of scholarly journals, including *Ethics, Mind, Philosophical Studies, Philosophy and Phenomenological Research*, and *Oxford Studies in Normative Ethics*. In recent years, he has been an academic visitor at Australian National University, the University of Turku (Finland), and the Hastings Center. He is the founder of the International Association for the Philosophy of Death and Dying and serves on the editorial boards of the *Journal of Applied Philosophy, Social Theory and Practice, Ergo*, and the *Journal of the American Philosophical Association*. His current research interests include Kantian ethics, particularly respect for persons, equality, and rational agency; death and dying, including suicide and assisted dying, immortality, and grief; the ethics of work and labor; paternalism; and procreative and parental ethics.

Tommy J. Curry, Personal Chair in Africana Philosophy and Black Male Studies at the University of Edinburgh, is the author of *The Man-Not: Race, Class, Genre, and the Dilemmas of Black Manhood* (Temple, 2017), winner of the 2018 American Book Award. He also authored *Another White Man's Burden: Josiah Royce's Quest for a Philosophy of Racial Empire* (SUNY Press, 2018) and republished the forgotten philosophical works of William Ferris as *The Philosophical Treatise of William H. Ferris: Selected Readings from The African Abroad or, His Evolution in Western Civilization* (Rowman & Littlefield, 2016). He is the editor of the first book series dedicated to the study of Black males titled *Black Male Studies: A Series Exploring the Paradoxes of Racially Subjugated Males* with Temple University Press.

Brandon Hogan is Associate Professor of Philosophy at Howard University. He writes about legal punishment, racial justice, Hegel's political philosophy, and Wittgenstein's later philosophy. His work has appeared in *Contemporary Pragmatism*, *The Journal of Pan African Studies*, and the *Berkeley Journal of African American Law and Policy*. He earned a PhD from the University of Pittsburgh under the supervision of Robert Brandom and a JD from Harvard Law School.

Mark Norris Lance is Professor of Philosophy at Georgetown University. He has published two books and around forty articles in philosophy of language, epistemology, logic, metaethics, and applied political philosophy. He is also the cofounder, current codirector, and professor in the Program on Justice and Peace. He has served as national cochair of the Peace and Justice Studies Association and the Consortium on Peace Research Education and Development. He has also been an activist and organizer for over thirty years on a wide range of peace and social justice issues, speaking to audiences around the world and working directly with activist campaigns.

Alex Madva is Associate Professor of Philosophy and Director of the California Center for Ethics and Policy at Cal Poly Pomona. He coedited *An Introduction to Implicit Bias: Knowledge, Justice, and the Social Mind* (Routledge, 2020), and his work has appeared in journals, including *Noûs, Ethics, The Journal of Applied Philosophy, Pacific Philosophical Quarterly, Ergo, Wiley Interdisciplinary Reviews (WIREs): Cognitive Science*, and the *International Journal of STEM Education*. He has led numerous workshops and training sessions on bias, stereotype threat, and impostor syndrome for schools, courts, and wider audiences.

Dana Francisco Miranda is Assistant Professor of Philosophy and Faculty Fellow for the Applied Ethics Center at the University of Massachusetts Boston, as well as a Research Associate for the Philosophy Department at the University of Connecticut. He earned his doctorate in philosophy at the University of Connecticut in 2019 and his bachelor's in philosophy at Bard College. His research is in political philosophy, Africana philosophy, and psychosocial studies. His current book manuscript, *The Coloniality of Happiness*, investigates the philosophical significance of suicide, depression, and well-being for members of the African Diaspora. His most recent work has been published in *Entre Letras, Disegno, Cosmos and History: The Journal of Natural and Social Philosophy*, and *The APA Blog: Black Issues in Philosophy*. He also currently serves as the Secretary of Digital Outreach & Chair of Architectonics for the Caribbean Philosophical Association.

Colleen Murphy is the Roger and Stephany Joslin Professor of Law and Professor of Philosophy and Political Science at the University of Illinois at Urbana-Champaign, where she is also Director of the Women and Gender in Global Perspectives Program. She is associate editor for the *Journal of Ethics and Social Philosophy, Journal of Human Development and Capabilities*, and the *Journal of Moral Philosophy*. Professor Murphy is the author of *The Conceptual Foundations of Transitional Justice* (Cambridge, 2017), which received the North American Society for Social Philosophy Book Award, and *A Moral Theory of Political Reconciliation* (Cambridge, 2010).

Ian Olasov is a doctoral candidate in philosophy at the CUNY Graduate Center. His research focuses on the philosophy of language, moral theory, and social epistemology. He is also the founder and director of Brooklyn Public Philosophers, a philosophy event series for a general audience. His is the author of *The Answers: Questions, Stories, and Insights from the Ask a Philosopher Booth* (St. Martin's, 2020).

Keyvan Shafiei is a PhD candidate in the department of philosophy at Georgetown University. He is currently working on a dissertation on the ideological and cultural underpinnings of mass incarceration in the United States. In this work, Shafiei explores the origins of the development of mass incarceration by investigating the ways in which ideologies, cultures, and persons are coconstitutive, and the ways in which mass injustices develop out of the interactions and interconnections therein.

Olúfẹ́mi O. Táíwò is Assistant Professor of Philosophy at Georgetown University. He completed his PhD at University of California, Los Angeles. He works on ethical theory and social/political philosophy, drawing from anticolonial thought, German transcendental philosophy, and the Black radical tradition.

Vanessa Wills is a political philosopher, ethicist, educator, and activist working in Washington, DC, where she is Assistant Professor of Philosophy at The George Washington University. Her areas of specialization are moral, social, and political philosophy, nineteenth-century German philosophy (especially Karl Marx), and the philosophy of race. Her research is informed by her study of Marx's work, and she focuses on the ways in which economic and social arrangements can inhibit or promote the realization of values such as freedom, equality, and human development. Her recent publications include "Revolutionary Admiration" and "'Man Is the Highest Being for Man': Marx's Radical Irreligion."

Benjamin S. Yost is Professor of Philosophy, Adjunct at Cornell University; he was previously Professor of Philosophy at Providence College. His specializations include the philosophy of punishment, especially punishment and inequality, and Kant's practical philosophy. His book *Against Capital Punishment* was published with Oxford in 2019. Other published work appears in journals such as *Utilitas, Journal of the American Philosophical Association, Kantian Review*, and *Continental Philosophy Review*.

Introduction

The Movement for Black Lives (M4BL) has reshaped how Americans think about activism and shined a light on the ongoing problem of police violence against Black and Brown communities.[*] The Movement began with a passionate Facebook post in response to the acquittal of George Zimmerman for the murder of Trayvon Martin. The post's author, Alicia Garza, intended her post to be a "Love Letter to Black People." At the conclusion of her post, she writes, "Black people. I love you. I love us. Our lives matter." This line morphed into the slogan "Black lives matter," which, along with the help of activists Patrisse Cullors and Opal Tometi, was transformed into the Black Lives Matter organization (BLM).

In 2015, BLM joined forces with a coalition of over 150 activist organizations to form the M4BL. While the Movement's first target was police violence, the M4BL has expanded the scope of its activism, issuing a platform titled "A Vision for Black Lives: Policy Demands for Black Power, Freedom and Justice." The platform includes a call to abolish the death penalty and private prisons, a demand for reparations for American slavery, a demand for the retroactive decriminalization of drug-related offenses, and a proposal for large-scale wealth redistribution, among other things. In short, the Movement seeks to tear down all laws and policies that evince a lack of concern for Black Life.

The M4BL is also notable because it resists the notion that Black activist organizations must be headed by a charismatic leader. The Movement seeks to empower individuals and local groups to imagine solutions to problems facing Black people. In this way, the Movement is self-consciously egalitarian. Further, the Movement seeks to give voice to Black persons who have been historically marginalized even within Black spaces. These persons include Black women, and gay, lesbian, formerly incarcerated, poor, disabled, and trans members of the Black community. The M4BL seeks to be both democratic and inclusive.

[*] The editors would like to thank Amy Ramirez for her help preparing this volume for publication.

The Movement for Black Lives. Edited by: Brandon Hogan, Michael Cholbi, Alex Madva, and Benjamin S. Yost, Oxford University Press. © Oxford University Press 2021. DOI: 10.1093/oso/9780197507773.003.0001

Sadly, the work of the M4BL is just as necessary today as it was at its inception. In the spring of 2020, the world was again reminded that police officers often treat Black life as disposable. On March 13, 2020, Breonna Taylor was murdered in her apartment in Louisville, Kentucky, by police officers executing a no-knock warrant as part of a drug investigation. Believing that the plainclothes police officers were burglars, Taylor's boyfriend fired a warning shot as deterrence. The police officers proceeded to fire thirty-two rounds into the apartment, killing Taylor only. Taylor was innocent, at home, and in her bed. No drugs were found. No officers were charged for her death.

On May 25, 2020, George Floyd was arrested for attempting to use a counterfeit $20 bill. During the arrest, Minneapolis police officer Derek Chauvin pinned Floyd to the ground, resting his knee on Floyd's neck for over eight minutes. Other officers stood by and did nothing. Floyd pleaded with the officer and called out for his mother, to no avail. Floyd later died due to injuries sustained during the arrest. The officers were filmed as onlookers pleaded with them to help Floyd. They did not care. Unlike the Taylor case, officers were charged in Floyd's death. Chauvin has been charged with second-degree murder, among other charges, and the onlooking officers have been charged with aiding and abetting. Hopefully, justice will be served in this case, though it is statistically unlikely.

Taylor and Floyd are the latest names to be added to a long list of Black people who were unjustly killed by the police. Until real changes are made, the list will continue to grow. Taylor and Floyd also serve as reminders that the work of the M4BL is far from over. Floyd's death in particular sparked worldwide protests, led to the creation of Black Lives Matter Plaza in Washington, DC, and brought greater public attention to the work of the organizations that comprise the M4BL.

The inspiring work of the M4BL has garnered much scholarly attention. Currently, there are over one hundred academic articles on the BLM organization alone. The Movement has also given rise to several academic books. These works include Christopher Lebron's *The Making of Black Lives Matter: A Brief History of an Idea*, Keeanga-Yamahtta Taylor's *From #BlackLivesMatter to Black Liberation*, and Barbara Ransby's *Making All Black Lives Matter: Reimagining Freedom in the Twenty-First Century*. While each book provides a take on the Movement's practical activities and theoretical underpinnings, these works primarily offer a historical analysis of BLM and the M4BL.

While contributions to this volume draw on the rich scholarship on BLM and the M4BL, this work offers critical *philosophical* engagements with the themes, platforms, language, and organizational model of the M4BL. Chapters in this volume address the context in which the Movement exists, and the contributors aim to offer critiques, appraisals, and insights based in their training in academic philosophy. The M4BL is deeply philosophical, and this volume seeks to respect and participate in the thoughtful philosophical discussion began by the Movement. To be clear, the authors in this volume do not claim to speak for the Movement nor do they presuppose that they have a better understanding of the Movement than those who participate on the ground. We view the M4BL as a dynamic, novel, and necessary social movement. The contributors only seek to think philosophically about the Movement as we do about other social phenomena. As such, they hope that participants in the Movement will engage philosophically with *their* work. The conversation should by symmetrical. Indeed, as an act of good faith and solidarity, any proceeds from the sale of this volume will be donated to causes supported by the Movement.

This volume is organized into five parts: Part I: The Value of Black Lives; Part II: Theorizing Racial Justice; Part III: The Language of the M4BL; Part IV: The M4BL, Anti-Black Racism, and Punishment; and Part V: Strategy and Solidarity. Naturally, themes from each part overlap, and the philosophers in this volume can easily be put into conversation with one another. As such, this work is organized so as to initiate a fruitful and comprehensive philosophical discussion about the M4BL. The remainder of this introduction will provide an overview of the contents of each section.

Part I: The Value of Black Lives

This first section addresses the ideological and theoretical underpinnings of the M4BL. Persons appear to disagree about the meaning of "Black lives matter." Some take the slogan to mean "Only Black lives matter," while others take it to mean "Black lives matter, too." In Chapter 1, "What 'Black Lives Matter' *Should* Mean," Brandon Hogan examines the meaning of the slogan, focusing on the assumptions about social reality undertaken by persons who say "Black lives matter." After reviewing several possible interpretations of the slogan, he concludes that there is no consensus about the meaning of "Black lives matter." He then turns to the question of what the slogan *should* mean, assuming that an attractive interpretation of "Black lives matter" should be both metaphysically plausible and useful to activists. He posits that the lives of Black people matter only in relation to a given population. As such, Black lives matter to some, but not to others. Thus, the slogan both expresses a truth (relative to some) and an aspiration (relative to others). He argues that both interpretations of the slogan are socially useful. It is useful, he argues, for activists to believe that Black lives do matter because this belief is a source of pride and inspiration. Hogan also argues that activists would do well to recognize that Black lives do not matter to some. This latter interpretation, Hogan argues, justifies certain forms of direct, nonsentimental activism.

One of the M4BL's central aims is to challenge the dominant systems of belief and value that reinforce the subordination of Black people. In other words, the M4BL aims to transform *racist ideology* root and branch. But this is, of course, no easy task. In Chapter 2, "'And He Ate Jim Crow': Racist Ideology as False Consciousness," Vanessa Wills argues that understanding the intransigence of racial oppression requires a deeper appreciation of racist ideology. Drawing from Marx and Engels, Wills argues that racist ideology is a form of *false consciousness*, which represents the world accurately at a very superficial level, but misrepresents the deeper facts that underlie the superficial appearances. Wills's analysis insightfully distinguishes between two types of racist ideology: (1) *first-order* false consciousness, or the inaccurate beliefs related to objective social arrangements (e.g., "this group is impoverished because they are lazy," rather than "this group is impoverished because they are oppressed"); and (2) *second-order* false consciousness, or the inaccurate beliefs about how our first-order beliefs are formed (e.g., "I believe this group is lazy because I am free-thinking rational person," rather than "I believe this group is lazy because I want to believe that the system is meritocratic and the world is fair"). The practical upshots of Wills's analysis are that we must both directly undermine oppressive social conditions and develop interventions that dislodge lay theories about the causes of race-based disadvantage.

Tommy J. Curry represents a dissenting voice. He is critical of BLM activists in particular. In Chapter 3, "He Never Mattered: Poor Black Males and the Dark Logic of Intersectional Invisibility," Curry argues that problematic ideological trends have caused BLM activists and their sympathizers to unjustifiably marginalize or downplay the unique struggles faced by Black men. BLM began as a reaction to the unjustified killings of Black men at the hands of police officers. As Curry explains, Black men are still more likely to face police violence than men or women in any other demographic. Curry contends that BLM activists have taken on a version of intersectional theory that contends that persons who suffer multiple forms of oppression (e.g., persons targeted by racism *and* heterosexism *and* classism) are rendered invisible in social justice movements. Because of this, Curry claims, activists seek to decenter the oppression of Black men. But, he claims, this decentering does not reflect the reality of Black male oppression. He further contends that this move has occurred because activists have become divorced from the Black communities they claim to serve, instead seeking praise and profits from white philanthropists. Curry calls on activists to move away from ideology and profit-seeking to focus on empirical findings about the nature and magnitude of anti-Black violence.

Part II: Theorizing Racial Justice

Chapters in this section engage directly with the vision of racial justice outlined in the M4BL platform. In Chapter 4, "Reconsidering Reparations: The Movement for Black Lives and Self-Determination," Olúfẹ́mi O. Táíwò provides a philosophical appraisal of the M4BL's call for reparations for American slavery and extends this discussion to address the issue of reparations for African colonization. Táíwò points out that many theorists justify reparations as a form of restorative justice. He contends that these sorts of views fail either because they operate on an underdeveloped notion of harm or because they fail to fully justify reparations, instead of, say, apologies, as the correct remedial measure. Táíwò instead argues for a forward-looking justification for reparations. Reparations, for Táíwò, provide historically oppressed groups with material resources that further the aim of group self-determination, that is, the tools necessary to take control of their own lives. This justification, Táíwò claims, is implicit in the M4BL policy platform.

In Chapter 5, "The Movement for Black Lives and Transitional Justice," Colleen Murphy proposes that the Movement be conceptualized as an effort at transitional justice. Transitional justice is the process of dealing with wrongdoing committed in the context of conflict or repression for the sake of recognizing victims, holding perpetrators to account, and, most fundamentally, contributing to societal transformation. Among the measures societies use to advance transitional justice are truth commissions, reparations programs, amnesty provisions, criminal trials, and memorials. Transitional justice succeeds to the extent that it transforms the political relationships among citizens and between citizens and their government. Contrasting US anti-racist movements in the Jim Crow era with similar movements in apartheid-era South Africa, Murphy highlights how the latter, unlike the former, succeeded in making the redressing of past racial wrongs a constitutive element of their social reforms. The M4BL thus operates in a contemporary American context wherein there remains widespread denial about the nature and scope of wrongdoing during Jim Crow, as well as inattention to ongoing structural inequality. Murphy sees the Movement as a catalyst for transitional justice within the United States, drawing attention to how racial facts continue to perpetuate inequality and human rights abuses. The Movement's focus on transitional justice has already borne fruit in greater political attention to racial reparations, the establishment of governmental commissions on lynching, and memorials and museums focused on slavery and mass incarceration.

Part III: The Language of the M4BL

After the emphasis in Part II on foundational questions of racial justice, Part III turns to the role of language in the M4BL. Three authors offer different perspectives on the nature and significance of the slogans and counter-slogans associated with the Movement, exploring, for example, the distinctive aims and consequences of chanting (or tweeting) "Black lives matter" in contrast to chanting "All lives matter" or "Blue lives matter."

One might think that all of these slogans are mere *propaganda*, public statements that primarily function to either undermine or undergird democratic ideals (rather than to, say, give reasons or add new information to our shared conversation). Thus, in Chapter 6, "Positive Propaganda and the Pragmatics of Protest," Michael Randall Barnes explores whether the "Black lives matter" slogan might simply be a "good" kind of propaganda, less about asserting information about Black lives than about pushing our nation toward justice. Taking Jason Stanley's *How Propaganda Works* as a point of departure, Barnes ultimately disagrees that "#BlackLivesMatter" is mere propaganda, and instead interprets it as a speech act of political protest. On Barnes's view—which generalizes to the moral and epistemic functions of protest more broadly—slogans like this foreground the *moral authority* of the protesters and challenge the *unjust authority* of the powerful.

Philosophers interested in social movement slogans often focus on their communicative nature, in particular the hermeneutical failures that arise in discourse. One of the most well-known of these is found in the infamous "All lives matter" retort to "Black lives matter." In Chapter 7, "Value-Based Protest Slogans: An Argument for Reorientation," Myisha Cherry contends that while highlighting and criticizing such failures provides insight into social movement slogans as a communicative practice, doing so risks placing too much importance on outgroup understandings. For Cherry, this emphasis on outgroups is misguided because social movement slogans need not gain external uptake in order to perform their functions. Cherry also worries that an outgroup emphasis can cause unproductive distractions for users. For her, protest slogans are first and foremost tools for their *users*. She urges a shift in focus to what these slogans (e.g., "Black is beautiful" and "Black lives matter") do for users, as well as what they demand from users and enable them to express. Among other things, "value-based protest slogans," as Cherry calls them, provide affirmation and comfort as well as moral and political guidelines for their users. As such, value-based protest slogans can successfully perform their key functions regardless of their uptake by nonusers.

Like Barnes and Cherry, Ian Olasov addresses the distinctive communicative tactics of the Movement. In Chapter 8, "The Movement for Black Lives and the Language of Liberation," Olasov observes that the Movement's tactics are continuous with those deployed in historical anti-racist, environmental, economic justice, and anti-war movements, including street protests, chants such as "No justice, no peace," and the incorporation of African-American Vernacular English. However, the Movement also uses several novel communicative tools. These include the online hashtag #BlackLivesMatter, videos of police violence, the naming of the dead, and what Olasov calls "stereotype engineering," wherein Movement supporters utilize known idioms (such as "white supremacist") in accordance with their literal meaning but in ways that challenge the associations surrounding those idioms (for example, using "white supremacist" to refer not only to members of overtly racist groups such as the Klan but to liberals who blame mass Black incarceration on features of Black culture). On Olasov's analysis, these novel tools respond to the distinctive challenges that Keeanga-Yamahtta Taylor has argued the Movement faces when compared to similar social movements. The Movement advances a systemic critique of long-standing institutions and practices, particularly in the United States, a critique that casts doubt on the popular embrace of color-blind policies, the trust in police and judicial institutions, and the entanglement of race with opposition to social welfare and support for mass incarceration. While these communicative tools have limits, Olasov understands them as an attempt to generate a new "language of liberation."

Part IV: The M4BL, Anti-Black Racism, and Punishment

The M4BL has been marked by a sustained focus on issues of criminal justice, including police brutality, the "criminalization" of blackness, and the harsh civil penalties and criminal sentences doled out to Black communities. As a result, the M4BL has demanded profound and radical reforms, with some members calling for the wholesale abolition of prisons. The two chapters in this section explore the relationships between the M4BL and criminal justice in greater depth.

In Chapter 9, "Can Capital Punishment Survive If Black Lives Matter?," Michael Cholbi and Alex Madva defend the Movement's claim that the death penalty is a "racist practice" that "devalues black lives" and ought to be abolished. They begin by surveying the jurisprudential history of race and capital punishment in the United States, noting that courts have occasionally expressed worries about racial injustice but have usually called for reform rather than abolition. Cholbi and Madva argue, however, that racial discrimination in capital contexts flows in part from implicit biases related to race, criminality, and violence. The body of research on implicit bias suggests that court-mandated reforms have and will continue to fail to remediate racial discrimination in capital punishment. Cholbi and Madva further argue that traditional debates about capital punishment have been overly individualistic, narrowly focused on the justice of the practice for particular defendants and victims. By contrast, drawing from the M4BL's *group-centered* approach, Cholbi and Madva investigate the justice of the practice for the community as a whole, and they claim that the case for abolition rests on understanding Black Americans *as a class* subject to bias and thereby not accorded equal status under the law.

However, calls for the abolition of capital punishment, or prisons more generally, lead to what Benjamin S. Yost calls the "decarceration dilemma." In Chapter 10, "Sentencing Leniency for Black Offenders," Yost seeks to resolve this dilemma. The M4BL's platform urges an end to policing and punishment "as we know them." This exhortation responds to the well-documented racial disparities that infect the American criminal justice system root and branch. Decarceration movements aim to reduce both the intensity and scope of policing and imprisonment. But, as Yost points out, letting violent offenses go unpunished leaves Black communities vulnerable. Wholesale penal abolition thus threatens to undermine the rights and liberties of Black Americans. Hence the dilemma: the most straightforward way to remedy the racial injustice of punishment imposes injustices of its own. After discussing how Tommie Shelby and Christopher Lewis attempt to resolve the dilemma, Yost lays out his procedural alternative, which he contends has advantages over Shelby and Lewis's substantive, culpability-based approach. Yost's view relies on the principle of expanded asymmetry, which holds that it is better to underpunish than overpunish. This principle obtains only under conditions of sentencing uncertainty; thus, Yost makes the case that virtually all trials of Black offenders meet this condition. If this effort is successful, he concludes, sentencing authorities are obliged to treat Black offenders leniently, though need not forgo punishment altogether.

Part V: Strategy and Solidarity

Part V concludes the volume by examining the M4BL's forward-looking strategies for social change. One of the most striking departures of the M4BL from prior racial justice movements is its collective refusal to anoint figurehead leaders who purport to "speak for" the interests of the entire community. As a result, the Movement is often criticized for being "leaderless." But members of the Movement reject this characterization. As the Founder of the Pasadena Chapter of #BlackLivesMatter, Jasmine Abdullah Richards, explains, "This is a leader-full movement. We empower each other. If we just have one leader then that depletes that person of all their resources, their energy and everything. But if we have more than one person then, when I fall I have this person and this person on the right and left of me to pick me up and give me some of their energy." In Chapter 11, "The Violence of Leadership in Black Lives Matter," Dana Francisco Miranda explains and defends the Movement's alternative "leader-full" model, which replaces traditional hierarchical forms of leadership with more collaborative, decentralized, and democratized organizational structures and practices. Miranda draws from work by Barbara Ransby, Patrisse Khan-Cullors, and Frantz Fanon to contrast decentralized Black liberation movements—which boast an abundance of locally situated leaders—from their centralized leadership forebears. The leader-full model, Miranda argues, represents a viable alternative to group accountability, service, and collective well-being.

Using concepts from the philosophy of language, Mark Norris Lance, in Chapter 12, "Speaking for, Speaking with, and Shutting up: Models of Solidarity and the Pragmatics of Truth Telling," provides three distinct models of how those who are not members of an oppressed group can express solidarity with that group or advocate for its political goals. Lance is particularly concerned with the pragmatics of assertions that nonmembers make, that is, with how assertions intersect with facts about who makes the assertions, the language in which the assertions are couched, and the institutional context in which the assertions are made. The norms applicable to assertions about the M4BL made by white academics such as Lance will not be the same as the norms applicable to equivalent assertions made by Black activists allied with the Movement, for example. Inattention to such norms, Lance argues, can result in harm to the oppressed groups or to their causes due to "structural epistemic violence." Lance's three models of solidarity engagement are "speakingfor" an oppressed community, "speakingwith" members of an oppressed community, and "shuttingup" so as to cede the discourse to the testimony of the affected members of the oppressed group. Each of these can be defensible in particular contexts, but "speakingfor" and "speakingwith" have negative pragmatic effects that, according to Lance, must be taken into account in all speech contexts.

Many social and political theorists are openly hostile to utopian theorizing, such as the vision of racial justice outlined in the M4BL platform. In Chapter 13, "Sky's the Limit: A Case Study in Envisioning Real Anti-Racist Utopias," Keyvan Shafiei attempts to vindicate the claim that utopias can, and should, inform attempts to carry out programs of radical change. But on his view, social and political organizing has to be grounded in *realisticutopian* visions, even when it is responding to deeply intractable issues like systemic racial injustice. Refining Erik Olin Wright's concept of realistic utopia and incorporating Elizabeth Anderson's depiction of social movements as offering unique experiments in living morally, Shafiei argues that realistic utopian visions highlight the potential for radical change and force us to acknowledge the structural contestability of the boundaries of the possible. The M4BL serves as a valuable case study in how we can experiment with realistic utopias. For Shafiei, the M4BL is an experiment in transformative politics, one which draws on the resources of the present but also calls for strategizing about new forms of organizing and activism that move us beyond the constraints of what is presently feasible.

This volume stems from both an admiration and a desire to think deeply about the work of the M4BL. This work should be viewed as a sustained engagement with the philosophical thought initiated by the Movement. Indeed, both the Movement's platform and this collection are a part of a larger and older conversation about the nature of justice and equality for Black Americans and other oppressed groups. Further, while our contributors may disagree about substantive issues, this volume is rooted in the belief that Black lives do matter and the hope that philosophy can play a role in the struggle for Black liberation.

PART I
THE VALUE OF BLACK LIVES

1
What "Black Lives Matter" *Should* Mean

Brandon Hogan

"Black lives matter" is both a slogan and a movement. The slogan traces its origins to Alicia Garza's impassioned response to the 2013 acquittal of George Zimmerman for the murder of Trayvon Martin. Martin was an innocent Black teen who was killed by Zimmerman, a racist vigilante. Prosecutors in Sanford, Florida, seemed reluctant to bring charges against Zimmerman. After a lackluster effort by the state prosecutor, Zimmerman was acquitted by a mostly white jury. To many Black Americans, Zimmerman's acquittal was a clear sign that Black lives were not valuable. Responding to this sentiment, Garza posted a message on Facebook that concluded "Black people. I love you. I love us. Our lives matter" (Cobb 2016).

Patrisse Cullors, a friend of Garza's, created the hashtag #BlackLivesMatter as a rewrite of the last three words of Garza's post. Cullors and Garza later contacted fellow activist Opal Tometi to discuss ways of organizing around the theme of police violence. The slogan itself gained increased popularity and became the name of a movement after the killing of Mike Brown in Ferguson, Missouri. Brown, an unarmed teen, was gunned down by Ferguson police officer Darren Wilson. According to eyewitnesses, Brown raised his hands in surrender before he was shot. Black Lives Matter now names a social justice organization that is part of a larger coalition of activist organizations, the Movement for Black Lives.

"Black lives matter" is used as a hashtag, a rallying cry, and appears on t-shirts, flags, and signs across the world. The slogan bears a striking structural similarity to slogans used by past Black activists. Consider "I AM a man," which was employed by striking Black sanitation workers in Memphis in 1968. Consider also "We shall overcome," the title of a protest song and a chant used by civil rights activists in the 1950s and 1960s. These slogans resemble "Black lives matter" in that they appear to be straightforward declarations but can also be read as aspirational claims. "We shall overcome" illustrates this structure most straightforwardly. It could be that protesters

Brandon Hogan, *What "Black Lives Matter" Should Mean* In: *The Movement for Black Lives.* Edited by: Brandon Hogan, Michael Cholbi, Alex Madva, and Benjamin S. Yost, Oxford University Press. © Oxford University Press 2021. DOI: 10.1093/oso/9780197507773.003.0002

expressed the belief that it is an established fact that they will overcome racial oppression. This interpretation is buttressed by the fact that many civil rights leaders were Christians and that "We shall overcome" has its origins in gospel music. If overcoming is guaranteed by God, then one can easily understand "We shall overcome" as a straightforward factual claim.

However, we know that civil rights activists in the 1950s and 1960s faced daunting obstacles. Because overcoming was far from certain, we have to believe that many activists understood this. Given this, one can also interpret the slogan as an aspiration to overcome racial oppression. That is, one can understand the slogan as a hopeful claim, as a way to affirm one's actions in the face of danger and uncertainty. On this is reading, "We shall overcome" means something like "We will act with the firm hope that our actions will not be in vain." Here, overcoming is far from an established fact.

"I AM a man" admits of similar alternative interpretations. On the surface, this slogan also appears to be a straightforward assertion of fact. One who employs the slogan informs his audience that he is a man. In this way, "I AM a man" is similar to the Cartesian declaration of existence, for example. Descartes claims that "I am, I exist" is necessarily true when uttered by himself or another (Descartes 1996: 17). For Descartes, a declaration of existence is necessarily factual. We know, however, that the sanitation worker's declaration of manhood carries a significance not found in the Cartesian claim. In this context, a declaration of manhood is a declaration that one deserves to be treated as a man. Thus, on this reading, "I AM a man" does aim to express a fact, but not a fact about one's gender. The slogan aims to express a moral fact, that the declarant deserves to be treated with a certain amount of dignity.

However, the fact that the slogan was part of a protest points to an alternative, more forward-looking or aspirational interpretation. The slogan was directed at the city of Memphis. The sanitation workers believed that they were not being treated with dignity and went on strike to demand better working conditions. Thus, they had an aspiration, a goal. The slogan could express not an established fact about what men deserve, but a demand to be treated with dignity. On this interpretation, "I AM a man" means, roughly "I have a conception of how I would like to be treated that stems from my understanding of manhood. I refuse to work until you act in accord with this conception." In a sense, on this interpretation, the slogan is an ultimatum to the city of Memphis: treat us with dignity or pay the price. On this interpretation, the slogan is more confrontational and less metaphysically weighty. The declarant isn't making claims about moral facts, but about what he is willing to tolerate.

The slogans "We shall overcome" and "I AM a man" admit of distinct interpretations, one straightforwardly factual, one more aspirational. "Black lives matter" follows this pattern. Again, on the surface, "Black lives matter" appears to be a value claim, namely, the claim that there are many things that matter and that Black lives are among those things. Thus, this interpretation entails a version of moral realism, the metaphysical view that moral facts exist independent of human beliefs or perceptions. On this interpretation, "Black lives matter" is a reminder to those who disregard, degrade, and take Black life. The declarant, on this interpretation, expresses the idea that many Americans, including Black Americans, have forgotten that Black people are deserving of respect, that their lives are valuable. The moral claim that Black lives matter is treated as a foundational truth.

But "Black lives matter" is a protest chant. Members of various Black Lives Matter organizations publicly declare that Black lives matter at demonstrations, protests, and on social media. The targets of these declarations are often individuals and groups that treat Black life as expendable. Most prominently, law enforcement is the target of the Black lives matter declaration.[1] Thus, one could understand "mattering" in this context as a way of being treated. To matter is to be treated with dignity and respect. Black life did not matter to Zimmerman and Wilson. We could understand "Black lives matter" as a demand that police officers and policymakers treat Black lives and white lives with equal regard. Here, the slogan is a demand and an aspiration. Black Lives Matter activists, on this interpretation, claim that Black lives matter in order to push others to change their attitudes and actions toward Black people. Here, the slogan entails fewer metaphysical commitments. Mattering is treated not as a moral fact, but as an attitude and form of treatment.

Given that each protest slogan I discuss is similarly ambiguous, we are naturally led to ask which interpretation should be preferred. Should these protest slogans be understood as expressing facts or aspirations? A satisfactory interpretation of a protest slogan will be both metaphysically plausible and socially useful. That is, the interpretation should not be out of touch with reality or the aims of the activist who uses the slogan. In this chapter, I attempt to provide such an interpretation. While the focus of this chapter will

---

[1] See Chapters 6, 7, and 8, this volume, for alternative interpretations.

be "Black lives matter," the conclusions I argue for apply to "We shall overcome" and "I AM a man." Thus, the claims I make in this chapter should help us to think more clearly about the meanings of past civil rights slogans.

There seems to be no scholarly or popular consensus about what "Black lives matter" means. Given this, I argue that we should understand mattering as a relationship between a person and a person or a person and a thing. Black lives matter to some and do not matter to others. I believe that this take on "Black lives matter" is metaphysically plausible. Both the matter-of-fact interpretation and the aspirational interpretation are true, relative to a set of persons. I argue further that both interpretations are socially usually, depending on context. In establishing these claims, I argue that other existing and possible interpretations of "Black lives matter" are either metaphysically implausible or not socially useful.

1. What does "Black lives matter" mean?

In this section, I discuss how activists and scholars have understood "Black lives matter" to better situate my interpretive suggestion. Garza's statements about the meaning of the slogan seem to be in tension with one another. Philosophers Luvell Anderson and Ashley Atkins provide consistent interpretations of "Black lives matter," but they do not delve into the metaphysical underpinnings of the slogan. Finally, political theorists Jonathan Havercroft and David Owen come closer to taking a stance on the metaphysics of "Black lives matter," but their interpretation would likely be rejected by Black Lives Matter activists. I conclude that based on resources provided by scholars and activists, it is not at all clear what "Black lives matter" means.

In an *n+1* magazine article "A Love Note to Our Folks," Garza discusses the origins and meaning of "Black lives matter." About her Facebook post following the Zimmerman verdict, she writes:

> I was basically sending love notes to black people and saying, "We're enough. We are enough, and we don't deserve to die, and we don't deserve to be shot down in the streets like dogs because somebody else is fucking scared of us. And our presence is important, and we matter. Our lives matter, black lives matter." (Garza and Kauffman 2015)

Here Garza understands herself as making factual claims about the importance of Black lives and what Black people deserve. Of course, Garza herself may not be explicitly committed to some version of moral realism, but she appears to believe that the issue of whether Black lives matter is settled not by individual attitudes, but by facts about human dignity that would be true whether or not anyone took them to be true.

Later, Garza discusses the creation of a Black Lives Matter Facebook page along with Cullors and Tometi. She explains that the Facebook page was designed for activists and those sympathetic to the cause to share their ideas, stories, and collaborate. Garza writes, "[w]e were really asking people to share with us what they were doing to build a world where Black lives matter" (Garza 2015). This claim about the aim of the Facebook page seems to contradict Garza's sentiments about her original Facebook post and the meaning of "Black lives matter." If Garza's implicit moral realism is correct, then there is no need to build a world where Black lives matter since we already live in that world. But if our actions can determine whether Black lives matter—that is, if facts about human worth are socially constructed—then Garza's implicit moral realism is simply false.

Garza could be drawing a distinction between the fact that Black lives matter and the failure of some to recognize that fact. So, for Garza, it can be the case that Black people deserve respect and dignity, but that some fail to treat Black communities as important and worthy of esteem. Conversely, Garza could have in mind that while Black lives matter to some, they do not matter to all. On this interpretation, Black lives matter in that Black people and others treat Black life as worthy of esteem. The mattering, so to speak, is a social fact. Garza may take it that the aim of Black Lives Matter is to make it the case that all individuals and institutions treat Black life as worthy of recognition.

In sum, Garza appears to contradict herself in claiming that the importance of Black life is established outside of individual attitudes and social institutions and also that activists must work to make it the case that Black lives matter. We can resolve this tension by attributing a version of moral realism to Garza, interpreting the claim that we should work to make Black lives matter as consistent with realism. Or we could also resolve the tension by attributing a social construction view to Garza, interpreting the seemingly realist claim in a constructivist manner. To be fair, Garza's philosophical/metaphysical commitments are at most implicit. I claim, though, that it is unclear which metaphysical picture best fits her explicit claims. Thus, it is unclear how she understands the meaning of "Black lives matter."

While Garza's stance on the meaning of "Black lives matter" is not clear, Luvell Anderson provides a relatively straightforward explanation of the meaning of the slogan. In "Hermeneutical Impasses," he writes "when members of the movement chant 'Black lives matter,' they view themselves as declaring that Black people should be treated with the same value and respect as others" (Anderson 2017: 1). Anderson believes that "Black lives matter" is a moral claim primarily directed at others. He believes that those who employ the slogan are primarily making claims about how they should be treated, not metaphysical claims about which persons matter, objectively. Anderson is primarily concerned with understanding how people come to misinterpret "Black lives matter." He recognizes the slogan as a moral claim, a demand, but he does not explicitly commit to a view about the implicit metaphysical commitments entailed by "Black lives matter."

Ashley Atkins also does not take a stance on the metaphysics of "Black lives matter." She believes that popular interpretations of "Black lives matter" often miss the larger point of the slogan. Some respond to the slogan by claiming that all lives matter, such that Black lives need not be singled out. Those who respond in this way understand "Black lives matter" to mean "*Only* Black lives matter." This, of course, is a mistake. In response to those who assert that all lives matter, some defenders of "Black lives matter" claim that "Black lives matter" really means "Black lives matter, too." Atkins dismisses this second interpretation succinctly:

> I would like to propose that just as "Black Power" implied that there was need to call for black, not white, power because power was white, so too, I understand "Black lives matter" as articulating the need to affirm the worth of black, not white, lives because the lives that are shown to have worth are white. (2019: 8–9)

Later she writes, "'Black lives matter' could no more be said to mean 'Black lives matter, too' than 'Black power' could be said to mean 'Black power, too'" (Atkins 2019: 9). Atkins's point is subtle. For her, the slogan aims to highlight structural inequality. There is no need to mention the value of white lives because the value of white lives has never been in question. Atkins believes that to interpret "Black lives matter" as "Black lives matter, too" is to rob the slogan of its radical force. For Atkins, "Black lives matter" is a powerful rejection of white supremacy.

Garza, Anderson, and Atkins offer interpretations of "Black lives matter." Garza's claims are in tension with one another and she does not make any explicit metaphysical commitments. Anderson and Atkins offer straightforward interpretations of the slogan but also do not commit to any view about the metaphysical picture that undergirds "Black lives matter." These observations do not serve as a critique of Anderson or Atkins. I simply wish to point out that their aims and questions are different from mine.

Havercroft and Owen come closer to thinking through the metaphysical views implicit in "Black lives matter." They offer a brief explanation of the complex meanings of the slogan:

> The hashtag #BlackLivesMatter is an exclamation, a complex avowal, that may be, at once, an expression of pain, of anger, of indignation, of resilience and, even perhaps, of hope. It is also a reminder that within the police orders that compose the history of the United States of America, black lives have not, or have only exceptionally been seen as mattering. (2016: 751)

For Havercroft and Owen, "Black lives matter" has several meanings, any one of which can be emphasized in a given context. They believe that the point of speaking or writing the slogan is to influence those who do not already see Black lives as significant and worthy of protection.

Central to Havercroft and Owen's account is the concept of soul blindness. The concept itself has an intriguing genealogy. The concept traces its origins to Ludwig Wittgenstein's discussion of aspect blindness in the *Philosophical Investigations*. In part II of the *Investigations*, Wittgenstein discusses the phenomenon of seeing aspects. To see an aspect is to come to recognize a familiar object in a new light. Wittgenstein uses the famous duck-rabbit illusion to explain the concept of seeing aspects. The image of the duck-rabbit can either be seen as a duck or as a rabbit, depending on one's orientation toward the image. The duck and rabbit are aspects of the image (Wittgenstein 1974: 194). In many cases, one or another of the aspects do not appear immediately to viewers, but must be pointed out. An aspect can strike a person who once did not see it.

Wittgenstein questions whether there could be a person who is unable to see aspects, unable to see either the duck or the rabbit. He labels this possible state "aspect blindness" (1974: 213). The aspect blind person sees the same objects that we do but is unable to see them *as* something else. Stanley Cavell picks up on Wittgenstein's discussion of aspect blindness and develops the concept of soul blindness (Cavell 1979: 378). The soul-blind person is unable to see other human beings (or some subset of human beings) as moral objects, as deserving of recognition and respect.

Havercroft and Owen claim that many persons who resist the "Black lives matter" slogan and the Black Lives Matter movement are guilty of soul blindness; they are unwilling or incapable of seeing Black Americans as full persons. Havercroft and Owen claim that this soul blindness is reflected in persons who respond to "Black lives matter" with "All lives matter" or "Blue lives matter." Soul blindness is also illustrated by persons who fail to fully appreciate or pay attention to the demands of Black Lives Matter activists (Havercroft and Owen 2016: 750–752). One of the purposes of claiming that Black lives matter, they argue, is to change the hearts of those who do not respect Black life, to cure the soul blindness of persons who practice anti-Black racism.

Of course, Havercroft and Owen do not believe that Black Lives Matter activists self-consciously employ Cavell's concepts. Their claim is that the aims of Black Lives Matter activists are not merely political in the sense that activists only want policy change. Activists, on this account, also want to be seen as worthy of dignity and respect. This, according to Havercroft and Owen, is a necessary condition for sustained racial justice (2016: 752). While not their intention, by relying on Wittgenstein and Cavell, Havercroft and Owen provide a take on the implicit metaphysics of "Black lives matter." If Black Lives Matter activists are relying on an implicit understanding of aspect perception, then it may be that the slogan itself relies on a metaphysical picture that is similar to that of Wittgenstein and Cavell's.

I take it that both Wittgenstein and Cavell are committed to a metaphysics that neither aligns with the matter-of-fact interpretation of "Black lives matter" nor the aspirational interpretation. Wittgenstein rails against Platonist understandings of linguistic meaning, on which words mean what they mean outside of how they are used or interpreted. He instead prefers to understand meaning as a product of how words are used within a community. Thus, the meaning of a word, sentence, or rule can change with changing attitudes and interpretations. Cavell also rejects Platonism about meaning. He takes his cues from Wittgenstein and the Oxford ordinary language philosophers, namely J. L. Austin. For Cavell, too, the best way to understand what a term means is to investigate the myriad of ways that the term is used.

Following Wittgenstein and Cavell (and, to an extent, Havercroft and Owen), we could argue that "Black lives matter" does not mean any one thing, but that its meaning is reflected in how the slogan is used in various contexts. Sometimes the slogan is a demand, sometimes a matter-of-fact statement, sometimes an aspiration, sometimes an expression of frustration. But if Black Lives Matter activists have an implicit understanding of soul blindness, this Wittgensteinian/ordinary language response will not settle the question of which metaphysical picture best fits the slogan when used to change the hearts of those who do not have regard for Black life. Does the slogan rely on there being a fact of the matter about whether Black lives matter or is seeing Black lives as mattering optional, such that one who is blind to the importance of Black life does not miss anything that is there, objectively?

According to one tradition, Cavell and Wittgenstein would answer in the following way. Just as there are many ways to see (understand) "Black lives matter," there are many ways to see Black people. Some see Black people as full persons who are entitled to rights and respect. Some do not. This does not mean that Black people do not matter or that their mattering isn't something that is there to be seen. We are sometimes able to see new aspects of words, objects, and people when we develop new concepts or are subjected to novel experiences. Thus, the importance of any person isn't something out there in the world, completely independent of human practices, just as the humor of a joke isn't out there, completely independent of personal experiences. However, one can be made to see others as important just as one can be made to get a joke (Cavell 1979: 378).

Admittedly, an answer that compares the mattering of persons to the humor of a joke would likely be unsatisfactory to many persons who claim that Black lives matter. I assume that many who employ "Black lives matter" and, indeed, "We shall overcome" and "I AM a man" take it that the humanity of Black people is not like an aspect of a drawing or the humor of a joke, but that Black humanity is simply there, objectively. Though, the soul-blindness interpretation of "Black lives matter," as I articulate it, denies not that aspects are there to be seen, but only that some are incapable of seeing aspects.

In sum, many who discuss "Black lives matter" do not directly address the implicit metaphysics of the slogan. Garza's claims about the slogan seem to be at odds with each other. Anderson and Atkins are concerned to understand why "Black lives matter" is misinterpreted. Their questions are not metaphysical in nature. Havercroft and Owen provide a framework to construct a plausible metaphysical interpretation of "Black lives matter," but this interpretation would likely face opposition from Black Lives Matter activists and those nonactivists who employ the slogan.

In conclusion, then, it is unlikely that we will be able to settle on the meaning of "Black lives matter" by referencing previous discussions of the slogan or by thinking about how persons use the slogan. There is no definite answer to the question "What does 'Black lives matter' mean?" Thus, I think we should focus on a related question, "What *should* 'Black lives matter' mean?"

In answering this question, I appeal to both metaphysical and pragmatic considerations. An interpretation of "Black lives matter" should be metaphysically plausible. That is, the interpretation should not rest on metaphysical assumptions that are contradictory, conceptually muddled, or wildly out of touch with common sense. A social movement should embrace metaphysical foundations that are coherent and seem reasonable to most who participate. An interpretation should also be socially useful. I take it that an interpretation of a slogan that is attached to a social or political movement is socially useful if it promotes, encourages, or justifies the type of actions that promote the ends of that movement. An interpretation is deficient to the extent that it fails to justify a certain type of activism. With these guidelines in mind, I evaluate several possible interpretations of "Black lives matter" in the following section.

2. What *should* "Black lives matter" mean?

In the previous section, I noted that the soul-blindness interpretation of "Black lives matter" would likely face opposition from persons who employ the slogan. This, however, does not entail that the soul-blindness interpretation is metaphysically implausible or that activists would not do well to accept this interpretation. Indeed, I believe that the soul-blindness interpretation of the slogan *is* metaphysically plausible. It just seems true that there are aspects in the world. It also seems true that seeing a person as a hero, or an automaton, or as having a soul is similar to seeing an aspect of a painting. The question, then, is whether the soul-blindness interpretation is socially useful.

I think the answer is no. First, seeing an aspect is a unique state, both cognitively and perceptually. To see the duck-rabbit is a rabbit is not necessarily to *believe* that the drawing is of a rabbit, but the state is subjective, like a belief. The state is also perceptual. In seeing the duck-rabbit as a rabbit, persons have the same perceptual experience that they would have if they were just seeing a drawing of a rabbit. Similarly, seeing another as having a soul, as being a human like oneself, is both a cognitive and perceptual state. To see someone as fully human is both to have a subjective conception of that person as being like oneself in some sense but also to experience that person differently.

But, as a cognitive/perceptual state, nothing specific follows from seeing a person as a full human being. One could believe that it is permissible to threaten full human beings, or to tease them, or to shoot or jail those humans who one believes pose a danger to others. Further, one could believe that all human beings should be treated equally, yet also believe that unequal treatment is justified in certain instances or for certain humans. In short, that one sees another person as human, or as having a soul, or as having a robust internal life does not entail anything about how that person should or will be treated. Admittedly, there are psychological facts about how persons are likely to treat others once they recognize them as fully human, but these psychological facts are not logical entailments. Thus, I believe that a socially useful conception of "mattering" should be more robust than is allowed on the soul-blindness interpretation. Cognitive/perceptual states do not entail specific forms of treatment.

Further, even if seeing another as having a soul did entail specific forms of treatment, the soul-blindness interpretation of "Black lives matter" would be unsatisfactory. Aspect perception is fleeting. I can see the duck-rabbit as a duck in one instance and as a rabbit in another. It seems that the same has to be true for seeing persons as ensouled. I can see another as having a robust interior life, but I can also put myself in the state of mind to see others as automatons. No doubt, Cavell envisions the state of seeing others as having a soul as a permanent state, which comes to one as a revelation and that shapes one's future actions with others. But it need not be this way. Just as one can have an experience that causes one to see an aspect, one can have an experience that causes one to see a contrasting aspect.

Thus, aspects are weak and fleeting in a way that is unsuitable for an interpretation of "mattering" in "Black lives matter." Persons who use this slogan speak out against various forms of violence and mistreatment of Black Americans by the state and by private citizens. They do not simply want these actors to perceive Black people differently, but to consistently act differently. No doubt, a change in the perception of Black people would be welcomed by Black Lives Matter activists, but this change is not itself sufficient. Thus, the soul-blindness interpretation of "Black lives matter" is not socially useful.

In my introduction, I contrasted the matter-of-fact interpretation of "Black lives matter" and other slogans with an aspirational interpretation. The soul-blindness interpretation straddles the line between these two interpretations. To matter is to be seen as mattering, as being fully human. The mattering is there to see, so to speak, but not everyone sees it. On this reading, "Black lives matter" is somewhat aspirational on this reading because those who use the slogan wish to make it the case that others see Black lives as mattering. Given that this interpretation is not fully satisfactory, one may be tempted to go for the matter-of-fact interpretation, where "Black lives matter" expresses an objective, mind-independent fact about the world. As I argue, many interpretations of this type are unsatisfactory.

If "Black lives matter" is a straightforward fact, then something must make it true. What could make it the case that Black lives matter? We could say that Black lives matter because Black lives matter. But this plain response is not informative. It does not tell us what mattering is or what distinguishes persons or things that matter from those that don't matter. We could also say that Black lives matter because God believes that they matter. According to some strands of the Judeo-Christian tradition, human beings matter because they are products of God and are loved by God. While compelling to some, this interpretation entails robust religious commitments, many of which are seemingly contradictory or admittedly incomprehensible (at least according to some Christian traditions). Further, such an interpretation would be divisive among persons who use the slogan.

A Kantian interpretation may be more attractive. We could say that Black lives matter because Black people are rational and thus capable of moral reasoning. On this interpretation, Black people matter because they are able to reason about right and wrong and have a robust conception of themselves and others as moral beings. According to Kantians, it is wrong to treat any being of this type as a mere means to an end. Moral beings, for the Kantian, must be treated as ends in themselves, as mattering. On this interpretation, to matter is to be deserving of rational engagement, that is, to be deserving of reasons and to be entitled to give reasons. To matter in this sense is also to have one's reasons taken seriously. George Zimmerman shot Trayvon Martin without any rational engagement and without regard for Martin's interests. Officer Daniel Pantaleo choked Eric Garner to death despite Garner claiming that he could not breathe (Southall 2019). In both cases, the victims were treated as if they did not matter.

The Kantian and Judeo-Christian conceptions of human value parallel one another. In the Judeo-Christian tradition, persons are valuable because they are children of God; they are made in God's image and thus have something that other things in the world don't have. For the Kantian, persons are valuable (that is, they matter) because they are rational. Persons have something (rationality) that other creatures do not have. However, one may wonder, as many critics of the Kantian tradition have, why rationality should be valued, that is, why rational beings should be treated with respect.

The Kantian answer to this question is complex and nuanced. I will not have space to discuss it in full here.[2] The core of Kant's position is that rationality itself is a rule-governed enterprise. Persons are only rational to the extent that they follow certain rules. One such rule is that rational persons should not use other rational persons, but should instead treat them having beliefs and interests that are deserving of respect. Respect for others, according to Kantians, is partially constitutive of rationality. For a Kantian, to ask why a rational person should value other rational persons is to ask why a basketball player should abide by the rules of basketball. One is only a basketball player to the extent that one abides by these rules. Likewise, according to at least some interpreters of Kant, to be rational is to respect others as moral beings.

The Kantian understanding of human value, of mattering, is metaphysically plausible. I believe that nonphilosophers would provide an answer similar to Kant's if asked why persons matter generally, and why Black lives matter specifically. For instance, most would agree that persons matter because they are robustly self-conscious, capable of rational, independent thought, and have life plans. I speculate that most would also agree that part of what it means to be a good person is to respect the interests of others.[3] The Kantian position is plausible and, I believe, matches some of our pretheoretical intuitions about what makes human life valuable.

I believe that the Kantian interpretation, while the most plausible of the matter-of-fact interpretations considered, is not as socially useful. According to the Kantian interpretation of "Black lives matter," Black lives matter

---

[2] For helpful reconstructions of Kant's moral philosophy, see Korsgaard (1996, 2009).
[3] To be clear, it is not Kant's position that one should respect others to the extent that one desires to be a good person. Kant believes that all rational persons are bound by morality, unconditionally.

because Black people are rational and are capable of moral reasoning. Black lives should be respected because part of what it means to be rational is to respect other rational persons. According to this folk version of the Kantian position, Black lives matter because Black people are autonomous moral agents with robust self-conceptions and life plans. Thus, rational people are bound to respect Black lives. This interpretation of "Black lives matter" is problematic because it fails to recognize the strength of anti-Black racism. I take it that the main targets of Black Lives Matter protests are those who are either hostile or indifferent to Black lives. These persons are the police officers, policymakers, and citizens who promote or tolerate actions and institutions that are inimical to Black flourishing. Such persons have little concern with Kantian rationality or liberal conceptions of goodness, at least as these concepts apply to Black life.[4]

The Kantian interpretation is unlikely to support actions that would motivate the main targets of Black Lives Matter to think or act differently about Black life.[5] For a person who is indifferent to the welfare of Black Americans, being told that Black people are rational or have robust life plans is unlikely to remedy their indifference.[6] Facts about Black people may serve as reasons for some, but not all. Further, it is not clear that all persons would act irrationally in failing to treat these facts as reasons. In fact, persons who benefit from racialized privilege have reason to suppress the interests of racial minorities. Thus, a social movement based in Kantian notions of rationality and morality is unlikely to be able to motivate those who are indifferent to Black life or those who have reason to suppress Black interests.

Thus far, I have discussed and rejected several interpretations of "Black lives matter." I claimed that the soul-blindness interpretation is unattractive because it relies on the concept of aspect perception. Seeing Black persons as ensouled does not entail any particular forms of treatment, and aspect perception can be fleeting. I claimed further that Kantian interpretations of the slogan are problematic because they are unlikely to motivate actions that will have an impact on the main targets of Black Lives Matter activists. In the

---

[4] A Kantian would hold that such persons do care about rationality, but simply don't understand the requirements of rationality. My point is that the concept of rationality is unlikely to motivate committed racists.

[5] For an opposing view, see Cherry, Chapter 7, this volume. Cherry believes that Black activists are the main targets of the "Black lives matter" slogan.

[6] For a further development of this idea, see Kate Manne's "In Ferguson and Beyond, Punishing Humanity," *The New York Times*, https://opinionator.blogs.nytimes.com/2014/10/12/in-ferguson-and-beyond-punishing-humanity/.

remainder of this chapter, I will articulate and defend an interpretation of "Black lives matter" that is both metaphysically plausible and socially useful.

3. "Black lives matter" as fact and aspiration

According to most matter-of-fact interpretations of "Black lives matter," mattering is a one-place predicate. That is, the predicate "matters" only implicates one person or thing. To say that a person matters, according to these interpretations, is to say that that person has certain features that entail their mattering. In this way, the predicate "matters" is treated like the predicates "is red," "weighs a ton," or "is a horse." A thing can be red, weigh a ton, or be a horse on its own, that is, not in relation to other things.

This is the wrong way to think about mattering. I suggest that we think of mattering the same way we think about the concept of love, that is, as a two-place predicate. Both love and mattering exist between a person and a person, or a person and a thing. A person is not simply loved; a person is loved *by* someone or something that is capable of loving. In the same way, a person does not simply matter, but matters *to* some person or to some group of persons. Of course, this is not to deny that there can be many features of persons that give rise to love or concern. A person may love someone simply because that person reminds them of their father. Relatedly, mattering may arise from self-interest. An employer's employees may matter to him because he wants them to work diligently and help him turn a profit. I claim only that mattering itself is inherently relational and attitudinal. If this is true, then it is possible for a person or thing to matter to some persons, but not all persons, or to not matter at all.

To be clear, I do not claim that a relational understanding of mattering is necessarily true or that there are not strong arguments against it. I do believe that the relational understanding is metaphysically plausible. It is not contradictory, incomprehensible, or wholly out of line with common sense. With this understanding of mattering in hand, I will now consider its implications for the interpretation of "Black lives matter."

It is clear that the lives of Black Americans matter to some people. It is equally clear that the lives of Black Americans do *not* matter to some people. If this is the case, and the relational understanding of mattering is true, then the claim that Black lives matter is only true relative to certain populations. Relative to most Black Americans and those non-Black Americans who oppose anti-Black racism, Black lives do matter. Relative to those who endorse or are indifferent to anti-Black racism, Black lives do not matter. If interpreted relative to this former class, then "Black lives matter" can be interpreted as a matter-of-fact claim. If interpreted relative to the latter class, then "Black lives matter" is at most an aspirational claim. We are left to ask which class is the relevant class for interpretation.

I contend that we have reason to interpret the slogan relative to both classes. Garza's original Facebook post was later titled "A Love Letter to Black People" (Fessler 2018). The letter was intended to be an affirmation of Black life directed to Black people. Many current uses of "Black lives matter" carry this connotation. The slogan is, at times, a self-affirmation. Thus, we could interpret "Black lives matter" in the following way. Black lives matter because Black people value their own lives and this valuing is sufficient to make it the case the Black lives matter. Under this interpretation, following Garza, the slogan is a declaration that *we* (Black people) are enough.

This interpretation is socially useful. Regardless of which actions activists take to promote their ends, self-confidence and group pride are essential to those actions being undertaken successfully. Activism is draining and stressful. Absent hope and a belief in oneself and in the merits of one's cause, activism will likely peter out. I take it that this is why previous civil rights activists chanted "We shall overcome." The slogan expresses a form of self-affirmation and hope. The implicit message, under this line of interpretation, is that the group's belief in its own success can bring about that success. Thus, as a form of self-affirmation, the relational interpretation of mattering, understood relative to the Black community and those who oppose anti-Black racism, is socially useful.

But the slogan is also directed at those who do not value Black lives. Activists direct the slogan toward police officers, policymakers, and citizens who fail to treat Black Americans with dignity and respect. These uses invite an interpretation relative to persons who support or are indifferent to anti-Black racism. If we understand mattering as relational, then the slogan rings false in these contexts. At most, "Black lives matter" is an aspiration under this interpretation. While Anderson takes it that "Black lives matter" is a moral demand directed toward those who do not value Black lives, on this interpretation, the slogan is false, yet exists as an aspiration. One may think that such an interpretation is not socially useful because it runs counter to the sentiments of Black Lives Matter activists and seems to invite despair. But I believe that the opposite is true. I believe that this second interpretation justifies certain forms of direct, nonsentimental activism. Indeed, this latter interpretation may be *more* socially useful than the former.

To make this argument, I turn to critical race theorist Derrick Bell. Bell argues that Black activists should embrace a form of pessimism about the prospects for racial justice in America. Bell writes,

> Black people will never gain full equality in this country. Even those herculean efforts we hail as successful will produce no more than temporary "peaks of progress," short-lived victories that slide into irrelevance as racial patterns adapt in ways that maintain white dominance. This is a hard-to-accept fact that all history verifies. We must acknowledge it and move on to adopt policies based on what I call: "Racial Realism." (Bell 1992: 373)

Bell contrasts Racial Realism with approaches to activism and civil rights litigation that presuppose a "right" way to interpret the Constitution or a fixed truth regarding the moral content of racial justice. Bell believes that those Americans who oppose Black progress will always act to promote their own interests, only benefiting Black Americans when doing so will advance those interests. Thus, for Bell, there is no set of arguments or appeals that would cause racists to "see the light."

Instead of appealing to Kantian notions of rationality or Christian conceptions of goodness, Bell encourages activists to appeal to the interests of white Americans in positions of political power, seeking to exploit areas of "interest convergence" (Bell 1980: 523). According to Bell, all social and political progress for Black Americans is a result of interest convergence. Understanding this, Bell contends, is essential for activists who wish to create opportunities for future progress. This form of activism requires a certain amount of creativity. Activists who embrace Bell would have to ponder, for example, how reforming police tactics could benefit police departments as well and the Black community. For Bell, appealing to the value of Black life in these scenarios is a losing strategy.

While Bell's claims about Black progress and interest convergence may seem extreme, the attitude that animates these ideas is a natural outgrowth of the relational conception of mattering. If Black lives only matter in relation to some populations, then appealing to the value of Black life to those populations for which Black lives do not matter makes little sense. A form of outward-facing activism that interprets "Black lives matter" only in relation to the Black community runs the risk of missing Bell's core insight, namely, that powerful persons and institutions are rarely swayed by moral arguments.[7] Thus, if Bell is at least partially correct, interpreting "Black lives matter" relative to those who do not value Black lives may be more socially useful than a self-affirming interpretation.

To be sure, both interpretations are socially useful and should be embraced fully depending on context. To those who oppose anti-Black racism, Black lives do matter and the affirmation of this truth can inspire activism. To those who either promote or are indifferent to Black lives, Black lives do not matter and activists should keep this truth in mind as they strategize. The aspiration in this instance is to create a world in which Black lives matter to all.

One might object that strategies based in pessimism about the efficacy of moral arguments are insufficient to bring about a world in which Black lives matter to all *for the right reasons*. I take it that when Garza expresses the goal of building a world where Black lives matter, she intends that world to be one in which Black people are respected, loved, and treated with dignity. Strategies based in the notion of interest convergence, however, are likely to build a world in which Black lives matter to many for purely instrumental reasons. Persons who only act to benefit Black Americans when it is in their own interest do not, it seems, value Black life. This objection is compelling. Ideally, all persons would promote the interests of Black Americans because they value Black life. Activist strategies based on Bell's insight seem to foreclose the possibility of this ideal.

But, as we know, the world is far from ideal. Given that Black Lives Matter activists wish to combat the effects of anti-Black racism, a strategy that appeals to instrumental reason is not out of place. As I mention earlier, the mattering relation need not be driven by love or concern. One person can matter to another for purely self-interested reasons. For instance, Black voters may matter to a politician only to the extent that they are willing to vote for her. But, in this case, the politician will take actions (or at least promise to take actions) that benefit the Black community. In this sense, the Black community matters to the politician. Likewise, if individuals and institutions cater to the concerns of Black Americans out of self-interest, it follows that Black lives matter to those individuals and institutions. This form of mattering may not be ideal, but it is nevertheless a form of mattering. Indeed, this form of mattering may be all that activists can hope for from individuals and institutions that have traditionally been indifferent to Black life.

---

[7] I borrow the term "outward-facing activism" from Grant (2018).

I have argued for a relational understanding of mattering. On this understanding, "Black lives matter" is only true relative to certain groups. I argue further that this understanding of mattering sets an aspiration for activists who embrace the "Black lives matter" slogan. The aspiration is that Black lives matter to all and not just some. Following Bell, I believe that activists should aim for a form of mattering that stems from the interests of individuals and institutions that currently devalue Black life. To be sure, my suggestion does not rule out appeals to morality. I only claim that there is good reason to believe that such appeals will oftentimes be willfully ignored.

What should "Black lives matter" mean? It should mean that Black lives are valuable because they are valuable to those who oppose anti-Black racism. It should also signal an agenda to make it the case that Black lives matter to all and not merely some. Both interpretations are socially useful and should help us think more clearly about the meanings of past civil rights slogans like "We shall overcome" and "I AM a man."

References

Anderson, Luvell (2017). "Hermeneutical Impasses." *Philosophical Topics* 45 (2): 1–19.

Atkins, Ashley (2019). "Black Lives Matter or All Lives Matter? Color-blindness and Epistemic Injustice." *Social Epistemology* 33 (1): 1–22.

Bell, Derrick (1980). "*Brown v. Board of Education* and the Interest-Convergence Dilemma." *Harvard Law Review* 93: 518–533.

Bell, Derrick (1992). "Racial Realism." *Connecticut Law Review* 24: 363–379.

Cavell, Stanley (1979). *The Claim of Reason: Wittgenstein, Skepticism, Morality, and Tragedy*. Oxford: Oxford University Press.

Cobb, Jelani (2016). "The Matter of Black Lives." *New Yorker*. https://www.newyorker.com/magazine/2016/03/14/where-is-black-lives-matter-headed.

Descartes, Rene (1996). *Meditations on First Philosophy*. Translated by J. Cottingham. Cambridge: Cambridge University Press.

Fessler, Leah (2018). "How the Leader of Black Lives Matter Defines 'Power.'" *Quartz*. https://qz.com/1391762/black-lives-matter-co-founder-alicia-garzas-definition-of-power/.

Garza, Alicia, and L. A. Kauffman (2015). "A Love Letter to Our Folks." *n+1*. https://nplusonemag.com/online-only/online-only/a-love-note-to-our-folks/.

Grant, Keneshia (2018). "Common Ground: A FAMUan's Observation of Howard University Student Activism." *The Hilltop*. https://thehilltoponline.com/2018/03/30/common-groud-a-famuans-observation-of-howard-university-student-activism/.

Havercroft, Jonathan, and David Owen (2016). "Soul-Blindness, Police Orders and Black Lives Matter: Wittgenstein, Cavell, and Rancière." *Political Theory* 44 (6): 739–763.

Korsgaard, Christine (1996). *The Sources of Normativity*. Cambridge: Cambridge University Press.

Korsgaard, Christine (2009). *Self-Constitution: Agency, Identity, and Integrity*. Oxford: Oxford University Press.

Manne, Kate (2014). "In Ferguson and Beyond, Punishing Humanity." *The New York Times*. https://opinionator.blogs.nytimes.com/2014/10/12/in-ferguson-and-beyond-punishing-humanity/.

Southall, Ashley (2019). "Daniel Pantaleo, Officer Who Held Eric Garner in Chokehold, Is Fired." *The New York Times*. https://www.nytimes.com/2019/08/19/nyregion/daniel-pantaleo-fired.html.

Wittgenstein, Ludwig (1974). *Philosophical Investigations*. Oxford: Oxford University Press.

2
"And He Ate Jim Crow"
Racist Ideology as False Consciousness

Vanessa Wills

A thorny tangle of racist oppression and naked capitalist exploitation—a phenomenon for which historian Cedric Robinson coined the term "racial capitalism"—forms perhaps the single most defining feature of life in the United States (2000: 10). Movements for Black liberation are thus prompted to ask precisely how it is that racism and capitalism mutually condition and reinforce one another. What is it about the interrelations between race and class that make both racist oppression and capitalist exploitation seem so inescapable and intractable?

Any thoughtful answer to this question must look, ultimately, to the concrete methods and mechanisms by which the whole of society is produced and reproduced generally and, therefore, to whom in that society is empowered to shape it and its ideas, and by what means. However, attending to the material conditions of capitalist society does not license inattention to ideology. Indeed, it helps bring into focus ideology's inner development and ways of reinforcing the existing material relations of unjust domination, of acting as a bulwark for them, and of making human emancipation from them more or less likely. Ideas are not merely epiphenomenal to the material conditions from which they emerge, but ideas themselves also have a causal impact on those conditions and partially determine them. As Marx wrote, "The weapon of criticism cannot, of course, replace criticism by weapons, material force must be overthrown by material force; *but theory also becomes a material force as soon as it has gripped the masses*" (1843: 182).

Movement slogans such as "Black lives matter," "I am a man," and others, conceptual interventions made in the context of building mass power, constitute attempts to realize theory as a material force. These slogans function discursively in (at least) three key ways. First, they directly contradict a prevailing conception about Black people and their lives—in the first case, that they do not matter, and in the second, that Black people never attain the moral status of adult human beings. Second, these slogans highlight an existing but suppressed truth about the existing state of affairs (for example, that Black lives *do* matter even if they are not generally treated as though they matter). And third, they put forward a positive, transformative vision of the world that ought to be created and insist that the germ of such a world already exists in the present one, even if only in early developmental form. It is not only that Black lives will be made to matter, or that adult male Black persons will attain social recognition as men. More than this, Black lives matter *now*, and insofar as the world is organized in such a manner that Black lives do not matter to the institutions that control their circumstances, or to whites generally, it is the existing state of affairs that is wrong about the truth of Black lives.

I argue here that to adequately describe and explain the persistence of racist ideology, to specify its role in the maintenance of racial capitalism, and to imagine the conditions of its abolition, we must understand racist ideology as a form of *false consciousness*. False consciousness gets things "right" at the level of appearance, but it mistakes that appearance for a "deep" or essential truth. In the case of anti-Black racism in the United States, it can be no mystery that it looks, by all superficial appearances, as though Black lives do not matter. It is very much obviously and objectively the case that they do *not* matter to the criminal justice system, to politicians, to economic elites, or to the majority of whites at large.

The person who holds the racist belief that Black lives do not matter is not simply guilty of an individual lapse of epistemic hygiene (although in most cases, they are guilty of that, too). Racist beliefs are consistently ratified and reinforced by the material circumstances in which agents find themselves. It is these objective material conditions that make racist belief so stubborn and intractable, even while we also recognize that people operating on the basis of racist belief further entrench the racist material conditions. As Martha Augoustinus warns in "Ideology, False Consciousness, and Psychology,"

> The Marxist notion of false consciousness can be misappropriated by psychologists and others who construct it simply as a psychological-cognitive phenomenon located in the mind, rather than as a socially emergent product of the reality of capitalism. Recognizing that contemporary social life itself is mystifying and distorting allows us to preserve and

maintain the long tradition of Marxist social and ideological critique which makes social change and societal transformation possible. (1999: 309)

The maintenance of racist ideology requires not only the ability to disseminate racist propaganda through the news media, the academy, and the pulpit (to name a few of the sites from which it might be promulgated) but also the ability to produce concrete structures that instantiate and provide evidentiary support for stereotypes and negative attitudes regarding racially oppressed groups. To dismantle racist ideology therefore requires movements that craft theoretical interventions highlighting the inessentiality and contingency of the despised racial groups' oppressed status, as well as practical interventions aimed at directly undermining the oppressive conditions that are reflected in racist beliefs about the "naturalness" or "appropriateness" of these groups' degraded status.

The concept of false consciousness has its origins in Marxist theory, especially as developed by Karl Marx's collaborator, Friedrich Engels, who coined the term. Here, I articulate a false consciousness concept that is rooted in Marxist theory, but I extend it beyond what Engels himself first meant when he developed the concept. I argue for a distinction between what I call "first-order false consciousness," which occurs in the case of false beliefs about the world that are sustained and superficially justified by objective social arrangements, and "second-order false consciousness," which occurs in the case of false beliefs about how one came to hold the beliefs that one does. (While I focus here on belief, false consciousness can also include other psychological states such as affective attitudes. The racist antipathy that many white Americans feel toward Black people, and that is in some ways constitutive of whiteness as a social category, is also an element of false consciousness.)

In what follows, I first put forward a positive account of false consciousness, which I employ as a term of art to describe a particular way in which one might come to be in error as a result of the way the world is arranged. In cases of false consciousness, the agent who holds beliefs holds them not just because of poor epistemic practice on their individual part, but because their beliefs reflect some stable aspect of social reality accurately, albeit only superficially or partially. That is to say, the causes of false consciousness are in large part structural. Additionally, structural features of the society are arranged such that the phenomenon of false consciousness itself functions as part of the infrastructure maintaining the oppressed racial groups' privation and subjugation. In this section of the chapter, I also disambiguate my false consciousness concept from interest-relative accounts of false consciousness which construe false consciousness primarily as a matter of believing things that are not in one's interest to believe. These accounts are quite reasonably described as false consciousness, but they are importantly different phenomena from the ones I identify here. In this section of the chapter, I invoke James Baldwin's 1963 remarks regarding the origin of the "nigger" concept as a brilliant example of the kind of critical intervention that a useful account of false consciousness could guide us in generating more of.

I then progress to an analysis of Martin Luther King Jr.'s 1965 speech on the march from Selma to Montgomery, Alabama. This speech included comments regarding the emergence and persistence of racist belief and sentiment in the Southern United States during the so-called Redemption period of racist reaction to the Black civil rights and human rights gains of Reconstruction. Few Americans have done as much as King to analyze racism as a problem of psychological states such as hatred, fear, and false belief. Yet King's 1965 speech is also a clear and compelling account of how the genesis of those states, their ubiquity and seeming ineradicability, is rooted in the material conditions associated with capitalist exploitation. Racist beliefs (and racist attitudes generally) emerge from these conditions and react back upon them to make them more deeply entrenched.

I argue that in order to capture the insights of King and similar thinkers, a concept of false consciousness is necessary. Such a concept allows us to articulate how it is that a system of false belief could hold such sway among such large swathes of the population, even when these beliefs justify their own ill treatment and guide them to act against their own objective interests. This, of course, commits me to the view that there is an objective fact of the matter about what is or is not in one's interests, and that one might be mistaken about this fact of the matter. I address one common complaint against the concept of false consciousness, which is that the concept is elitist, patronizing, or problematically vanguardist because it does not defer to individuals' subjective judgments about their interests. I argue that the false consciousness concept is no worse off in this respect than all sorts of utterly mundane judgments we make daily regarding others' interests, and how their preferences would be arranged if they had fuller information than they do.

I close by making a case for the indispensability of the false consciousness concept to anti-racist struggle today. Understanding the workings of false consciousness helps highlight the need not only for intellectual interventions that challenge racist ideology in the realm of ideas but also for political activism up to and including direct action aimed at transforming the material conditions that are reflected in racist ideology.

1. Varieties of false consciousness

To invoke the term "false consciousness" is immediately to suggest that there might be such a thing as true consciousness. In such cases of true consciousness, one's beliefs about the world would robustly reflect the world as it is. In speaking of false consciousness, we also implicitly presume that there are at least some objectively true facts of the matter about what the world is like.

Lest the notion of false consciousness seem somehow cryptic or mysterious, note that here we are proceeding from one relatively straightforward and widely held view about the nature of belief, namely that, as Bernard Williams famously put it, belief aims at the truth (1973: 136). One needn't embrace much or any of Marxist theory in order to think this. It is therefore at least in principle possible to develop a concept of false consciousness that is rooted in Marxist theory but sensible from within a broad range of philosophical and political perspectives. One need only embrace the notion of objectivity and that there is a robust sense in which one might be genuinely incorrect regarding facts of the matter about the world. The chief operating background assumption for the false consciousness concept is simply that if all is epistemically in order, then an agent will believe p just in case that p. And so, the activity of believing is at least weakly teleological: its aim is to reflect the world as it truly and objectively is.

Of course, this *does* rule some perspectives out as suitable theoretical bedfellows for a concept of false consciousness, since for any consciousness of the world to count as false, there must be some objective, universally valid sense in which the world genuinely is as described in p. If there is no objective and universally valid fact of the matter, then there can be no sense (at least, no obvious sense) in which statements about the world are objectively true or false. Thus, a concept of false consciousness is intrinsically tied to a metaphysical claim that there is, indeed, some objective fact of the matter about how the world is arranged.

Here, one might object that claims to objectivity have been weaponized against marginalized populations in order to invalidate their perspectives and ways of knowing. This is undoubtedly the case; however, this observation does not suffice to impugn objectivity altogether. Here, we ought to be guided by an observation made by Mari Matsuda: "the powerless have always relied on claims of objective truth and on the existing structures of knowledge to critique dominant society on its own terms" (1990: 1769). A final judgment on whether we ought to embrace the liberationist potential of claims to objectivity, or reject such claims in favor of a deep relativism about truth, is outside the purview of this chapter. I do, however, adopt the aim here of offering reasons to think claims to objectivity are not inherently at odds with marginalized peoples' demands that the validity of their perspectives be respected. Quite the opposite: the false consciousness concept provides us with a tool for diagnosing and dismantling the facile "obviousness" of racist beliefs and their veneer of objective validity within the context of racist social structures.

Our beliefs aim at the truth, but sadly for us, they often fall short. They generally fail in quite straightforward ways. If I believe that the time is not later than 4:45 a.m. when actually it is 4:47 a.m., then I have a straightforwardly false belief about what time it is. Investigating my mistake, and the conditions of my having made it, may not reveal much that is particularly deep about the world. I was just mistaken about the time; I glanced at my watch too quickly, or I was drawn into deep philosophical reflection and the time "got away from me." There is no sense, weak, strong, partial, or otherwise, in which my *belief* that it was earlier than 4:45 a.m. reveals some special sense in which it truly *was not* any later than then.

If I believe that I have sung an E flat perfectly when in fact I was a quartertone sharp, then I have a false belief. I believe the boss is calling me into her office to admonish me, but in fact she is authorizing a pay raise—or vice versa. Plenty of beliefs are just mundanely false in this way. The false consciousness concept does not subsume all or perhaps even most instances of false belief. But as Jim Boettcher notes, "racist beliefs, for example, are not only plainly false; historically they have often gained widespread and enduring acceptance through false consciousness and have served to legitimate various forms of legally sanctioned, class-structured oppression" (2009: 242). The beliefs that occur in false consciousness are ones that describe a stable, structurally maintained appearance of social reality, and that additionally function to further justify, maintain, and entrench that reality. These beliefs are "false" insofar as they mistake what is contingent for what is necessary and also insofar as they take themselves to merely discover what they in fact help constitute and produce.

Still, part of what makes false consciousness so stubborn to crack or dislodge is that it does "truly" describe the world at the level of superficial appearance. Evidence to support falsely conscious beliefs is everywhere to be found, allowing the falsely conscious agent to consider themselves reasonably epistemically responsible, while failing to recognize that the world around them has been arranged precisely to produce their racist beliefs *and* their misled confidence in these beliefs' objectivity and correctness.

To distinguish between the two key aspects of false consciousness, I employ the term "first-order false consciousness" to refer to falsely conscious beliefs about the world and "second-order false consciousness" to speak of falsely conscious beliefs about how one forms one's beliefs about the world.

"False consciousness" is a term of art here, describing a process of belief formation that routinely and systematically mistakes a partial, obscured (and sometimes even heavily stage-managed) perspective for a freely and autonomously produced "view from nowhere," thereby in turn reinforcing and lending theoretical justification to the material conditions that produce the flawed belief. The false consciousness concept is rooted in a Marxist historical materialist analysis of how human beings form their ideas about the world. A particularly important source for this concept is Marx and Engel's *Critique of the German Ideology*:

> Men are the producers of their conceptions, ideas, etc.—real, active men, as they are conditioned by a definite development of their productive forces and of the intercourse corresponding to these, up to its furthest forms. Consciousness can never be anything else than conscious existence, and the existence of men is their actual life-process. If in all ideology men and their circumstances appear upside-down as in a *camera obscura*, this phenomenon arises just as much from their historical life-process as the inversion of objects on the retina does from their physical life-process. (Marx and Engels 1846: 36)

While here Marx and Engels do not specifically employ the term "false consciousness," they do identify the first-order phenomenon of ideology in which "men and their circumstances appear upside-down." This inversion occurs in thought not mainly or merely because of a subjective error in one's thinking, but because one's real-life circumstance is objectively arranged in such a way as to give rise to that appearance as its reflection.

The reflection metaphor appears twice in this passage, first in the example of the *camera obscura*, and second in the example of the retina. It is crucial not to misinterpret the reflection metaphor to suggest that consciousness is formed only passively. Rather, on the Marxist view, the world is represented to human beings in thought, in a manner that is mediated all the way down by human beings' active interaction with their natural and social environment. The examples of the *camera obscura* and the retina are therefore heuristically valuable, but importantly inexact.[1] What is reflected in human beings' thought is not a static image of the world outside themselves, but rather the whole developing complex of themselves and the world, in dynamic interaction over time. In producing the world that is represented in thought, they thereby indirectly produce their own consciousness. In this way, it would be mistaken to interpret Marx's materialism about the sources of consciousness as evidence of a strict determinism on his part that would rule out genuine human agency. False consciousness is produced, at bottom, by actual social, economic, and political conditions that constitute the object of thought in false consciousness, and that ratify claims and perspectives developed within its frame. It is the result of human beings' active cognizing of the world of which they are a part.

False consciousness *is true* in the sense of reflecting stable, systemic features of the world, albeit in a partial or superficial way. Here, my account of false consciousness is indebted to the work of György Lukács, who writes:

> The dialectical method does not permit us simply to proclaim the "falseness" of this consciousness and to persist in an inflexible confrontation of true and false. On the contrary, it requires us to investigate this "false consciousness" concretely as an aspect of the historical totality and as a stage in the historical process. (1923: 50)

A chief danger of false consciousness is that in accepting this "false" or superficial *truth* and mistaking it for a "deep" truth, we risk reifying and reinforcing the "false reality" that false consciousness reflects. The challenge, then, is to interrogate the contents of false consciousness so as to ascertain their connections to the circumstances that give rise to them, and to discover what they reveal about the historical moment from which they emerge.

---

[1] Michael Rosen addresses some of the pitfalls in taking this analogy too literally (1996: 179).

Here, we ought also look to Herbert Marcuse's remarks in *One-Dimensional Man*, where he writes of this phenomenon, "To the degree to which they correspond to the given reality, thought and behavior express a false consciousness, responding to and contributing to the preservation of a false order of facts. And this false consciousness has become embodied in the prevailing technical apparatus which in turn reproduces it" (Marcuse 1964: 149).

It's worth noting that the notion of a "false reality" or a "false order of facts" is involved in a framework familiar to much religious sentiment that decries worldly injustice and iniquity as a mere temporary trial or illusion, beyond which lies the just reality of Heaven where human souls truly belong. Of course, we are after a somewhat different model with the false consciousness concept. But the danger such religious teachings warn against is one we recognize as well: namely, to mistake specific, contingent, and temporary conditions of domination and oppression for absolute, just, necessary, and permanent states of affairs. When we speak of a "false reality," this is what we have in mind—a state of affairs that is indisputably existent and real, yet that obscures its own contingency, mutability, and status as a condition that could be transcended and transformed.

In James Baldwin's reflections on the concept of the "nigger," we find a clear and elegant example of what it might look like to investigate false consciousness "concretely as an aspect of the historical totality," in the manner that Lukács prescribes. In a 1963 interview, Baldwin explains:

> We have invented the nigger. *I* didn't invent him. White people invented him. [...] What you were describing was not me, and what you were afraid of was not me. It had to be something else. You had invented it, so it had to be something you were afraid of. You invested me with it. Now if that's so, no matter what you've done to me, I can say to you this, and I mean it [...] I've always known that I'm not a nigger. But if I am not the nigger, and if it's true that your invention reveals you, then who is the nigger? I am not the victim here. I know one thing from another. [...] But you still think, I gather, that the nigger is necessary. Well he's unnecessary to me, so he must be necessary to you. So I give you your problem *back*. You're the "nigger," baby. It isn't me. (Baldwin 1963)

Baldwin's counternarrative here is a resistance ontology. A key tenet of 1960s racist ideology in the United States, of course, is that some people—if they are even recognized as "people"—*are* niggers, and that Baldwin is typical of this category. Baldwin resists this, denying that "nigger" captures some essential quality in him and identifying it as something he has instead been "invested with" by racist whites. His question then, is what does this social fact, the existence of the category of "the nigger," reveal about the society from which it emerges? It is in this sense that he gives the problem of "the nigger" *back* to white America. Understanding it as not just any simple error, but as *false consciousness*, opens up the possibility of problematizing what seems, from the standpoint of false consciousness, obvious and natural, and of inquiring into the conditions that give rise to it.

Racist ideology, I claim, is a form of false consciousness. Insofar as all consciousness is produced by, and reflects, however imperfectly, the real-life process of human beings, false consciousness is no exception. It reveals a real aspect of social being. But false consciousness does so problematically, not only because it mistakes superficial appearance for deep, essential truth, and thereby misunderstands the world, but also because agents acting from within the grip of false consciousness go on, in turn, to act upon the world in a way that reinforces and reproduces the original mistake, the epistemological and ontological *wrongness* of the world under description.

The superficial evidentiary support for anti-Black racist belief in the United States is everywhere to be found. To gather *seeming* evidence for the claim that Black people are inferior to whites, one may note, for example, that they are paid less for their labor, that they live in the worst areas, that they are mistreated without consequence, and that their needs are routinely ignored. They die sooner and spend their lives in more suffering, more poverty, and deeper abasement. The indignation a white person might feel at being asked to consider herself equal with a Black person in a racist, anti-Black society is, in part, the indignation of one asked to consider herself equal with what multiple factors in the society tell her is clearly a degraded, subhuman being. She mistakes the socially produced, artificially maintained subjugation of Blacks for an essential fact about their nature, which she takes to be revealed in their conditions of life. Armed with racist ideology and the social conditions that reinforce it, she goes on to act in racist ways, further entrenching the very subjugation that she takes as evidence of Blacks' lower status vis-à-vis whites. The conspiracy of mutually reinforcing oppressive material conditions and racist ideology thus makes the problem of racial capitalism seem intractable, utterly without solution. As György Markus observes, the ideas contained in false consciousness "render the totality completely opaque, transforming it into a matter of unintelligible naturalness or technical necessity" (1981: 92). It is a state of affairs that the false consciousness concept helps us to name, to diagnose, and as we will see later in this chapter, to confront and dismantle.

Before we do that, however, let us first address the phenomenon of what I call here "second-order false consciousness," which is false consciousness about how one's beliefs come to be formed. In cases of second-order false consciousness, an agent persists under the delusion that he comes to his beliefs through a process that is fully autonomous from determination by the material world. With this in mind, Engels writes:

> Ideology is a process accomplished by the so-called thinker consciously, indeed, but with a false consciousness. The real motives impelling him remain unknown to him, otherwise it would not be an ideological process at all. Hence, he imagines false or apparent motives. Because it is a process of thought he derives both its form and its content from pure thought, either his own or that of his predecessors. He works with mere thought material which he accepts without examination as the product of thought, he does not investigate further for a more remote process independent of thought; indeed its origin seems obvious to him, because as all action is produced through the medium of thought it also appears to him to be ultimately based upon thought. The ideologist who deals with history (history is here simply meant to comprise all the spheres—political, juridical, philosophical, theological—belonging to society and not only to nature), the ideologist dealing with history then, possesses in every sphere of science material which has formed itself independently out of the thought of previous generations and has gone through an independent series of developments in the brains of these successive generations. True, external facts belonging to its own or other spheres may have exercised a co-determining influence on this development, but the tacit presupposition is that these facts themselves are also only the fruits of a process of thought, and so we still remain within that realm of pure thought which has successfully digested the hardest facts. (Engels 1893: 164)

Take, for example, a garden variety sincere white racist in the United States. Asked how it is that he has come to hold his beliefs about Black people, he may offer what he takes to be some independently derived arguments for his racist conclusions. He may recount some experiences in which he was involved in negative encounters with Black individuals. He might even reference ideological products such as the Moynihan Report or *The Bell Curve* and offer what he takes to be objective reasons for accepting their conclusions as valid. What he is unlikely to do is explain his beliefs as themselves the utterly predictable result of a campaign of racist propaganda, or as post hoc justifications for the racist hierarchy in which he exists—which they in large part, in fact, are.

My interpretation of Engels here departs from the one offered by Tommie Shelby. Shelby interprets Engels's account as amounting to the claim that "To hold a belief with a false consciousness is to hold it while being ignorant of, or self-deceived about, the real motives for why one holds it. [. . .] Those with a false consciousness cling to a system of belief, not because of its epistemic warrant, but because it serves some noncognitive interest" (Shelby 2003: 170).

Shelby's remarks here on the Marxist concept of false consciousness pertain strictly, of course, to what I refer to as second-order false consciousness: false beliefs about how one comes by the beliefs one has. He understands Engels to be arguing that in such cases, one comes by one's beliefs because one is motivated to do so by hidden, clandestine, inner psychological drives which are satisfied by holding the belief in question. This reading hangs crucially upon what it is, exactly, that is being denoted by the English word *motive* in the *Marx-Engels Collected Work* translation that Shelby cites.

The contrast Engels draws is not between cognitive and noncognitive *psychological* factors that give rise to belief. For Engels, the chiefly relevant contrast here is the same one that he and Marx insist upon elsewhere as in *The Critique of the German Ideology*—it is between ideal and *material* determinants of belief. This is made clear later in the letter, where Engels condemns idealist histories of ideas for depicting intellectual advance "as a sheer victory of thought; not as *the reflection in thought of changed economic facts* but as the finally achieved correct understanding of actual conditions subsisting always and everywhere" (Engels 1893: 165).

In English, the word *motive* can quite readily be understood as referring to a kind of subjective purpose in virtue of which one selects one course of action or another. Engels's word in the original German is *Triebkraft*, and in Engels's usage, *Triebkraft* is not most readily understood as a subjective psychological motivation. It is better understood here as an *external* cause or mover, acting upon an agent and shaping his belief processes, generally unbeknownst to him. It is the agent's failure to appreciate the ways in which his beliefs are shaped by utterly nonpsychological and nonideal factors—such as the economic conditions in which they arise—that constitutes false consciousness for Engels.

In his *The Condition of the Working Classes in England*, Engels writes of the spinning throstle that "After the steam-engine, this is the most important mechanical invention of the 18th century. It was calculated from the beginning for mechanical motive power [*Triebkraft*], and was based upon wholly new principles" (1845: 312). Later, in his "Revolution and Counterrevolution in Germany," Engels writes, "It is this rapid and passionate development of class antagonism which, in old and complicated social organisms, makes a revolution such a powerful agent [*Triebkraft*] of social and political progress" (1852: 32). In his synopsis of Marx's *Capital*, Engels says of the Industrial Revolution that it "started with the machine tool. What characterises it is that the tool—in a more or less modified form—is transferred from man to the machine, and is worked by the machine under the operation of man. At the outset it is immaterial whether the motive power [*Triebkraft*] is human or a natural one" (1867: 300). Considered in this context, it seems more consistent with Engels's typical usage to understand *Triebkraft* as a kind of force that acts upon the believer.

That Engels is making a metaphysical point about the relationship between matter and ideas, and not a purely psychological point about the relationship between cognitive and noncognitive mental states, is further confirmed by the manner in which he concludes his discussion of false consciousness in the letter to Mehring quoted earlier. Engels writes:

> Hanging together with this too is the fatuous notion of the ideologists that because we deny an independent historical development to the various ideological spheres which play a part in history we also deny them any effect upon history. The basis of this is the common undialectical conception of cause and effect as rigidly opposite poles, the total disregarding of interaction; these gentlemen often almost deliberately forget that once an historic element has been brought into the world by other elements, *ultimately by economic facts*, it also reacts in its turn and may react on its environment and even on its own causes. (Engels 1893:165)[2]

The issue at hand, for Engels, is to insist upon the possibility of mutually conditioning causal interaction between ideal and material aspects of Being.

---

[2] Emphasis mine.

In the following section, we will address some ways in which Black counternarratives of US history reveal racist ideology's rootedness in second-order false consciousness—the opacity, to whites, of their own processes of racist belief formation, and of the factors, both internal *and external* to consciousness, that shape these beliefs. We will then understand more about what it means for Baldwin to have given their "nigger problem" back to them.

2. Reconstruction and redemption: "the public and psychological wage" as an object lesson in false consciousness

Given the embeddedness of anti-Black racism in the fabric of American life, it is not altogether surprising that it should seem a permanent and intractable feature of it. The events occurring in the immediate aftermath of the US Civil War tell a different story, however, highlighting some key ways in which racist hierarchy has been meaningfully confronted and, tragically, deliberately reinforced and maintained. The story is a familiar one. During the Reconstruction era, Blacks in the American South achieved rapid political gains, including the right to vote and to hold elected office. Historians have identified over 1,500 Blacks who held elected office during this period. Once Reconstruction was defeated by the Southern white planter class (who overwhelmingly identified politically as "Bourbon Democrats"), Blacks did not hold elected office in the American South again until the civil rights movement of the 1960s began to challenge the hegemony of Jim Crow (Foner 2000: 166). The stirrings of interracial working-class solidarity in the South were stamped out in "Redemption," the elite Southern white planter class's response to the gains of Reconstruction.

In remarks delivered at the end of a civil rights march from Selma to Montgomery, Alabama, King described this period in the following terms:

> Toward the end of the Reconstruction era, something very significant happened. That is what was known as the Populist Movement. The leaders of this movement began awakening the poor white masses and the former Negro slaves to the fact that they were being fleeced by the emerging Bourbon interests. Not only that, but they began uniting the Negro and white masses into a voting bloc that threatened to drive the Bourbon interests from the command posts of political power in the South.

To meet this threat, the southern aristocracy began immediately to engineer this development of a segregated society. I want you to follow me through here because this is very important to see the roots of racism and the denial of the right to vote. Through their control of mass media, they revised the doctrine of white supremacy. They saturated the thinking of the poor white masses with it, thus clouding their minds to the real issue involved in the Populist Movement. They then directed the placement on the books of the South of laws that made it a crime for Negroes and whites to come together as equals at any level. And that did it. That crippled and eventually destroyed the Populist Movement of the nineteenth century.

If it may be said of the slavery era that the white man took the world and gave the Negro Jesus, then it may be said of the Reconstruction era that the southern aristocracy took the world and gave the poor white man Jim Crow. (King 1965)

Here are echoes of W. E. B. Du Bois, who remarked in *Black Reconstruction* that during this period of Bourbon reaction, white workers

were admitted freely with all classes of white people to public functions, public parks, and the best schools. The police were drawn from their ranks, and the courts, dependent upon their votes, treated them with such leniency as to encourage lawlessness. [. . .] White schoolhouses were the best in the community, and conspicuously placed, and they cost anywhere from twice to ten times as much per capita as the colored schools. The newspapers specialized on news that flattered the poor whites and almost utterly ignored the Negro except in crime and ridicule. (Du Bois 1935: 701)

King's assertion that the Southern aristocracy "engineered" segregation and "clouded the minds" of white workers similarly echoes Du Bois's claim that

the theory of race was supplemented by *a carefully planned and slowly evolved method*, which drove such a wedge between the white and black workers that there probably are not today in the world two groups of workers with practically identical interests who hate and fear each other so deeply and persistently and who are kept so far apart that neither sees anything of common interest. (Du Bois 1935: 700)

To effectively produce racist false consciousness requires not only ideological hegemony but also the economic and political power to transform society in such a manner that it seems to offer an objective confirmation of racist ideology. In this way, material and ideal aspects of existence are co-constituting and mutually reinforcing. Blacks in positions of political power were a concrete affront to white supremacist doctrine—they were hounded out. Proximity between whites and Blacks gave the lie to racist anti-Black caricatures and stereotypes—segregation law ensured that such opportunities for interracial solidarity and understanding would be fewer and further between.

For poor white workers in the South who adopted white supremacism, racist anti-Black ideology exhibited features of both first-order and second-order false consciousness. It is first-order false consciousness because they regard Blacks' low position in the social hierarchy as a just consequence of some inherent, natural, and essential inferiority of Black people. It is second-order false consciousness because at least some of the reasons—the *Triebkräfte*—causing them to believe this are opaque to them. Invoking the concept of false consciousness allows us to capture the insights of Du Bois, King, Baldwin, and others, with respect to the socially constructed nature of race and racism. Without it, we unnecessarily deprive ourselves of a resource for describing the complicated ways that the "false reality" of a racist social order is generated and maintained.

One common critique of historical analyses of Reconstruction that foreground elite Southern whites' cynical use of racist ideology to split the working class is that such analyses wrongfully let white workers "off the hook" and erase their agency in perpetuating a white supremacist social order. But the false consciousness concept specifically articulates the way in which the relationship between matter and ideas is not unidirectional but mutually conditioning and co-constitutive. While we insist that successful ideology critique must be grounded in an analysis of power, and must name those elements in society that enjoy the greatest opportunity to shape its ideology, the notion of false consciousness also proceeds from Marcuse's observation that in acting from false consciousness, one in turn "contributes to the preservation of a false order."

Thus, the activities of white workers acting on the basis of false consciousness are not to be simply swept away as an accidental, inessential, unreal, or merely epiphenomenal feature of racial capitalism. Rather, they demand close attention as one of the chief mechanisms that maintain it. That said, in seeking to divorce false consciousness from the objective conditions that give rise to it, and to instead reduce it entirely to a matter of individual moral failing, we run an even greater risk, one that Du Bois, King, and others warn us against: that of letting racist elites off the hook for the ways in which they deliberately exercise power to promote a white supremacist order from which they stand to benefit most.

3. False consciousness, class consciousness, and rational self-interest

So far, I have said little about the relationship between false consciousness and enlightened self-interest, aside from referencing Du Bois's observation that Blacks and poor whites in the Reconstruction-era South shared similar interests yet nonetheless confronted one another as enemies in the system of white supremacy. The false consciousness concept as I develop it here is not defined principally in terms of a belief's usefulness for advancing the interests of the believer in question. This is, however, one common way of conceiving of false consciousness—that it amounts primarily to believing things that are not in one's interest to believe.

One typical such account of false consciousness is offered by John Jost and Mahzarin Banaji, who describe the phenomenon of false consciousness as "the holding of beliefs that are contrary to one's personal or group interest and which thereby contribute to the maintenance of the disadvantaged position of the self or the group" (1994: 1). I depart from such an account for two main reasons. The first is that this account proceeds from a picture of belief that is very different from the one we started with: namely, it implies a pragmatism that understands the value of belief chiefly in terms of its usefulness to the believer. One could, of course, develop a perfectly tenable account of false consciousness on such a basis; it simply would not be one that is shared by those philosophical perspectives which take it that one ought to believe that p just in case that p (and not just in case it is *useful* to believe that p).

A capitalist in a capitalist society might adopt anti-capitalist beliefs; capitalists even sometimes do. It would be a mistake to say that such a capitalist exhibits false consciousness just because she holds beliefs that conflict with her interests *qua* capitalist, and that if implemented, would serve to diminish her class advantage. Such an anti-capitalist worldview would not count as false consciousness for the capitalist. In this case she might well be abandoning a limited and partial perspective in favor of one that allows a fuller and deeper understanding of the social reality within which she operates (whether or not she does so will depend on the variety of anti-capitalism she adopts). Indeed, capitalist ideology counts as false consciousness for the capitalist (just as it does for everyone else in a capitalist society), *regardless* of the fact that endorsing and promoting capitalist ideology further her economic class interests. Guenter Lewy captures this point well when he writes that for the bourgeois class, "false consciousness hides the true nature of bourgeois class rule—from itself and from those whom it dominates and oppresses. [. . .] Bourgeois false consciousness thus sustains the belief in the eternal rule of the bourgeoisie" (1982: 4).[3]

While in the case of working-class people who embrace capitalist ideology, it might seem immediately intuitive to argue that they labor under false consciousness just in virtue of the fact that they adopt the perspective of an economic class whose interests are opposed to their own, to characterize false consciousness in this way downplays and obscures a key presupposition for the concept: that there is an objective fact of the matter about how the world is arranged, and one can be genuinely mistaken about it.

The second reason that I do not define false consciousness mainly in terms of personal or group interest is that to the extent that we want to deploy the false consciousness to describe the ways in which one might be wrong about what is in one's own interests, such beliefs are only species of a general category that is already captured in our account of first-order false consciousness. In cases of first-order false consciousness, recall, one mistakes a partial and superficial appearance for an essential and permanent feature of reality. In this sense, first-order false consciousness is a particular way of being wrong about objective facts of the matter. This includes facts about what is in one's own interests. As W. G. Runciman points out, "blindness to one's interests is, in effect, merely ignorance of the facts of the case" (1969: 303). False consciousness does not have to be construed primarily in terms of its specific relation to self-interest, in order to capture the ways that operating under false consciousness can be counterproductive to effectively pursuing one's self-interest.

Belief that whites are entitled to white privilege is an example of false consciousness that simultaneously accurately reflects an existing social schema, a "false reality" in which whites are privileged over Blacks; that obscures the

---

[3] See also Christopher Pines (1993: 87).

objective and essential truth of human equality; *and* that is counter to the objective material interests of white workers who hold it, insofar as it encourages them to uphold a white supremacist order that they, too, would be better off without. This last point is what King had in mind at Montgomery, Alabama, in 1965:

> The southern aristocracy took the world and gave the poor white man Jim Crow. And when his wrinkled stomach cried out for the food that his empty pockets could not provide, he ate Jim Crow, a psychological bird that told him that no matter how bad off he was, at least he was a white man, better than the black man. And he ate Jim Crow. (King 1965)

4. Black lives matter: "true" consciousness in anti-racist struggle

Effective political slogans become rallying cries, pithily articulating demands and galvanizing mass momentum behind them. "Black power," "I am a man," "Black lives matter"—each of these poses a direct challenge to prevailing social conditions of Black disempowerment and of white refusal to acknowledge Black humanity and worth. Anti-racist thought faces an uphill battle. It must not only cut through the fog of racist ideology, but it must also make itself sensible within a social order that seems to belie it.

In the course of their discussion of stereotypes as elements of false consciousness, Jost and Banaji aptly describe the way that ideal and material conditions intertwine in false consciousness to constitute a formidable obstacle to the liberation of the oppressed:

> [S]tereotypes serve ideological functions, in particular that they justify the exploitation of certain groups over others, and that they explain the poverty or powerlessness of some groups and the success of others in ways that make these differences seem legitimate and even natural. This position is consistent with a large body of social psychological research which finds that "one of the most commonly observed characteristics of social existence is that people imbue social regularities with an 'ought' quality." (1994: 10)

It is in this sort of context that a simple, seemingly anodyne declarative statement such as "Black lives matter" can engender the kind of harsh ridicule, anger, and backlash that it does. It is (quite rightly!) perceived to be a statement that threatens to disturb and upend the prevailing racist social order. It directly contradicts the correct description of that order, in which Black lives obviously *do not* matter, and it suggests a potential future reality that may be nurtured within the current one. The claim that "Black lives matter" thus functions both descriptively and prescriptively, suggesting that Black life is, although not socially valued, *already valuable*. It indicts prevailing conditions as a false and inessential reality to be swept away.

Employing the false consciousness concept here permits us to diagnose the harsh, often incredulous response to the claim that "Black lives matter," as well as offering a guide to anti-racist activism. If it is true that false consciousness is upheld by specific material conditions that lend it plausibility, then to dislodge racist ideology requires both intellectual arguments and appeals to emotion but also, crucially, practical and concrete interventions aimed at dismantling the material conditions that are reflected in it.

5. Conclusion

A common complaint against the concept of false consciousness is that it is in some sense inherently paternalistic. This paternalism is taken to consist in the fact that in suggesting that someone else is wrong about objective facts of the matter, I imply that I, of course, am right. But in this respect, the false consciousness concept is not any worse off than everyday analyses of disagreement and error. Imagine that I know that you are hurrying to board the last departing train of the night, and I also know that you wrongly believe that you have an hour to get to the station when in fact the train departs in fifteen minutes. In this circumstance, I know something about the train schedule that you don't know, and I further know that while you believe you would be furthering your interests by arriving at the station half an hour from now, you would most likely not be. There is nothing about false consciousness as I have articulated the concept that is any more "paternalistic" than what is going on in this case.

Paternalism does not inhere in the mere fact of my knowing some things that you don't know, or even in my believing that I know some things that you don't know. There are numerous ways I could proceed in the train example, knowing what I know. One of those ways would be to grab your bag, force it into your hands, physically push you toward the door, and bark an order into your stunned face: "To the station! Now!"

Maybe there will be some exceptionally rare and dire circumstances in which such domineering behavior would be acceptable or even called for, but mostly we'd find it condescending and rude. What we might instead expect is that I present my evidence to you for the conclusion that you'd really better go, and allow you the opportunity to decide how to proceed on the basis of it. In this way, I respect your autonomy even while I may remain in disagreement with you about what you ought to do.

Being wrong about whether or not Black lives matter is not like being wrong about the train schedule. But the difference between these cases, with respect to whether I should physically intervene or take the time to patiently explain and to respect your autonomy, is primarily one of elevated stakes. If your wrong beliefs lead you to enact racist violence, there will be many more cases in which my response should take the form of direct action to impede you. But that is not because of anything distinctive about false consciousness. It is because of general background commitments we have regarding the immorality of my standing by idly to let you unjustly harm others, lest you should feel condescended to.

My aim in this chapter has been twofold. It has been to develop the false consciousness concept as an analytical tool that stems from Marxist theory but is in principle available to theorists and activists from a broader swathe of political and philosophical perspectives, and to argue that racist ideology is helpfully thought of as a form of false consciousness. Marxist theory is frequently accused of a one-sided economic determinism that dismisses the specific impact of ideal factors in determining social reality. My discussion of false consciousness, however, draws its inspiration from Engels's insistence that "once an historic element has been brought into the world by other elements, ultimately by economic facts, it also reacts in its turn and may react on its environment and even on its own causes." In the case of racism and capitalism, this mutual co-conditioning can make the nexus of oppressive material conditions and reactionary ideology seem impenetrable, immutable, and inescapable. Critical analytical tools such as the false consciousness concept help to make it less so.

Postscript

The preceding analysis was written before the dramatic uptick in anti-racist struggle that occurred throughout the spring and summer of 2020, as the police murder of George Floyd sparked Black Lives Matter protests in Minneapolis, across the country, and around the world. These events have borne out a central claim made here: that activism and especially direct action are key drivers in producing the objective material conditions that transform consciousness. At the height of the protests, a Pew Research Center poll showed that 67 percent of adults in the United States supported the Black Lives Matter movement (Parker et al. 2020). Similarly, June 2020 analysis in *The New York Times* found that pro–Black Lives Matter sentiment had increased nearly as much over two weeks of protest as it had in the preceding two years (Cohn and Quealy 2020).

In a society in which the deaths of Black people have long been treated as inconsequential, the public perception of racist policing has been profoundly altered by Black Lives Matter activism. Argument, moral suasion, and appeals to conscience have all played a role, but most significant has been the movement's concrete demonstration of its capacity to meet continued racist brutality with social consequences. Thousands of people in the streets night after night, actions that challenged the sanctity of capital and private property, and even direct attacks on policing infrastructure (as in the burning of the Minneapolis Police Department's Third Precinct) all made it immediately and viscerally indisputable that George Floyd's life mattered and was not inconsequential. It also introduced into popular discourse slogans that, like "Black lives matter," fundamentally challenged existing social norms. These were "Abolish the police" and "Defund the police."

Police abolitionism is a political project developed over decades of grassroots anti-racist struggle. It is theorized in the pioneering work of scholars such as Ruth Wilson Gilmore (2007) and Angela Davis (2003), who apply abolitionist politics to the context of resistance against the criminal justice system. "Black lives matter" challenges an apparent social reality in which Black lives do not matter. "Abolish the police" challenges an apparent social reality in which the institution of modern policing—and the social ills it is purported to address—are all regarded as necessary and permanent. It seeks to force open a conversation about what else in our social reality might also be contingent and mutable, and about what kinds of broader social transformations would be required in order to abolish the police.

Critics of the Black Lives Matter movement have argued that slogans such as "Abolish the police" or "Defund the police" alienate "moderate" audiences (Hamby 2020). Whether consciously or unwittingly, such critics peddle a false conception of how social change occurs and progressive alliances are made. Activists must stand with the oppressed and yet also stand visibly against the prevailing narratives that function as apologias for the status quo—a delicate balancing act, given that for a particular discourse to be dominant in a society is in part for it to shape the consciousness of even many of those whose oppression it justifies.

The task for activists is not to restrict themselves entirely to those demands that most faithfully mirror existing mass sentiment, however damaging and reactionary majority attitudes might be with respect to specially oppressed populations. Activists must raise a rallying cry for people whose consciousness is shifting in the course of struggle. Activists must develop slogans, politics, and analyses that aid in building a movement capable of creating those conditions within which the shift of consciousness on a mass scale can occur and in which a revolutionary force, capable of advancing the cause of human emancipation, can emerge and carry out its work.

References

Augoustinus, Martha (1999). "Ideology, False Consciousness, and Psychology." *Theory & Psychology* 9 (3): 295–312.
Boettcher, Jim (2009). "Race, Ideology, and Ideal Theory." *Metaphilosophy* 40 (2): 237–259.
Cohn, Nate, and Kevin Quealy (2020). "How Public Opinion Has Moved on Black Lives Matter." *The New York Times*. https://www.nytimes.com/interactive/2020/06/10/upshot/black-lives-matter-attitudes.html.
Davis, Angela (2003). *Are Prisons Obsolete?* Toronto: Seven Stories Press.
Du Bois, W. E. B. (1935). *Black Reconstruction in America: An Essay toward a History of the Part Which Black Folk Played in the Attempt to Reconstruct Democracy in America, 1860–1880.* New York: Russell & Russell.
Engels, Friedrich (1845). *The Condition of the Working Classes in England. Marx and Engels Collected Works.* Vol. 4. London: Lawrence & Wishart.
Engels, Friedrich (1852). "Revolution and Counterrevolution in Germany." *Marx and Engels Collected Works.* Vol. 11. London: Lawrence & Wishart.
Engels, Friedrich (1867). "Review of Volume One of *Capital*." *Marx and Engels Collected Works.* Vol. 11. London: Lawrence & Wishart.
Engels, Friedrich (1893). "Letter to Franz Mehring." *Marx and Engels Collected Works.* Vol. 50. London: Lawrence & Wishart.
Foner, Eric (2000). "South Carolina's Black Elected Officials during Reconstruction." *At Freedom's Door: African-American Founding Fathers and Lawyers in Reconstruction*

South Carolina. Eds. J. L. Underwood and W. L. Burke. Columbia: University of South Carolina Press: 166–176.

Gilmore, Ruth Wilson (2007). *Golden Gulag: Prisons, Surplus, Crisis, and Opposition in Globalizing California*. Berkeley: University of California Press.

Hamby, Peter, and Barack Obama (2020). "Peter Hamby Interviews Barack Obama." *Snapchat: Good Luck America*. https://www.youtube.com/watch?v=Yj-eNGfeG0o.

Jost, John, and Mahzarin Banaji (1994). "The Role of Stereotyping in System-justification and the Production of False Consciousness." *British Journal of Social Psychology* 33: 1–27.

King, Martin Luther (1965). *Address at the Conclusion of the Selma to Montgomery March*. https://kinginstitute.stanford.edu/king-papers/documents/address-conclusion-selma-montgomery-march.

Lewy, Guenter (1982). *False Consciousness*. New York: Routledge.

Lukács, György (1972). *History and Class Consciousness: Studies in Marxist Dialectics*. Cambridge, MA: MIT Press.

Marcuse, Herbert (1964). *One-dimensional Man*. Boston: Beacon.

Markus, György (1983). "Concepts of Ideology in Marx." *Canadian Journal of Political and Social Theory* 7 (1–2): 84–103.

Marx, Karl (1843). "Contribution to a Critique of Hegel's Philosophy of Law." *Marx and Engels Collected Works*. Vol. 3. London: Lawrence & Wishart.

Marx, Karl, and Friedrich Engels (1846). *Critique of the German Ideology Marx and Engels Collected Works*. Vol. 5. London: Lawrence & Wishart.

Matsuda, Mari (1990). "Pragmatism Modified and the False Consciousness Problem." *Southern California Law Review* 63: 1763–1782.

Parker, Kim, Juliana Horowitz, and Monica Anderson (2020). "Amid Protests, Majorities Across Racial and Ethnic Groups Express Support for the Black Lives Matter Movement." *Pew Research Center*. https://www.pewsocialtrends.org/2020/06/12/amid-protests-majorities-across-racial-and-ethnic-groups-express-support-for-the-black-lives-matter-movement/.

Pines, Christopher (1993). *Ideology and False Consciousness: Marx and His Historical Progenitors*. Albany: State University of New York Press.

Robinson, Cedric (2000). *Black Marxism: The Making of the Black Radical Tradition*. Chapel Hill: University of North Carolina Press.

Rosen, Michael (1996). *On Voluntary Servitude: False Consciousness and the Theory of Ideology*. Cambridge, MA: Harvard University Press.

Runciman, W. G. (1969). "False Consciousness." *Philosophy* 44 (170): 303–313.

Shelby, Tommie (2003). "Ideology, Racism, and Critical Social Theory." *The Philosophical Forum* 34 (2): 153–188.

Take This Hammer (1964). Directed by Richard O. Moore [Film]. San Francisco: WNET.

Williams, Bernard (1973). "Deciding to Believe." *Problems of the Self*. Ed. Bernard Williams. Cambridge: Cambridge University Press: 136–151.

3

He Never Mattered

Poor Black Males and the Dark Logic of Intersectional Invisibility

Tommy J. Curry

> *How representative were Garza's slaps at "hetero-patriarchy" and "charismatic Black men" of the black community in whose name she spoke? Would it be too hetero-patriarchal of me, I wondered, to suggest that maybe a black male or two with experience of oppression in the nation's racist criminal justice system ought to share some space front and center in a movement focused especially on a police and prison state that targets black boys and men above all?*
>
> —Paul Street, "What Would the Black Panthers Think of Black Lives Matter"

In the fall of 2016, I was invited to be part of a panel on Black lives at a Midwestern university. The topic of my talk was the unacknowledged sexual assault and rape Black men and boys suffer at the hands of police in the United States (Harris 2016). Earlier that year, a thirty-two-year-old Black man and father named Kevin Campbell was anally penetrated and sexually assaulted by a white police officer named Daniel Mack. Mr. Campbell was stopped by the white officer because his license plate was not visible. Mr. Campbell explained that "he had just bought a minivan for his wife, and it still had the temporary paper license plate taped to the window" (Catallo 2016). This explanation did nothing to stop the aggression of Mack. In a video of the illegal body cavity search, Mr. Campbell can be heard yelling at officer Mack, "You can't do that. Why you putting your fingers in my ass? Why you feeling my [shit]?" Officer Mack violated Mr. Campbell despite Mr. Campbell's pleas. Mr. Campbell said that this haunted him and that "It was very dehumanizing.

What he did was unconstitutional, violated my civil rights and violated me as a man period." Like many Black men, Mr. Campbell was exhausted by fear. He feared that at any moment any physical protest against being sexually assaulted could be construed as aggression toward the office and result in his death. So like with many other Black men, compliance even in the face of sexual violation and rape is a life-saving strategy (PoliceCrime 2016).

I offered the audience several other cases of Black male victims suffering sexual assault by police. I mentioned the case of Coprez Coffie, who was anally sodomized by a white Chicago police officer named Scott Korhonen in 2004 (England 2016). I described the horror experienced by Abner Louima, who was raped by a police officer with the handle of a bathroom plunger. I reported the pain of teenage Black boys, children, who had their genitals tased, as in the case of Andre Little, or stomped while on the ground, like Darrin Manning (Watkins 2013; Younge 2014). After recounting these stories, I reminded the audience that these occurrences of sexual violation and anal penetration (which would be considered rape if ever mentioned regarding a female body) were being ignored and erased within the discussions of police violence toward Black men and boys and replaced with the idea that the only violence that Black males suffer from in the United States is death at the hands of a white vigilante or another Black man.

Not surprisingly, no one in the audience knew anything about the rates of sexual assault and rape at the hands of police. In fact, even after explicitly documenting that Black men were 248 of the 258 deaths among Black Americans in fatal police shootings in 2015 and 223 of the 243 victims of fatal police shootings in 2016, the comments on my paper said nothing about whether my interpretation of the data was correct and showed both that Black males comprised well over 90 percent of the victims of fatal police violence and an unknown number of sexual assault and rape victims at the hands of the police,[1] but denied that the sexual abuse of Black men *even mattered*. The single comment about my research was that in the era of Black Lives Matter (BLM), we have had enough discussions about Black men and consequently should not be discussing them as the majority of those killed by police, even though we know this to be the case, and furthermore as rape victims by police, even though we did not know that they were. I urged the BLM activists and academics to integrate mental health services and trauma protocols for Black men and boys who were survivors of rape and sexual assault at the

---

[1] https://www.washingtonpost.com/graphics/investigations/police-shootings-database/.

hands of police. Their indifference was stunning. There was a tacit agreement from the BLM representative and the intersectional feminists in attendance that Black men simply were not to be centered as victims of lethal or sexual violence in any discussions, despite the evidence showing that Black males are more at risk than their female counterparts, given the political charge to concentrate on Black women and girls.

Black Lives Matter, like any other group, articulates its political vision through its constituency. Consequently, the focus on Black women, Black queer, and Black transgender peoples, while immensely important to understanding societal violence, misconstrues the violence against cis Black men and boys as simply a matter of racism. This chapter questions the organizational strategy and historiography of BLM. The first section will argue that BLM engages in a class strategy that actually silences poor working-class organizers and distances BLM activism from the majority of the victims of police violence and mass incarceration, which are Black men. In the second section, I argue that SayHerName and the associated academic theories influencing the organizational ideology of BLM deliberately ignore the sexual assault of Black men and boys by police officers. I conclude with a reflection on the erasure of Black men as sexual victims at the hands of police and how ignoring Black males as victims of rape undermines any attempt to deal with police violence. I am particularly interested in the way the concept of invisibility in intersectionality theory is used to "decenter" the sex-specific oppression, rape, or sexual trauma of Black males within the political coalitions of BLM and intersectional feminist theorists.

1. The philanthropist capitalist model of Black Lives Matter

For many academics and activists, BLM has been interpreted as a new civil rights movement (Edgar and Johnson 2018). Barbara Ransby explains that BLM arose in 2013 as a response to the murder of Trayvon Martin in 2012 in Sanford, Florida, and the police killing of Michael Brown in 2014 in Ferguson, Missouri (2018). BLM originated from a hashtag shared on Twitter by Alicia Garza, Patrisse Cullors, and Opal Tometi as a call for Black Americans to be treated as human beings rather than disposable bodies. According to Ransby, it has transformed into a consciousness-shifting movement: "It has penetrated our consciousness and our lexicon, from professional sports to prime time television, to corporate boardrooms, and to all sectors of the art world" (2018: 1–2). Because of its timeliness and unorthodox coalitional leadership styles, BLM is often described as decentralized and is praised for being adaptive as well as representing the emerging political consciousness of Black Millennials who see social media platforms and the anti-hierarchical discourse of the movement as pivotal to twenty-first-century social justice agendas. Even philosophers such as Chris Lebron have commented upon this aspect of BLM: "#BlackLivesMatter represents an ideal that motivates, mobilizes, and informs the actions and programs of many local branches of the movement. Much like the way a corporate franchise works, minus revenue and profit, #BlackLivesMatter is akin to a social movement brand that can be picked up and deployed by any interested group of activists inclined to speak out and act against racial injustice" (2017: xii).

Lebron underestimates the profitability of BLM over the last several years and the specific relationship to engaging poor Black communities this corporate mode entails. For the award-winning journalist Paul Street, comparing the activist model of BLM's founders Alicia Garza, Patrisse Cullors, and Opal Tometi to the class politics of Martin Luther King Jr. and Fred Hampton highlighted some unsettling and exploitative practices. According to Street, BLM practices a corporatism that seems more interested in "brand value and narrow identity than social justice" (2017). Since BLMS's inception, working-class Black communities have been distrustful of the celebrity-like culture of BLM and well aware of the extraordinary violence that would be exacted against them when the cameras went off. The leaders of BLM made their career working for nonprofits. They were not activists grown from urban Black communities in any way that would suggest to poor working-class Blacks that BLM would take their interests to heart or understood the kind of violence and political coercion poor Black people in the United States experience. According to Street:

> Black Lives Matter—founded by three veteran, professional-class, nonprofit activists and fundraisers (Garza, Cullors, and Opal Tometi) with long prior "close ties to corporations, foundations, academia and government-sponsored agencies"—poses no comparable threat to the established order. Its expertly marketed slogans, "Black Lives Matter" and "Hands Up, Don't Shoot," are defensive and pale reflections of "Black Power" and "Power to the People." BLM has little, if any, direct service relationships with the poor black communities in whose name it speaks.... The U.S. ruling class, whose

capitalist system is the historical midwife of modern racism, is not threatened by the racialist and black-capitalist BLM. But just to make sure that black anger is kept within safe political boundaries, a critical, cash-rich arm of concentrated wealth agreed last year to lavishly fund the group and a significant number of black middle class-led policy and advocacy groups coming in under its rubric. (2017)

As a Marxist, Street insists that BLM is a corporate-sponsored platform instrument that markets capitalist programs supporting democratic and liberal political platforms under the guise of Black radicalism. The 2016 democratic primaries serve as a prime example. Bernie Sanders and his supporters were repeatedly attacked by BLM as inattentive to police brutality and anti-Black racism in the United States. He was effectively the only candidate deplatformed by BLM, while Hillary Clinton and the Democratic National Convention were allowed to meet with BLM and incorporate BLM slogans into electoral strategy (Lind 2015; Street 2017). Clinton and the Democratic National Convention actually passed resolutions supporting BLM. In 2016, the Democratic National Convention invited the Black mothers of dead Black boys on stage to show their solidarity with BLM (Friedersdorf 2015; Seitz-Ward 2015). Despite the harm Hillary and Bill Clinton's crime bill and economic policies had on Black men and boys, the mothers of the dead Black boys that inspired protests against police brutality and state violence overwhelmingly endorsed Hillary Clinton's platform and candidacy (Alexander 2016).

Careful to distance himself from the implicit Marxist assertion of race as epiphenomenal or secondary to the objective reality of class, the sociologist Tamari Kitossa writes that:

> Street opens up questions about the radical pedigree of BLM and the complex ways that it becomes the dominant framing for Black resistance movements. Whereas prior to the emergence of BLM localized grass-root organizations challenged and protested without any media attention, this changed when BLM became the public face of the new civil rights movement. Its central distinction is that it explicitly centres queer politics mixed with an odd variant of Black capitalism and racial tribalism. The official BLM organization teamed up with OneUnited Bank to launch, in February 2017, a Black Lives Matter credit card. Leaders of BLM insist there is no role for white people in the Black liberation struggle, so the cross-race working

class solidarity of the sort advocated by Fred Hampton is beyond consideration. Most recently, Garza and company have been showered with one hundred million dollars from the Ford Foundation to distribute to various approved community based organizations, some which are directed by BLM organization leaders. (2019: 92)

Kitossa maintains that the capitalist drive exacerbates a class barrier to mass social activism and revolutionary consciousness: "BLM USA operates from the vantage point of Black philanthropic capitalism and that as a result are at odds with the organic resistance of many African-American communities such as Ferguson" (2019: 101). The corporatist drive of BLM commodifies poor Black Americans—makes them into products consumed by the liberal white public. Because BLM works from a sectarian logic, its class-based sociopolitical analysis and its ability to consider the dehumanization of specific members of the Black community based on gender, class assignment, and political ideology is limited.

BLM's inception involved a national marketing strategy to the Black community. The organization was sold to poor, overpoliced Black communities as a grassroots resistance to the police state and urban poverty. It asserts that there are policies, travesties, and political strategies that need no specific class analysis, but simply appeal to all Blacks through Blackness. In sum, there has been little analysis of how working-class Black communities could be comprised in ways that are economically, culturally, or politically different from those of BLM's platform. The absence of a class analysis within the movement allows a lack of reflexivity concerning whose Black politics come to occupy the trope of radicality. As the journalist Jon Jeter writes, "Almost since its inception four years ago, the BLM leadership has come under fire for its lack of a class analysis. This lack has been underscored by BLM's close ties to multinational corporations such as Google, nonprofit donors like the Ford Foundation, and pro-market strategies that are inconsistent with a radical black polity" (2018). Rather than responding to contextual problems of racism and poverty that might differ by region or community, BLM used poor Black communities' vulnerability to police violence, poverty, and political marginalization to brand Black suffering, not alleviate it. There was no concrete investment in poor Black communities or the hundreds of Black men and boys comprising the majority of the unemployed and most heavily policed and incarcerated throughout the movement (Alexander 2010).

BLM has now retreated from the forefront of social protest, leaving these communities to fight for themselves. The retreat of BLM from communities like Ferguson has resulted in harsher forms of violence and force directed at these communities (Hansford 2019; Salter 2019). Black Agenda Report recently featured an editorial by Tory Russell, a Ferguson organizer, who shared the consequences the celebrity activist culture has on the poor Black people who remain marginalized and cut off from the liberal white networks established by activist brokers like BLM, which are selling the pain of their lives. The Ferguson activist, reflecting on the last five years since Michael Brown was shot in 2014, explains:

> The actual contours of the protest as it shape-shifted into a full-blown uprising are still misunderstood 'til this day. Folks know the basics. They know the name of the officer (Darren Wilson) who pulled the trigger; they know some of us organizers and organizations. And they know that Ferguson and its people, unrepentant and righteous, kicked off "the movement" as we know it. But here's the thing, most don't know the deep toll the movement—the suppression and commodification of it—has taken on our lives or what we're still up against right now. To put it bluntly, people stopped giving a damn the second the QuikTrip stopped burning, before the ashes could even blow away in the wind. (Russell 2019)

The retreat from the suffering and violence imposed on Ferguson has put Mr. Russell and other activists who risked their lives to confront police that patrol his community in far greater danger than the leaders of BLM. He battles depression, anxiety, and fear of retribution, but most of all the disappointment from a movement that used the pain of his community to build a brand. According to this activist, their lives and ultimately their deaths have been commodified and sold to white liberals as a product. He explains:

> We were in the streets, attempting to construct the narrative of us, to share our truths, to heal, protect, and build our Ferguson; while our so-called movement brothers, sisters, and allies were building their platforms on our backs and redirecting resources to their pockets. We have been forced to watch the movement turn away from the masses of Black people activated by Mike's death and become mainly focused on lucrative mainstream acceptance from white media and white funders. (Russell 2019)

Instead of a world eager to hear from the activists and residents of Ferguson who suffered under the draconian brutality of the Ferguson police, Russell experienced censorship and media blackballing. "Our ability to shut any and everything down made the vast majority of us a liability on university panels and television roundtables. They couldn't predict what we would say, according to TV producers I spoke with behind the scenes on many occasions" (Russell 2019). While academics were touting their radical credentials for #BlackLivesMatter, the very Black lives rendered disposable and made silent were forgotten. The academic production of radical intersectional scholarship continued unabated for years, while the actual casualties of the Ferguson tragedy remained confined to their condition.

Perhaps Mr. Russell's most tragic realization was that the world silenced him and others like him because it resented his voice, the messages that would slip over his lips as truth. He was told that the world would be allowed to watch his death as well as the death of his fellow activists, but that he must not speak. "Even now, though several of the Ferguson organizers have been shot and burned to death, they're in their graves while some people who claim to love the people have been on MSNBC and haven't even mentioned their names. Some of us have had to endure interrogation rooms, while they've been sipping tea in greenrooms" (Russell 2019).

This is not the first time that local activists have made this criticism of the global BLM network. In July 2018, the Cincinnati branch of BLM left the organization. The organizers of the Cincinnati branch clarified in an open letter:

> We can no longer use or identify with the name Black Lives Matter—a rally cry that still has meaning, even if perverted by those pushing it as a brand. The depth and scope of betrayal of struggles against police brutality and the families fighting for their loved ones is too great. The continuous shift towards electoral and liberal Democratic Party politics and away from revolutionary ideas is too great. The consequences for Black, brown, and poor people are too great. (Harmon 2018)

The exploitation of poor Black people is nothing new in this country, but what makes BLM such a problem is the complacency of the Black academic class in the appropriation of the movement. As the former BLMC chapter, now known as Mass Action for Black Liberation, explains: "BLM did not create or build this new grassroots movement against police brutality and racism; they capitalized off a nameless groundswell of resistance sweeping the nation, branded it as their own, and profited from the deaths of Black men and women around the country without seriously engaging, as a national formation, in getting justice for fighting families" (Harmon 2018). Because poor Black people are not thought to be able to represent themselves and their communities, intellectuals deliberately deny integrating the people themselves into structures and systems that would allow them to voice and express their positionality.

The problem that emerges from the support of Black and white intellectuals who write the narratives that legitimize the celebrity activism of BLM is that of the interpreter. Zygmunt Bauman explains in *Legislators and Interpreters: On Modernity, Post-Modernity, and Intellectuals*: "The typically post-modern strategy of intellectual work is one best characterized by the metaphor of the 'interpreter' role. It consists of translating statements, made within one communally based tradition, so that they can be understood within the system of knowledge based on another tradition" (Bauman 1987: 5). The intellectual then comes to re-present the group Bauman terms "the new poor" (those marginalized and subject to violence and repression) to systems of power and publics such that they can be translated as something other than the wretched and disposable (1987: 177). The poor remain victims of a managerial logic and repression, so the racialized poor, which is a class separate from the bourgeois aspiring Black academic, is explained away as a category of political preference—an intersectional subject of democratic interest. The white liberal can see the image constructed of the Black poor. They can see the Black queer woman, Black straight woman, these democratic voters, the Black transgender man/woman, the Black activist, the Black feminist, because those are the political entities US liberals are willing to recognize. These constituencies have been publics of great concern to 2020 democratic candidates and the party at large (McNamara 2019; Elliot 2019; Finnegan 2019). No such political appeals by democratic candidates exist for Black males specifically, despite their overrepresentation as unemployed, imprisoned, or dead (Kinnard 2019). So the Black intellectual class creates these entities from the rawness of Black bodies and flesh that are unrecognizable within the configurations of state power and academic knowledge. The Black object is created so that the Black academic can present *it* to the world as distant and distinct from themselves (Curry 2017: 104–136).

BLM has been rewarded for being proxies for the Black poor, a class of academics and activists to manage this marginal population that liberal whites aim to maintain distance from. The corporatist message of BLM has escaped critique by Black academics and opinion makers in some part due to the harsh social penalties that disagreement with the movement entails. Under the blanket of liberal identity politics, criticizing BLM can lead to blackballing from jobs, bullying, and character assassinations. Even criticisms of BLM for not achieving its explicitly stated goals can ignite any number of social media attacks and calls for the publishing venue to retract said publication (Szetela 2019; Rojas 2019; Zevallos 2019).

Another explanation for the branding of BLM as de-emphasizing the deaths of Black males compared to Black women and Black gay and transgender populations could also be about white liberal support. In "Black Men, White Women, and Demands from the State: How Race and Gender Jointly Shape Protest Expectations and Legitimate State Response," Corrine McConnaughy (2017) argues that the support white liberals are willing to lend to protest movements may be determined by the extent to which they perceive the movement to be violent and, in the case of Black movements, the support they lend to Black males. Building on her previous article showing that racist stereotypes about Black people are driven by the negative stereotypes whites have of Black men, she and a coauthor found that "it is black men that are most likely to be distinguished from the other race-gender groups, and to be particularly negatively evaluated when they are. [They also found] those negative evaluations of black men seem particularly influential on assessments of blacks as a group—suggesting that whites may be more likely to conjure their notions of black men when thinking about blacks as a group" (McConnaughy and White 2011: 15).

McConnaughy argues that "public sentiment about protest matters not simply for the opportunity to influence public opinion on a policy issue, but much more fundamentally because public support of the act of protest, itself, can shape the likelihood of the repression of activists by the state" (2017: 26). The perception that BLM is about Black men, and that Black men comprise the movement, associates the movement with more violence, higher aggression, and less intelligence in the minds of white Americans. This is of consequence for how white Americans are able to empathize with the movement and, more importantly, the amount of violence they accept from the state toward members of BLM. As McConnaughy concludes: "That Black Lives Matter is about black men, associated in the minds of white Americans with violence, has consequence: among the stereotype measures only stereotypes of black men are significant predictors of opposition to the protest movement" (2017: 26). In this sense, branding BLM as nonviolent, not straight Black male focused, and led by three lesbian Black women enables greater sympathy and social support for the movement. A recent study by the media studies scholar Ethan Zuckerman found that the "peak of attention to Black Lives Matter was in July 2016, when Michael Xavier Johnson opened fire on Dallas Police who were protecting marchers protesting the deaths of Alton Sterling and Philando Castille" (Zuckerman et al. 2019). Put differently, the one incident of a Black man killing cops in Dallas was more strongly associated with BLM than all of the more often reported of killings of Black people since 2013 (Zuckerman et al. 2019). The relation of BLM with Black male lives thus has a noticeable consequence in the minds of whites, associating BLM with violence. This problem could explain why Black Lives Matter Global Network does not mention that Black males are peculiarly the most disproportionately affected by police brutality, incarceration, and death compared to other groups (Black Lives Matter Global Network 2019).

Even though BLM has been internationally recognized as an organization led by three queer women, their leadership has not stopped Black male activists from being killed and prosecuted more than their female counterparts for their involvement in the organization. In 2017, Americans became aware of an FBI program targeting Black activists as domestic terrorist threats. This program labeled Black activists fighting against anti-Black racism as "Black Identity Extremists." In December 2017, Mr. Rakem Balogun became the first person to be arrested by the FBI for Black Identity Extremism (Levin 2018; Speri 2019). The growth of BLM has come with a disproportionate share of death for Black male activists. Darren Seals, DeAndre Joshua, and Darnel Johnson were all killed for their activism surrounding police violence in Ferguson (Kenney 2016). And historically organizations led by women spare Black men and boys from lethal violence. According to the historian Robyn Spencer, even when the Black Panthers were under female leadership, "law enforcement officials adhered to gendered assumptions about leadership when determining their targets. . . . When the police arrested and killed, they tended to seek out men, thinking that men were the leaders" (2016: 94). But recently there has been a widespread media campaign publicizing the leadership of three Black women in BLM. Why then do Black males remain the primary targets of state lethal violence?

Decentering Black men in BLM follows from its ideological commitments to intersectionality, but it is also profitable for the organization within a white philanthropic complex that views Black men as violent and irredeemable bodies. Stereotypes of Black men as thugs and innately violent influence how white Americans judge the legitimacy or illegitimacy of violence against Black men and boys. Political movements focusing on Black men in the United States offend white America. The deaths of Black men and boys and the political movements and their challenges that emerge as a response to the demonization of Black males have led to state violence, government misinformation and assassinations, and Black men and women associated with these organizations being exiled or imprisoned. To avoid this fate, BLM has distanced itself from the victimization of Black males at large.

The celebrity activism from BLM could allegedly speak for everyone, while the victims of police violence remained no one(s). BLM proclaimed it would deliver humanity to the wretched but failed to make good on that proclamation. It promised an act of transubstantiation, an act akin to turning water into wine, or the Nigger into a Human (Warren 2018). Sylvia Wynter has previously articulated how poor Black men in America are liminal beings, disposable—No Human Involved. Because of this peculiar dehumanization, poor Black men and boys have been the stepping stone for the Black middle classes (Wynter 1992). They have literally paid for the class ascension of Black America with their lives. Unfortunately, BLM perpetuated this problem rather than arresting it.

2. SayHerName and the logic of intersectional invisibility

BLM is not tabula rasa in its organizational models of leadership. BLM has been decidedly reactionary to older, more radical forms of Black political resistance. The feminist leaders of BLM have been adamant in declaring the movement to be nonviolent and intersectional, as a way to distinguish it from the decadent Black Power and armed self-defense politics originating in the late 1960s and early 1970s (Garza 2014). The call to value Black life begins with the paradigmatic decentering of Black male political presence, or as Garza (2014) says of the movement: "It goes beyond the narrow nationalism that can be prevalent within some Black communities, which merely call on Black people to love Black, live Black and buy Black, keeping straight cis Black men in the front of the movement while our sisters, queer and trans and disabled folk take up roles in the background or not at all." Garza depicts the leadership of the movement as being opposed to the previous era precisely because of the role that straight Black men have in political organizations and political organizing. This does not come as such a surprise, given the theoretical trajectory of intersectionality in the early 1990s. Legal theorist Mari Matsuda writes, "In coalition, we are able to develop an understanding of that which Professor Kimberlé Crenshaw has called 'inter-sectionality'" (1991: 1190–1191).

These coalitions, however, are not simply an objective strategy for liberation and anti-subjugation work. The intersectional coalitional model is thought to be opposed to and superior to the race-first strategies of Black men from the mid-twentieth century. As Matsuda states: "perhaps the most progressive reason for moving beyond race alone is that racism is best understood and fought with knowledge gained from the broader anti-subordination struggle. Even if one wanted to live as the old prototype 'race man,' it is simply not possible to struggle against racism alone and ever hope to end racism" (1991: 1191). As a political theory, intersectionality presumes a reductionist interpretation of Black militancy and Black male anti-racist activism where every Black charismatic leader only focuses on race and racism in an effort to establish patriarchal manhood to the detriment of gender or class liberation (Crenshaw 2016). Black men become caricatures of single-axis thinking, as if they characterize race as the defining aspect of social hierarchy and Black oppression. Considerations of sexuality, economic oppression, and imperialism go unremarked, despite these topics occupying center stage in their writings, speeches, and organizational platforms (Curry and Keheller 2015; Sawyer 2020).

Drawing attention to the epistemic insiderism of BLM, where the identity of activists and writers are privileged as an expertise and authority, Szetela writes: "The rhetoric and images deflect reflexive attention away from the fact that all the identity-based problems that crippled black nationalism in the 1960s epistemological insiderism, proclamations to bank and vote black, etc. remain present in Black Lives Matter. Only this time, the calls to 'close ranks' emphasize black Americans who are not cisgender, heterosexual, and able-bodied men" (Szetela 2019: 19). Perhaps the greatest irony of a BLM movement dedicated to understanding police and state violence is that the organizers, theorists, and writers of the movement see no need to learn from the experience of cis Black males who remain the majority of those targeted and killed by police and extralegal state violence.

BLM, informed by both the political call and academic resources of SayHerName, insists that analyses of and activism against police brutality concern themselves with the gender-based violence Black women, queer, and transgender people suffer (Crenshaw and Ritchie 2015). In *Say Her Name: Resisting Police Brutality against Black Women*, Kimberlé Crenshaw and Andrea J. Ritchie argue that "the failure to highlight and demand accountability for the countless Black women killed by police over the past two decades . . . leaves Black women unnamed and thus underprotected in the face of their continued vulnerability to racialized police violence" (2015: 1). Intersectional feminists have asserted that the recognition of Black women killed is not merely honorific but ameliorative. Crenshaw and Ritchie claim that racial justice movements have solely focused on Black men and as such have "developed a clear frame to understand the police killings of Black men and boys, theorizing the ways in which they are systematically criminalized and feared across disparate class backgrounds and irrespective of circumstance" (2015: 1). Black women, they claim, are unaccounted for in the literature and not placed before the public's eyes. "Black women who are profiled, beaten, sexually assaulted, and killed by law enforcement officials are conspicuously absent from this frame even when their experiences are identical. While their experiences with police violence are distinct—uniquely informed by race, gender, gender identity, and sexual orientation—Black women remain invisible" (2015: 1).

Crenshaw and Ritchie claim that "acknowledging and analyzing the connections between anti-Black violence against Black men, women, transgender, and gender-nonconforming people reveals systemic realities that go unnoticed when the focus is limited exclusively to cases involving Black nontransgender men" (Crenshaw and Ritchie 2015: 6). However, this claim is misleading, since Black men experience the very same issues that the AAPF report suggest are uniquely experienced by Black women, Black queer, and Black nonbinary peoples. By suggesting that gender is invisible because of the attention to cis, heterosexual Black males, intersectional feminists maintain that intimate partner violence, rape, and other forms of sexual violence do not affect Black males.

In the AAPF report, Crenshaw and Ritchie assert that the decentering of Black males and the inclusion of all Black victims demonstrate that police violence is not about "fix[ing] individual Black men and bad police offers" (2015: 6), but they provide no evidence that any scholars or opinion makers analyzing anti-Black violence and Black men are making such arguments. Social scientists are quite adamant that Black men's murder by police officers is driven by a particular hatred and fear of Black males as criminals and thugs, and is not a matter of bad police officers (Smiley and Fakunle 2016; Hall et al. 2016; Adedoyin et al. 2019). Perhaps the authors are assuming they can change white liberals who believe this, but if this is the case, they have offered no evidence that focusing on multiple Black bodies who are not Black and male would in fact resocialize whites to not fear the group most disproportionately killed and harassed by the police.[2]

Invisibility stands in stark opposition to recognition and understanding in the literature on SayHerName. While there are no specific policies or laws proposed to remedy the distinct suffering of Black women, Crenshaw and Ritchie suggest that "the solution to their absence is not complex; Black women can be lifted up across the movement through a collective commitment to recognize what is right in front of us" (2015: 5). By making the cases of Black women killed and brutalized by police visible, there is a hope that the frame would be expanded. As Crenshaw and Ritchie write, "The challenge here is to expand the existing frames so that this violence too is legible to activists, policy makers and the media" (2015: 5). The appeal to recognition in much of this literature is somewhat surprising given the specific naming of anti-Blackness and the insistence upon a twenty-first-century Black politics (Garza 2012). This appeal assumes that there is a power in being seen, and that grasping the suffering of specific racial groups will inspire policy and opinion maker to address societal inequalities. This is an empirically tenuous position to hold, given that the claim by intersectional theorists is that the deaths of Black men garner all the attention and those of Black women very little. Intersectional theorists provide no evidence that the greater attention paid to Black male police killings, which outnumbers those of Black women by hundreds, forms a viable strategy to save the lives of Black males. It is asserted that despite the inability of recognition to save Black men and boys, recognition can indeed save Black women and girls.

---

[2] Crenshaw and Ritchie offer no evidence that recognition is a necessary condition to prevent police violence against any group of Black people in the United States. By their own admission, Black men are currently recognized as victims, and no analyses or acknowledgments have lessened their deaths. We simply do not know what is or is not part of the solution, so there is no empirical basis by which inclusion, recognition, or political representation in fact decreases Black deaths. The irony of such a claim is that it puts an unwarranted faith in political systems responding to the efforts of Black people to respond to racism. This view is based in an optimism and liberalism that is the direct target of Derrick Bell and Richard Delgado's work in critical race theory. These authors argue that American racism is permanent, and that legal and political systems do not respond to Black demands for justice, only the economic interests and pressures that affect various white constituencies (see Curry 2009).

In Andrea Ritchie's *Invisible No More: Police Violence against Black Women and Women of Color*, she argues that BLM alongside the efforts of SayHerName and the Black Woman's Blueprint "emphasized the need to incorporate women's experiences into discussions of police violence and develop systematic approaches to sexual abuse by police" (2017: 219). The SayHerName report draws from the Black Woman's Blueprint document, *Invisible Betrayal: Police Violence and the Rapes of Black Women in the United States*, which argues that "Black women in the United States specifically, fully accounting for the ways in which their experiences of sexual assault, or rape more specifically, constitute an act of torture requires understanding the historical context and institutional legacy of slavery and the contemporary burden placed on victims of police sexual assaults" (2014). Throughout the reports, editorials, and articles from intersectional scholars exploring the invisibility of Black women and state violence, rape is assumed to be a kind of violence specifically imposed on Black women. According to the legal scholar Michelle S. Jacobs, "Both Black men and women could be killed, maimed, mutilated at the will of the slave holder with no redress or sanctuary for the so gravely injured. Certainly, Black men were killed and maimed, as were Black women, but women were also violently raped and sexually abused by both the slave holder, and his employees" (2017: 44). This exclusion of Black males from considerations of sexual violence and rape shows that there is an ideological bias motivating which groups are viewed as victims and what counts as violence when it is perceived.

BLM and their intersectional interlocutors offer ahistorical assertions about the nature of rape and sexual assault singularly affecting Black women without any consideration of the sexual vulnerability and rape of Black men. It has been well-documented that Black men were victims of rape and sexual assault at the hands of white men and women during slavery and Jim Crow (Foster 2011, 2019). Black men were anally sodomized, made to penetrate other bodies under the threat of death, and endured genital mutilation under America's racial order (Sweet 2003; Aidoo 2018). Contrary to the lens deployed by intersectional feminism to evaluate sexual violence and policing, Black men were raped throughout history and are routinely raped within our society, even in their own communities (Curry and Utley 2018). The fundamental difference between the rape of Black men and women resides in the fact that while both were and are victims of rape, only the Black male is demonized as the savage Black rapist. As I have argued previously in *The Man-Not: Race, Class, Genre and the Dilemmas of Black Manhood*, the history of Black male victimization at the hands of police involved a (homo)eroticism that has endured since slavery (Curry 2017). While the history of American racism provides ample examples of Black men being raped and sexually assaulted throughout the centuries, SayHerName activists have refused to acknowledge and include the rape and sexual assault of Black males in any of their analyses or activism. Because gender requires a difference between men and women, BLM and SayHerName have insisted that gender-based violence comprises that difference and consequently does not affect Black male death or dying. Black men have been interpreted primarily through their corpses, not their victimization to sexual violence.

Intersectional feminism asserts that the sexual violence Black women and girls suffer during police encounters is causally related to their enslavement and victimization as women. As the SayHerName report emphasizes, Black women are also victims of sexual assault at the hands of police. It rightly highlights and condemns the abuse of Black women by police officers, specifically Daniel Holtzclaw and Ernest Marsalis, who raped Black women and girls without harsh penalties or even an acknowledgment of the systemic nature of this abuse (Crenshaw and Ritchie 2015: 26). But Black men are routinely subjected to rape by police officers in the United States (Curry 2016). Most recently, a Black man in Tennessee was anally sodomized and beaten by officer Daniel Wilkey during an illegal cavity search. The injuries Wilkey received required surgery and hospitalization (Stack 2019). Black men's sexual assault and rape by police has been a normalized, yet routinely ignored aspect of policing. In February 2017, a Black man under the alias of Theo was raped with an extendable baton by French police officers in Aulnay-sous-Bois (Chrisafis 2017). This twenty-two-year-old man was held down, beaten, and had injuries to his rectum so severe that they required emergency surgery. Despite occurring two decades later, these stories are eerily similar to the rape of Abner Louima. On August 9, 1997, Abner Louima, a Haitian man, was sexually assaulted by Officer Justin Volpe in a Brooklyn police station. Volpe forced Louima into a bathroom in the police station, grabbed his testicles, kicked him in the groin, and then anally penetrated him with a bathroom plunger. After he raped Louima, Volpe paraded the bloody plunger around the police station as evidence of his conquest (Fried 1999). Black men suffer tremendous amounts of sexual violence at the hands of the police, yet they are not included or even mentioned as sexual victims by BLM activists or within the SayHerName literatures. As mentioned earlier, there is a refusal to even acknowledge these assaults of Black men as rape.

Invisibility, as an intersectional concept, offers little guidance as to how to discern what is or is not to be ignored in pursuit of social justice. Consequently, there is no criterion offered by intersectional theory or politics under the nomenclature of gender-based or sexual violence that becomes clearer by saying one should also account for sexual violence in police encounters or as part of racism. As demonstrated by the aforementioned literature, these calls for recognition simply assert the most intuitive aspects of violence, not necessarily the most truthful. Much of intersectional theory has remained indifferent to the findings and theoretical advancements in masculinities studies, specifically work showing how Black men suffer specific gender-based violence because they are male (Mutua 2013; Curry 2017). Building on a second wave theory of gender by Catherine MacKinnon, which asserts "the congealed form of the sexualization of inequality between men and women" (1987: 6), intersectionality suggests that that maleness forms a border between certain kinds of violence—between gendered violence and other forms of violence (Crenshaw 2010). These ideas of gender and patriarchy are analytically fixed on male domination and privilege over women regardless of economic, racial, or ethnic social positioning, even when little historical or social scientific evidence establishes that all men actually do benefit within various patriarchal systems more than women in that society. Central to understanding what constitutes gender-based violence are the ideological and historical presumptions of male-to-female violence. If men are imagined primarily, if not solely, as perpetrators of sexual violence, there is a tendency to exclude these males from consideration as victims of sexual violence altogether. It has been well documented that Western patriarchal societies tend toward the elimination and systematic extermination of racialized male groups. The work of Errol Miller, Adam Jones, Jim Sidanius, and Felicia Pratto has shown that throughout history, patriarchal societies imposed harsher sanctions on and targeted racialized men with lethal violence. The systematic removal of Black males from society has previously been referred to institutional decimation where the murder of Black males, their unemployment, and incarceration are meant to keep them outside of civil society (Stewart and Scott 1978). This criticism of intersectionality's failure to consider how higher rates of police violence, incarceration, and homicide are in fact forms of gender-based violence targeting Black men has been made before; however, within intersectional theory these gender-disparities have been theorized as racism and consequently erase the sex-specific disadvantages affecting Black men and boys (Harris 2000). Rather than simply being a function of different masculinities where some males are dominated by other males, Miller (1991, 1994, 2004), Jones (2000), and Sidanius and Pratto (1999) suggest that patriarchy, as an actual system, thrives by oppressing outgroup males, or racialized males who fall outside of the kinship bonds of the dominant racial groups. For these authors, patriarchy is a system that thrives on systems of gendercidal violence (police brutality, mass incarceration, and lethal violence), or practices of violence that systematically separate racialized males outside the dominant racial group from society.

Whereas "feminists characterize patriarchy as primarily a misogynist structure driven by male hatred of and contempt for women ... empirical research shows that patriarchy is primarily associated with paternalism (i.e. the intersection of discriminatory intent and positive affect) rather than with misogyny" (Sidanius and Veniegas 2000: 48). Social dominance theory does not suggest that women are not oppressed within patriarchal and capitalistic societies; rather, it argues that "arbitrary-set discrimination" violently targets outgroup men while women experience patriarchal oppression primarily through coercion and hegemony. The idea that subordinate men are lethally targeted by men of the dominant group is called the subordinate male target hypothesis. Sidanius and Pratto explain that the subordinate male target hypothesis "does not imply the absence of discrimination against women, for such discrimination clearly occurs and is part of the gender system of group-based social hierarchy (i.e., patriarchy). Rather, what we are suggesting is that, everything else being equal, subordinate males rather than subordinate females are the primary objects of arbitrary-set discrimination" (1999: 50). Arbitrary-set discrimination contains the most extreme forms of lethal and genocidal in human history (1999: 34). In housing, incarceration, employment, and policing, social dominance theorists have found that subordinate group males suffer more occurrences of direct discrimination and lethal violence than subordinate and dominant group females within the same society (Sidanius and Veniegas 2000; McDonald et al. 2011).

The intersectional invisibility literature, which responds to social dominance theory, has conceded that Black males or subordinate group males are in fact the primary targets of the most virulent forms of violence in patriarchal societies. The visibility of subordinate males spares subordinate group females, like Black women, from direct oppression. Despite the vulnerability of Black males within these systems, some authors would like to suggest the targeting of Black males in patriarchal societies is not evidence of their powerlessness under the predatory regimes of patriarchy, but their privilege. Valerie Purdie-Vaughns and Richard Eibach (2008) argue that invisibility protects subordinate females from being the direct targets of lethal violence. But they also argue that subordinate males become targets of lethal violence because patriarchal societies value men over women. They explain that an intersectional invisibility model "views the oppression of subordinate group men as a reflection of the general tendency in an androcentric society to view all men—both those of dominant groups and those of subordinate groups—as more important than women. It is this marginalization of women in an androcentric society that causes subordinate women to be relatively ignored as direct targets oppression of compared to subordinate men" (2008: 383). Recent social science investigations of intersectional invisibility have shown that Black males are seen as more dangerous, and that Black women and girls are affected by the arbitrary-set discrimination and racism to a lesser extent that Black men and boys are. Black females are generally perceived as less dangerous and less threatening than their male counterpart by white society and white police officers (Todd et al. 2016; Thiem et al. 2019).

A reoccurring theme among SayHerName activists and social scientists deploying the language of invisibility is that of recognition. For Purdie-Vaughns and Eibach intersectional invisibility actually means "the general failure to fully recognize people with intersecting identities as members of their constituent groups" (2008: 381). For Crenshaw and Ritchie, by contrast, the experiences of Black women are unseen and unheard and require exposure if their negative experiences with police are to be solved. These calls by BLM and SayHerName build on a shared premise in the intersectional invisibility literature, namely that while subordinate males suffer from greater levels of violence, discrimination, and death, as well as unacknowledged sexual violence and rape, the primary struggle of multiple subordinate groups is one of recognition, where members of these groups "struggle to have their voices heard and, when heard, understood" (Purdie-Vaughns and Eibach 2008: 383).

The political power of this invisibility frame can be seen in the recent push to decenter the murder of George Floyd Jr. as the face of police brutality in the United States. Mr. Floyd was killed in broad daylight on May 25, 2020, by Derek Chauvin. Chauvin kneeled on Mr. Floyd's neck for eight minutes and forty-six seconds while three other police officers stood by and allowed Mr. Floyd to die from asphyxiation. Since his death, various national news outlets and social media sites have suggested that Black men still receive most of the news coverage and outrage, thereby furthering Black women's invisibility regarding police killings (Gupta 2020). From January to October 2020, Black men are roughly 99 percent of the Black people shot by police; out of 150 Black people killed, Black men are 149 of the victims (Muysken and Fox 2020). These numbers do not actually include the murder of Mr. Floyd, because he was not killed by a "police shooting." The tendency of Black men and boys to be killed by police indicates that Black male life is not highly valued in the United States. Being the target of lethal violence is a consequence of dehumanization and subhuman status. In this sense, Black male deaths are *thought* to be normal. It is the normality of these deaths that make them so easily dismissed.

Theorists and policymakers have historically asserted that the higher prevalence of violence against a specific group is an indication of their disadvantage and oppression, or a sign that their suffering deserves special attention and remedy. Recognizing Black men and boys as the primary victims of lethal violence after their deaths is not privilege. Mr. Floyd's corpse represents the aversion white America has toward Black males. He was killed publicly for the world to see. His corpse demonstrated that there was no power in being seen. Because he was not a human being, his death—even as spectacle—could not be stopped. It was simply the fate of his body. While there are marches against the killings of Black males, the death of Black males is not exceptional. Black male life is not valued as human, so the deaths of Black men and boys are easily used as political currency for any numbers of groups other than Black males themselves. The Black male is detested by the world, so his death can easily be replaced by the life of other Black bodies. It is these other groups who can be recognized, since he is doomed by his maleness, confined to death. This transubstantiation of the Black male is at the core of invisibility politics.

Intersectional invisibility focuses on who recognizes the death of Black men, not that being a Black male makes one more likely to suffer death. The specific targeting of Black men and boys has no significant consequence for intersectionality scholars. Instead of focusing on the seemingly causal relationship and risks associated with being Black and male in the United States, and consequently being a member of the most at-risk population for police encounters and negative police engagements, invisibility scholars assert that not being *seen* as the primary victims of police homicide is just as bad as being part of the group most *likely to be killed* by police. Because the criterion of oppression for intersectional invisibility is recognition, not actual injury or lethal harm, Black male suffering is interpreted as irrelevant to the outcome of being recognized. Consequently, the grotesque public murder of Mr. Floyd is thought to be a privileged kind of suffering since others *see* his death This standard which ignores that his particular Black male body is more prone to injury and death than his female counterpart ultimately usurps his humanity and ignores the magnitude of the oppression and violence that brought about his death. Both Breonna Taylor and George Floyd were killed because the police targeted Black men. Ms. Breonna Taylor was a victim of racist police officers' attempt to apprehend her ex-boyfriend Jarmarcus Glover; she was not the intended target of the raid (Joseph and Andone 2020). This distinction is crucial to how one assesses the analytic import of intersectional thought.

Invisibility advocates suggest that there is a need—both morally and politically—to recognize the death Black women and nonbinary Black bodies suffer. In principle, this cannot be disputed. However, this very same need is not extended to Black males suffering similar rates of sexual violence, intimate partner violence, or political marginalization in any of the analyses or literatures coming from intersectional activists and BLM. How does one assign consequences to invisibility? Is there an injustice to ignoring women, same-sex, and transgender Black bodies as victims of police killings, but no such concern regarding the conversations about sexual violence that fail to recognize the sexual victimization of Black men and boys and consequently make their rape by police unsolvable? The precariousness of the politics associated with invisibility is worrisome in a world where Black people are dying. Who should be seen, which disparities, and which resources should be allocated? Answers based on actual evidence of death and dying have thus far been in short supply.

3. Concluding thoughts

BLM has announced itself as an intersectional Black feminist movement. To include forms of Blackness thought to be deviant or unworthy of respect by the civil rights movements of the 1960s and 1970s, the founders of BLM have sought to create a political movement focused on Black women, queer, and transgender bodies. Garza, for instance, suggests that Black women suffer racism just like cis Black males but also "experience police violence in distinctly gendered ways, such as sexual harassment and sexual assault" (Garza

2014). This author disagrees with the assertion that the suffering and death of Black males can be understood simply under our present understandings of racism offered by intersectionality theory. Rather, Black men are affected by both race- and sex-specific violence, including rape and sexual assault. Despite the coordination of BLM and the African American Policy Forum on issues of incarceration and police brutality, Black men have remained in the background even when their sexual victimization mirrors that of other groups (Clark et al. 2018).

A similar problem emerges in how Black intimate partner violence is discussed by BLM and the African American Policy Forum. Highlighting the disproportionate rates of Black female victimization compared to whites, BLM and the AAPF suggest that Black women endure more abuse at the hands of partners and risk further abuse if they call police to intervene. The research cited by the SayHerName report interprets domestic violence solely through a male perpetrator and female victim lens (Crenshaw and Ritchie 2015: 22). The article "Why Black Women Struggle More with Domestic Violence" cited by the report actually suggests that the only time Black men are victims of domestic violence by Black women is when the women are trying to defend themselves (Jones 2014). The problem in this discourse is that while there is a move to better situate the myriad of ways that various forms of violence affect Black people, Black men are excluded from being considered victims of domestic and sexual abuse, and they are confined to the status of perpetrators. For example, in the very same economic strata that produce high levels of Black female victims of domestic abuse, social scientists observe extraordinarily high reports of male victims and female perpetrators and high levels of bidirectional violence (Field and Caetano 2005; Hampton and Kim 2005; Caetano et al. 2005; West 2016). Contrary to the female-as-victim perspective taken by the SayHerName report, all Black Americans are vulnerable to disproportionately higher rates of intimate partner violence and homicide.

> The stressors and oppressive systemic forces that disproportionately affect African Americans place them at greater risk for domestic violence . . . despite the overrepresentation of African American male victims of domestic violence and female-perpetrated homicides, there is a dearth of literature on Black male victims. This omission seems to reflect an assumption that males alone are responsible for intimate violence and are not themselves harmed by abuse. On the contrary, data show that for African American

males as well as females, "involvement in abusive relationships is likely to result in depression, stress, and alcohol abuse"—outcomes placing the entire family system at risk. (Malley-Morrison et al. 2007: 325)

The research by psychologists, epidemiologists, and clinicians shows that domestic violence in the Black community is bidirectional. This means that the violence in Black couples is perpetrated by both men and women at different times in the relationship. Put differently, the men and women in same-sex or heterosexual relationships are both the aggressors and the victims at different times (West 2012, 2016). All Black couples (straight or gay, gay or lesbian) have disproportionately higher rates of violence than whites. Unlike the theories used to describe white domestic violence in white populations, the theories for Black intimate partner violence show that economics, racism, and cycles of abuse must be considered as more likely causes of domestic conflict rather than the trope of patriarchy and toxic masculinity. Because racism and peculiar misandric stereotypes cast Black men as violent and misogynistic, scholars and public health officials use Black men as scapegoats for domestic violence and deny resources to poor Black communities (such as economic programs and mental health access) that would actually decrease domestic violence (Al'Uqdah et al. 2016: 880). BLM activism and writings continue to assert that patterns of intraracial violence are predominantly male, are causally related to masculinity, and that Black women and girls are primarily victims and not perpetrators of similar acts of violence (Caetano et al. 2005; Curry and Utley 2018). This belief is simply false, yet it dictates popular understandings and descriptions of intraracial violence, especially by feminist authors who refuse to account for current CDC victimization studies or cultural differences in intimate partner violence and homicide within the Black race.

Black maleness marks a specific social location of disposability and victimization in the United States that has not seriously been acknowledged nor seems able to be acknowledged by BLM. When Black males have been sexually assaulted and taken their cases against police to court, BLM has neither supported their cause nor highlighted their assault. In fact, as the sociologist Tamari Kitossa points out:

> BLM has taken an approach to critiquing heterosexual Black men that has an undertone of competitiveness and misandry. More complex readings of heterosexual Black masculinity, such as that presented by Curry and

Mutua, are not considered. The call is for straight Black men to "decentre" themselves and stop "taking up space"—a curious demand, since much of BLM's mobilizing is built around the destruction of Black men by the necropolitical state. (2019: 97)

This is curious indeed as Black males are victimized in ways that should be within the purview of BLM and the African American Policy Forum. The debates concerning male incarceration ignore that being Black and *male* produces vulnerabilities that have effects far beyond criminalization. Even when compared to their female counterparts and other race/sex groups in the United States, Black males endure the highest levels of lethal violence, social marginalization, and dehumanization, and for the last decade they have reported the highest levels of contact sexual violence and made-to-penetrate victimization in the United States (Smith et al. 2017; Curry 2019). As Jennifer A. Hartfield, Derek M. Griffith, and Marino A. Bruce explain:

Being Black, but more distinctively, being a Black male in America seems to increase dramatically the chances that someone is likely to have an encounter with the police where the civilian ends up dead. Being Black and male also is a robust marker of who is likely to experience unfavorable and unfair outcomes in criminal justice and across other key sectors of American society. . . . Black males are the only group for which legal intervention is a leading cause of death. (2009: 157)

These vulnerabilities certainly deserve attention or, better yet, serious study; however, the experience of Black males shows that the recognition of their corpses does not in fact inspire sympathy or action to stop them from dying.

Black males in the United States are roughly 96 percent of the Black people killed by police from 2013 to 2019 (Muysken and Fox 2020). Among all groups, Black males have the highest lifetime risk of being killed by police (Edwards et al. 2019: 16793). Roughly 96 per 100,000 Black men will be killed over their life course as compared to 5.4 per 100,000 Black women (2019: 16794). "Between the ages of 25 y and 29 y, black men are killed by police at a rate between 2.8 and 4.1 per 100,000. . . . Women's risk of being killed by police use of force is about an order of magnitude lower than men's risk at all ages. Between the ages of 25 y and 29 y, we estimate a median mortality risk of 0.12 per 100,000 for black women" (2019: 16795). While is it certainly true that both Black men and women are disproportionately killed by police, Blackness and maleness make Black men more likely to be a direct target of police brutality and death. Women are less likely to be killed by police as a group than all groups of men. Because of racism, Black women are certainly less safe than white women, but Black men are exterminated and endangered more than white men, white women, and Black women, because they are both Black and male. This is a reality that must be dealt with if we are truly committed to liberation and resistance to the state.

References

Adedoyin, A. Christson, Sharon Moore, Michael Robinson, Dewey Clayton, Daniel Boamah, and Dana Harmon (2019). "The Dehumanization of Black Males by Police: Teaching Social Justice—Black Life Really Does Matter." *Journal of Teaching in Social Work* 39 (2): 111–131.

Aidoo, Lamonte (2018). *Slavery Unseen: Sex, Power, and Violence in Brazilian History.* Durham, NC: Duke University Press.

Alexander, Michelle (2010). *The New Jim Crow: Mass Incarceration in the Age of Colorblindness.* New York: The New Press.

Alexander, Michelle (2016). "Why Hillary Clinton Doesn't Deserve the Black Vote." *The Nation*, February 16. https://www.thenation.com/article/hillary-clinton-does-not-deserve-black-peoples-votes/.

Al'Uqdah, Shareefah N., Calisda Maxwell, and Nichole Hill (2016). "Intimate Partner Violence in the African American Community: Risk, Theory, and Interventions." *Journal of Family Violence* 31: 877–884.

Bauman, Zygmunt (1987). *Legislators and Interpreters: On Modernity, Post-Modernity, and Intellectuals.* Cambridge: Polity Press.

Black Lives Matter Global Network. 2019. https://blacklivesmatter.com/what-we-believe/.

Black Women's BluePrint and Yolande M. S. Tomlinson (2014). *Invisible Betrayal: Police Violence and the Rapes of Black Women in the United States.* New York: Black Women's BluePrint.

Caetano, Raul, Suhasini Ramisetty-Mikler, and Craig A. Field (2005). "Unidirectional and Bidirectional Intimate Partner Violence among White, Black, and Hispanic Couples in the United States." *Violence and Victims* 20 (4): 393–396.

Catallo, Heather (2016). "Allen Park Police Sued after Man Says He Underwent an Illegal Body Cavity Search." *Wxyz.xom*, September 16. https://www.wxyz.com/news/monday-at-11-disturbing-video-captures-dehumanizing-jailhouse-incident?fbclid=IwAR1BMmFJblaFbq1mD_YedmM4L6XtAcdvMk5pT-YCKTDMaMqOTV1xeHRXqNM.

Chrisafis, Angelique (2017). "French Police Brutality in Spotlight Again after Officer Charged with Rape." *The Guardian*, February 6. https://www.theguardian.com/world/2017/feb/06/french-police-brutality-in-spotlight-again-after-officer-charged-with.

Clark, Amanda D., Prentiss A. Dantzler, and Ashley E. Nickels (2018). "Black Lives Matter: (Re)Framing the Next Wave of Back Liberation." *Research in Social Movements, Conflicts and Change* 42: 145–171.

Craven, Julia (2016). "Black Mothers Get a Standing Ovation at the DNC." *Huffington Post*, July 27. https://www.huffingtonpost.co.uk/entry/black-mothers-dnc_n_57980493e4b0d3568f8517ca?ri18n=true.

Crenshaw, Kimberlé (2010). "Close Encounters of Three Kinds: On Teaching Dominance Feminism and Intersectionality." *Tulsa Law Review* 46 (1): 151–189.

Crenshaw, Kimberlé (2016). *On Intersectionality*. https://www.youtube.com/watch?v=-DW4HLgYPlAandt=20s.

Crenshaw, Kimberlé, and Andrea J. Ritchie (2015). *Say Her Name: Resisting Police Brutality against Black Women*. New York: Center for Intersectionality and Social Policy Studies.

Curry, Tommy J. (2009). "Will the Real CRT Please Stand Up: The Dangers of Philosophical Contributions to CRT." *The Crit: A Journal in Critical Legal Studies* 2: 1–47.

Curry, Tommy J. (2015). "Robert F. Williams and Militant Civil Rights: The Legacy and Philosophy of Pre-emptive Self-Defense." *Radical Philosophy Review* 18 (1): 45–68.

Curry, Tommy J. (2016). "Eschatological Dilemmas: The Problem of Studying the Black Male only as the Deaths that Result from Anti-Black Racism." *I Am Because We Are*. Eds. Jonathan Lee and Fred Lee Hord. Amherst: University of Massachusetts Press: 479–499.

Curry, Tommy J. (2017). *The Man-Not: Race, Class, Genre and the Dilemmas of Black Manhood*. Philadelphia: Temple University Press.

Curry, Tommy J. (2019). "Expendables for Whom: Terry Crews and the Erasure of Black Male Victims of Sexual Assault and Rape." *Women Studies in Communication* 42 (3): 287–307.

Curry, Tommy J., and Ebony A. Utley (2018). "She Touched Me: Five Snapshots of Adult Sexual Violations of Black Boys." *Kennedy Institute of Ethics Journal* 28 (2): 205–241.

Edgar, Amanda Nell, and Andre Johnson (2018). *The Struggle over Black Lives Matter and All Lives Matter*. Lanham, MD: Lexington Books.

Edwards, Frank, Hedwig Lee, and Michael Esposito (2019). "Risk of Being Killed by Police Use of Force in the United States by Age, Race-Ethnicity, and Sex." *PNAS* 116 (34): 16793–16798.

Elliot, Philip (2019). "2020 Hopefuls Are Talking Transgender Rights, Signaling a Political Shift on the Issue." *Time.com*, August 21. https://time.com/5657157/2020-election-candidates-transgender-lgbt-rights/.

England, Charlotte (2016). "US Police Officer Who Sodomised Black Man with Screwdriver Allowed to Keep Working." *The Independent*, October 7. https://www.independent.co.uk/news/world/americas/chicago-police-coprez-coffie-screwdriver-assault-scott-korhonen-gerald-lodwich-a7350006.html.

Field, C. A., and R. Caetano (2005). "Longitudinal Model Predicting Mutual Partner Violence among White, Black, and Hispanic Couples in the United States General Population." *Violence & Victims* 20 (5): 499–511.

Finnegan, Michael (2019). "Thou Shalt Not Serve the Gay Meatloaf? Democrats Disagree." *Los Angeles Times*, October 11. https://www.latimes.com/politics/story/2019-10-10/democrats-vow-to-reverse-trumps-rollback-of-lgbtq-rights.

Foster, Thomas (2019). *Rethinking Rufus: Sexual Violations of Enslaved Men*. Athens: University of Georgia Press.

Fried, Joseph (1999). "In Surprise, Witness Says Officer Bragged about Louima Torture." *The New York Times*, May 20. http://www.nytimes.com/1999/05/20/nyregion/in-surprisewitness-

Friedersdorf, Conor (2015). "A Conversation about Black Lives Matter and Bernie Sanders." *The Atlantic*, August 21. https://www.theatlantic.com/politics/archive/2015/08/a-dialogue-about-black-lives-matter-and-bernie-sanders/401960/.

Garza, Alicia (2014). "A Herstory of the #BlackLivesMatter Movement." *The Feminist Wire*, October 7. http://thefeministwire.com/2014/10/blacklivesmatter-2/.

Garza, Alicia (2017). "Interview." *How We Get Free: Black Feminism and the Combahee River Collective*. Ed. Keeanga-Yamahtta Taylor. Chicago: Haymarket Books: 145–176.

Glick, Peter, and Susan Fiske (1996). "The Ambivalent Sexism Inventory: Differentiating Hostile and Benevolent Sexism." *Journal of Personality and Social Psychology* 70 (3): 491–512.

Gupta, Alisha H. (2020). "Why Aren't We All Talking About Breonna Taylor?" *New York Times*, June 4. https://www.nytimes.com/2020/06/04/us/breonna-taylor-black-lives-matter-women.html

Hall, Allison, Ericka Hall, and Jamie Perry (2016). "Black and Blue: Exploring Racial Bias and Law Enforcement in the Killings of Unarmed Black Male Civilians." *American Psychologist* 71 (3): 175–186.

Hampton, Robert, and Joan Kim (2005). "Domestic Violence in African American Communities." *Domestic Violence at the Margins: Readings on Race, Class, Gender, and Culture*. Eds. Natalie J. Sokoloff and Christina Pratt. New Brunswick, NJ: Rutgers University Press: 127–141.

Hanford, Justin (2019). "5 Years after Ferguson, We're Losing the Fight Against Police Violence." *The New York Times*, August 9. https://www.nytimes.com/2019/08/09/opinion/ferguson-anniversary-police-ra. ce.html.

Harmon, Mark (2018). "Why Black Lives Matter Cincinnati Is Changing Its Name." *Libcom.org*. April 30. https://libcom.org/library/why-black-lives-matter-cincinnati-changing-its-name.

Harris, Angela (2000). "Gender, Violence, Race, and Criminal Justice." *Stanford Law Review* 52: 777–807.

Harris, Ashley (2016). "Panel Discusses the History of Black Lives at the University." *The Daily Illini*, October 16. https://dailyillini.com/news/2016/10/17/panel-discusses-history-black-lives-university/?fbclid=IwAR3Q3vWHKIFHowgGnogam_uV7-o2sriS7XYu1Tjs-nq6v8lCy3rfbcrpVvQ.

Hartfield, Jennifer, Derek Griffith, and Marino Bruce (2009). "Gendered Racism Is a Key to Explaining and Addressing Police-Involved Shootings of Unarmed Black Men in America." Inequality, Crime, and Health among African American Males. *Research in Race and Ethnic Relations* 20: 155–170.

Jacobs, Michelle (2017). "The Violent State: Black Women's Invisible Struggle against Police Violence." *William and Mary Journal of Race, Gender, and Social Justice* 24 (1): 39–100.

Jeter, Jon (2018). "Speaking Fees, Selfies, Sucking Up to Power: How BLM Lost Its Mojo." *MPN News*, April 17. https://www.mintpressnews.com/speaking-fees-selfies-sucking-up-to-power-how-blm-lost-its-mojo/240592/?fbclid=IwAR29sIRcf1BiqsNv9AHud4v-cMQnAS6tSIN5VPTHdLn_iV-x4EFd8rVHPNc.

Jones, Adam (2000). "Gendercide and Genocide." *Journal of Genocide Studies* 2 (2): 185–211.

Jones, Feminista (2014). "Why Black Women Struggle More with Domestic Violence." *Time*, September 10. https://time.com/3313343/ray-rice-black-women-domestic-violence/.

Joseph, Elizabeth, and Dakin Andone. "Breonna Taylor's Ex-boyfriend Has Been Arrested and Says She Had Nothing to Do with Alleged Drug Trade." August 28, 2020. https://edition.cnn.com/2020/08/27/us/breonna-taylor-jamarcus-glover-arrest/index.html.

Kenney, Tanasia (2016). "Activist Darren Seals Wasn't the First Ferguson Man to Be Shot, Torched in His Car." *Atlanta Black Star*, September 8. https://atlantablackstar.com/2016/09/08/activist-darren-seals-wasnt-the-first-ferguson-man-shot-torched-car/?utm_content=bufferd65b0andutm_medium=socialandutm_source=facebook.comandutm_campaign=bufferandfbclid=IwAR2dFDq1ZdC7wo4ZDo0miIUq9j9bbDI_cX3dQ64IGoczd1Aac-8.

Kinnard, Meg (2019). "Booker Extends 2020 Campaign Outreach to Black Men in South." *APNews.com*, December 2. https://apnews.com/d8694c2859564c989ea77904e4685468.

Kitossa, Tamari (2019). "African Canadian Leadership and the Metaphoricality of Crisis: Towards Theorizing, Research, and Practice." *African Canadian Leadership: Continuity, Transition, Transformation*. Eds. Tamari Kitossa, Erica Lawson, and Philip Howard. Toronto: University of Toronto Press: 71–100.

Lebron, Chris (2017). *The Making of Black Lives Matter*. New York: Oxford Press.

Levin, Sam (2018). "Black Activist Jailed for His Facebook Posts Speaks Out about Secret FBI Surveillance." *The Guardian*, May 11. https://www.theguardian.com/world/2018/may/11/rakem-balogun-interview-black-identity-extremists-fbi-surveillance.

Lind, Dara (2015). "Black Lives Matter vs Bernie Sanders, Explained." *Vox.com*, August 11. https://www.vox.com/2015/8/11/9127653/bernie-sanders-black-lives-matter.

MacKinnon, Catherine (1987). *Feminism Unmodified*. Cambridge, MA: Harvard University Press.

Malley-Morrison, Kathleen, Denise Hines, Doe West, Jesse Tauriac, and Mizuho Arai (2007). "Domestic Violence in Ethnocultural Minority Groups." *Family Interventions in Domestic Violence*. Eds. John Hamel and Tonia L. Nicholls. New York: Springer: 319–341.

Matsuda, Mari (1990). "Beside My Sister, Facing the Enemy: Legal Theory Out of Coalition." *Stanford Law Review* 43 (6): 1183–1192.

McConnaughy, Corrine (2017). "Black Men, White Women, and Demands from the State: How Race and Gender Jointly Shape Protest Expectations and Legitimate State Response." *Dannyhayes.org*. http://www.dannyhayes.org/uploads/6/9/8/5/69858539/mcconnaughy_race_gender_protest_workshop_june2017.pdf.

McConnaughy, Corrine, and Ishmael White (2011). "Racial Politics Complicated: The Work of Gendered Race Cues in American Politics." https://polisci.osu.edu/sites/polisci.osu.edu/files/mcconnaughy_white.pdf.

McDonald, Melissa, Carlos D. Navarrete, and Jim Sidanius (2011). "Developing a Theory of Gendered Prejudice: An Evolutionary and Social Dominance Perspective." *Social Cognition, Social Identity, and Intergroup Relations*. Eds. Roderick Kramer, Geoffrey Leonardelli, and Robert Livingston. New York: Psychology Press: 189–220.

McMahon, Jean M., and Kimberly Barsamian Kahn (2018). "When Sexism Leads to Racism: Threat, Protecting Women, and Racial Bias." *Sex Roles* 78: 591–605.

McNamara, Brittney (2019). "Cory Booker Called for Protection of Black Transgender Women during Democratic Debate." *Teen Vogue*, June 27. https://www.teenvogue.com/story/corey-booker-black-transgender-women.

Miller, Errol (1991). *Men at Risk*. Kingston: Jamaica Publishing House.

Miller, Errol (1994). *Marginalization of the Black Male: Insights from the Development of the Teaching Profession.* Barbados: Canoe Press.

Miller, Errol (2004). "Male Marginalization Revisited." *Gender in the 21st Century: Caribbean Perspectives, Visions and Possibilities.* Eds. Elsa Leo-Rhynie and Barbara Bailey. Kingston: Ian Randle: 99–133.

Mutua, Athena (2013). "Multidimensionality Is to Masculinities what Intersectionality Is to Feminism." *Nevada Law Review* 13: 341–367.

Muysken, John, and Joe Fox (2020). "Fatal Force." *The Washington Post*, October 1. https://www.washingtonpost.com/graphics/investigations/police-shootings-database/.

PoliceCrime (2016). "Officer Performing Forced Anal Cavity Search on Innocent Man." https://www.youtube.com/watch?v=IxNN1cS8nhc.

Purdie-Vaughns, Valerie, and Richard Eibach (2008). "Intersectionality Invisibility: The Distinctive Advantages and Disadvantages of Multiple Subordinate-Group Identities." *Sex Roles* 59 (5): 377–391.

Ransby, Barbara (2018). *Making All Black Lives Matter: Reimagining Freedom in the 21st Century.* Oakland: University of California Press.

Ritchie, Andrea J. (2017). *Invisible No More: Police Violence against Black Women and Women of Color.* Boston: Beacon Press.

Rojas, Fabio (2019). *Commentary on Szetela's 2019 Critique of Black Lives Matter.* July 30. https://orgtheory.wordpress.com/2019/07/30/commentary-on-szetelas-2019-critique-of-black-lives-matter/.

Russell, Tory (2019). "A Ferguson Organizer Reflects on the Aftermath." *Black Agenda Report*, September 11. https://blackagendareport.com/ferguson-organizer-reflects-aftermath?fbclid=IwAR1-LbobdzqVfgaWQsxvLTxNnRMa-Ln6WtmO5CMZ-d2XSTyO5XJyvHds2cM.

Salter, Jim (2019). "5 Years after Fatal Shooting of Michael Brown in Ferguson, Racial Tensions Might Be More Intense." *Fortune.com*, August 9. https://fortune.com/2019/08/09/michael-brown-ferguson-race/.

Sawyer, Michael (2020). *The Political Philosophy of Malcolm X.* London: Pluto Press.

Seitz-Wald, Alex (2015). "DNC Passes Resolution Supporting Black Lives Matter." *MSNBC.com*, August 28. http://www.msnbc.com/msnbc/dnc-passes-resolution-supporting-black-lives-matter.

Sidanius, Jim, and Felicia Pratto (1999). *Social Dominance: An Intergroup Theory of Social Hierarchy and Oppression.* New York: Cambridge University Press.

Sidanius, Jim, and Rosemary Veniegas (2000). "Gender and Race Discrimination: The Interactive Nature of Disadvantage." *Reducing Prejudice and Race Discrimination.* Ed. Stuart Oskamp. Mahwah, NJ: Lawrence Erlbaum Associates: 47–69.

Smiley, Calvin John, and David Fakunle (2016). "From Brute to Thug: The Demonization and Criminalization of Unarmed Black Male Victims in America." *Journal of Human Behavior in the Social Environment* 26 (3–4): 350–366.

Smith, Sharon G., Jieru Chen, Kathleen C. Basile, Leah K. Gilbert, Melissa T. Merrick, Nimesh Patel, Margie Walling, and Anurag Jain (2017). *The National Intimate Partner and Sexual Violence Survey: 2010–2012 State Report.* Atlanta: National Center for Injury Prevention and Control, Centers for Disease Control and Prevention. https://www.cdc.gov/violenceprevention/pdf/NISVS-StateReportBook.pdf.

Spencer, Robyn C. (2016). *The Revolution Has Come.* Durham, NC: Duke University Press.

Speri, Alice (2019). "Fear of a Black Homeland." *The Intercept*, March 23. https://theintercept.com/2019/03/23/black-identity-extremist-fbi-domestic-terrorism/.

Stack, Liam (2019). "Tennessee Sheriff's Deputy Indicted on 44 Charges, Including Rape and Stalking." *The New York Times*, December 11. https://www.nytimes.com/2019/12/11/us/tennessee-deputy-daniel-wilkey.html.

Stewart, James B., and Joseph Scott (1978). "The Institutional Decimation of Black American Males." *Western Journal of Black Studies* 2 (2): 82–92.

Street, Paul (2017). "What Would the Black Panthers Think of Black Lives Matter?" *TruthDig*, October 29, 2017. https://www.truthdig.com/articles/black-panthers-think-black-lives-matter/.

Sweet, James Hoke (2003). *Recreating Africa: Culture, Kinship and Religion in African-Portuguese World, 1441–1770*. Chapel Hill: University of North Carolina Press.

Szetela, Adam (2019). "Black Lives Matter at Five: Limits and Possibilities." *Ethnic and Racial Studies* 43 (3): 1–26.

Thiem, Kelsey C., Rebecca Neel, Austin Simpson, and Andrew Todd (2019). "Are Black Women and Girls Associated with Danger? Implicit Racial Bias at the Intersection of Target Age and Gender." *Personality and Psychology Bulletin* 45 (10): 1427–1439.

Todd, Andrew, Kelsey Thiem, and Rebecca Neel (2016). "Does Seeing Faces of Young Black Boys Facilitate the Identification of Threatening Stimuli." *Psychological Science* 27 (3): 384–393.

Warren, Calvin L. (2018). *Ontological Terror: Blackness, Nihilism, and Emancipation*. Durham, NC: Duke University Press.

Watkins, Angela (2013). "Officer May Be Liable for Tasering Teen's Scrotum." *Courthouse News Service*, October 22. http://www.courthousenews.com/2013/10/22/62249.html.

West, Carolyn (2012). "Partner Abuse in Ethnic Minority and Gay, Lesbian, Bisexual, and Transgender Populations." *Partner Abuse* 3 (3): 336–357.

West, Carolyn (2016). "Living in a Web of Trauma: An Ecological Examination of Violence among African Americans." *The Wiley Handbook on the Psychology of Violence*. Eds. Carlos Cuevas and Callie Marie Rennison. Malden: Wiley-Blackwell: 649–665.

Wynter, Sylvia (1992). "No Humans Involved: An Open Letter to My Colleagues." *Voices of the African Diaspora* 8 (2): 13–16.

Younge, Gary (2014). "If Darrin Manning Were a High School Dropout, He'd Still Have the Right to Walk the Streets Unmolested." *The Guardian*, January 27. https://www.theguardian.com/commentisfree/2014/jan/27/darrin-manning-high-school-deserving-victims.

Zevallos, Zuleyka (2019). *Whitewashing Race Studies*. https://othersociologist.com/2019/07/29/whitewashing-race-studies/.

Zuckerman, Ethan, J. Nathan Mathias, Rahul Bhargava, Fernando Bermego, and Allan Ko (2019). "Whose Death Matters? A Quantitative Analysis of Media Attention to Deaths of Black Americans in Police Confrontations." *International Journal of Communication* 13: 4751–4777.

PART II
THEORIZING RACIAL JUSTICE

4
Reconsidering Reparations

The Movement for Black Lives and Self-Determination[*]

Olúfẹ́mi O. Táíwò

> *Now, how does this issue of self-determination have a relationship to the demand for reparations today? Simple. The necessary corollary to self-determination is that there must exist the capacity for putting self-determination into effect.*
>
> —Nkechi Taifa

Recent police killings and controversies, including the killing of Breonna Taylor in Louisville, Kentucky, and of George Floyd in Minneapolis, Minnesota, set off protests across the United States, which then spread across the globe.[1] Perhaps one reason why these protests were embraced globally is that anti-Black state violence is a global phenomenon: in Nigeria, the world's largest Black nation, widespread police impunity contributed to endemic torture, sexual assault, and killings. Tina Ezekwe and Kazeem Tiamiyu join Taylor and Floyd on the list of those dead due to anti-Black state violence.[2]

The Movement for Black Lives policy platform is an attempt to construct and articulate a broad set of positions on Black liberation that achieve consensus or plurality support among Black political organizations. It succeeds, at least, in building a foundation that can productively orient ideological

---

[*] Thanks to David Ragland, Marya Hannun, Keyvan Shafiei, Brandon Hogan, Alex Madva, Benjamin Yost, Michael Cholbi, Mark Lance, Rose Lenehan, Emilee Chapman, Laura Gillespie, Johannes Himmelreich, and all others who helped.

[1] Rashaan Ayesh and Rebecca Falconer, "In Photos: People around the World Rally in Solidarity of U.S. Protests and against Racism," *Axios*, https://www.axios.com/george-floyd-death-sparks-global-protests-photos-790f29a4-588f-4ce1-b66d-e4dc86bfaafd.html.

[2] "Eight pipo wey dia death from 'suspected' police brutality shake Nigeria," *BBC News Pidgin*, https://www.bbc.com/pidgin/tori-54493376.

Olúfẹ́mi O. Táíwò, *Reconsidering Reparations* In: *The Movement for Black Lives*. Edited by: Brandon Hogan, Michael Cholbi, Alex Madva, and Benjamin S. Yost, Oxford University Press. © Oxford University Press 2021. DOI: 10.1093/oso/9780197507773.003.0005

struggle between competing contemporary visions. Though many of the contributing organizations are based in the United States and many of its policy proscriptions are directed at the United States in particular, I'll argue that the approach set out in this document provides a useful basis for response to the global problem of anti-Black racism and racial justice.

Historically, political organizations and activists have released similarly scoping documents in periods of heightened political activity, including A. Philip Randolph and Bayard Rustin ("A Freedom Budget for All Americans"), Harry Haywood ("A Revolutionary Position on the Negro Question"), the Honorable Elijah Muhammad of the Nation of Islam ("What the Muslims Want"), and the Black Panther Party for Self-Defense (the "Ten-Point Program"). There are many ideological divergences between the positions articulated in these documents, but a consistent theme is self-determination as an organizing principle for advancing Black liberation. The visions of reparatory justice offered in many of these documents are no exception to this general orientation.

In contrast, the positions developed by philosophers have largely failed to acknowledge the central role of self-determination in reparatory justice, instead focusing either on arguments that portray reparations in overly legalistic conceptions of harm repair, or refocusing it on symbolic or communicative conceptions of the needed repair of social relations between Black people, their neighbors, and the relevant political and social institutions. Here I explore another argumentative possibility for reparations made possible by critical engagement with the arguments and proposals historically put forth by activists and other political actors, and the role of self-determination in their efforts.

The arguments for reparations for colonialism, the trans-Atlantic slave trade, and their aftermath are necessarily different from reparations in many other contexts, and we should be cautious in applying insights from other reparations debates to this particular discussion. The historical patterns and events that jointly constitute the history of colonialism and slavery involved hundreds of millions of people, scattered across all of the world's inhabited continents, and have taken place over five centuries. This particular reparations discussion, then, greatly differs in scale from the events or patterns that are the topic of many other discussions, even other mass atrocities—for example, those that were the subject of International Criminal Court tribunals after genocides in Yugoslavia and Rwanda.[3] Partly owing to

---

[3] For more on the International Criminal Court's tribunals, see Owiso (2019: 505–531).

the scale of colonialism and trans-Atlantic slavery—especially their temporal scale—is a set of philosophical puzzles and problems that has no clear analog in many other reparations cases.[4]

These observations point to a deeper difference between this reparations conversation and other reparations conversations. Reparations, as such, seek repair or recompense in response to harm or wrongdoing. But in many reparations discussions, the harm or wrongdoing occurs between parties in a given historical context. The challenge, then, is to figure out what repair looks like in such a context. Trans-Atlantic slavery and colonialism certainly involve and involved harm and wrongdoing at the level of individuals and communities, and responding to these is a very important part of what they ought to achieve. But trans-Atlantic slavery and colonialism are the historical forces that built the modern world, that built world politics as we know it. The world historical context is *itself* an important part of the wrongdoing, which reparations ought to concern itself with.

The implications of this point for the stakes and aims of reparations have been appreciated by activists and actors, particularly those among anti-colonial movements (including radical Indigenous activism) and the Black radical tradition, most notably the vision articulated and acted upon by the Republic of New Afrika in the early 1970s. This paper's aim is to review problems with existing views and to sketch an alternative critical reconstruction of the aforementioned ignored contributions.

That distinctive view, which I call the *constructive view* of reparations, is rooted in distributive justice. Distributive justice deals with how we understand, justify, or condemn distributions of goods and resources (broadly construed) to people, and the processes and social facts that explain these distributions. It also issues forward-looking recommendations about whether and how to change our current distribution of goods and resources. Reparations are about how to distribute resources between an aggrieved party and a party held responsible.

In section 1, I will examine current views of reparations in mainstream Anglo-American academic philosophy. In section 2, I will survey rationales and demands put forward by activists and thinkers throughout the African diaspora more widely. Then I will briefly sketch the philosophical features of a distributive justice-based argument for reparations that articulates what

---

[4] For a thoughtful discussion of the difference scale makes to reparatory justice, see Yepes (2009: 625–647).

I call the "constructive view" of reparations, drawing from the Movement for Black Lives, Nkechi Taifa and the Republic of New Afrika, and Dr. Martin Luther King Jr.

1. Repair views

Many accounts of reparations defend it primarily in terms of restorative justice. This position is best exemplified by Margaret Walker, which describes reparations as "creating trust and hope in a shared sense of value and responsibility" (2006: 28). On this view, reparations, where appropriate, are such because they repair the moral relationship of the aggrieved with the party held responsible. Something like this view is also instantiated by what I call this broad family of views: the *repair view*.

There are two broad subfamilies of repair views: harm-based repair and relationship repair.

Harm-repair views treat potential claimants of reparations (individuals or collectives) to have been harmed by the paying party, and they view reparations as repairing these harms. On this family of views, the welfare of affected parties is typically treated as the broken thing to be fixed by successfully petitioning for reparations (e.g., Verdun 1992: 597).

Relationship-repair views likewise consider the claimants as having been harmed, but they view the relationship between the parties as the primary locus of importance (Kumar and Silver 2004; Shiffrin 2009). On these views, reparations aim either at repairing the relationship broken by the harm and subsequent nonreparation (which cause additional injury) or at rightfully navigating whatever relationship remains between the parties by a performance of obligations arising out of that relationship. On such views, reparations are required because of what they communicate, and in turn because of the terms of amicability or détente which parties can reach. I will review objections to both subfamilies of views.

1.1. Against harm-repair views

Harm-repair views give reparations the role of fixing present harms causally connected to or constituted by previous harm. The view of harm typically underlying these arguments is welfarist: considering the aggrieving party to have harmed the victim by lowering them from some baseline of welfare that they would have enjoyed but for the offense. Reparations "repair" this damage by distributing benefits to the victim that close the gap between their current state of wellness and this purported baseline, perhaps with some interest for their trouble.[5] This way of thinking about the harm resembles discussions of liability contract and tort law, and many arguments for reparations in legal literature take this form, including the prominent recent argument offered in *From Here to Equality* by Sandy Darity and A. Kirsten Mullen, who argue that reparations should end racial disparities in wealth, incarceration, and other socially and economically important areas.[6]

I have no objection to the harm-repair view in other domains of political and legal philosophy, or for other cases that demand reparatory justice. However, this strategy runs into difficulties in dealing with reparations claims grounded in trans-Atlantic slavery and colonialism.

The conceptual problems with the harm-repair view in this context are about finding the right baseline of welfare. Even had reparations been paid shortly after the abolition of slavery: how could one "repair," say, whatever harm was done to a child born in the condition of slavery? For this individual's life, there is no "before" to return to. Put generally: it may be impossible to make sense of an individual "harm" claim on the repair view if the action or process being charged with harm is also responsible for creating the harmed agent. According to this objection, there is no possible world or relevant counterfactual in which the agent is better off without the harming action, because every world in which the harming action does not exist is a world in which the agent who claims they were harmed does not exist either.

Kumar and Silver term this problem the "existential worry," following Christopher Morris's treatment of the problem in ethical theory.[7] If successful, there are no backward-looking considerations that could possibly establish that processes like slavery or colonialism harmed the people formed as a result of those processes (the descendants of enslaved or colonized

---

[5] To take an example from international criminal law, see the ruling of the Permanent Court of Justice in *Factory v. Chorzow*, which informs the current policy of the International Criminal Court under the Rome Statute on reparations; http://www.worldcourts.com/pcij/eng/decisions/1928.09.13_chorzow1.htm. Also see McCarthy's (2009) discussion of the aforementioned.

[6] See, for example, Verdun 1992; Levitt 1997: 1; Roman 2002: 380; and McCarthy 2009: 256.

[7] Christopher Morris discusses how descendants of slaves would not exist at all but for the facts of slavery, which renders false counterfactual claims constructed along the lines of the repair view. Subsequent treatments of the philosophical problem have termed it the "nonidentity problem" (see Morris 1984; Kumar and Silver 2004; Roberts and Wasserman 2009).

people) and claims of harm cannot underwrite a successful argument for reparations for descendants of aggrieved parties.[8]

The welfarist conception of harm demands a comparison between levels of welfare, real or counterfactual. But it is unclear which contrast cases to use to ground claims of harm. For example, take the 1965 debate between James Baldwin and William Buckley. Buckley favorably compared Blacks' lives in the United States to those of Black Africans at the time (Baldwin et al. 1965). What if, as Buckley pointed out to a packed Oxford audience, Blacks in the United States are "better off" than their African counterparts?[9] If so, reparations face an even stronger objection than the existential worry: if a Buckley-style objector is right, there's no harm to repair![10]

But this genre of response faces its own "existential worry." If the existential worry is a reason that Blacks could not have been harmed by slavery, then it is also a reason that they could not have benefited from it. Put generally: if the existential worry rules out counterfactuals that establish harm, it in the very same way also rules out those that establish benefit—either for Blacks or whites whose opportunities and life chances (or lack thereof) owe themselves to a history fueled by a slave system and global colonial capitalism.

Perhaps this doesn't mean that Blacks are advantaged by slavery, but simply that they are not disadvantaged or harmed. But conceptual difficulties remain. The disparities in quality of life between Black Americans and Black Africans are themselves produced by the very historical process that led to the claims for redress, namely colonialism and the slave trade. Those processes figure into the economic development of nations like the United States and the relative lack thereof in Africa. Then they also help explain the very gap in living conditions appealed to by the Buckley-style objector.[11]

---

[8] Kumar and Silver's own view (2004) is an interesting intermediate case between the categories of arguments I've termed "harm repair" and "relationship repair." Like the relationship-repair theorists, Kumar and Silver reject a solely or primarily welfarist conception of harm as the moral impetus for reparations. They also spend the bulk of their essay on "rectification," which shares argumentative concerns with moral repair theorists, and the inheritance of wrongs (much like the particularly Lockean brand of relationship repair). Nevertheless, they characterize reparations and rectification as responses and remedies to injury (in a nonwelfarist sense) to African Americans, so I tend to group them with the harm-repair theorists. I don't yet see that anything of interests hangs on this categorization.

[9] A closely related style of response is to credit "the West" for any positive developments on the continent (access to modern technology or public health) while blaming African corruption or endogenous environmental and cultural factors for negative developments (war, famine). I'm not sure which argumentative strategy is less philosophically serious, but Mazrui has the stuff of a reply to this concern (1994: 8–10).

[10] For a more in-depth discussion of this web of problems, see Perez (2012: ch. 2).

[11] Shiffrin makes this point about the dependence of everyone, not just descendants of slaves, to the historical legacies of slavery and colonialism (2009: 334–335). For some historical treatments

Even if we were to confine our search for contrasts to a particular state, it is unclear that we would escape counterfactual problems. Take, for example, the United States. Some might use white workers' levels of payment or political privileges as a contrast case, arguing that the extent of harm caused to enslaved Black Americans can be measured by the quality of education whites received or the level of wage payments whites got. But this strategy runs headfirst into counterfactual problems.

First: were it not for slavery, there would be no United States at all. Historian Eric Williams argued that slavery was a stage of a process of colonization, a stopgap measure used to build a building a colony up to the point of development where it can attract free labor.[12] The settling and development of the British empire's American colonies follow something like the pattern that Williams describes: the first colonies imported enslaved African workers and indentured European workers to produce tobacco for the world market and defend the territory taken from the Piscataway and Nacostine peoples.[13] This labor was necessary for the bare survival of the colony and also to attract capital investment and workers to expand Britain's colonial possessions on the continent—that is, for the existence of what became the United States of America. While these sorts of facts are often appealed to by Black activists rightly pointing out the critical importance of slavery and its legacy for American history, they cut against the counterfactual argument.

Even setting aside larger explanation fail, we don't need a historical explanation quite so elaborate to see the counterfactual difficulties. That's because whites' wage levels and levels of political privileges throughout history were a result of the power structures set by the same social system that rendered Blacks enslaved. Both wages and political privileges are set by contestation across power divides: between employer and workers, political elites and nonelites.[14] The politics of slavery and racial domination, then, also determined the economic destiny of white workers. The question of white workers' complicity doesn't change this basic fact: in the counterfactual case where

---

of both sides of the comparison, see Amin 1972; Rodney 1972; Osabu-Lke 2000; Táíwò 2010; and Williams 2014.

[12] "When slavery is adopted, it is not adopted as the choice over free labor; there is no choice at all" (2014: 6–7).

[13] See Rountree 1990; Thornton 1998: 421–434; Asch and Musgrove 2017; and *History Magazine* 2019.

[14] Fields makes the point about how this should inform our historical understanding of English working-class rights, but the point as I understand it is general (Fields 1990: 102–103).

there is no social reality of systematic racial domination, there is nothing for them to be complicit in.

This same reasoning cuts against Buckley's preferred comparison of Black Americans' levels of income and Black Africans'. Historically, the slave trades involved a transfer of labor power from the African continent so large that, by 1850, the continent's population was half of what it would have been without them (Nunn 2008: 142). The trans-Atlantic slave trade, by volume, was responsible for double the amount of depopulation as all other slave trades on the continent combined. The labor power that the abducted people possessed then became an economic input in the macroeconomies of the countries where they were forced to work. That was of immense economic and strategic importance to colonial powers. For example, the total economic value of enslaved people in the US South was greater than the entire country's combined industrial capital until well into the nineteenth century (Piketty and Zucman 2014: 1255–1310; Williams 2014). The incentive structure generated by the existence of such a lucrative market for kidnapping resulted in the decline of previously stable societies, the creation of a continental bandit class, and interethnic divisions that continue to undermine political institutions on the continent (Rodney 1972: ch. 4; Nunn 2008). These factors powerfully shape the political circumstances and characteristics of African nation-states today.

Conceptually, the explanation for why we should always expect to find counterfactual problems is much simpler than the historical case. The very same racialized social system that constitutes a person as a slave (or potentially so) also constitutes other people as slave owners (or potentially so), and the same colonial social system that constitutes persons as members of the colonized group constitutes other people as members of the colonizing group. Then, the disadvantages being placed in one group (e.g., the enslaved) have the same structural causes as the advantages of being in the other group (e.g., potential slave owner): the overarching system that creates these categories to begin with.

A fuller treatment of the causal entanglements appreciated by a historical view shows that there are more existential worries than we initially bargained for. Neither the United States, nor developed countries, nor African countries, nor formerly colonized countries, nor the various gaps between the life chances of their current inhabitants would be what they are but for colonialism and the slave trade (Shiffrin 2009). This is clear both as an historical, empirical, and conceptual matter.

Then, what point in whose history can we appeal to establish a baseline of harm without triggering the existential worry? I don't think there is a satisfying answer to that question.[15] Harm-repair views that treat the relevant harm as having occurred in the distant past don't seem to survive the existential worry.

1.2. Against relationship-repair views

The problems with the harm-repair view have not gone unnoticed. Some authors, like Coates (2014) and Bittker (2003), emphasize the importance of racial domination more broadly than the considerable wrongdoing of slavery. This gets something important right, since the harms of racial domination did not end with abolition.

But this strategy also risks incentivizing narrowed attention to individual components of the larger system of racial injustice. Focusing on school segregation as Bittker does, for example, runs into the same problem as trying to calculate the damages of slavery in terms of unpaid wages (see Morse and Ross 2018). This approach may make it easier to calculate legal damages than an entire system of racial domination, but for the very reason that they represent a fraction of the injuries that provide the moral force behind reparations claims. The extent and scope of reparations that are likely to result from this reparations programs targeted to redress these might not be of the right scale to address the full system of racial injustice that I argue reparations ought to respond to. Racial domination was much more than wage theft or inadequate schooling, and the moral atrocities it involved demand a reparations project that matches their scale and breadth. Unsatisfied with this option, others opted to shift toward a family of argumentative strategy that gives up on the welfarist assumptions behind reparations-as-restitution entirely (Yamamoto 1998: 491–493).

Relationship-repair views task reparations with fixing damaged relationships: typically between the aggrieved party (and those who inherit their identity) and the aggrieving party (and those who inherit their identity).

---

[15] Daniel Butt (2012) offers a noteworthy attempt to do just this, proposing a "double counterfactual" which invites us to imagine any particular colonized community not simply without the particular colonial past it has but without having been colonized at all. I suspect this strategy will run into significant hurdles at the calculation stage, and in any event, the constructive view that will be introduced later in this paper obviates the need for it by shifting from "harm" to a more general sort of explanation.

These authors tend to reject a welfarist conception of harm both as an exhaustive explanation of what it is to harm someone and as the relevant kind of harm to appeal to in making reparations arguments. Instead, these authors take wrongdoing, the violation of the right sort of normative expectations, as the target of their take on reparations arguments. Authors advancing these arguments often frame relationship-repair views as a response to the difficulties with harm-repair arguments, most notably the nasty philosophical problem of identifying the right contrast class that arises on arguments that presume a welfarist conception of harm. Whatever else slavery and colonialism were, they involved significant moral wrongdoing. This damaged the moral relations that sustain political community, or that enjoy some kind of independent or intrinsic importance. Reparations are then tasked with fixing these moral relations.

One subfamily of relationship-repair views, which I call *inheritance arguments*, treats reparations claims as a straightforward payment of a debt. The injustice of slavery generated an obligation to pay and a right to demand payment, thus creating a creditor–debtor relationship between those who are identified with the former and those identified with the latter. Both the moral credit and debt are inheritable on this view: the moral credit is passed on to the descendants of the enslaved, the moral debt onto the descendants of those who were culpable in the slave system, and thus the relation itself is sustained from generation to generation. Reparations, then, alters the moral relationship between the debtors and those to whom the debt is owed, ending a state of war or enmity and restoring the possibility of fully cooperative relations, or simply (on a contractualist view, perhaps) achieving whatever non-instrumental moral value lies in fulfilling one's obligations.

An important set of inheritance arguments follows a Lockean approach based on a philosophical commitment to reparations as a moral or political right. Locke thought that the right to reparation of harm was a natural right, one that each person would have over every other person whether in a "commonwealth" or even in the state of nature.[16] Further, on his historical view of reparations, he argued that the children of those dispossessed by war, even where the war is just, retain moral rights to the possession of their ancestors (Book XVI, sec. 190–196). Where their rights to those possessions, or any other property, are infringed, the claimants are to be considered "slaves under

---

[16] See Locke's *Second Treatise of Government*, Book II, sec. 6–12. Bernard Boxill points to this passage in "Black Reparations" (2011).

the force of war" rather than free people (Book XVI, sec. 192). That is, the infringement of their rights harms a political relation between the claimants and the broader political community; this relation is degraded into conflict and adversity, where the relationship could and should be a cooperative one. Reparations repair by removing one set of barriers between the claimants and the broader political community, and thus help create the conditions for nonadversarial political relations.

Finding these sorts of theoretical claims congenial, a number of prominent philosophers have made similar if not explicitly Lockean arguments for Black reparations in the United States. This view is most obviously exemplified by Bernard Boxill (2003), though Catherine Lu (2015), Lawrie Balfour (2005), J. Angelo Cortlett (2005), and Robert Fullinwider (2000) also provide reparations arguments that make similar moves.

Margaret Walker gives a different kind of relationship-repair argument than the Lockean sort in her book *Moral Repair*. She argues that reparations construed as restorative justice for anti-Black racism are aimed at the "restoration of relationships" between Black citizens and other citizens, seeing the alienation of Blacks from their (now) fellow citizens and from the government they live under as a primary harm (2006: 224). Lu (2015), Kumar and Silver (2004), and Shiffrin (2009) argue similarly.

The harm to the relationships is constituted by wrongdoing—the violation of the right kind of normative expectations (Shiffrin 2009). Moreover, the refusal to take reparative steps when one has injured another (or otherwise ought to) can send a further signal that the ongoing moral commitment that the injured party morally deserved their injury or need not be regarded as a moral equal. Refusal can also be criticized for the culpable failure to signal the opposite commitment (Boxill 1972: 113–123; Shiffrin 2009). The past history of racial discrimination, disrespect, and the current living conditions of much of the Black world, to the extent that these owe their character to slavery and colonialism, would qualify as harm on these conceptions.

Since these views aren't committed to a merely welfarist conception of harm, we needn't appeal to a colonized person's being made "worse off" relative to an actual past baseline or a counterfactual scenario. These views, then, avoid the so-called nonidentity problem or existential worry. Instead, the important aspect of the ongoing wrongs of slavery (and, presumably, colonialism) for these theories is the ongoing failure of the relevant parties to repudiate the ills of slavery. Failing to provide reparations, these theorists argue, risks tacit endorsement of or some other kind of continuity with the racist attitudes of the past, on which African, African-descended, and other colonized peoples were deserving of inferior social status and treatment.[17] Then, the value of reparations is to be understood as communicative, an expression of serious and sincere regret of the past (Shiffrin 2009: 335).

This second group of relationship-repair views, however, faces a more important worry. Granted, they don't explicitly rule out material redress, and many even call for it. But the *grounds* for calling for material redress only contingently relate to the purpose of reparations as these groups conceive of it. After all, there are many ways to repair relationships and communicate an intention to change one's ways—verbal apologies, constructions of memorials, and other symbolic gestures might well suffice.

But there's another way to think about reparations, the same kind that motivated the harm-repair view: that the reason for and moral force of reparations claims are somehow bound up with the present-day living conditions of the potential recipients of reparations, and the consequences of those conditions for the self-determination of the people who live under them. Judged from this perspective about what reparations are about, any "reparations" view that isn't organized around material redress isn't really a defense of reparations at all. In the next section, I try a different approach, one that aims to hit the target set by the harm-repair view without falling prey to the counterfactual troubles of the nonidentity problem.

2. Toward the constructive view

2.1. *A difference in emphasis*

In my view, consideration of reparations claims demands a historical view of distributive justice, since the motivations for a present claim of reparations are intrinsically backward looking and discussions of distributive justice tend to focus on the present.[18] Reparations as such, after all, respond to past harm or wrongdoing.

---

[17] Kumar and Silver are speaking about the US context in this section (2004: 152), but I take it that this specific point of theirs generalizes.

[18] McGary (2010: 546–562) argues that this plays a distinctive role in the moral evaluation of reparations claims, where this evaluation is taken to be separable from an evaluation of future-looking, consequence-based analyses. Boxill (1972: 117) distinguishes reparations programs, which are necessarily backward looking, from mere compensatory accounts, which need only be forward looking.

Outside of the philosophical literature, many advocates of reparations for trans-Atlantic slavery and colonialism causally link current conditions faced by people living today to the historical phenomena they are responding to. For these thinkers, reparations are primarily considered based on what it is hoped that they will do for the recipients' lives in particular: give them access to the resources they need to determine their own fates, and pursue opportunities unencumbered by either discrimination or deprivation. Such views rest on stronger argumentative ground than those taken up more commonly in the philosophical and legal literature of the ivory tower. While a full defense of that claim is outside of the scope of this paper, I aim to both explain the basic structure of the reconstructed view and gesture at the commitments a full defense of it would take on.

A view centered on self-determination seems to be part and parcel of the Movement for Black Lives platform generally, to which its reparations platform is no exception. The very first sentence of the reparations platform tasks it with addressing "past and continuing harms" and goes on to propose policy initiatives aimed at empowering Black people directly with money and education, rather than spiritual healing or symbolism.[19] These include a universal basic income, provisions to deal with physical and mental trauma, and access and control of food sources, housing, and land. The rationale for the provisions, particularly "control of food sources, housing, and land," seems motivated by considerations of self-determination and neither makes reference to nor relies on any conception of reconciliation with or friendship to white or non-Black citizens.

This focus puts them in good company in the history of Black liberation movements. Dr. Martin Luther King Jr. argues that we should generally understand the stakes of movements for Black liberation in the following way:

> The Negro today is not struggling for some abstract, vague rights, but for concrete and prompt improvement in his way of life. What will it profit him to be able to send his children to an integrated school if the family income is insufficient to buy them school clothes? What will he gain by being permitted to move to an integrated neighborhood if he cannot afford to do so because he is unemployed or has a low-paying job with no future? During the lunch-counter sit-ins in Greensboro, North Carolina, a nightclub comic observed that, had the demonstrators been served, some of them could not

---

[19] "Reparations." https://m4bl.org/policy-platforms/reparations/.

have paid for the meal.... The struggle for rights is, at bottom, a struggle for opportunities. (2000: 129)

More specifically, on the topic of reparations, Nkechi Taifa writes:

Now, how does this issue of self-determination have a relationship to the demand for reparations today? Simple. The necessary corollary to self-determination is that there must exist the capacity for putting self-determination into effect. (1989: 10)

I contend that, like the Movement for Black Lives platform, both King and Taifa's comments are based in the importance of self-determination. They view their target as giving Black people the tools with which to meet their own needs and control their own lives, rather than fighting to achieve the good terms on which to beg, borrow, or get charity from those who have the power to determine their own destinies.

Activists, organization leaders, and actors in multinational or international contexts seem to advocate a different purpose for reparations than many academic philosophers have. Despite different justifications, argument styles, and concrete goals, a theme that emerges among these disparate views is a focus on the changes reparations could make to the lives of recipients in material terms, and the resultant empowerment of African-descended peoples within the power structures and institutions that construct and limit their individual and collective agency to operate within. This strategic gambit toward reclaiming self-determination for African-descended peoples stands in stark contrast both to the moralizing, obligation-based arguments of harm-repair views and the symbolic and communicative value emphasized in many versions of the relationship-repair views.

2.2. *Reparations and distributive justice*

These views share a commitment to a conception of the import of reparations as primarily emanating from a concern with the present material and social conditions of Blacks across the diaspora today, especially as these interact with the ability of Black people to govern their own lives. But that might be the very reason you're wondering: where's the *reparations*? Talk about self-determination and just distribution of resources is all well and good, but we don't need a history lesson to do that. What is the difference between a view of reparations that centers on the living conditions and self-determination of present-day people and regular old policy conversations, which also are concerned with living conditions in the ordinary sense? Why do we need the kind of backward-looking considerations that come up in reparations conversations to answer questions about whether or not to have this tax or that housing initiative?

But this is a virtue of the constructive view of reparations, not a vice. Every "regular policy" is itself a continuation of history, a use of the institutions and resources the past made available to the present. As such, every such policy constitutes a success or failure to break with the legacies of oppression that define our present. Redlining, sharecropping, Jim Crow, and mass incarceration were all constituted and preserved by a web of often individually banal policy conversations about zoning, property taxes, and price regulation.

Recall that principles of distributive justice govern how we understand, justify, or condemn distributions of benefits and burdens to people. It is possible to stop there. I call a *snapshot view* of distributive justice one that conceptually "starts over" and analyzes the appropriateness of the current distribution of wealth, resources, and social goods in abstraction from the historical processes that produced the distribution in question a *snapshot* view of distributive justice.[20] On such an approach, the only considerations that ought to bear on reparations are forward looking—for example, disincentivizing the past aggressor to take future harmful actions, or creating the possibility of future moral relations by signaling the aggressor party's stance on past injustices (Wenar 2006: 403–405). Many academic philosophers defend such views of distributive justice (Wenar 2006: 396–397).

Reparations are concerned with distributive justice, viewed as the distribution of the conditions for self-determination. But we can't see how from a snapshot view of distributive justice, since that elides the backward-looking

---

[20] Rawls's *A Theory of Justice* gives a famous ideal theory of political philosophy that gives considerable attention to distributive justice, but not to corrective justice (1999). Charles Mills (2017) points out that Rawls does not explicitly discuss rectificatory justice and seems to openly admit that the principles he outlines will be of limited application to (what Mills terms) "ill-formed" societies, those whose actual history does not sufficiently resemble the "well-formed" society. There is some disagreement in the literature about whether the view Rawls develops can adequately account for corrective justice: for example, see the exchange between Tommie Shelby (2003) and Charles Mills (2013), with Shelby dissenting, preferring a view that Rawls's theory provides adequate resources for the corrective justice needed for racial justice specifically.

considerations that make reparations what it is. A different view of distributive justice is required.[21]

Moreover, the view of distributive justice implicitly held by the activists and thinkers in section 3 explicitly appeal to backward-looking considerations of past racial domination and violence to explain their reparations demands. A *historical* view of distributive justice takes into account both welfarist considerations the snapshot theorist would consider (how well the distribution in question meets the needs of the people it affects) but also historical considerations explaining how that distribution was fairly or unfairly established are relevant.[22] The historical causes of present-day living conditions figure prominently, but as an explanation for who is on the hook for paying the costs of fixing the downstream effects of those historical trajectories.

2.3. Laying out the constructive view

The constructivist views reparations as the project of constructing the just world, in which the advantages and disadvantages of the transition to the just world are distributed in ways sensitive to past injustice. The constructive view relies on a division of labor between backward-looking considerations and forward-looking considerations. Forward-looking considerations establish the *target* state of affairs, and backward-looking considerations bear upon potential distributions of the costs of transition to the target state of affairs.

We can only get from the status quo distribution to a stable world characterized by the recommended distributions by expense of considerable effort, labor, investment, and other costs. In the transitory period where this work is done, there will be winners and losers across a host of domains of human interaction, resulting in a field of benefits and burdens. These transitional burdens must also be distributed. Another way to describe the constructive view of reparations, then, is concerned with the distributive justice of a

---

[21] Rawls seems to offer a stronger claim, one that implies that the views I've labeled "snapshot" views are somehow incoherent: "Thus in this kind of procedural justice the correctness of the distribution is founded on the justice of the scheme of cooperation from which it arises and on answering the claims of individuals engaged in it. A distribution cannot be judged in isolation from the system of which it is the outcome or from what individuals have done in good faith in the light of established expectations" (1999: 76). I won't lean on a claim this strong here.

[22] Nozick's "entitlement theory of acquisition" counts as historical in the technical sense considered here (1974: 150–151).

particular sort of transition—the transition from unjust social structure to a just one.

The constructive view thus sharply distinguishes two questions about distributive justice that are too often run together: diagnostic questions identifying problems with how resources are distributed in the status quo (stages 1 and 2) from prescriptive questions about distributive justice that ask what we should do about our current distribution of resources. Further, it provides a way of relating them to each other that clarifies what they have to do with one another.[23]

The vision emanating from the 1972 Black Political Convention in Gary, Indiana, is particularly instructive as a historical example of the theory of the constructive view. The conference endorsed reparations as part of a broader "Anti-Depression Program" advanced by the Republic of New Afrika, which included provisions for the construction of a literal Black nation-state by plebiscites. Each location or region could vote in the plebiscite to join or abstain from the nation, and the territorial borders of the resultant nation-state would thus be literally constituted by election, since the Black nation would be composed of all and only the areas that elect to join (Berger 2009: 50). It also called for a cession of land and a $300 billion initial payout to help finance the nation-building process, justified by the history of "slavery and unjust war against the black nation."

Taifa provides a clear articulation of the philosophy of the constructive view in the broader section that the epigraph to this piece originates from:

> If the self-determining decision is to accept the U.S. offer of citizenship in the United States, then that citizenship must be unconditional and carry with it the requisite affirmative measures needed to effectively integrate the Afrikan into American society. If the self-determining decision is to return to a country in Afrika, those persons must have transportation resources plus those additional reparations necessary to restore enough of the Afrikan personality for the individual to have a reasonable chance of success in reintegrating into African society in the motherland. If the self-determining decision is to emigrate to a country outside of Afrika, the person must have the same reparations as persons emigrating to countries inside Afrika. If, finally, the decision is for an independent New Afrikan

---

[23] For discussion of the problems relating distributive justice to reparatory justice (more conventionally understood), see Yepes (2009).

nation-state on this soil, then the reparations must be those agreed upon between the United States government and the New Afrikan government. The reparations must be at least sufficient to assure the new nation a reasonable chance of success in solving the problems imposed upon us by the Americans in our status as a colonized people. (1989: 10)

Though Taifa certainly may have a preference between these options, she is clear and careful to say that reparations for slavery and colonialism are consistent with a variety of choices at the level of the individual Black region or even person. For Taifa, reparations are the achievement of a state of affairs where the ability to choose between these disjuncts is meaningfully materially accessible to Black people, which requires material reparations to provide access to the resources required to make the choices practically available. This is also implicit in the Republic of New Afrika's decision to populate and demarcate the borders of the ex-U.S. Black nation-state through plebiscite rather than imposition.

Finally, something like the constructive view seems at work in the Movement for Black Lives policy platform. The platform's reparations section uses the word "harm" to describe the "past and continuing" effects stemming from "colonialism to slavery" through food, housing, redlining, and mass incarceration policies, and wisely asks for race specific policies to remedy these effects.[24] But this section of the proposal is situated within the full platform's larger vision of deep structural change, including its "Invest-Divest" section, which describes fundamentally renegotiating the distributions of resources and social advantages from the status quo, and its "Economic Justice" section, which specifies general and universal political rights that should be upheld for all.[25] Taken together, the document represents a comprehensive view of justice that reparations contributes to, which I would describe as the constructive view in action.

In this respect, we can sharply contrast the success of the Movement for Black Lives platform as an instance of the constructive view with another approach descriptively nearby but normatively far from the mark. Reparations paid by Germany for the crimes of the Holocaust to the state of Israel provide a clear historical example of something approaching the constructive view in action. The atrocities of the Holocaust—like those of the trans-Atlantic

---

[24] https://m4bl.org/policy-platforms/reparations/.
[25] Both can be found at https://m4bl.org/policy-platforms/.

slave trade and of European colonialism—involved incalculable and unjustifiable human suffering (Honig 1954: 564–578). The reparations paid Israel, however, neither represented an attempt to calculate the welfare losses associated with these grave injustices (as one might on the harm-repair view) nor primarily a making of amends (as on relationship-repair view). Nor did they represent the responsibilities of just *any* well-off country to just any displaced and aggrieved people. Instead, the reparations payment was calculated based on the estimated costs of resettling those who would become citizens of Israel—that is, according to forward-looking considerations that aimed to bring about a specific political outcome in the future.[26] Furthermore, the parties of this transfer were also nonaccidentally related to the history that produced the reason for the transfer. This example is explicitly appealed to by Taifa in her explication of the case for reparations, for reasons that the constructive view more or less restates: snapshot considerations established the outcome that needed to be pursued (resettlement and the construction of a state) and historical distributive justice principles identified Germany as the party that ought to bear the lion's share of the costs (Taifa 1989: 10). Many of the recognizable features of the constructive view are at play in this example.

But this example is also instructively different from the constructive view. Pointing out this respect in which the financial relationship between Germany and Israel on the resettlement question is not to endorse where and under what circumstances the now-Israelis were resettled—that is to say, not to endorse the prices paid by *Palestinians*, who were disempowered and displaced by the resettlement scheme devised by other parties (Massad 2000: 52–67). The ethical problems brought up by the occupation of Palestine underscore a virtue of the constructive view's demand for justice over the harm-repair and relationship-repair views, which demand reparations for specific target relationships or zones of welfare but often relegate questions about what will happen to everyone else to the background. Only an act of restructuring of the world *toward justice* counts as reparations on the constructive view, for which redress of past grievances is a necessary but insufficient condition. This is also a particular virtue of the Movement for Black Lives platform, which calls for targeted reparations for the descendants of American slavery but also for general structural changes that address what the resulting system

---

[26] I refer here specifically to the rationale for the resettlement payments, not the selection of land for resettlement, which needs to be justified on independent grounds. As such, this point provides no defense for either Israel's or the international community's treatment of Palestinians. I'm indebted to Samia Hesni, Deidre Nelms, and Keyvan Shafiei for this point.

will be like for all involved: including demands for the protection of political rights for workers of any ancestry to organize collectively, as well as divestment from fossil fuels to protect everyone's environment.

Settling the amount of reparations monies to be demanded is an important question. Some argue that the amount of reparation demanded should be sufficient to return the total amount of wealth generated due to trans-Atlantic slavery and colonialism, which would undoubtedly be an astronomical amount on any serious calculation—hearkening back, implicitly, to the failed harm-repair argument.

But on the most natural extension of the philosophically reconstructed version of the constructive view, backward-looking considerations primarily establish *who*: who is to be burdened (and how) with the costs of correcting the distribution of goods and resources and who is to be benefited. They do not establish the extent to which each side is to be burdened and benefited—that target is set by the future-looking considerations that aim to establish a just distribution of resources, goods, and other determinants of political self-determination. Then, wealth and capital transfer demanded by corrective justice as I have construed it here would not be queued to the immeasurable amount of value plundered from colonized nations by colonizing nations, but rather to whatever amount is required to produce a just future. Moreover, they would be limited by the ability of the relevant liable parties to pay in quite conventional ways, given that a *just* distribution is the target goal. Attempts to achieve this by burdening the poor or less powerful beyond what they can reasonably be asked for present a contradiction in terms.[27]

Admittedly, this philosophical reconstruction is in some tension with various activist arguments for reparations, most notably with respect to arguments attempting to calculate how large the costs of reparations ought to be. Though the broad contours of the arguments for reparations considered in the previous section are concerned with distributive justice, rationales for the amounts demanded often proceed on the harm-repair model, which I have rejected here. For example, the account given of the constructive view here doesn't provide rationale or support for calculations of reparations amounts that construe them as back wages for unpaid labor during slavery (Conley 2002: 13–20).

---

[27] Again, for further discussion of the seeming conflict between corrective justice and distributive justice conventionally understood, see Yepes (2009).

3. Conclusion

I've sketched a constructive view of reparations that takes self-determination and distributive justice as its goal and subject matter. This critical reconstruction of activists' views clashes directly with the repair and relationship views' ways of making out the harms of slavery and, especially, the extent of reparations owed that have been articulated by these peoples.

Maybe the descendants of the colonizers and inheritors of their spoils are sorry; maybe they are not. Maybe we'll be bosom buddies; maybe we won't. Maybe paying reparations will confer political and moral legitimacy on the paying states; perhaps it will not. But I side with voices like the Movement for Black Lives and the Republic of New Afrika in insisting that none of these possibilities is the point. Reparations are about the just construction of a better world.

References

Amin, Samir (1972). "Underdevelopment and Dependence in Black Africa—Origins and Contemporary Forms." *The Journal of Modern African Studies* 10 (4): 503–524.

Asch, Chris Myers, and George Derek Musgrove (2017). *Chocolate City*. Chapel Hill: University of North Carolina Press.

Baldwin, James, and William F. Buckley (1965). *Debate: Baldwin vs Buckley*. Cambridge Union Society (University of Cambridge) and National Educational Television and Radio Center. New York: National Educational Television and Radio Center.

Balfour, Lawrie (2005). "Reparations after Identity Politics." *Political Theory* 33 (6): 786–811.

Berger, Dan (2009). "The Malcolm X Doctrine: The Republic of New Afrika and National Liberation on US Soil." *New World Coming: The Sixties and the Shaping of Global Consciousness*. Eds. Karen Dubinsky et al. Toronto: Between the Lines: 46–55.

Bittker, Boris I. (2003). *The Case for Black Reparations*. Boston: Beacon Press.

Boxill, Bernard (1972). "The Morality of Reparations." *Social Theory and Practice* 2 (1): 113–123.

Boxill, Bernard (2003). "A Lockean Argument for Black Reparations." *The Journal of Ethics* 7 (1): 63–91.

Boxill, Bernard (2011). "Black Reparations." *Stanford Encyclopedia of Philosophy*. https://plato.stanford.edu/entries/black-reparations/.

Butt, Daniel (2012). "Repairing Historical Wrongs and the End of Empire." *Social & Legal Studies* 21 (2): 227–242.

Coates, Ta-Nehisi (2014). "The Case for Reparations." *The Atlantic*. https://www.theatlantic.com/magazine/archive/2014/06/the-case-for-reparations/361631/.

Conley, Dalton (2002). "Forty Acres and a Mule: What If America Pays Reparations?" *Contexts* 1 (3): 13–20.

Corlett, J. Angelo (2005). "Race, Racism, and Reparations." *Journal of Social Philosophy* 36 (4): 568–585.

Darity, Jr., William, and A. Kirsten Mullen (2020). *From Here to Equality: Reparations for Black Americans in the Twenty-First Century*. Chapel Hill: University of North Carolina Press.

Fields, Barbara Jeanne (1990). "Slavery, Race and Ideology in the United States of America." *New Left Review* 181 (1): 95–118.

Fullinwider, Robert K. (2000). "The Case for Reparations." *Report from the Institute of Philosophy Public Policy* 20 (2/3): 1–8.

History Magazine (2019). "400 Years Ago, Enslaved Africans First Arrived in Virginia." https://www.nationalgeographic.com/history/magazine/2019/07-08/virginia-first-africans-transatlantic-slave-trade/.

Honig, Frederick (1954). "The Reparations Agreement between Israel and the Federal Republic of Germany." *The American Journal of International Law* 48 (4): 564–578.

King, Martin Luther (2000). *Why We Can't Wait*. New York: Penguin.

Kumar, Rahul, and David Silver (2004). "The Legacy of Injustice. Wronging the Future, Responsibility for the Past." *Justice in Time: Responding to Historical Injustice*. Ed. Lukas Meyer. Baden-Baden: Nomos Verlagsgesellschaft: 145–158.

Levitt, Jeremy (1997). "Black African Reparations: Making a Claim for Enslavement and Systematic De Jure Segregation and Racial Discrimination under American and International Law." *S.U.L. Review* 25: 1–41.

Locke, John (1980). *Second Treatise of Government*. Indianapolis: Hackett.

Lu, Catherine (2015). "Reconciliation and Reparations." *The Oxford Handbook of Ethics of War*. Eds. Seth Lazar and Helen Frowe. New York: Oxford University Press: 538–557.

Massad, Joseph (2000). "Palestinians and Jewish History: Recognition or Submission?" *Journal of Palestine Studies* 30 (1): 52–67.

Mazrui, Ali A. (1994). "Global Africa: From Abolitionists to Reparationists." *African Studies Review* 37 (3): 1–18.

McCarthy, Conor (2009). "Reparations under the Rome Statute of the International Criminal Court and Reparative Justice Theory." *International Journal of Transitional Justice* 3 (2): 250–271.

McGary, Howard (2010). "Reconciliation and Reparations." *Metaphilosophy* 41 (4): 546–562.

Mills, Charles (2013). "Retrieving Rawls for Racial Justice? A Critique of Tommie Shelby." *Critical Philosophy of Race* 1 (1): 1–27.

Mills, Charles W. (2017). *Black Rights/White Wrongs: The Critique of Racial Liberalism*. New York: Oxford University Press.

Morris, Christopher (1984). "Existential Limits to the Rectification of Past Wrongs." *American Philosophical Quarterly* 21 (2): 175–182.

Morse, Joel, and Jetaime Ross (2018). "A Forensic Economics Approach to Reparations." *Baltimore Sun*, January 6.

The Movement for Black Lives. "Economic Justice." https://m4bl.org/policy-platforms/economic-justice/.

The Movement for Black Lives. "Invest-Divest." https://m4bl.org/policy-platforms/invest-divest/.

The Movement for Black Lives. "Reparations." https://m4bl.org/policy-platforms/reparations/.

Nozick, Robert (1974). *Anarchy, State, and Utopia*. New York: Basic Books.

Nunn, Nathan (2008). "The Long-Term Effects of Africa's Slave Trades." *The Quarterly Journal of Economics* 123 (1): 139–176.

Osabu-Kle, Daniel Tetteh (2000). "The African Reparation Cry: Rationale, Estimate, Prospects, and Strategies." *Journal of Black Studies* 30 (3): 331–350.

Owiso, Owiso (2019). "The International Criminal Court and Reparations: Judicial Innovation or Judicialisation of a Political Process?" *International Criminal Law Review* 19 (3): 505–531.

Perez, Nahshon (2012). *Freedom from Past Injustices: A Critical Evaluation of Claims for Inter-Generational Reparations*. Edinburgh: Edinburgh University Press.

Piketty, Thomas, and Gabriel Zucman (2014). "Capital Is Back: Wealth-Income Ratios in Rich Countries 1700–2010." *The Quarterly Journal of Economics* 129 (3): 1255–1310.

Rawls, John (1999). *A Theory of Justice*. Rev. ed. Cambridge, MA: Harvard University Press.

Roberts, Melinda, and David Wasserman, eds. (2009). *Harming Future Persons: Ethics, Genetics and the Nonidentity Problem*. Dordrecht: Springer.

Rodney, Walter (1972). *How Europe Underdeveloped Africa*. London: Bogle-L'Ouverture.

Roman, Ediberto (2002). "Reparations and the Colonial Dilemma: The Insurmountable Hurdles and yet Transformative Benefits." *Berkeley La Raza Law Journal* 13 (2): 369.

Rountree, Helen C. (1990). *Pocahontas's People: The Powhatan Indians of Virginia through Four Centuries*. Norman: University of Oklahoma Press.

Shelby, Tommie (2003). "Race and Social Justice: Rawlsian Considerations." *Fordham Law Review* 72 (5): 1697–1714.

Shiffrin, Seana Valentine (2009). "Reparations for US Slavery and Justice over Time." *Harming Future Persons: Ethics, Genetics and the Nonidentity Problem*. Eds. Melinda Roberts and David Wasserman. Dordrecht: Springer: 333–339.

Taifa, Nkechi (1989). "Reparations and Self-Determination." *Reparations Yes!* Eds. Chokwe Lumumba, Imari Obadele, and Nkechi Taifa. Baton Rouge, LA: House of Songhay Commission and Malcolm Generation Inc.: 1–13.

Táíwò, Olúfẹ́mi (2010). *How Colonialism Preempted Modernity in Africa*. Bloomington: Indiana University Press.

Thornton, John (1998). "The African Experience of the '20 and Odd Negroes' Arriving in Virginia in 1619." *The William and Mary Quarterly* 55 (3): 421–434.

Verdun, Vincene (1992). "If the Shoe Fits, Wear It: An Analysis of Reparations to African Americans." *Tulane Law Review* 67: 597.

Walker, Margaret Urban (2006). *Moral Repair: Reconstructing Moral Relations after Wrongdoing*. Cambridge: Cambridge University Press.

Wenar, Leif (2006). "Reparations for the Future." *Journal of Social Philosophy* 37 (3): 396–405.

Williams, Eric (2014). *Capitalism and Slavery*. Chapel Hill: University of North Carolina Press.

Yamamoto, Eric K. (1998). "Racial Reparations: Japanese American Redress and African American Claims." *Boston College Third World Law Journal* 19 (1): 477–523.

Yepes, Rodrigo Uprimny (2009). "Transformative Reparations of Massive Gross Human Rights Violations: Between Corrective and Distributive Justice." *Netherlands Quarterly of Human Rights* 27 (4): 625–647.

5
The Movement for Black Lives and Transitional Justice

Colleen Murphy

Transitional justice is the process of dealing with wrongdoing committed in the context of conflict or repression for the sake of recognizing victims, holding perpetrators to account, and, most fundamentally, contributing to societal transformation (Murphy 2017). Dozens of countries across the globe have engaged in the pursuit of transitional justice, establishing truth commissions, reparations programs, amnesty provisions, criminal trials, and memorials. This chapter considers, from the perspective of transitional justice, the Movement for Black Lives (M4BL).[1] M4BL is comprised of a wide range of groups rooted in Black communities who share a platform demanding a wide range of structural changes so as to achieve economic and reparative justice, freedom, and control. This movement was created as a response to violence targeting Black communities both in the United States and around the world. My analysis is comparative. Throughout, I compare and contrast the United States with one of the most central cases of transitional justice that has shaped both scholarship and practice, South Africa.

Specifically, I focus on the armed struggle to end apartheid in South Africa and the pursuit of transitional justice in the aftermath of apartheid's end with the civil rights movement in the United States. Both movements were a response to decades-long regimes of racial segregation which were preceded by slavery in the United States and colonialism in South Africa. Underpinning and justifying both regimes was white supremacy, providing an ideological basis of support for racial segregation and subordination and shaping and distorting race relations in both contexts historically and to this day. While sharing these similarities, the two contexts are also different in important ways. Although the achievement of transitional justice in South Africa is

---

[1] For the official platform and associated groups, see https://m4bl.org/policy-platforms/.

Colleen Murphy, *The Movement for Black Lives and Transitional Justice* In: *The Movement for Black Lives*. Edited by: Brandon Hogan, Michael Cholbi, Alex Madva, and Benjamin S. Yost, Oxford University Press. © Oxford University Press 2021. DOI: 10.1093/oso/9780197507773.003.0006

unfinished in important respects, explicit steps in that direction were made in South Africa that were not made in the United States. Dealing with legacies of wrongdoing was a central component of the terms that enabled the transition to democracy. By contract, efforts to end Jim Crow in the United States, culminating in the passage of the Civil Rights Act, did not make the redressing of past wrongs a constitutive element. Against the background of the absence of processes of transitional justice, as a consequence today there remains within the United States denial about the nature and scope of wrongdoing during Jim Crow and about the existence and depth of ongoing structural inequality. My account conceptualizes M4BL in the United States in part as a response to the absence of transitional justice in this context, and as calling for mechanisms of transitional justice to explicitly address past wrongs as part of the pursuit of broader societal transformation.

This paper has three sections. In the first section I discuss two important features of the contexts of apartheid and of Jim Crow, which are paradigmatically found in societies where transitional justice is needed: pervasive structural inequality and normalized collective and political wrongdoing. I detail the specific forms such inequality and wrongdoing took in each context. The second section discusses the movements to end apartheid and Jim Crow, emphasizing the role of Black intellectuals and Black resistance movements in articulating the necessity and justifiability of resistance. In both cases such resistance was crucial in enabling a negotiated transition away from apartheid to multiracial democracy in South Africa and the passage of the Civil Rights Act in the United States. The third section compares transitional justice in both countries. In South Africa, transitional justice was explicitly pursued, but the work of transitional justice remains unfinished. Indeed, current discussions about land inequality are in part a product of the choice of wrongs on which to focus in transitional justice processes that took place during the transition to multiracial democracy. In the United States, by contrast, transitional justice has still to begin, given the absence of any systematic effort to pursue transitional justice to date. The Civil Rights Act was a forward-looking document, but it did not deal with the legacy of past wrongdoing or the underlying conditions that made discrimination and other forms of wrongdoing possible. Because transitional justice has not yet begun in the United States, the challenges for dealing with our own legacies of wrongdoing are much greater as a result.

1. Contexts of transition: pervasive structural inequality and normalized collective and political wrongdoing

Processes of transitional justice are characteristically established in contexts of what I have called in other work *pervasive structural inequality* and *normalized collective and political wrongdoing* (Murphy 2017: ch. 1). These are two of the four circumstances of transitional justice I defend. After providing a very general definition of these two features, I focus on their presence in apartheid South Africa and Jim Crow United States.

Pervasive structural inequality focuses on the terms for interaction among citizens and between citizens and officials as mediated by a wide range of institutions (Murphy 2017). Economic institutions, social institutions, political institutions, and legal institutions set terms for interaction by defining obligatory, permissible, and impermissible terms for interaction. Such terms are enforced in a wide range of formal and informal sanctions for violations. Terms for interaction can be unequal, in my view, in two main respects. First, they may structure different opportunities for various groups of citizens to do and become things of value, such as being educated, being employed, and being recognized as a member of the political community. Second, various groups of citizens may have differential opportunities to define the terms of interaction themselves. When pervasive, inequality is such that the legitimacy of the institutional order can be challenged; there can exist a right to rebel on the part of citizens.

Normalized collective and political wrongdoing refers to human rights violations that become a basic fact of life for (certain targeted groups) of citizens. Citizens who are members of a targeted group must take into account the possibility of becoming a victim of a human rights violation when determining how to act. Such wrongdoing is political in two senses. It implicates members of the state; perpetrators of wrongdoing include characteristically state security agents at times acting within their official capacity and at times outside of it. Perpetrators can also include private citizens acting with the permission of or in coordination or collusion with state agents. Wrongdoing can also implicate groups contesting the state. Second, wrongdoing is committed for political reasons, such as to enforce or contest state policies, to defend or acquire land, or to maintain political control. Wrongdoing is collective in the sense that individuals are targeted on the basis of a group membership, and it is individuals acting in a group that are perpetrators of wrongdoing.

The description of these features is at a certain level of abstraction. Here is what pervasive structural inequality and normalized collective and political wrongdoing looked like in apartheid South Africa and Jim Crow United States.

The Rome Statute of the International Criminal Court (2002) in Article 7 categorizes apartheid as a crime against humanity. A nonexhaustive list of other crimes against humanity recognized by the Rome Statute includes enslavement, torture, enforced disappearances, and sexual slavery. Apartheid itself is defined as "inhumane acts of a character similar to those referred to in paragraph 1, committed in the context of an institutionalised regime of systematic oppression and domination by one racial group over any other racial group or groups and committed with the intention of maintaining that regime."

The National Party in South Africa began to implement apartheid in 1948. The National Party platform in elections for that year included a commitment to promoting the Afrikaner identity and white racial goals.[2] More specifically, apartheid was implemented in the name of white supremacy. Underpinning apartheid was the view that there were four races in South Africa (White, Indian, Coloured, and African), each with its own "inherent culture." Apartheid was designed to keep the four races separate and segregated; the word itself draws from the Afrikaans word for "apart." There was no pretense to "separate but equal" in the South African context. White interests should prevail over Black. Segregation entailed no obligation for facilities or infrastructure to be equal for the various racial groups (Thompson 2001; Dyzenhaus 2003).

A sample of legislation passed to realize apartheid includes the following. The Population Registration Act of 1950 required all South Africans to register their race. Racial classification was determined by government officials on the basis of stereotypical characterizations of phenotypic features of each racial group, leading in a number of cases to the breakup of families whose members were categorized in different racial groups. The Prohibition of Mixed Marriages Act of 1949 and the amended Immorality Act of 1950 rendered unlawful sexual contact across racial lines. The Reservation of Separate Amenities Act required segregated facilities across a wide range of domains, including churches, parks, hotels, schools, beaches, public toilets, and ambulances. Interracial contact in sports was also forbidden. The Group

---

[2] Afrikaner South Africans are Dutch-descended white South Africans.

Areas Act of 1950 led to most Africans losing their land rights, as millions of Indians, Coloured, and Africans were forcibly relocated to townships outside of urban cities. Urban zones were redistricted for white South Africans, including the infamous case of Sophiatown, which had been a thriving Black area. Pass laws required Africans to have a permit to enter urban areas, and violations of pass laws led to hundreds of thousands of arrests. Three hundred thousand Africans were arrested for violations of pass laws in 1975-1976 alone. Wage differences across racial lines were pervasive, with Black laborers earning six times less than white laborers in construction and twenty-one times less in mining. Higher rates of unemployment existed for Black workers relative to white. Public expenditure for education of white students was significantly higher than for Black students, and facilities for education reflected that public investment difference. Censorship was widespread. Government appointees ran the South African Broadcasting Corporation, which enjoyed a monopoly on TV and radio. Voting rights of Blacks were eliminated. Security forces were given wide latitude to arrest anti-apartheid activists. Such forces often acted outside of such latitude, in many cases torturing and murdering anti-activists. A number of legislative measures (including the Suppression of Communism Act, Riotous Assemblies Act, Terrorism Act, and Internal Security Act) made protest effectively illegal, as the government authorized the banning of organizations and inhibiting of individuals from joining organizations, as well as powers to arrest and detain and place under house arrest individuals deemed problematic. Gun laws were such that while almost all white South Africans owned firearms, few Black South Africans held gun licenses (Truth and Reconciliation Commission of South Africa 1999; Thompson 2001).

A cumulative consequence of the apartheid structure was that South Africa became, and still remains, one of the most unequal countries globally. White South Africans under apartheid enjoyed a high standard of living, high-quality public services, high life expectancy, and low infant mortality rates, and they experienced racial interaction always from a position of power and authority. By and large, white South Africans lived in denial about the vast gap between the lives they led and the lives Black South Africans were able to lead and about the violence used to maintain apartheid. White South Africans were told at church and in the news they consumed about the justifiability of the current arrangement, and they chose to take at face value the claim that death, torture, and suffering inflicted on anti-apartheid fighters was simply communist propaganda. Some white South Africans were actively involved in participating in such violence. Only a small minority of white South Africans fought against apartheid either form within or from outside the system (Dyzenhaus 2003).

By contrast, the life of Black South Africans was in the words of Nelson Mandela (1995: 95), "poor, unarmed and insecure, most experienced life as a continual struggle for survival.... His life is circumscribed by racist laws and regulations that cripple his growth, dim his potential and stunt his life. This was the reality, and one could deal with it in a myriad of ways." Two-thirds of Africans lived below the Minimum Living Level, "the lowest sum on which a household could possibly live in South African social circumstances"; for Africans living in Homelands—the areas that Africans were moved into when they were removed from urban centers—that number was 80 percent (Thompson 2001). Public facilities and services were nonexistence or inadequate. In many areas, electricity, running water, sewage, and public telephone services were rare. Infant mortality rates were significantly higher than for whites, with the highest levels among Africans. Hunger and undernourishment were chronic problems. Black South Africans faced constraints on movement, obstacles to education, restrictions on employment opportunities, and lived with the daily humiliation of second-class citizenship. The experience of apartheid was not uniform. It varied to some extent for Blacks who lived in cities versus white farming areas versus the Homelands. It varied for Black women and Black men; for example, women in the Homelands were tasked with keeping households together as men migrated outside of the Homelands looking for work.

Life expectancy was thirteen years less for Black South Africans than white South Africans, with murder the most common cause of death among Africans and Coloureds (Thompson 2001: 202). Normalized wrongdoing in the form of physical violence was a defining feature of the lived experience of Black South Africans (Gobodo-Madikizela 2004). Twenty thousand individuals who had been victims of killing, abduction, torture, or severe ill treatment from 1960 to 1994, either at the hands of armed anti-apartheid groups or at the hands of South African security forces, appeared before the South African Truth and Reconciliation Commission (TRC; see section 3). While some white South Africans, especially those involved in the anti-apartheid movement, were among those who testified as victims at the TRC, the overall lived experience of white South Africans was free from the fear of or exposure to violence.

Apartheid's end left a society with deep divisions and deep inequality, both features present along racial lines. Reflecting these divisions, the anticipation of many was that apartheid's end would bring not democracy but racial civil war (Thompson 2001). Recognizing its extraordinary achievement is compatible with acknowledging that white South Africans in many cases resented apartheid's end, as the establishment of equality entailed the loss of unjustified privilege, a loss which for many was instead experienced as unjust loss. White South Africans feared what democracy would bring and what would happen when exclusive power was ceded. Black South Africans emerged from the end of apartheid with deep distrust and with high expectations for what democracy would mean.

The situation in the United States bore both important similarities and differences from that of South Africa. In the United States following the end of the Civil War, there was a brief period of Reconstruction which included efforts, ultimately undermined or unfulfilled, to establish conditions of equality for freed slaves, one form famously in a federal promise to provide "forty acres and a mule" (Myers 2017; Foner 2019). This period also saw the passage of the Thirteenth Amendment, which abolished slavery; the Fourteenth Amendment, which enshrined birthright citizenship and a commitment to equal protection under the law; and the Fifteenth Amendment, guaranteeing the right to vote for all regardless of race. With the end of Reconstruction came the onset of Jim Crow, an almost hundred-year period between ca. 1870 and 1965 in which there was a strict regime of legalized racial segregation in the southern United States.

Jim Crow was motivated and justified by white supremacy (Packard 2003). Like apartheid, racial segregation under Jim Crow encompassed all public facilities, including churches, schools, the military, theaters, and educational facilities. Unlike apartheid, however, separate was officially claimed to be compatible with equality. This principle existed in theory only, for in practice separate was unequal. Separate but equal was the official principle, but not reflective of the institutional structure or lived experience of Black Americans. Facilities for Blacks were inferior in quality and funding for such facilities unequal in practice relative to facilities for whites. Discrimination in employment and wages, segregation in housing, and discriminatory bank lending practices, in the North as well as in the Jim Crow South, all served to artificially and unjustly constrain wealth acquisition on the part of Blacks (Mitchell and Franco 2018). Interracial sexual relationships and marriage were illegal. Though legally enjoying the right to vote, the effective exercise of that right was undermined for Blacks through methods such as poll taxes (setting a fee to be paid before someone could vote), literacy tests (setting reading requirements for eligibility to vote, which were intentionally aimed at disenfranchising Black voters), and grandfather clauses (which enabled illiterate whites to vote but not illiterate Blacks by granting the right to vote to anyone whose grandfather or father had voted prior to 1867).

Like apartheid, Jim Crow was maintained through violence. Blacks living during the period of Jim Crow faced the persistent threat of a distinctly American form of wrongdoing in lynching, which is extrajudicial punishment carried out by white citizens with impunity (Dray 2003). Lynching was often vicious and gruesome, implicated government officials as either active participants or passive enablers, and occurred in public in some cases with thousands of white citizens as onlookers and bystanders. Unsubstantiated claims of rape, in particular of white women by Black men, often accompanied the white public's justification of the need for vigilante justice, while in most cases lynching was the result of wage or work condition disputes between white employers and Black employees (Dray 2003). The Equal Justice Initiative (2019) has documented more than 4,084 Blacks who were lynched; the real number is likely higher. Lynching represented the de facto absence of effective protection of basic rights to liberty, bodily integrity, and due process for Black citizens during the Jim Crow era. White citizens could inflict violence with impunity on Black citizens during this era. Lynching became a basic fact of life around which Black Americans had to orient their conduct.

The life of Black Americans during Jim Crow, as captured powerfully in memoirs like *Black Boy*, was filled with constraints on movement as well as on opportunities for education and employment, with the subsequent poverty, hunger, and illness that such constraints generated. The ever-present threat of violence at the hands of whites for contesting or challenging the injustice of the status quo aimed to motivate Black Americans to submit to the status quo and adjust life expectations to what the Jim Crow order permitted. Black Americans quickly learned how to calibrate responses and actions to accord with White expectations. Life under Jim Crow was for Black Americans a life of stress, exhaustion, tension, and terror. As *Black Boy* articulates in the chapter where the author, Richard Wright (2007), moves north with his family, for many Black Americans living under Jim Crow the options presented to them were to learn to accept the status quo of injustice: "to submit and live the life of a genial slave," to fight either the system or fellow Blacks, or to seek to escape from the struggles of everyday life in alcohol. In his words:

> That winter my mother and brother came and we set up house-keeping, buying furniture on the installment plan, being cheated and yet knowing no way to avoid it.... My brother obtained a job and we began to save toward the trip north ... I told none of the white men on the job that I was planning to go north; I knew that the moment they felt I was thinking of the North they would change toward me. It would have made them feel that I did not like the life I was living, and because my life was completely conditioned by what they said or did, it would have been tantamount to challenging them.
>
> I could calculate my chances for life in the South as a Negro fairly clearly now.
>
> I could fight the southern whites by organizing with other Negroes, as my grandfather had done. But I knew that I could never win that way.... If I fought openly I would die and I did not want to die. News of lynchings were frequent.
>
> I could submit and live the life of a genial slave, but that was impossible ... if I did that, I would crush to death something within me, and I would hate myself as much as I knew the whites already hated those who had submitted. Neither could I ever willingly present myself to be kicked, as Shorty had done. I would rather have died than do that.
>
> I could drain off my restlessness by fighting with Shorty and Harrison. I had seen many Negroes solve the problem of being black by transferring their hatred of themselves to others with a black skin and fighting them. I would have to be cold to do that, and I was not cold and I could never be.
>
> I could, of course, forget what I had read, thrust the whites out of my mind, forget them; and find release from anxiety and longing in sex and alcohol. But the memory of how my father had conducted himself made that course repugnant....
>
> I had no hope whatever of being a professional man. Not only had I been so conditioned that I did not desire it, but the fulfillment of such an ambition was beyond my capabilities. Well-to-do Negroes lived in a world that was almost as alien to me as the world inhabited by whites.
>
> What, then, was there? ... My days and nights were one long, quiet, continuously contained dream of terror, tension, and anxiety. I wondered how long I could bear it. (Wright 2007: 252–253)

2. Generating a transition

Both apartheid and Jim Crow proved unsustainable, and a fundamental factor that explains the transition from apartheid to democracy in the case of South Africa and from Jim Crow to the Civil Rights Act in the case of the United States was mobilized mass Black resistance.

In South Africa, nonviolent resistance to apartheid was initially used by organizations such as the African National Congress (ANC). However, in the wake of the Sharpeville massacre, when thousands of unarmed protestors marched to a police station in Sharpeville to protest pass laws and police shot directly into the crowd killing sixty-nine and injuring many more, the struggle against apartheid took the form of armed resistance. The overarching objective of the armed struggle was ending apartheid. Armed struggle between South African security forces and anti-apartheid armed groups such as Umkhonto weSizwe (Spear of the Nation), the armed wing of the ANC occurred co-founded by Nelson Mandela, occurred both inside South Africa and across borders of neighboring states. It involved torture, assassination, bombings, and necklacing. In necklacing, suspected Black collaborators with the South African apartheid government were subjected to extrajudicial punishment and death. A tire was placed around their torso and arms and then set on fire, burning the victim to death. Their public death aimed to serve as a deterrent for others considering collaborating with the South African government.

The struggle against apartheid was not only through arms. Philosophically underpinning the struggle against apartheid were the ideals articulated in the Black Consciousness movement, emphasizing the beauty and value of Black lives. Leaders like Steve Biko, founder of the Black Consciousness movement in South Africa, emphasized the value, worth, and beauty of Black South Africans, rejecting the daily messaging of devaluation and daily experience of humiliation. Steve Biko died after being severely beaten during police detention, but the police officers involved were exonerated from wrongdoing.[3] Other leaders spent years in prison in the course of pursuing the freedom for Black South Africans. Mandela himself spent twenty-seven years in prison on Robben Island, after being tried and convicted for sabotage and sentenced to life in prison in 1963.[4]

---

[3] The officers involved in the beating of Steve Biko later applied for amnesty at the TRC; their application was denied.
[4] https://www.nelsonmandela.org/content/page/biography.

The armed struggle between anti-apartheid organizations and the South African government increased in intensity, reaching the greatest intensity in the 1980s. It became clear that neither side would win in the armed struggle. Negotiations between the National Party and the ANC paved the way for the crafting of an Interim Constitution (1993) and democratic elections. The work of President F. W. De Klerk and Nelson Mandela resulted in their joint receipt of the Nobel Peace Prize. Mandela was also the first democratically elected president, assuming office on May 10, 1994, following the first democratic elections. The final Constitution of South Africa (1996) begins with a commitment to nonracialism and nonsexism. As I discuss in greater detail in the next section, the Interim Constitution that preceded the final Constitution took up the question of past wrongdoing and included a commitment to amnesty for some perpetrators of wrongdoing.

Turning now to the United States, in the 1954 case of *Brown v. Board of Education*, the United States Supreme Court declared segregation in schools unconstitutional, violating the equal protection clause of the Fourteenth Amendment. *Brown II* the next year affirmed the unconstitutionality of school desegregation and held that southern school boards, with the power to desegregate, should do so with "all deliberate speed."

In his analysis of the period from *Brown* through the Civil Rights Act of 1964, legal historical Michael Klarman (2006) shows how *Brown* had the effect of radicalizing Southern politics. It mobilized sustained efforts to impede school desegregation on the part of white Southerners, which resulted in broad delay in any school desegregation occurring. School boards would not desegregate without court orders, which meant that desegregation turned on the ability and willingness of Black parents to file suits and on federal judges to order desegregation. However, few Black families could afford the fees to litigate and, moreover, lacked a pressing incentive since their children would likely be grown by the time a suit was settled. It took the efforts of the National Association for the Advancement of Colored People (NAACP) to bring suits, though here, too, the NAACP faced obstacles as Black families feared violent retribution for becoming litigants, worried about the impact of having their children in predominantly white schools, and worried about the impact of desegregation on Black teachers. White southern politicians attacked the NAACP, asking for lists of members and charging alleged communist infiltration. Even for those suits that were brought, white judges from the South faced intense pressure to keep segregation in place. Some judges independently favored maintaining segregation, while those who did not faced hate mail, harassment, burned crosses, and house bombings for ordering desegregation (Klarman 2006). It took federal troops being sent in to enforce desegregation orders at Little Rock High School in 1957, three years after *Brown*, to see movement toward integration. Federal interference in order to facilitate desegregation generated a powerful backlash by white citizens. The white supremacist Klu Klux Klan reemerged. Efforts after World War II to expand voting rights were reversed. Public school teachers and university professors lost jobs for supporting integration, while the social costs for opposing segregation among whites increased through threats, ostracism, and physical violence. Even greater threats of violence faced Black citizens in the South opposing segregation. Threats to jobs, credit, and mortgages occurred for voicing support for integration, as did police harassment (Klarman 2006).

Mass action by Black citizens was required to effectively end Jim Crow, which occurred through the passage of the Civil Rights Act of 1964. Voter registration campaigns aimed to increase the participation and voice of Black citizens. And targets for boycotts and lawsuits extended beyond education into other areas of segregation such as buses and parks. A bus boycott by Black men and women started in Montgomery in 1955 that lasted eighteen months focused on ending the humiliation of Black bus passengers by white bus drivers, who would verbally insult Black passengers, drive off after Black passengers had paid but before they could board, and in some cases physically abuse Black passengers. More than 100,000 individuals protested in this manner. The 1956 Supreme Court case *Browder v. Gayle* used the precedent of *Brown* to invalidate bus segregation.

1960 was a watershed year for direct action protests. On February 1 of that year, Black college students sat at a segregated lunch counter at Woolworths in Greensboro, North Carolina. This began a period of sit-ins in which Black students would sit at white-only spots in segregated restaurants, demand to be served, and refuse to leave if denied service. More than seventy thousand participated in sit-ins over the course of one year, of whom four thousand were arrested. The result was the desegregation of more than one hundred public accommodations in over twenty states. Following the *Boynton v. Virginia* Supreme Court Case of 1960 which declared segregation in interstate bus and rail travel unconstitutional, freedom riders traveled on buses to enforce the decision. Many were arrested and severely beaten, including former Georgia Congressman John Lewis. Finally, the Birmingham Campaign of 1963 included an organized boycott of merchants, sit-ins at lunch counters, and a march. Martin Luther King, Jr. joined the boycott, getting arrested after participating in a protest in violation of a court injunction; in prison he penned the famous "Letter from a Birmingham Jail." The images of violence against freedom riders proved transformative of public opinion, in particular in the North, of white southerners and their actions. The 1961 US Commission on Civil Rights recommended sweeping changes for accelerating desegregation, including the withholding of 50 percent of federal education money for segregated districts and requiring that all districts in southern states submit desegregation plans.[5]

Unlike in South Africa, in the United States Black mobilization and mass action aimed not at overturning the constitutional framework governing the United States, but rather at seeing the ideals and normative commitments in the constitutional framework realized and satisfied for Black Americans. The 1964 Civil Rights Act passed by the US Congress effectively ended Jim Crow era de jure segregation, outlawing discrimination on the basis of race, color, sex, religion, or national origin; outlawing racial segregation in public facilities, workplaces, and schools; and ending differential and unequal application of voter registration requirements.[6] Also unlike the South African case, the question of redressing past wrongs was not addressed as the Civil Rights Act outlined commitments to be addressed moving forward.

3. Transitional justice: justice not yet begun and, where begun, unfinished

The context in which the 1964 Civil Rights Act was passed in the United States and the first democratic elections were held in South Africa was characterized by a third feature paradigmatically present in transitional contexts, what I call *serious existential uncertainty* (Murphy 2017). The specific uncertainty at issue concerns what the political trajectory of a community is at a particular period in time and, more broadly, whether transformational change sought will be achieved or undone. This uncertainty in the South African context was alluded to earlier, where it was far from obvious that democratic elections promised would be held, or that results would be respected. Nor was it clear whether the new democratic era would be peaceful or resisted with

---

[5] The five-volume report of the 1961 US Commission on Civil Rights submitted to the President of the United States and US Congress is available at http://www2.law.umaryland.edu/marshall/usccr/chrolist.html#1961.

[6] Available at https://www.govinfo.gov/content/pkg/STATUTE-78/pdf/STATUTE-78-Pg241.pdf.

violence. In the United States, uncertainty about whether segregation would in fact end stemmed from violent responses to nonviolent opposition to racial segregation and the refusal of white citizens to adhere to Supreme Court mandates, effectively challenging the legitimacy of the federal government.

During such periods of uncertainty, whether and how past wrongdoing is dealt with often assumes an existential importance for a community, as it comes to signal whether a transition will be realized or whether repression and conflict will resume as before. This is why the phrase "looking back, reaching forward" has come to symbolize transitional justice. As processes look back at the wrongdoing that is part of their mandate, they are at the same time looking forward at helping to establish and entrench conditions for long-term transformation change in the political relationships structuring a community (Murphy 2017).

Processes for dealing with past wrongdoing stand in precarious positions, in which moral failure is an ever-present possibility. Criminal trials may become mere show trials or mechanisms for victor's justice; reparations may become mechanisms used to silence victims rather than provide justice; truth commissions may document abuses but not provide any meaningful condemnation or impetus for changes in the conditions that enabled widespread wrongdoing.

In South Africa, the issue of dealing with past wrongdoing was explicitly addressed in the 1993 Interim Constitution. A product of the negotiations to end apartheid, the Interim Constitution included a commitment to amnesty for past wrongdoing. Following the first democratic elections in 1994, the newly elected South African Parliament decided to respect this commitment to amnesty by building it into the structure of a truth commission. The South African Truth and Reconciliation Commission (TRC) (1999) was established by the South African Parliament via the Promotion of National Unity and Reconciliation Act, no. 34 of 1995. Its charge was documenting killing, abduction, torture, and severe ill treatment committed from 1960 to 1994 by either members of the South African government's security forces or members of liberation organizations. The TRC was comprised of three committees, a Committee on Amnesty, a Committee on Human Rights Violations, and a Committee on Reparation and Rehabilitation. Perpetrators of wrongs that fell under the mandate of the commission were eligible for amnesty provided they met two conditions: they fully disclosed the acts for which they were responsible and could demonstrate that their actions were done for political reasons. The overarching purpose of the TRC, as the name suggests, was to promote reconciliation specifically at the national level among South Africans.

The TRC has been profoundly influential in the scholarship and practice of transitional justice. Within philosophy and political theory specifically, it sparked conversations about the moral justifiability of amnesty and the nature of the justice realized by the TRC (Allais 2012; Allen 1999; Dyzenhaus 2000; Rotberg and Thompson 2000). Other conversations focused on the extent to which the South African model of transitional justice could and should be exported and how successful the TRC was in achieving its overarching objective (e.g., Gibson 2006). Critical conversations of the TRC have focused on particular aspects of its functioning, including the gendered experience of how witnesses were treated and the absence of psychosocial support for victims (Hamber 1998; Ross 2003).

There is one specific critique of the TRC, articulated powerfully by Mahmood Mamdani (2002), that is worth dwelling on, for it foreshadows the current discussions in South Africa about the remaining work to be done in dealing with apartheid's legacy, which is still visibly present and reflected in the vast economic inequality that continues to characterize South Africa. It also reflects the limits of any single process of transitional justice as a mechanism for transformational change. The TRC made a choice to focus on the extraordinary violence of apartheid, that is, the extrajudicial violence committed in the name of defending or ending apartheid. Though justifications can and have been given for this particular selection, especially when it comes to countering a certain kind of white denialism about the intrinsic role of violence in maintaining apartheid, critics like Mamdani highlight the limitations of this focus. In particular, it left the institutionalized regime of apartheid itself unexamined. Apartheid was a crime against humanity, and yet the perpetrators of apartheid effectively got impunity (Mamdani 2002). The ordinary violence in the name of which apartheid was achieved, in the forms of forced removals of Black South Africans and bulldozing of their homes, arrests for pass law violations, and breaking up of families, was excluded from consideration. The inequality that permeated educational institutions and economic institutions was not altered by the TRC and its functioning. While there have been important reform efforts in employment and education, twenty-five years after the end of apartheid, South Africa remains the most unequal country in the world (Sulla and Zikhali 2018; Beaubien 2018). Tackling this inequality was not part of the TRC's mandate.

The road to reconciliation may be through mechanisms like the TRC, but the establishment of the truth by itself cannot fully repair damaged political relationships. No single process of transitional justice can achieve relational transformation on its own. Even if the truth commission had had a different mandate, it would have been unable on its own to rectify apartheid's legacy of inequality. Transforming political relationships that are deeply unjust is a long-term, intergenerational project. The incomplete satisfaction of claims of transitional justice can be seen in the current discussions to amend Article 25 of the South African Constitution to allow for land appropriation without compensation (Daniel 2018a, 2018b; Mbatha and Cohen 2018). One central justification for this change is its role in rectifying historic injustice stemming from land confiscation during apartheid. In universities, protests in recent years rejected the increase in student fees and emphasized the necessity of decolonizing the curriculum (Mgqwashu 2016). Disillusionment with the African National Congress, and with politics more generally, especially among Black youth, is in part a product of the failure to mitigate the poverty and inequality that apartheid generated (Bearak 2019).

In the United States, the story of transitional justice's contemporary demands looks different, because we are not continuing, but rather beginning, the pursuit of transitional justice. There has been no effort analogous to the TRC to begin the work of dealing with past wrongs and their legacy. The Civil Rights Act of 1964 drew a line between a past predicated on segregation and discrimination, and a future in which such practices would no longer be permissible. However, unlike the South African Interim Constitution, the Act marking the beginning of a new era was silent on the question of how to deal with the legacy of the past. Whereas discrimination would no longer be tolerated, the legacy of discrimination that was legally sanctioned in the past was not unaddressed. Lynching, and the ways law enforcement officials were implicated in its practice, was not confronted. Nor were the cumulative economic consequences of slavery, lynching, and the policies of Jim Crow in the South or policies like redlining in the North. The racial wealth gap maps the difference in net worth between white and Black families; white families have close to ten times the wealth of Black families today. The median wealth of white families in 2016 was $171,000, whereas for Black families it was $17,600 (Jan 2017; Dettling et al. 2017). Most fundamentally, the Civil Rights Act did not provide a method for addressing the white supremacist ideology underpinning and justifying Jim Crow and slavery before it; though its commitment to nondiscrimination rested on a repudiation of white supremacy, the Civil Rights Act itself did not provide guidance as to how to dismantle the ideology of white supremacy.

Subsequent to the passage of the Civil Rights Act, there have been attempts to deal with slavery and Jim Crow. However, the relatively limited impact of each of these measures is reflected in the absence of widespread knowledge among American citizens that they occurred; as an anecdote, whenever I teach transitional justice, it is rare for even one student to know about the measures I now list. The Greensboro Truth and Reconciliation Commission (2006), explicitly modeled on the TRC, was established in Greensboro, North Carolina, with a mandate to investigate the "the context, causes, sequence and consequence of the events of November 3, 1979" for the purpose of healing transformation for the community. Known as the Greensboro Massacre, five demonstrators in a low-income area of Greensboro arguing for racial and economic justice were killed by members of the Klu Klux Klan. Affirmative action programs have been established, though they are increasingly coming under court scrutiny. The United States House of Representatives issued an apology for slavery in 2008 in H.Res.194 (https://www.congress.gov/bill/110th-congress/house-resolution/194/text), with the Senate issuing a concurrent resolution apologizing for slavery a year later (https://www.congress.gov/bill/111th-congress/senate-concurrent-resolution/26).

More recently, however, interest in pursuing what I would characterize as transitional justice seems increasing. The M4BL is explicit about this pursuit insofar as it ties programs for transforming contemporary relations and the conditions characterizing the lives of Black Americans with efforts to deal with the legacies of injustice. In addition to such comprehensive efforts, specific processes of transitional justice are occurring. A memorial to lynching and a museum on the history from slavery through the present mass incarceration were opened in Alabama by the Equal Justice Initiative last year. The first state-wide commission to deal with lynching was established in Maryland in 2019 (https://www.wbur.org/hereandnow/2019/09/12/maryland-commission-sets-out-to-investigate-states-lynching-history). A motion on reparations for slavery, HR40, was introduced in the House of Representatives in January 2019 "To address the fundamental injustice, cruelty, brutality, and inhumanity of slavery in the United States and the 13 American colonies between 1619 and 1865 and to establish a commission to study and consider a national apology and proposal for reparations for the institution of slavery, its subsequent de jure and de facto racial and economic discrimination against African-Americans, and the impact of these forces on living African-Americans, to make recommendations to the Congress on appropriate remedies, and for other purposes" (https://www.congress.gov/bill/116th-congress/house-bill/40/text). Ta-Nehisi Coates's testimony in the House of Representatives was widely covered and powerfully argued that the legacies of slavery and Jim Crow continue to influence and shape American institutions and lives (https://www.nytimes.com/2019/06/19/us/ta-nehisi-coates-reparations.html?searchResultPosition=1).

Much recent work among philosophers and lawyers analyzes how Black lives are discounted, overlooked, or actively harmed in the contemporary world; and by setting out a positive agenda for both political change and political philosophy itself. Christopher LeBron (2017) offers an intellectual history of the Black Lives Matter political movement, situating the contemporary origins as a protest against police brutality against and disproportionate killing by police of Blacks in the context of Black philosophers and thinkers grappling with how best to challenge and end white supremacy through their critiques of slavery, lynching, and through their use of various forms of political critique, including artistic expression. At the core of such debates was the question of whether the United States was redeemable, whether white supremacy could be dismantled, and whether Black equality could be achieved or was a utopian task. Tommy Curry (2017) develops an extended critique the conceptualization of Black males across academic disciplines, arguing for the need for the establishment of a field of Black male studies to conceptualize the place of Black men in American society and their vulnerability to violence and abuse both historically and continuing to this day (see Chapter 3, this volume). Tommie Shelby (2016) critically examines the American phenomena of Black urban ghettos, meticulously articulating the sources of injustice in these zones of limited opportunity. Charles Mills (2017) offers a searing critique of the inattention to issues of race and racism in dominant strands of Anglo-American liberal political theory, and argues that it leaves such ideal political theory unable to provide normative guidance to how to deal with the issues of racial injustice and their legacy in societies like the United States. Michelle Alexander (2010) tackles mass incarceration, arguing that the system of criminal punishment as it exists in the United States continues the control of Black bodies and exploitation of Black labor that were at the core of Jim Crow. Myisha Cherry (2019) defends the value of anger, as a form of social protest compatible with love and as a mechanism for calling attention to injustice.

All of these scholars contribute to articulating a program for social transformation in the United States, and what would be needed to truly enable the United States to become a post–white supremacist society. Lebron (2017: xiv) notes that Black Lives Matter as a political movement "exists because many feel, believe, and hope that the past is not necessarily an augur of the future, that the arc of the universe does bend toward justice, and that good and conscientious people might sharpen that trajectory before many more black lives are loss or ruined." For Mills, philosophy needs to take as its starting point the presence of injustice and then articulate ideals that provide guidance for what the rectification of historic injustice would look like. To engage in this project and provide this normative guidance is to articulate a roadmap for achieving the relational transformation that is the orienting aim of transitional justice using the specific means for pursuing relational change, which is through processes for dealing with past wrongs and their ongoing legacy.

References

Alexander, Michelle (2010). *The New Jim Crow: Mass Incarceration in the Age of Colorblindness*, 4th ed. New York: New Press.

Allais, Lucy (2012). "Restorative Justice, Retributive Justice, and the South African Truth and Reconciliation Commission." *Philosophy & Public Affairs* 39 (4): 331–363.

Allen, Jonathan (1999). "Balancing Justice and Social Utility: Political Theory and the Idea of a Truth and Reconciliation Commission." *University of Toronto Law Journal* 49: 315–353.

Bearak, Max (2019). "The Promises Are Empty: South Africans Vote, But the Nation's Young People Abstain in Droves." *Washington Post*, August 5. https://www.washingtonpost.com/world/africa/the-promises-are-empty-south-africans-vote-but-its-youth-abstain-in-droves/2019/05/08/407fc728-6b95-11e9-bbe7-1c798fb80536_story.html?utm_term=.63d160365d86.

Beaubien, Jason (2018). "The Country with the World's Worst Inequality Is…" *National Public Radio*, April 2. https://www.npr.org/sections/goatsandsoda/2018/04/02/598864666/the-country-with-the-worlds-worst-inequality-is.

Cherry, Myisha (2019). "Love, Anger and Racial Injustice." *The Routledge Handbook on Love in Philosophy*. Ed. Adrienne Martin. New York: Routledge: 157–168.

The Constitution of the Republic of South Africa, Act 108 of 1996. http://www.justice.gov.za/legislation/constitution/SAConstitution-web-eng.pdf.

Curry, Tommy (2017). *The Man-Not: Race, Class, Genre, and the Dilemmas of Black Manhood*. Philadelphia: Temple University Press.

Daniel, Luke (2018a). "Land Expropriation without Compensation: What the Constitution Says." *The South African*, September 16. https://www.thesouthafrican.com/land-expropriation-constitution-september-2018/.

Daniel, Luke (2018b). "Land Expropriation without Compensation: What's Next for South Africa." *The South African*, January 14. https://www.thesouthafrican.com/land-expropriation-update-south-africa-2019/.

Dettling, Lisa, Lisa J. Dettling, Joanne W. Hsu, Lindsay Jacobs, Kevin B. Moore, and Jeffrey P. Thompson with assistance from Elizabeth Llanes (2017). "Recent Trends in Wealth-Holding by Race and Ethnicity: Evidence from the Survey of Consumer Finances." *Fed Notes*, September 27. https://www.federalreserve.gov/econres/notes/feds-notes/recent-trends-in-wealth-holding-by-race-and-ethnicity-evidence-from-the-survey-of-consumer-finances-20170927.htm.

Dray, Philip (2003). *At the Hands of Persons Unknown: The Lynching of Black America*. New York: Modern Library.

Dyzenhaus, David (2000). "Survey Article: Justifying the Truth and Reconciliation Commission." *Journal of Political Philosophy* 8: 470–496.

Dyzenhaus, David (2003). *Judging the Judges, Judging Ourselves: Truth, Reconciliation, and the Apartheid Legal Order*. Oxford: Hart.

Equal Justice Initiative (2019). "The Legacy of Lynching." https://eji.org/racial-justice/legacy-lynching.

Foner, Eric (2019). "Reconstruction." *Encyclopaedia Brittanica*. https://www.britannica.com/event/Reconstruction-United-States-history.

Gibson, James (2006). *Overcoming Apartheid: Can Truth Reconcile a Divided Nation*. New York: Russell Sage Foundation.

Gobodo-Madikizela, Pumla (2004). *A Human Being Died That Night: A South African Woman Confronts the Legacy of Apartheid*. Boston: Mariner Books.

Greensboro Truth and Reconciliation Commission (2006). http://www.greensborotrc.org.

Hamber, Brandon (1998). "The Burdens of Truth: An Evaluation of the Psychological Support Services and Initiatives Undertaken by the South African Truth and Reconciliation Commission." *American Imago* 55 (1): 9–28.

Interim Constitution of South Africa (1993). http://www.justice.gov.za/trc/legal/sacon93.htm.

Jan, Tracy (2017). "White Families Have Nearly 10 Times the Net Worth of Black Families. And the Gap Is Growing." *Washington Post*, September 28. https://www.washingtonpost.com/news/wonk/wp/2017/09/28/black-and-hispanic-families-are-making-more-money-but-they-still-lag-far-behind-whites/?utm_term=.c73449f96a7b.

Klarman, Michael (2006). *From Jim Crow to Civil Rights: The Supreme Court and the Struggle for Racial Equality*. New York: Oxford University Press.

LeBron, Christopher (2017). *The Making of Black Lives Matter: A Brief History of an Idea*. New York: Oxford University Press.

Mamdani, Mahmood (2002). "Amnesty of Impunity? A Preliminary Critique of the Truth and Reconciliation Commission of South Africa." *Diacritics* 32 (3–4): 33–59.

Mandela, Nelson (1995). *The Autobiography of Nelson Mandela*. Boston: Back Bay Books.

Mbatha, A., and M. Cohen (2018). "Why Land Seizure Is Back in South Africa: QuickTake." *Washington Post*, November 15. https://www.washingtonpost.com/business/why-land-seizure-is-back-in-the-news-in-south-africa-quicktake/2018/11/15/8bf70278-e8ac-11e8-8449-1ff263609a31_story.html?utm_term=.35a2f169ae8e.

Mgqwashu, Emmanuel (2016). "Universities Can't Decolonise the Curriculum without Defining It First." *The Conversation*, August 22. https://theconversation.com/universities-cant-decolonise-the-curriculum-without-defining-it-first-63948.

Mills, Charles (2017). *Black Rights, White Wrongs: The Critique of Racial Liberalism*. New York: Oxford University Press.

Mitchell, Bruce, and Juan Franco (2018). "HOLC 'Redlining' Maps: The Persistent Structure of Segregation and Economic Inequality." National Community Reinvestment Coalition. March 20. https://ncrc.org/holc/.

Murphy, Colleen (2017). *The Conceptual Foundations of Transitional Justice*. New York: Cambridge University Press.

Myers, Barton (2017). "Sherman's Field Order No. 15." *New Georgia Encyclopedia*. https://www.georgiaencyclopedia.org/articles/history-archaeology/shermans-field-order-no-15.

Packard, Jerrold (2003). *American Nightmare: The History of Jim Crow*. New York: St. Martin's Press.

Rome Statute of the International Criminal Court (2002). U.N. Doc. A/CONF.183/9. http://legal.un.org/icc/statute/romefra.htm.

Ross, Fiona (2003). *Bearing Witness: Women and the South African TRC*. London: Pluto Press.

Rotberg, Robert, and Dennis Thompson (2000). *Truth v Justice: The Morality of Truth Commissions*. Princeton, NJ: Princeton University Press.

Shelby, Tommie (2016). *Dark Ghettos: Injustice, Dissent, and Reform*. Cambridge, MA: Harvard University Press.

Sulla, Victor, and Precious Zikhali (2018). "Overcoming Poverty and Inequality in South Africa: An Assessment of Drivers, Constraints, and Opportunities." *World Bank*, March 22. http://documents.worldbank.org/curated/en/530481521735906534/Overcoming-Poverty-and-Inequality-in-South-Africa-An-Assessment-of-Drivers-Constraints-and-Opportunities.

Thompson, Leonard (2001). *A History of South Africa*, 3rd ed. New Haven, CT: Yale University Press.

Truth and Reconciliation Commission of South Africa (1999). Truth and Reconciliation Commission of South Africa Report. 5 vols. London: Macmillan. http://www.justice.gov.za/trc/report/.

Wright, Richard (2007). *Black Boy: A Record of Childhood and Youth*. New York: Harper.

PART III
THE LANGUAGE OF THE M4BL

6
Positive Propaganda and the Pragmatics of Protest[*]

Michael Randall Barnes

> *I think it's silly when people want to add things to [the phrase "Black lives matter"] or feel worried that it's too divisive. What's divisive is cops killing black people. What's divisive is vigilantes shooting up churches. That's divisive.*
>
> —Patrisse Khan-Cullors[1]

The phrase "Black lives matter" has cemented itself as a political speech act of great importance. For better or worse, media discussions on Black Lives Matter (BLM) protests often focus narrowly on the slogan that gives the group their name. It therefore offers a unique route to a greater understanding of the pragmatics of protest as a speech act.

By reflecting on the significance of "Black lives matter" as a speech act, I argue that it is the distinct pragmatic features of protest—its entitlement conditions and the uptake it aims at—that best reveal its moral, political, and epistemic significance. In short, we must understand protest as paradigmatic socially located speech that reveals the moral authority of the protester. And the conception of authority here must account for the basic moral status of

---

[*] This chapter has benefited from helpful feedback from audiences at a number of conferences, including the 2016 North American Society for Social Philosophy meeting; the 2017 Canadian Philosophical Association meeting; the University of Toronto's 2017 Graduate Conference; the 2018 Central division meeting of the American Philosophical Association; and the 2018 Columbia-NYU Philosophy Graduate conference. I owe special thanks to Hamish Russell, Eric Tracy, Olúfẹ́mi Táíwò, and Philip Yaure for providing written comments at the latter four of those meetings, respectively, and also to my dissertation committee, Quill Kukla, Alisa Carse, Madison Powers, and Lynne Tirrell, who helped me work through early versions of these ideas.

[1] See Bell and Kondabolu (2017).

Michael Randall Barnes, *Positive Propaganda and the Pragmatics of Protest* In: *The Movement for Black Lives*. Edited by: Brandon Hogan, Michael Cholbi, Alex Madva, and Benjamin S. Yost, Oxford University Press. © Oxford University Press 2021. DOI: 10.1093/oso/9780197507773.003.0007

the speaker, their situated knowledge, as well as the contextual and interpersonal relations that inform the "total speech situation"—to borrow a term from Austin (1962). These elements shape the pragmatic force of protest.

To better approach these issues, I consider Jason Stanley's account of "positive propaganda," which he takes to be an important avenue of antioppressive resistance. I evaluate his suggestion that some instances of protest—such as the 1964 March on Montgomery—are paradigmatic examples of positive propaganda (2015: 113). I argue that Stanley's model is an unhelpful tool to apply to most forms of protest, and an examination of BLM protests illustrates why.

This is because, as I argue, we lose sight of what makes egalitarian protest distinct if we think of it as engaging in argument.[2] A focus on content, even unarticulated content, leads us to evaluate the claims of protesters separately from the context that produced them. Stanley's model encourages this abstraction, as does the greater attention it gives to the audience in place of the speaker(s). The crucial role of the speaker is thus obscured, as is the relationship between speaker(s) and audience. In this way, by using Stanley's account of propaganda as a starting point, I consider what protest is from a pragmatic point of view and argue that the speakers of protest make demands backed by a type of authority not detachable from the context in which they are embedded.

In what follows, I first sketch Stanley's account of positive propaganda. Next, I consider how this might be applied to BLM protests, and I discuss what this account leaves out. I then examine the pragmatic function of protest in more detail, drawing on a variety of philosophical sources to develop an account of the authority that protest, as a speech act, both calls upon and makes explicit. I then consider protest as it functions as *provocation*—for example, how the assertion of "Black lives matter" gives rise to the dismissive counterslogan "All lives matter." This demonstrates an important relation between protest and (part of) its audience, namely, how protest implicates the status of its target—that is, the more powerful—making vivid their social position as well.

---

[2] I focus on what I call "egalitarian" protest for the sake of narrowing my topic to a more manageable size. Much more would need to be said about protest in general to fully capture its many features. This, however, is beyond my scope.

1. Propaganda: positive and negative

In *How Propaganda Works*, Jason Stanley examines a sometimes subtle, but nonetheless dangerous type of subordinating speech.[3] According to Stanley, propaganda is dangerous because of how it can erode important political values in liberal democracies (2015: especially ch. 3). To get a firmer grasp on this, let's consider some useful distinctions and examples.

To begin, Stanley discusses propaganda as it is a "contribution to public discourse that is presented as an embodiment of certain ideals, yet is of a kind that tends to erode those very ideals" (2015: 53). Climate change denial campaigns provide a useful example. When oil companies promote the views of the few climate scientists who deny anthropogenic climate change, they engage in this type of *undermining* propaganda, because they appeal to a worthy ideal—scientific objectivity—in the service of a goal that tends to undermine that ideal.

When the ideals are specifically *political* values, Stanley calls it "demagoguery," which is:

> A contribution to public discourse that is presented as an embodiment of a worthy political, economic, or rational ideal, but is in the service of a goal that tends to undermine that very ideal. (2015: 69)

Demagoguery is always anti-democratic because "it wears down the possibility of democratic deliberation" (2015: 82). Arguments for racist voter ID laws that exploit "ideals like 'one man, one vote,' together with the appeal to voter fraud," are a clear example of this type demagoguery, as well as its undemocratic effects (2015: 68–69).

One political ideal that Stanley discusses in detail is the ideal of *reasonableness* in the realm of public reason—that is, the norms and standards that ought to guide public discourse. Following the ideal of reasonableness here means that debate and discussion about matters of public interest are "guided by equal respect for the perspective of everyone subject to the policy under debate" (2015: 94). At the heart of this norm of reasonableness is the capacity for empathy—which, following Stanley, we can understand as the ability to imaginatively position oneself in the situation of another. To say

---

[3] For different contemporary analyses of propaganda, see Smith (2012) and Tirrell (2012).

that public discourse is guided by reasonableness, then, is to say that public policy discussions don't exclude the voices of anyone who might be affected.

On the assumption that something close to reasonableness is an operative ideal in a democracy, cases of propaganda will then typically look to make the appearance of being reasonable, while actually serving to make debate on a topic biased and unjust. It will do so by making it harder for some members of the community to participate on fair terms, in part by diminishing the capacity for empathy within dominant members of that community. As Stanley puts it, "paradigm cases of propaganda will be ones that represent it to be reasonable not to take certain perspectives into account" (2015: 108). This can occur, he suggests, when propaganda presents "the perspectives of some of our fellow citizens as unworthy of consideration" (2015: 122).

One method that makes this erosion of empathy possible is the prevalence of persistent negative stereotypes about certain social groups. Negative stereotypes of Black Americans, abetted by the use of terms like "superpredator," can have the effect of eroding empathy and set the stage for anti-Black policies (Stanley 2015: 123; see also Cholbi and Madva, Chapter 9, this volume). And this can occur as part of seemingly reasonable contributions to a debate, in part by the foregrounding of "reasonable" topics like public safety.

While Stanley defines propaganda primarily in terms of its *effects*, the *mechanism* of propaganda that he elaborates most clearly focuses explicitly on the expressed content of utterances. That is, propaganda works by communicating propositions that strengthen or weaken certain ideologies.[4] On Stanley's model, utterances contribute new propositional content to the shared conversational background—the "common ground"—that then informs future linguistic and nonlinguistic moves. Crucially, utterances can do so covertly and indirectly. This often occurs through the careful use of presupposed or "not-at-issue" content, which enables the addition of new propositional material to the conversational participants' common ground without their conscious assessment of this material.[5] As Stanley says, the not-at-issue content of an utterance "is not advanced as a proposal of a content to

---

[4] These mechanisms are discussed more fully in chapter 4 of Stanley (2015), while the general definition of propaganda appears in chapter 2. It is worth nothing, however, as others have, that Stanley's stated definition of propaganda seems to be inconsistent with his general use of the term throughout the book. See Wolff (2016) or Brennan (2017).

[5] See Stanley (2015: 134). Stanley draws on work from Potts (2005). For a criticism of the implications Stanley draws from this to the case of propaganda, see McKinnon (2018). For another illuminating criticism, see Táíwò (2017).

be added to the common ground. Not-at-issue content is directly added to the common ground" (2015: 135).

For example, Stanley argues that repeated associations of the term "welfare" with images depicting Black Americans as lazy has made the generic claim "Blacks are lazy" part of the not-at-issue content of the term "welfare" (2015: 138). This means that a contribution to political discourse may be presented as an embodiment of reasonableness, but due to the use of the term "welfare," it will also communicate not-at-issue content that erodes reasonableness, further reducing empathy for Black Americans (among non-Black Americans). This is what makes the skillful deployment of not-at-issue content fertile ground for propagandists, and explaining this process in detail is Stanley's main project in the book.

1.1. Positive propaganda

Let's turn now to what Stanley calls acts of "positive propaganda." These, unlike demagoguery, are contributions that *strengthen* democratic ideals. Following W. E. B. Du Bois (1926), Stanley calls this "civic rhetoric":

> A contribution to a debate [that] can improve the subsequent reasonableness of the debate, even though the contribution itself is not a rational contribution, in the sense that its informational content contributes to the debate's resolution. (Stanley 2015: 112)

This type of speech is, according to Stanley, "structurally . . . the opposite of demagoguery" (2015: 112; see also Stanley 2018: 506). Both are (according to Stanley) nonrational contributions, and both have an effect on reasonableness. That is, both have an impact on the level of empathy within a political community.[6] But where demagoguery results in *less* empathy and *less* reasonableness, civic rhetoric *increases* empathy and therefore reasonableness.[7]

---

[6] I do not have room here to fully explain Stanley's distinction between rational and nonrational means of persuasion. However, I do want to briefly acknowledge that this is a fraught distinction, and one that I do not believe is ultimately tenable.

[7] It should be noted that there may be significant drawbacks to dominant members attempting to themselves occupy the perspective of oppressed people, as the *aspiration* to empathy can itself backfire, as Iris Marion Young (1997) and others have noted. One worry concerns the temptation to speak *for* another and, in doing so, undermine their own (moral) authority. Thanks to Philip Yaure for pushing me on this.

Beyond this functional similarity between demagoguery and civic rhetoric, Stanley also says there is a "structural problem in certain imperfectly realized liberal democracies that necessitates civic rhetoric" (2015: 115). If a group lacks political power and has no say in a policy that affects them, their perspective is illegitimately left out, and—because of the prevalence of flawed ideologies—cannot easily be included through rational debate.

In short, inequality creates conditions where positive propaganda is necessary, in that it offers a path toward a more reasonable politics (see, e.g., Stanley 2018: 507). Drawing on an example from Du Bois, Stanley suggests civic rhetoric can play this role by employing liberal democratic ideals "against a certain understanding of their application": freedom, solely for whites; or democracy, only for men.

One example Stanley uses to explain this potential for positive propaganda comes from the civil rights movement. The 1964 Selma to Montgomery March, Stanley says, "is a paradigm case of democratically acceptable propaganda: manipulation of the media to draw attention and empathy to the predicament of an otherwise invisible group." What kind of manipulation is this? Stanley answers: King "manipulated white Southerners into revealing their hatred on national media, thereby turning the opinion of the country against them" (2015: 113–114).

While this is a roughly true description of historical events, this is where I will begin to sketch my criticism of Stanley's application of positive propaganda to protest. First, Stanley's main linguistic model of propaganda won't apply, as it's not obvious what utterance is expressed via the march, or how we could begin to demarcate the at-issue versus not-at-issue content.[8] Second, this description centers the discussion on King's manipulation of white Southerners' cruelty—and the reactions of the white population more generally. While King and others certainly utilized this method to great effect, this ignores other core tenets of the movement that concerned the character of the resistors themselves, and how the anti-hierarchical and democratic ethos of nonviolent direct action are virtues in and of themselves (King 1963, especially ch. 2). In this way, Stanley's model focuses exclusively on the *audience*

---

[8] The content of utterances at protests are, of course, relevant, in part because they can help up distinguish egalitarian protest from bigoted protest, and so could perhaps play this role. Rather than take this route, I'm interested here in how content contributes to the pragmatic structure—who it's calling on and how. That is, how the speech acts of protest function as second-personal transactions. For more on this, see Kukla and Lance 2009; Lance and Kukla 2013; Herbert and Kukla 2016.

of the protest rather than the protesters themselves. There is a significant cost to this, as it de-emphasizes the agency of the protesters themselves.

As I see it, there is much more that distinguishes positive and negative propaganda at the structural level than their effects—at least when discussing *protest* as a form of positive propaganda. To make this more explicit, and to demonstrate what is left out, I now turn to a contemporary example: BLM.

1.1.1. BLM as positive propaganda

Much has been written about the Movement for Black Lives in general, and Black Lives Matter protests in particular (e.g., Taylor 2016; Lebron 2017), and my aim isn't to give a definitive analysis of the ongoing movement. Rather, I aim to show that analyses of protest that focus at the level of expressed content—like Stanley's mode of positive propaganda—obscure important aspects of the pragmatic of protests. Namely, they obscure protest's function to foreground the moral authority of the protester in a way that challenges the unjust authority of the powerful. Discussions of BLM protest are illuminating examples in part because so much attention has been given to the phrase that serves as both the group's name and their main slogan. Consider two popular—and in my eyes *revealing*—discussions of BLM protest.

The first comes from comedian and activist Franchesca Ramsey's video titled "4 Black Lives Matter Myths Debunked" (2016). There, Ramsey makes the point that the phrase "Black lives matter" is not a racist statement directed against non-Black people; rather, it should be interpreted as saying "Black lives *should* matter." She says:

> This movement isn't saying Black lives matter more than anyone else's. It's saying that Black lives should matter, but the way that our justice system, our media, and our police have been operating suggests that they do not. (2016)

Ramsey tries to clarify a surprisingly common (among whites) misconception about the origins and meaning of these protests. And she does so by uncovering the meaning—that is, semantic content—of the slogan.

In another example, law professor Patricia Leary takes this approach a bit further in her viral letter written in response to anonymous student complaints about her wearing a BLM pin to class. Leary carefully analyzes the claims of her student detractors and points out that their argument rests on a false premise, namely, that "there is an invisible 'only' in front of the words 'Black lives matter.'" As Leary goes on to say, while this assumption is false, she suggests that:

> there *are* some implicit words that precede "Black lives matter," and they go something like this: "Because of the brutalizing and killing of Black people at the hands of the police and the indifference of society in general and the criminal justice system in particular, it is important that we say . . ." (cited in Jaschik 2016)

This, as she points out however, doesn't nicely fit on a shirt.

These examples, of course, represent only one way in which BLM has been talked about. And there is much more to discuss about the mainstream analysis of BLM protests than I can fit in here. But what I hope to bring out is how these analyses suggest that the phrase "Black lives matter," and the protests it symbolizes, fit the model of positive propaganda that Stanley articulates and may be productively analyzed as such. Through their provocative slogan, BLM deploys (what Stanley might call) nonrational means of persuasion that aim to extend empathy to an oppressed group. We can see this because:

(1) the message "Black lives matter" embodies a cherished moral ideal—moral value, civic equality;
(2) extending this ideal to group that has been unjustly excluded from the dominant interpretation of that ideal reveals how it is, in practice, restricted to whites;
(3) in doing so, it undermines the existing, restricted ideal of moral value; and
(4) this has the effect of—or aims at—increasing empathy for the excluded group.

We see this, moreover, when we engage in the kind of excavation of hidden meaning that Stanley's account encourages, searching for the unarticulated constituents that reveal the true power of the slogan.

A similar analysis could be provided for the counterslogan "All lives matter" that explains how, given the context in which this phrase emerged—that is, in direct response to BLM protests—the expressed content of "All lives matter" contains implicit associations that function to silence Black protest, and ultimately reduce empathy. A worthy political ideal—moral and legal equality—is appealed to in a fashion that in fact serves to undermine that very ideal, by presenting BLM protestors as racially partisan, and therefore ignorable. And, without that context, it's so abstract as to be meaningless.

1.1.2. What's missing
While I don't disagree with the earlier analyses, I worry that this type of analysis, with its focus on semantic content—including implicit or presupposed content—comes at a cost.[9] It tends to push the analysis and subsequent discussion in a specific direction. Namely, it presents these protests as though they are *moves in a debate*, as if they, and the counterspeech they generate, are competing claims to be evaluated in a similar fashion.[10] This is, I will argue, an inadequate approach to take for protest. As Bernard Boxill states:

> Typically, people protest when the time for argument and persuasion is past. They insist, as Du Bois put it, that the claim they protest is "an outrageous falsehood," and that it would be demeaning to argue and cajole for what is so plain. Responding to a newspaper article that claimed "The Negro" was "Not a Man," Frederick Douglass disdainfully declared, "I cannot, however, argue, I must assert." (1976: 63–64)

As Boxill might put it, treating "Black lives matter" and "All lives matter' " as claims competing in a debate obscures some of the central features that are inherent in protest, namely, that moral protest involves a *demand*. It is a type of demand, moreover, that asserts the protester's moral entitlement to make such a demand—that is, their *authority* to demand.

While the policy proposals put forward by BLM ought to be evaluated and debated, the act of protest itself does not deserve to be argued over. The call of "Black lives matter" is not put forth as a claim to be contested, as if it were a premise in an argument in a seminar room. Recognizing it as protest means recognizing it as an assertion *to be heard*. As I see it, this is a difference in the *uptake* the speech act aims at, which is obscured when we focus on the proposition being expressed. Recognizing it as such is the first step toward seeing the speech act of protest for what it is.

---

[9] For an examination of the further nonsemantic features of the protest slogans of 2011 Egyptian revolution, see Colla (2013), where he argues that "the context of performance demands that we consider slogans not just in terms of semantic meaning or as discursive genre, but also as embodied actions taking place in particular situations" (45).

[10] To urge a shift of attention away from semantic content is not to say that the founders of Black Lives Matter did not think long and hard about their choice of phrasing; they did. For more, see Khan-Cullors and bandele (2018).

Beyond this basic difference in uptake, the entitlement conditions that the speech act of protest presumes are another area worthy of attention. And since uptake is partly determined by the speaker's entitlements to make certain speech acts, this deserves more attention. That is, one contribution that protest makes to a political culture concerns not simply what's being said, but *who is saying it*. From what *perspective*, or social location, is the protest being asserted? Herbert and Kukla (2016) point out the existence of "community-specific speech," which has both community-specific input and uptake. On the input side, they note how "speech acts that have community-specific inputs are of a sort that are felicitous only when performed by insiders" (580). In the following section, I will show how this is an important feature of the input of protest, one that I explain in terms of collective authority.[11] To build toward a conception of protest that foregrounds these aspects, I first turn to Elizabeth Anderson's analysis of the function of social movements (see also Shafiei, Chapter 13, this volume).

2. The moral-epistemological function of social movements

Elizabeth Anderson argues that social movements tend to do three things to correct for the biases of the powerful:

(1) Inform the powerful of the needs and interests of the less powerful ...
(2) Express what is required to respect these needs and interests *as claims or demands* on the powerful ...
(3) Enable the less powerful to display their worthiness, so that they can assume some moral authority to contest the counterclaims of the powerful, and put authority behind their own claims. (2014b: 8, emphasis in original)

An analysis of protest must address these features, which are informed by elements such as speaker, audience, and context, and cannot be captured in impersonal propositional terms. This follows from recognizing that most

---

[11] Though, because it is (most often) directed at outsides, it is not itself community-specific speech in Herbert and Kukla's (2016) sense.

protests occur as part of broader social movements. That is their context, and this must be kept in view.

The protests of social movements, according to Anderson, function to reject the authority of the unjust norms of the dominant. In their place, they foreground the authority of the protesters themselves. They position their own voices as voices in need of being heard. This act, when performed by oppressed persons, directly threatens an unjust hierarchy, and this is in some ways distinct from the specific content they express.[12] And so, as instances of positive propaganda—where they aim to or manage to increase the empathy of their audience—protests achieve this end through a distinct and more direct means than that highlighted by Stanley. Focusing too closely on content tempts us to mischaracterize protest as argument, rather than as a platform foregrounding the moral authority of the protesters. This threatens to make us lose sight of important aspects of protests, including the concrete social context that produced them.

To offer a clearer picture of what I mean by the "moral authority of the protester," I'll next consider how similar concepts are discussed in two distinct, but related contexts: the (meta)ethics of moral demands and the pragmatics of hate speech. Looking to these two areas offers a richer picture of the authority—the entitlements—protesters are invoking in their (speech) acts.

2.1. Egalitarianism and second-personal calls

To better approach the role of authority in protest, I turn to a branch of egalitarianism known as "relational egalitarianism" (see Wolff 1998; Anderson 1999; Scheffler 2010; and Fourie et al. 2015). What makes relational egalitarianism distinctive is its central concern with social hierarchies and interpersonal power.[13] The central questions for many relational egalitarians

---

[12] As Judith Butler (2017) says: "Before we ask what it means to speak truth to power, we have to ask who can speak. Sometimes the very presence of those who are supposed to remain mute in public discourse breaks through that structure. [. . .] [And] we [can] understand the extraparliamentary power of assemblies to alter the public understanding of who the people are. Especially when those appear who are not supposed to appear. [. . .] Of course, they make specific demands, but assembly is also a way of making a demand with the body, a corporeal claim to public space and a public demand to political powers."

[13] This is opposed to the focus on material inequality that resource egalitarians about distributive justice adopt. However, it should be noted that both forms of egalitarianism are concerned with inequalities of different sorts—social, material, welfare, and so on; the difference lies mainly in what is given greater explanatory power, along with distinct metaethical commitments. See Anderson (2010, 2012).

then become: what is it that we *owe* one another, and what can we *demand* from each other?[14] In being so focused, relational egalitarians highlight the "second-personal" dimensions of many core ethical concepts, like rights, duties, and justice.

On this view, complaints of injustice are best seen as demands, and this casts them as second-personal utterances rather than impersonal expressions of propositions. A second-personal utterance is a speech act that is directed at and calls upon a second person, a "you," to give it specific uptake.[15] And so, a moral claim is a performative utterance, where one makes a claim—a demand—on another, and at the same time asserts their entitlement to do so. "A claim of justice," Anderson (2012: 3) says, "is essentially expressible as a *demand* that a person makes *on* an agent whom the speaker holds accountable." Therefore, on this reading, it matters on whom one makes a claim, and whether the speaker is entitled with the proper moral authority to do so.

Inspiration for relational egalitarianism comes directly from egalitarian social movements. For instance, both Anderson (2014a, 2014b) and Iris Marion Young (2011) take such social movements as the civil rights movement, LGTBQ+ rights advocates, and more to be crucial for both our theorizing about concepts like justice and to be themselves a core engine of moral progress. As Anderson (2014a: 260) writes, social movements are "the source of egalitarian ideas."

This appreciation of the second-personal nature of moral claims recognizes that protests and demands are distinct from mere moral arguments, which are often indifferent to elements like speaker, audience, context, and so on. Pure moral arguments—the type we might read and discuss in an ethics classroom—are often expressed in third-personal language to emphasize their presumed universality. There is a difference, therefore, between the *argument* that all moral agents should refrain from hurting other sentient beings, and the second-personal *demand* that you stop stepping on my toe (Darwall 2006: 18). The latter, but not the former, highlights and grounds itself in my authority to make a claim upon you and hold you accountable. It is this (metaethical) difference in address that places protests in between the poles of "pure moral argument," on the one hand, and "riots, war, and other violent acts," on the other (Anderson 2014b: 9). Understanding moral

---

[14] The notions of second-personality found in this literature, including the centrality of demands, are mainly inspired by Darwall (2006).
[15] See also Kukla and Lance (2009) and Lance and Kukla (2013).

claim-making in the real world requires taking stock of these broader contextual features that give moral life its richness and specificity.

One element this attention to context reveals, then, is the invocation of the moral status of the person making a demand. In the case of protest, the status and position of the protester are essential to fully understanding the act being performed. In protesting, one does more than express dissatisfaction with the status quo. They position this complaint as originating from a specific social location. They call upon *their* moral standing and situated knowledge, issuing second-personal calls with distinct entitlements.[16] That is, they put some distinct authority behind their claims, and we must keep this in view.

2.2. The "authority" of hate speech

To further develop this notion of authority, I'll now turn to how it arises in hate speech.[17] This will further illuminate the roles of *context* and *social position*, and how these inform speaker authority and shape the pragmatic force of speech acts.

Unlike moral demands like "get off my toe," which requires only a general entitlement which most of us share, some speech acts require a *particular* entitlement, or authority, to be successfully carried out. For instance, only the umpire can call a strike.

With this in mind, we may ask why something like authority seems necessary to account for the force of hate speech. Consider what *act* is being done when one person hurls hate speech at another. These, in part, are *degrading* and *subordinating* acts. Speech acts like these—like *rankings* and *judgments*—however, have *verdictive* and *exercitive* force, and as such, they are authoritative speech acts. It is as illocutionary acts like these—to use the jargon of Austin (1962)—that authority has seemed a relevant feature of hate speech. In other words, to account for the *pragmatic force* of such speech acts, we're drawn to the idea that hate speakers draw on some form of authority to perform these acts with their words (Maitra 2012; Langton 2017).

---

[16] Reclamation projects are a helpful example of this, in part because reclamation depends on centering the perspective (and authority) of members of the group targeted by the contested term. That is, we cannot lose sight of the 'we' in "we're here, we're queer, get used to it." For discussion of these issues, see Herbert (2015) and Tirrell (1999).

[17] For an overview of some of the main themes of the broader subordinating speech literature, see Langton et al. (2012) and Maitra and McGowan (2012).

Seen in this way, hate speech relies on a *dominating relation* to perform its characteristic function of subordinating its targets. It is therefore *asymmetrical speech*, such that speaker and target are not equally situated in regards to their speech capacity—it's not the case that the target of hate speech can just turn on their assailant and return fire with fire (which shows the limits of the "more speech" response to hate speech). It is worth noting, however, that this authority is not tied to *formal positions* of authority, and is achievable even for so-called ordinary speakers (Maitra 2012; Barnes 2016). The authority at issue here relies on a richly contextual network of features that grant some, but not all, people distinct normative powers in particular situations. Informal distinctions of power and privilege along lines of race, gender, ability, and so on play a large role in distributing this authority, significantly affecting the type of speech acts available to different speakers.[18] This reveals how authority can be thoroughly contextual and interpersonal.

Like moral demands, then, hate speech *calls* upon another to give uptake, and in doing so it also presupposes a certain (contextual) entitlement for the speaker. Putting this together with the features described earlier, we're led to a conception of the elements of authority that accounts for the basic moral status of the speaker, including their situated knowledge, as well as the contextual and interpersonal relations in a given situation. These elements—the entitlement conditions—together inform and constrain the pragmatic force of the (second-personal) calls at a speaker's disposal.

Moreover, an important but neglected type of subordinating authority is what I'll call *collective authority* (Barnes 2019). This is a type of speaker authority generated through the repeated use of the same of similar utterances by a group of speakers. Where each individual utterance would seem to lack authority when considered in isolation, it is by noting the pattern of repetition and amplification that we can understand these as authoritative—and potentially subordinating—speech acts. Through this process, individual speakers fall from view, and instead, a mass of speakers join to produce speech with a distinct, and stronger, pragmatic force.

Protest, I believe, functions similar to this. The speech acts of protest gain a significance and strength that are incomprehensible when considered as simply originating from individual speakers. And to fully understand the speech acts of protest, we must attend to this aspect of its pragmatic output.

---

[18] For a structural account of the harms of injustice in speech in terms of speech capacity, see Ayala (2016).

Colla (2013) describes this feature of a protest slogan in terms of how it "is intended to circulate as an authorless text." He goes on to say that:

> one index of a slogan's power is the degree to which it can detach itself from the specific conditions of its initial composition, and the degree to which it circulates as if it were the anonymous expression of a collective will. (Colla 2013: 38)

Of course, by anonymous, this does not mean that the speech acts of protest are identity-less. The social location of those protesting is obviously significant. But, as this shows, it's the identity of the *group* as a whole that's relevant. And, at least in one sense, it is *through speech* that this group comes into being and acts as a collective. This is, in part, what these collective speech acts do, as their pragmatic function. They create or solidify a group identity. "Slogans are performatives," Colla says, "in the sense they are deliberate compositions intended not so much to reflect collective will *but to create it*" (2013: 38, emphasis added).

In the final section, I examine how differences at the pragmatic level distinguish protest from Stanley's conception of (positive) propaganda. Specifically, I examine how protest functions as *provocation* in order to show how protest, like hate speech, draws on contextual features, like the relative statuses of speaker and target, to be the act that it is.

3. Protest as provocation

Thinking of protest as *provocation* helpfully demonstrates an important interplay between protest and (a subset of) its audience. Booker T. Washington's dismissal of protest out of prudence was partly based on this. Washington claimed that one danger of protest lies in its potential for provocation. "A provocation arouses an individual's resentment," Boxill (1976: 59) notes, "because it challenges his moral claim to a status he enjoys and wants to preserve, thus Black protest would have challenged the white South's justification of the superior status it claimed." The concern here is that protest arouses resentment because it constitutes a challenge to its targets, in part because it questions their status. White Southerners would not accept the (equal) entitlement Black protesters claimed *in protesting*, and thus would react with hostility.

Kate Manne (2014) raises a similar worry in her analysis of the violence and scorn directed at BLM protesters in Ferguson. She writes:

> The humanist line on Ferguson hence fails to explain what seems to provoke the aggression—namely, acts of political and personal defiance, which only people can demonstrate. Moreover, it is hardly surprising that historically subordinated people should be perceived in this way when they try to assert themselves around, or over, dominant group members. They are liable to be perceived as belligerent, "uppity," insubordinate or out of order.

Protest, because it both presumes a certain entitlement on the part of the speaker and makes a specific claim on its target, can serve to trigger hostile and resentful reactions from those on whom the claim is being made. As we saw, protest functions as a demand. But in a hierarchy, not everyone can (successfully) make a demand upon everyone else, as demands are also asymmetrical speech acts in this context.

In addition to the presumption of authority—the moral entitlement *of the protester*—protest also implicates the *status of its target*—the group to whom the protest is directed. As such, protest makes vivid not only the social position of the protesters themselves but also the social position of their audience, that is, the more powerful. It challenges the justification for their superior status, which means it is often interpreted as threatening—because, in important ways, it is. And yet, of course, it is the denial of equality and justice that make protest necessary.

Under conditions of oppression, "acts of personal and political defiance" on the part of the oppressed, like protest, are in and of themselves a challenge to the status quo, and it is the broader political and contextual features that make this vivid, rather than any particular aspect of the protest's content. Putting protest in context, seeing it as provocation that can lead to a range of reactions reveals this aspect more fully.

3.1. A strategic objection

This analysis, however, leads us to an important complicating factor, namely, that conditions of oppression lead many members of dominant social groups to dismiss oppressed people as sites of moral and epistemic authority. And hostile threats to the status quo are interpreted as proof of their unequal status. That is, anti-Black racism makes it difficult for non-Black people in a white-supremacist society to accept Black protesters as moral authorities in need of being listened to. To take one example, Shree Paradkar (2017) notes this in writing about how the 1992 Yonge Street riots in Toronto were reported by a (largely) white media. Through this lens, "Blacks who protest violently are thugs," while "whites who do so have a righteous anger." We see this double standard time and again.[19]

One possible implication might be that where there exist entrenched racisms and other forms of marginalization, talk of the moral authority of the protester is a luxury reserved for the more privileged. It is no accident that Anderson's analysis of British abolitionism focuses mainly on the white Britons who opposed the slave trade but weren't themselves at risk of enslavement. This may lead one to suggest that, given this racist resistance and the tendency to see protest as provocation, it might be strategically preferable to focus on the *content* of the claims being made rather than the people. If Black protesters are more likely to be perceived as violent criminals rather than authoritative voices on injustice—at least for white audiences—then maybe impersonal arguments are more effective.

This is a serious concern. I can offer only a partial response. A similar danger lurks when looking at protest in terms of presenting an argument, so perhaps this is no refuge. We see this when the particular claims being made by *certain* speakers—for example, people of color—are subject to heightened scrutiny. Melissa Harris-Perry (2011) notes that when she and other Black writers write on racism, they tend to "encounter a few common discursive strategies that are meant to discredit our perspectives." These tropes demonstrate the raised standards that claims of racial bias face.

While there is no doubt people of color encounter these "strategies" more severely than whites, part of Harris-Perry's point seems to be that in a racist society, the topic of racism itself invites frustrating skepticisms. As she notes, one strategy is simply to "scorn the study of race as an illegitimate intellectual pursuit." As I see it, this heightened scrutiny relates in some ways to Kristie Dotson's discussion of "risky" and "unsafe content" that can lead a speaker to silence herself, to preemptively avoid such scrutiny (2011). Where racial injustice is present, even when the focus becomes content, it is similarly likely for some—typically white—audiences to dismiss the concern being raised.

---

[19] For another example, Bierria (2014) discusses reporting in the aftermath of Hurricane Katrina.

And so, a retreat to the (disembodied) content being expressed offers no safe refuge from anti-Black racism.

Provocation, in other words, is inevitable when one calls out injustice. And despite the criticisms I have raised earlier, Stanley has a clear grasp of this sad feature of political speech. "A salient feature of many paradigm cases of propaganda," he says, "is that it is speech that owes its efficacy in ending rational debate not to its settling of the question, but rather to its erosion of second-personal ideals like reasonableness" (2015: 121). As such, we can see how many paradigm cases of propaganda would emerge as attempts to renounce the efforts of social movements. The "All lives matter" response to the call of "Black lives matter" demonstrates this very efficiently. Protests invoke a demand—which presupposes the moral authority to do so—and counter-protest propaganda looks to deny this entitlement. It helps to see these acts in conversation with each other. But as I have argued, an analysis that focuses at the level of content misconstrues the way these speech acts differ.

Indeed, this interplay works to reveal the element of protest that Stanley's account ignores. While Stanley sees civic rhetoric and demagoguery—positive and negative propaganda—as structurally parallel, his analysis of both focuses most extensively on the effect each has on its *audience*. Demagoguery reduces empathy; civic rhetoric increases it. But the role of the speaker is obscured, as is the relationship between speaker(s) and audience.

This is inappropriate in the case of protest, an act that fundamentally aims to reveal the moral authority of the protester. And it is in this way that protest may be a paradigmatic instance of positive propaganda. Not because it engages in clever (linguistic) manipulation, but because, through the act of protest oppressed people can claim what they are entitled to, and this assertion of one's authority in the face of injustice itself undermines unjust domination.

References

Anderson, Elizabeth (1999). "What Is the Point of Equality?" *Ethics* 109: 287–337.
Anderson, Elizabeth (2010). "Justifying the Capabilities Approach to Justice." *Measuring Justice: Primary Goods and Capabilities*. Eds. Harry Brighouse and Ingrid Robeyns. Cambridge: Cambridge University Press: 81–100.
Anderson, Elizabeth (2012). "The Fundamental Disagreement between Luck Egalitarians and Relational Egalitarians." *Canadian Journal of Philosophy* 36 (Suppl.): 1–23.

Anderson, Elizabeth (2014a). "A World Turned Upside Down: Social Hierarchies and a New History of Egalitarianism." *Juncture* 20 (4): 258–261.

Anderson, Elizabeth (2014b). "Social Movements, Experiments in Living, and Moral Progress: Case Studies from Britain's Abolition of Slavery." Paper presented at the University of Kansas as part of the Lindley Lecture Series, Lawrence, Kansas, February 11.

Austin, J. L. (1962). *How to Do Things with Words*. Cambridge, MA: Harvard University Press.

Ayala, Saray (2016). "Speech Affordances: A Structural Take on How Much We Can Do with our Words." *European Journal of Philosophy* 24 (4): 879–891.

Barnes, Michael (2016). "Speaking with (Subordinating) Authority." *Social Theory & Practice* 42 (2): 240–257.

Barnes, Michael (2019). "Subordinating Speech and the Construction of Social Hierarchies." PhD dissertation, Georgetown University.

Bell, W. Kumau, and Hari Kondabolu (2017). "Patrisse Khan-Collurs on Black Lives Matter and Resistance under 45." *Politically Reactive*, Season 2, Episode 1. https://www.politicallyreactive.com.

Bierria, Alisa (2014). "Missing in Action: Violence, Power, and Discerning Agency." *Hypatia* 29 (1): 129–145.

Boxill, Bernard (1976). "Self-Respect and Protest." *Philosophy and Public Affairs* 6: 58–69.

Brennan, Jason (2017). "Propaganda about Propaganda." *Critical Review* 29 (1): 34–48.

Butler, Judith (2017). "Reflections on Trump." *Cultural Anthropology* 18 (Jan.). https://culanth.org/fieldsights/1032-reflections-on-trump.

Colla, Elliott (2013). "In Praise of Insult: Slogan Genres, Slogan Repertoires and Innovation." *Review of Middle East Studies* 47 (1): 37–48.

Darwall, Stephen (2006). *The Second-Person Standpoint: Morality, Respect, and Accountability*. Cambridge, MA: Harvard University Press.

Du Bois, W. E. B. (1926). "Criteria of Negro Art." *The Crisis* 32 (Oct.): 290–297.

Dotson, Kristie (2011). "Tracking Epistemic Violence, Tracking Practices of Silencing." *Hypatia* 26 (2): 236–257.

Fourie, Carina, Fabian Schuppert, and Ivo Wallimann-Helmer, eds. (2015). *Social Equality: On What It Means to Be Equals*. Oxford: Oxford University Press.

Harris-Perry, Melissa (2011). "The Epistemology of Race Talk." *The Nation*, September 26. https://www.thenation.com/article/epistemology-race-talk/.

Herbert, Cassie (2015). "Precarious Projects: The Performative Structure of Reclamation." *Language Sciences* 52: 131–138.

Herbert, Cassie, and Rebecca Kukla (2016). "Ingrouping, Outgrouping, and the Pragmatics of Peripheral Speech." *Journal of the American Philosophical Association* 2 (4): 576–596.

Jaschik, Scott (2016). "The Law Professor Who Answered Back." *Inside Higher Education*, July 12. https://www.insidehighered.com/news/2016/07/12/law-professor-responds-students-who-complained-about-her-black-lives-matter-shirt.

Khan-Cullors, Patrisse, and asha bandele (2018). *When They Call You a Terrorist: A Black Lives Matter Memoir*. New York: St. Martin's Press.

King Jr., Martin Luther (1963). *Why We Can't Wait*. New York: Harper & Row.

Kukla, Rebecca, and Mark Lance (2009). *'Yo!' and 'Lo!': The Pragmatic Topography of the Space of Reasons*. Cambridge, MA: Harvard University Press.

Lance, Mark, and Rebecca Kukla (2013). "Leave the Gun; Take the Cannoli! The Pragmatic Topography of Second-Person Calls." *Ethics* 123: 456–478.

Langton, Rae (2017). "The Authority of Hate Speech." *Oxford Studies in Philosophy of Law*. Vol. 3. Eds. John Gardner, Leslie Green, and Brian Leiter. New York: Oxford University Press.

Langton, Rae, Sally Haslanger, and Luvell Anderson (2012). "Language and Race." *Routledge Companion to the Philosophy of Language*. Eds. Gillian Russell and Delia Graff Fara. New York: Routledge: 753–767.

Lebron, Christopher J. (2017). *The Making of Black Lives Matter: A Brief History of an Idea*. New York: Oxford University Press.

Maitra, Ishani (2012). "Subordinating Speech." *Speech and Harm: Controversies over Free Speech*. Eds. Ishani Maitra and Mary Kate McGowan. Oxford: Oxford University Press: 94–117.

Maitra, Ishani, and Mary Kate McGowan, eds. (2012). *Speech and Harm: Controversies over Free Speech*. Oxford: Oxford University Press.

Manne, Kate (2014). "In Ferguson and Beyond, Punishing Humanity." *The New York Times*, September 26. https://opinionator.blogs.nytimes.com/2014/10/12/in-ferguson-and-beyond-punishing-humanity/.

McKinnon, Rachel (2018). "The Epistemology of Propaganda." *Philosophy and Phenomenological Research* 96 (2): 483–489.

Paradkar, Shree (2017). "The Yonge St. Riots of 1992 . . . Or Was It an Uprising?" *The Toronto Star*, May 5. https://www.thestar.com/news/gta/2017/05/05/the-yonge-street-riot-of-1992-or-was-it-an-uprising-paradkar.html.

Potts, Christopher (2005). *The Logic of Conventional Implicatures. Oxford Studies in Theoretical Linguistics*. Oxford: Oxford University Press.

Ramsey, Franchesca (2016). "4 Black Lives Matter Myths Debunked." *MTV Decoded*. https://www.youtube.com/watch?v=jQ_0bqWKO-k.

Scheffler, Samuel (2010). *Equality and Tradition: Questions of Value in Moral and Political Theory*. Oxford: Oxford University Press.

Smith, David Livingstone (2012). *Less than Human: Why We Demean, Enslave, and Exterminate Others*. New York: St. Martin's Griffin Press.

Stanley, Jason (2015). *How Propaganda Works*. Princeton, NJ: Princeton University Press.

Stanley, Jason (2018). "Reply to Critics." *Philosophy and Phenomenological Research* 96 (2): 497–511.

Táíwò, Olúfẹ́mi (2017). "Beware of Schools Bearing Gifts: Miseducation and Trojan Horse Propaganda." *Public Affairs Quarterly* 31 (1): 1–18.

Taylor, K. Keeanga-Yamahtta (2016). *From #BlackLivesMatter to Black Liberation*. Chicago: Haymarket Books.

Tirrell, Lynne (1999). "Derogatory Terms: Racism, Sexism, and the Inferential Role Theory of Meaning." *Language and Liberation: Feminism, Philosophy, and Language*. Eds. Christina Hendricks and Kelly Oliver. Albany: SUNY Press: 41–79.

Tirrell, Lynne (2012). "Genocidal Language Games." *Speech and Harm: Controversies over Free Speech*. Eds. Ishani Maitra and Mary Kate McGowan. Oxford: Oxford University Press: 174–221.

Wolff, Jonathan (1998). "Fairness, Respect, and the Egalitarian Ethos." *Philosophy and Public Affairs* 27: 97–122.

Wolff, Jonathan (2016). "*How Propaganda Works* by Jason Stanley." *Analysis* 76 (4): 558–560.
Young, Iris Marion (1997). "Asymmetrical Reciprocity: On Moral Respect, Wonder, and Enlarged Thought." *Constellations* 3 (3): 340–363.
Young, Iris Marion (2011). *Justice and the Politics of Difference*. Princeton, NJ: Princeton University Press.

7
Value-Based Protest Slogans
An Argument for Reorientation

Myisha Cherry

When bringing philosophical attention to bear on social movement slogans in general, philosophers have often focused on their communicative nature—particularly the hermeneutical failures that arise in discourse. Some of the most popular of these failures are illustrated in "All lives matter" retorts to "Black lives matter" pronouncements. Although highlighting and criticizing these failures provide much needed insight into social movement slogans as a communicative practice, I claim that in doing so, philosophers and slogan users risk placing too much importance on outgroup understandings. This emphasis is misguided because gaining such uptake is not required of particular slogans to perform their functions; indeed, it is an inherent risk of them. I show how such an emphasis can also be distracting to users. Since social movement slogans that express values are first and foremost for *users*, I argue for a shift in focus in what these slogans (such as "Black is beautiful" and the more recent "Black lives matter") do for users, as well as what they demand from users and enable them to express. When slogans have done these things, regardless of uptake, we can say they have performed one of their key functions.

I begin, in section 1, by exploring what users of "Black lives matter" mean by the slogan and what the slogan is often taken to mean by nonusers. I also highlight the epistemic and moral sources that are believed to account for breakdowns in understanding. These range from lack of knowledge to a refusal to disrupt the racial status quo. In section 2, I describe characteristics of social movement slogans—specifically what I refer to as *value-based protest slogans* (VPSs). I do this not only to provide a basic account of our subject of inquiry but also to show that misunderstandings and even attempts to analyze and remedy them (of which many occur in section 1) are not required of slogans. In section 3, I claim that although uptake is not required for slogans to perform their function, an overemphasis on nonusers' understanding of them can be distracting to users—making users' overemphasis an obstacle to slogans performing their main function.

1. Understandings and misunderstandings

If you create a social movement slogan that you believe is precise and clear, you may expect some disagreement (particularly if it's provocative) but may be surprised and intrigued when others misunderstand your message. The surprise may be heightened when slogans ascribe value to marginalized groups like "Black lives matter" (BLM) as opposed to making demands like "Freedom now." One might contest the demand slogan over disagreements about timing. And we can imagine how issues like the "right timing" can be up for debate. Martin Luther King Jr.'s "Letter from a Birmingham Jail" engages such a debate. King wrote the letter in response to white clergymen's worry that the civil rights movement was moving too fast. King disagreed. He argued that not only had the movement taken timing into consideration in each nonviolent campaign, but also that the time for justice is always now. By contrast, we might not expect the value of human lives to be up for debate. Philosophers have helped us make sense of misunderstandings of value slogans. In analyzing "Black lives matter"—a slogan that speaks to the value of lives—philosophers have provided preliminary accounts of the BLM slogan, as well as the nature and reasons for its misunderstandings—particularly those found in "All lives matter" (ALM) retorts.

Luvell Anderson (2017) interprets BLM as *a demand* that black people be respected and treated as equals in society. However, he points out that when someone responds with All lives matter, they are taking BLM to mean that *only* black lives matter, and not others. Although BLM users explain that they do not intend the slogan in that way, ALM users continue to hold this interpretation. Anderson highlights a gap in understanding here brought about by interpretive challenges—obstacles "that leave us without understanding," which he calls *hermeneutical impasses*. These are "instances in which agents engaged in communicative exchange are unable to achieve understanding due to a gap in shared hermeneutical resources" (2017: 3).

One example of a hermeneutical impasse that occurs in ALM responses is, according to Anderson, due to a lack of knowledge. We probably have experienced such an impasse when watching a comedy performance. We may fail to get a comedian's joke because we do not have knowledge of a group's beliefs, experiences, or dialect—all of which an understanding is needed in order to get the joke. Understanding what the comedian's words mean will prove insufficient. To get the joke, we must share certain beliefs and experiences. ALM responses, for Anderson, fail in the same way. Responders cannot understand BLM users because responders lack the necessary knowledge of the experiences of African-Americans (e.g., a history of police brutality), experiences that lead African-Americans to have to publicly declare that black lives matter.

But lack of knowledge is not the only source of misunderstanding. Hermeneutical impasses are also caused by prejudice. ALM responders may claim to understand what is meant by the BLM slogan, but their understanding is distorted by prejudices toward those who express the statement or about the racial climate in general. Prejudice can short-circuit understanding by "creat[ing] a particular bias that causes the interpreter to privilege uncharitable interpretations over more charitable ones" (2017: 5). Impasses that arise from prejudice often occur in high-stakes contexts and when performance has major influence on uptake. That is to say, people tend to misinterpret in life-or-death scenarios and when the communication is performed in a particular place or with a particular tone that one has come to associate with danger. In these instances, ALM responders may fail to interpret BLM slogans because they are under racial stress and are resorting to what Robin DiAngelo (2018) describes as "white fragility." Or they may fail to interpret the slogan because it is being uttered by many people of color and they have come to associate large groups of racial minorities with danger. Anderson points out that these impasses are most resistant to linguistic remedies like clarity and precision. As a result, they are in need of extra-linguistic remedies—the least among them being racial knowledge.

Havercroft and Owen describe Black Lives Matter in the following way:

> [BLM] critiques an order of continuous racial perception enacted in and through everyday practices of racecraft. An exclamation, a complex avowal, that may be, at once, an expression of pain, of anger, of indignation, of resilience and, even perhaps, of hope. It is also a reminder that within the police orders that compose the history of the United States of America, black lives have not, or have only exceptionally, been seen as mattering, as of account, in the same way as white lives and that this condition is a product not of

the black community but rather of those who see themselves as white and, more specifically, of their becoming white. (2016: 13)

On their account, BLM is more than a demand. It is an expression and avowal of a range of emotions and experiences. It is also a reminder and a criticism of the racial reality for many blacks in the United States. The failure to understand these multiple meanings is to be struck by what Havercroft and Owen describe as *racial soul blindness*. Racial soul blindness occurs by refusing to see blacks as human—not just as a biological kind but as an ethical kind. Those who have racial soul blindness do not recognize their connection to blacks nor do they see blacks' suffering as being of the same kind as theirs. It "evidences [their] inability to understand how a demand to acknowledge the value of Black lives and the end of their legalized killing by the police is, in a fundamental way, a demand by the Black community to have equal standing to speak and act in American political life" (Havercroft and Owen 2016: 14). To remedy this gap in understanding, an ALM responder must overcome soul blindness. This requires them to be struck by the world in a particular way, and this can occur by coming to stand in the right relationship with blacks (i.e., by not seeing one's whiteness as superior).

For Ashley Atkins, "Black lives matter is a critical affirmation of what is known by black Americans, the referent of 'Our lives matter,' in response to threats, among other things, to that group-understanding" (2019: 3) Atkins points out that ALM responders may agree with the claim that "Black lives matter" but still respond with ALM since they might think that "Black lives mattering is a trivial consequence of All lives matter." Such an interpretation, some might argue, arises out of color-blindness—a phenomenon Michelle Alexander describes as "the widespread belief that race no longer matters... [a belief that] has [made us ignore] the realities of race in our society and facilitated the emergence of a new caste system" (2010: 11–12). However, Atkins disagrees that color-blindness is behind BLM misunderstandings. Atkins's analysis of historical receptions to "Black power" reveals similarities across time regarding misunderstandings of black political speech.

> That atmosphere of fear gave rise to repeated requests for the definition of "Black power" on the part of the white intelligentsia of Stokely Carmicheal's time, though one has to wonder why that is; its meaning was clear enough to the poor, uneducated, and disenfranchised blacks to whom it was, in the first instance, addressed. I would venture that its meaning was clear to

them, though not to white Americans, because it spoke to their exclusion from the field of power and articulated this exclusion in a way that wasn't calibrated to white racial sensibilities. (Atkins 2019: 5)

She concludes by claiming that misunderstandings and thus criticisms of BLM, like those regarding "Black power," are actually due to understanding too well white life and white power. Although this may appear to fly against the claims of race theorists and feminist philosophers who argue that the disadvantaged are sometimes better poised to know and understand the life and power of the advantaged than the advantaged, here, Atkins is pointing to the inability of whites to achieve a critical distance from white conceptions of power and value. According to Atkins, "they were terms within which whites had historically realized their collective power (of course, with legal, political, economic, and police force that made possible the enforcement of separation or segregation). The failure to see that "Black power" was not a call to perpetrate these wrongs was a failure to understand how power might be claimed by blacks in ways other than whites had claimed it" (2019: 8). For Atkins, BLM marks a feature of domination not exclusion. That is, it illuminates the reality of racial inequality—a reality in which blacks are at the bottom of a socially constructed hierarchy—rather than proclaiming superiority over all non-black others. BLM challenges a racialized system of value, and this explains the presence of recalcitrant defenses. BLM is not interpretive speech but resistance speech that "appear[s] to be saying what they [blacks] already know in the way that they know it and demanding that those who don't take responsibility for that" (2019: 17). BLM reflects for Atkins "the need to affirm the worth of black, not white lives because the lives that are shown to have worth are white" (2019: 8–9).

In summary, according to Anderson, Atkins, and others, users of the BLM slogan intend to affirm black life; criticize black disrespect; demand that blacks be respected; and challenge a racialized system of value. These philosophers help us make sense of the misunderstandings around these meanings. Such clarity is important for two distinct but related reasons.

First, moral agents seek to understand others—not just their words but also their struggles and needs. And if we as moral agents cannot understand, we might want to know what mistakes we are making and resolve them. Second, in terms of being contributors to collective political acts, we want our fellows to understand our political claims and demands and to take them seriously. Such understanding is important for political agreement, protest, collaboration, and solidarity. Making sense of hermeneutical failures is epistemically, morally, and politically important for these reasons.

I will argue, however, that the power of the BLM slogan for users is radically underappreciated in most discussions of the slogan, where the focus is disproportionately on the reactions and interpretations of *nonusers*. Although slogans can have an impact on both users and nonusers, discussion has exclusively focused on the latter. However, the overall value of the slogan cannot be appreciated without considering both. I will also show that nonuser misunderstandings of the slogan are less worrisome, as long as the slogan advances various user-directed goals and values.

2. Value-based slogans and their characteristics

In this section I will lay out the characteristics of a distinct kind of social movement slogan in order to provide a more detailed account of it, as well as show how misunderstanding does not affect its function for users.

I refer to social movement slogans like "Black lives matter" as well as "Black is beautiful" and "Black power" as *value-based protest slogans* (henceforth VPSs) because they express the value (i.e., respect, dignity, and moral worth) of a particular group *and* they are created in response to oppressive systems such as white supremacy—a system that aims to refute certain groups' claims to value. By "protest" I mean a challenge to and refusal of oppressive values and norms. Protest does not require that a perpetrator of that norm be the audience for a particular utterance of the slogan. While a slogan can be said to affirm a life, it can also be simultaneously protesting and pushing back against values that say that such a life does not matter. Just as saying that one loves oneself expresses a value (of the self), it also can protest against certain norms that say "certain people are too inferior to warrant love," particularly groups like immigrants or the working poor. When I refer to slogans in this essay, I am referring to VPSs.

While VPSs share characteristics found in mottos, other slogans, mission statements, song choruses, or persuasive speeches, VPSs also have unique features.[1] They are very brief and usually contain fewer words than a short sentence. Both "Black lives matter" and "Black is beautiful" are three words.

---

[1] I am indebted to Mike W. Martin (2010) for providing the blueprint for how I think generally about slogans in this paper.

"Black power" is two words. They are short so that they can be easily recalled, enjoyed, and repeated by a large group as a chant. A slogan might rely on alliteration or shock to appeal to users' ears and imaginations. "Black power," for example, is shocking and appeals to the political power it believes black people have and can obtain more of. "Black lives matter" appeals to the imagination; it announces value in a world that does not always see or acknowledge it as such.

VPS also specify the people to whom the slogans will apply. "I am a man" applied to black male sanitation workers in Memphis who were being economically exploited by the city in the late 1960s. "Black is beautiful" applied to black people who lived in a culture in which anti-black modes of judging beauty were pervasive, creating what Paul C. Taylor refers to as a *beauty gap*—which encompasses the ways in which "people who are socialized by hegemonic aesthetic norms, norms of bodily aesthetics in places like the US, have decided to act as if people of color are less attractive than white people" (Taylor and Cherry 2019).[2] Likewise, "Black lives matter" applies to those who identify as black and exist in a world in which there is what Eddie Glaude (2016) refers to as the *value gap*—the hegemonic idea that says that some lives (whites) are more valuable than others (non-whites).

Slogans also have users. A slogan needs people who will adopt and employ it. These will be people who "get the message" of the slogan. That is to say, in the case of BLM, users will have the necessary knowledge to understand the message; lack significant amounts of prejudice; see blacks as humans; and be unafraid to challenge a racialized system of value. Users will consist of people to whom the slogan applies, like blacks. But it will also consist of people to whom the slogan does not apply, like whites and Asians.

Nonusers of VPSs are those who lack the necessary knowledge; have significant amounts of prejudice; deny that certain groups are human; or are unwilling to challenge a racialized, gendered, or classist system of values. Those who respond to BLM with ALM are examples of nonusers. Nonusers will consist not only of those to whom the slogan does not apply but also those to whom it does apply. VPSs that apply to women will have nonusers who are also women. Slogans like "Equal women, equal pay" may be rejected by some women who believe that men—as heads of households—should be paid more, or that women should not work. VPSs that apply to the working class will have nonusers who are poor. For example, slogans like "Workers

---

[2] For more on the beauty gap, see Taylor's (2016) monograph on the topic.

are people too" may be rejected by low-skilled workers who believe that employers should not be coerced or that workers should accept their subordinate fates. Likewise, VPSs that apply to black people will also have nonusers who are black.[3] For example, Roy Wilkins, former executive director of the NAACP, was a nonuser of "Black power."[4] He rejected the slogan because for him, "no matter how endlessly they try to explain it, the term Black power means anti-white power" (cited in Aberbach and Walker 1970). Likewise, Martin Luther King, Jr. was a nonuser of "Black power." He thought that "it's absolutely necessary for the Negro to gain power, but the term 'Black power' is unfortunate because it tends to give the impression of black nationalism" (1966).[5] (It may be argued that both men were nonusers for pragmatic reasons related to their position as black leaders and not for reasons cited earlier.)

VPSs will also connect to users' needs, aspirations, vulnerabilities, or pride. "Black is beautiful" speaks to pride in one's natural appearance. "Black lives matter" speaks to the vulnerabilities in response to what seems like the disposability of black people. It also speaks to the pride in one's own value and need to be reminded of that value in the face of oppression. VPSs in particular will not aim merely to demand or make requests, but to state the moral, political, or aesthetic value of a particular group.

Who is the audience of VPSs? One might assume that because these slogans are protest slogans, they are directed to those to whom one is protesting. On this view, VPS users create and chant their slogans with hopes that outside groups like white nationalists, biased police departments, and indifferent citizens will understand their message. However, those to whom the slogan does not apply are not the only audience of VPSs. The origin story of Black Lives Matter is instructive here.

While one might assume that #BlackLivesMatter was originally created as a response to racists, Alicia Garza, cofounder of Black Lives Matter, says that her original audience were fellow blacks. After the acquittal of George Zimmerman in 2013, Garza wrote on Facebook: "Black people. I love you. I love us. Our lives matter, Black lives matter." She notes that BLM was

---

[3] African-American rapper A$AP Rocky and actors KeKe Palmer and Columbus Short, to name a few, publicly responded to BLM with ALM retorts on the social media platform Twitter. See Bragg (2016).

[4] In their 1970 study, Aberbach and Walker provide a detailed study on the different meanings as well as users and nonusers of "Black power." Wilkins is listed as a non-user and is quoted here.

[5] For more information on King's views on Black power (a mix of criticism and charity), see his statement on Black power (1966).

directed at blacks whose response to the verdict was "why are you surprised?" and "this was terrible, but that's why we need to make sure our kids get an education... pull their pants up" (Garza and Hayes 2019). These were black people! Note that these were not ALM responses. They were responses from people who had lost hope or perhaps thought that blacks could minimize threats directed at them through educational and aesthetic efforts. Nonetheless, the slogan was directed at those to whom the slogan applied—the subjects of the slogan. They, too, are the audience of VPSs.

Another feature of VPSs is their one-sidedness. One-sidedness is partly due to slogans' brevity (Martin 2010). When a slogan is two or three words, it is bound to omit other perspectives. Furthermore, slogans' function is to remind us of something important, so it is likely to leave out other things in the process—important things, but not so important to the context in which the slogan arises. Because the slogan indicates certain priorities, some things will be left out. "Black lives matter," a slogan that arises in a context of racial oppression, will focus on black identities over other racial identities and racial oppression as opposed to other kinds of injustices. It does not have this focus because other racial identities or types of injustice are unimportant. Rather, they focus on black identities because they are the disproportionate victims of this particular injustice. Importantly, this highlighting of one theme or one group over others makes misunderstanding or interpretive failures inherent to slogans. This risk is also connected to their brevity. When there are only three words in a slogan to interpret, it is highly likely that the slogan will be misunderstood. As a result, the brevity may facilitate ambiguity. As Mike W. Martin claims, "conciseness and compression carry a price" (2010: 52). But this risk is also connected to the unique political moment from which the slogan arises. Slogans will speak to and out of a particular moment in time. The exclusion of concerns that arise in other moments is bound to cause criticism.

Slogans function to "encapsulate attitudes, emotions, or habits and thereby to motivate and guide our actions and reflections" (Martin 2010: 51). VPSs like "Black lives matter" can express an attitude of respect, an emotion of love and anger, and anti-racist habits. It can also motivate users to defend black lives, value them, challenge racist systems and racists, and think about the ways in which users themselves can resist anti-black racism. VPSs also serve to guide, inspire, affirm, comfort, and unify. Garza talks openly about the origins of the slogan and how it performs this function.

And part of what I was trying to communicate is that I love black people, and I don't think that we are dysfunctional. I don't think there's anything wrong with us. I think that we are incredibly resilient under the worst kinds of circumstances. And that's really what Black Lives Matter was for me. And that's why I said black people, I love you. I love us. And that our lives matter. And that we matter. And that Black lives matter. . . . In order for us to be powerful, we have to believe that we are powerful. And after that verdict was announced, I don't think that people felt powerful. I didn't feel powerful. And from what I was seeing on social media, a lot of people didn't feel powerful. And I posted that and I woke up in the morning and there were some legs. (2019)

BLM expressed Garza's attitudes and emotions and is what motivated her to share the message online to other blacks. Garza hoped that BLM would affirm, comfort, and inspire black folks. "Black lives matter" affirms the inherent worth of people of African descent. It provides comfort from a world that doesn't value them. It inspires people to continue to fight for rights and equal treatment under the law. It guides and motivates antiracist actions. Similarly, a VPS like "Black is beautiful" affirms the internal and external beauty of blacks. It provides comfort from assaults of white supremacy that say that only white Western standards of beauty are acceptable. It inspires blacks to embrace themselves. It also guides action that might include wearing a natural hairstyle or being inclusive of such hairstyles as an employer.

We can see how affirmation and comfort function for black users—for they can employ the slogan as a self-affirming and comforting tool. But how about other users? When a white person adopts and employs "Black lives matter," it is not to affirm their own anti-racist attitudes or comfort their racial anxiety. Affirmation and conformation should go in the direction of the group to whom the slogan applies and not be directed at users to show that they are "good white people," for example. But the function of the slogan, when employed by users to whom it does not apply, is not necessarily to affirm and comfort black people either. If it were, it could promote "white saviorism"— the view that black people are in need of saving, and only white people can save (or affirm) them—as well as other forms of saviorism. Instead, adopting and employing the slogan can—in addition to publicly protest—serve as an *amen affirmation*.

An amen affirmation communicates "I agree" with what you say about your life. It is a humble response. It admits that while one's confirmation is not needed to make the VPS so, what a user (to whom the slogan applies) says about themselves is so true and powerful, that the most appropriate response to such a slogan is to agree with it by adopting and employing the slogan. When uttered by non-blacks, the slogan might still affirm and comfort some users to whom the slogan applies. But it needn't do so in order to perform its function in this case. It does perform its function in other ways. The slogan can still inspire the user. It can also express his attitudes and habits and guide his anti-racist actions. It can also function as a way for him to challenge racialized value systems. It can also unify him with others.

VPSs will also function by alluding to certain virtues and values and providing an implicit imperative for the group. "Black is beautiful" alludes to respect and self-respect. "Black power" alludes to racial pride. "Black lives matter" alludes to dignity. These slogans will not only allude to values but give imperatives, given such values. The imperative for the group who adopts "Black is beautiful" may be to resist normalizing white Western standards of beauty. The imperative for users who adopt "Black power" might be to participate in political action, given their belief in their power as political citizens. An imperative for "Black lives matter" is for users to view black victims brutalized by the police as significant and as having value. Or an imperative could be to push toward policy changes that embrace the humane treatment of blacks.

Again, the function of VPSs is to express attitudes and habits; motivate and guide actions of users through the imperatives they provide; and inspire, affirm, or comfort users. And the slogan will recur—for users will often use it to motivate conduct or influence their thinking. It performs its function when it has done these things. The slogan need not perform every function all at once for the user. A VPS might affirm a user at T_1. It might motivate her actions at T_2. It might provide her comfort at T_3. What's important to note here is that no matter what point on the timeline a user finds herself, the function of VPS will always be directed at the user and not nonusers. That is to say, VPS performs its function exclusively for the user. While we can admit that slogans are also able to *impact* nonusers by challenging, criticizing, and making demands of them, we should be careful not to confuse impact with function.

VPSs do not require accurate interpretation by nonusers in order to perform their function. A VPS does not require nonusers to understand its meaning in order for the slogan to inspire or affirm users. A VPS that defends black life and stimulates political action does not require that people who issue ALM retorts change their minds. As I argued earlier, slogans carry the inherent risk of misunderstanding by both users and nonusers. VPSs accommodate this misunderstanding—even misunderstandings that go beyond reasons of brevity and priority-setting. VPSs are not destroyed nor is their function blocked when a person is unable or unwilling to understand the values and virtues expressed through the slogan. Whether a nonuser adopts, misinterprets, or accuses the slogan of making no sense whatsoever has no bearing on the slogan advancing various user-directed goals and values.

The function I have alluded to earlier is slogans' *primary* function. This is not to say that it is the only function of the VPS. VPS can also have a *secondary function* and it might include, for example, making nonusers *aware* of certain attitudes and habits or even making some kind of *impact* on nonusers. But this secondary function will not be the primary function, and it need not occur in order to advance user-directed goals and values.

3. The interpretive distraction

My claim is not that interpretation is trivial. The less misunderstanding in the world, some might argue, the better—at least epistemically speaking. Instead, my claim is that even if there is misunderstanding, slogans can still perform vital functions. And if they can, we should draw our attention to their other functions, targets, and obstacles. Even if responders continue to provide ALM retorts, BLM could still express attitudes and habits. Even if other blacks are confused by its meaning, BLM can still inspire, comfort, and unify users. Although some might interpret BLM as racist speech, the slogan will still allude to certain values and place imperatives on its users. Since this is possible, I see no payoff in focusing on interpretive failures exclusively, *as if* they were deal breakers or major blockages to value-based slogans' function. This is not to say that interpretive failures are not important. This is only to say that functioning is possible even where hermeneutical failures exist.

One might object by pointing to the link between users and interpretation. It seems that you can only have users to the extent that they can, at least minimally, interpret the slogan. Without such user interpretation and thus adoption, for whom could the slogan function? I am not downplaying the need for interpretation; users are users because they are able to understand and employ the slogan. However, slogans cannot be said to appeal to everyone. Some will misinterpret the slogan. Others will reject it for other reasons. This is the price that slogans must pay. But this price will not cause VPSs to fail to function for users. This is not to say that misunderstanding has no impact on slogans. They do. But not in the ways we might assume. Let me explain.

While nonusers' uptake is not required for slogans to perform their function, users can allow retorts and outside misunderstandings to distract them from focusing on the slogan's function for them. I will now describe how this is done and what happens as a result. I do this with the aim of not just engaging in a descriptive project, but to offer up a cautionary tale to VPS users.

First, an overemphasis on misunderstanding rather than the function of the slogan hits the wrong target. In the case of VPSs, the right target is users. The wrong target is nonusers. Since VPSs are for users, we should give greater significance to slogans performing their function. Recall, the function of VPSs is to express attitudes and habits. This is not to say that users will not hope that hearers be persuaded by their expressions. It is only to say that VPSs function is expression and not persuasion.

But VPSs also function to guide the political and social action of users—actions that aim to bring about a world in which black lives will matter. This is not to say that in order for change to happen, everyone including nonusers must accept the value claim of the slogan. Nonusers can give into demands by VPS users or engage in policy reform (with users) without becoming users themselves or interpreting the slogan correctly. VPSs would have performed their function by guiding the action of users to bring about structural changes so that our institutions *treat* black lives with as much respect, dignity, and value as nonblack lives. These institutions needn't *understand* "Black lives matter" for these things to occur, and for VPSs to perform their function.

Secondly, focusing on the wrong target can also do the opposite of what the slogans aim to do. For example, one of the functions of BLM is to affirm black life. However, when users focus on certain targets' misunderstanding of that slogan (e.g., white people) at the expense of users, they can unintentionally privilege white people's understandings of black value. This puts whites at the center. It also may communicate that black lives cannot have value until white folks think that they do. This is the opposite of what VPSs aim to achieve, making the focus on misunderstanding both counterproductive and counterintuitive.

Thirdly, the function of VPSs is to affirm. But focusing on misunderstandings and trying to remedy them with arguments for why the slogan expresses a particular value can be dehumanizing—particularly for users to whom the slogan applies. Reminding myself, as a black person, that black lives matter is quite different from convincing a non-black person or nonuser that black lives matter. The reminder in the first instance is an affirming and comforting act. The reminder in the second case can be read and even feel like a humanity plea—an effort to convince another person of one's humanity. To do so in the latter case can be dehumanizing.

It can also be dehumanizing in another way. Audre Lorde talks about the expectation certain socially positioned groups have in respect to teaching others about their humanity when she writes:

> Black and Third World people are expected to educate white people as to our humanity. Women are expected to educate men. Lesbians and gay men are expected to educate the heterosexual world. The oppressors maintain their position and evade their responsibility for their own actions. (2007: 115)

What can be dehumanizing here is not just the fact that a person must teach others that she is human and that there is an expectation that she does so. It can be dehumanizing when the target of that education does not change himself, transform his world, or take responsibility given this new knowledge. We find this in ALM users who continue to use ALM after BLM has been fully clarified. We can also see this in cases in which a VPS like "Black is beautiful" is explained to nonusers but then refuted while the person continues—through their actions—to widen the beauty gap.

Lastly, an overemphasis of nonusers' understanding can distract users from taking full advantage of the slogan's function. Users adopt and employ slogans. Users employ the slogan by expressing values and virtues and by allowing the slogan to guide their actions. However, when users spend all their time attempting to get people to understand what BLM means or why their interpretation is mistaken, slogans are being debated rather than expressed. If I spend all my time telling you what something means, I lose the time I can spend on living out what that slogan means and benefitting from what it can do for me. Lorde helps make sense of this claim in the earlier passage. She continues: "This [teaching] is a constant drain of energy which might be better used in redefining ourselves and devising realistic scenarios for altering the present and constructing the future" (2007: 115). Trying to get uptake from nonusers for slogans that are first and foremost for users—as if it was necessary—is a drain of energy that is better used for expressing attitudes and habits, and performing more fruitful imperatives of

BLM like saying the names of cis and trans women victims of police violence or working for criminal justice reforms. These are of utmost importance as well as part of the primary function of VPSs.

4. Conclusion

Many questions about slogans' function and uptake remain. Is there a thin line between addressing nonusers' concerns and emphasizing them? How does one know the difference? Is there a group I have left out that treads the line between user and nonuser, and do we have different obligations to them? What other ways might users block the function of VPSs—irrespective of tending to interpretive failures? These are worthy of further research. What I have hoped to do here is to give an account of VPSs and show how their function does not depend on nonusers. I hope that my argument will show the limited power that outsiders have over what marginalized people and their allies express and perform through VPSs and the range of agency that users have with respect to them.

References

Aberbach, Joel, and Jack Walker (1970). "The Meanings of Black Power: A Comparison of White and Black Interpretations of a Political Slogan." *The American Political Science Review* 64 (2): 367–388.
Alexander, Michelle (2010). *The New Jim Crow: Mass Incarceration in the Age of Colorblindness*. New York: The New Press.
Anderson, Luvell (2017). "Hermeneutical Impasses." *Philosophical Topics* 45 (2): 1–19.
Atkins, Ashley (2019). "Black Lives Matter or All Lives Matter? Color-blindness and Epistemic Injustice." *Social Epistemology* 33 (1): 1–22.
Bragg, Ko (2016). "Celebrities Back 'All Lives Matter.' The Internet Goes Nuts." *NBCNews*, July 8. https://www.nbcnews.com/news/nbcblk/celebrities-back-all-lives-matter-internet-reacts-n606031.
DiAngelo, Robin (2018). *White Fragility: Why It's So Hard for White People to Talk About Racism*. Boston: Beacon.
Garza, Alicia, and Chris Hayes (2019). "Why Is This Happening? Remembering Why Black Lives Matter with Alicia Garza." *NBC News*, June 11. https://www.nbcnews.com/think/opinion/remembering-why-black-lives-matter-alicia-garza-podcast-transcript-ncna1013901.
Glaude, Eddie (2016). *Democracy in Black: How Race Still Enslaves the American Soul*. New York: Crown.

Havercroft, Jonathan, and David Owen (2016). "Soul-Blindness, Police Orders and Black Lives Matter: Wittgenstein, Cavell, and Rancière." *Political Theory* 44 (6): 739–763.

King, Martin Luther (1966). Statement. https://www.crmvet.org/docs/6610_mlk_power-poverty.pdf.

Lorde, Audre (2007). *Sister Outsider: Essays and Speeches*. New York: Crossing Press.

Martin, W. Mike (2010). "Of Mottos and Morals." *The International Journal of Applied Philosophy* 25 (1): 49–60.

Taylor, Paul C. (2016). *Black Is Beautiful: A Philosophy of Black Aesthetics*. Hoboken, NJ: Wiley-Blackwell.

Taylor, Paul C., and Myisha Cherry (2019). "Paul Taylor on Black Aesthetics." *UnMuted: Conversations on Prejudice, Oppression, and Social Justice*. Ed. Myisha Cherry. New York: Oxford University Press: 251–259.

8
The Movement for Black Lives and the Language of Liberation

Ian Olasov

When we think of philosophy that engages with the problems of its time, the problems that preoccupy our politicians and pundits and social movements, we're apt to think of moral and political philosophy. But it's not hard to find points of contact between our most pressing social problems and other branches of philosophy. There is work for philosophers of science to do on climate change, for metaphysicians to do on race and gender, for epistemologists to do on expertise and public reasoning. There is also urgent work for philosophers of language to do, reflected in the recent proliferation of research on speech used to oppress, disinform, or serve otherwise dubious political ends.[1] As I hope to show, philosophy of language, broadly construed, can also help us understand the Movement for Black Lives (M4BL) by helping us understand the speech that sustains and promotes the movement.

In particular, I hope to shed some light on two related problems. The first has to do with the content of the movement. What is M4BL about? The problem is more acute for M4BL than for many past black liberatory movements. Where those movements have often had some more or less unambiguous leadership structure, which could coordinate the actions of their members and enforce some messaging discipline, M4BL is a diffuse, largely unstructured group of people pursuing a broad range of goals (Taylor 2019).[2]

---

[1] Readers interested in this work might consult McKinney (2016) on extracted speech, Stanley (2015) on propaganda, Saul (2018) and Olasov (2016) on dogwhistles, Rini (2016) on microaggressions, and Tirrell (2018, 2012) on toxic and genocidal speech. There is also, in the spirit of this paper, increasing attention to pro-social political speech. Simpson (2016), Camp (2017), Anderson (2018), and Langton (2018) propose some tools we can use to combat slurs and insults. McKinney (2018) describes the backstage communication (and noncommunicative action) that makes public dissent possible.

[2] Strictly speaking, the institutionalized coalition called the Movement for Black Lives has the Black Lives Matter Global Network as a member, which in turn has various local chapters with their own organizational structure. There is also a much larger, looser group that has rallied behind the slogan "Black Lives Matter."

Ian Olasov, *The Movement for Black Lives and the Language of Liberation* In: *The Movement for Black Lives*. Edited by: Brandon Hogan, Michael Cholbi, Alex Madva, and Benjamin S. Yost, Oxford University Press. © Oxford University Press 2021. DOI: 10.1093/oso/9780197507773.003.0009

No one person or institution can speak for the movement, and the movement itself has clearly been interpreted differently by different audiences. Nevertheless, we can explicate M4BL's message in part by looking at some of the protest chants and other signals associated with the movement.

The second problem has to do with strategy. How does the characteristic speech and rhetoric of the movement (which I will call M4BL speech) address, or fail to address, the specific obstacles to black liberation we face today? Commentators have often remarked that M4BL is a movement that takes place online as much as in face-to-face encounters, and that the movement would not have been possible unless ordinary people were able to make and share video recordings of police violence. But how, exactly, has the movement exploited the resources afforded by social media and camera phones? What types of speech has the movement centered, and what are the strategic strengths and weaknesses of this speech?

I approach the first problem by looking at what is old in M4BL speech, and the second by looking at what is new. First, I describe some of the continuities between the speech of M4BL and past black liberatory and social justice movements, and explain how these continuities clarify the movement's message. Second, I briefly summarize and expand on Taylor's (2016) account of the specific challenges facing M4BL today. Third, I describe four new or newly prominent tools in M4BL speech: the slogan and hashtag #BlackLivesMatter, videos of police violence, naming the dead, and what I will call stereotype engineering. I argue that these four tools each serve to address some of the challenges identified by Taylor. I also note that they illuminate some topics of independent philosophical interest—how to remedy testimonial injustice, what it means to engineer a concept, what makes a mental state a moral attitude. Lastly, I explore some of the limitations of three of these tools.

My focus throughout will be on the illocutionary speech acts involved in M4BL speech, rather than on, say, the linguistic meaning of the words and sentences associated with the movement. I understand illocutionary acts in terms of the mental states they are used to express (Bach and Harnish 1979), but my account doesn't hinge on any particular theory of speech acts.[3] It is

---

[3] I don't endorse Bach and Harnish's theory entirely. My view is that communicative speech acts are expressions of mental states, where a speaker expresses a mental state if she either acts with a communicative intention to give an audience evidence that she is in that state, or she has no such intentions in acting that way, but does so primarily because a (biological or conventional) function of that action is to give others evidence that she is in that state (Millikan 2005). Conventional speech acts, whose performance depends on the speaker bearing an appropriate relation to a social institution, do not consist in the expression of mental states.

178 IAN OLASOV

important, however, that I am using "speech" (and, consequently, "speech act") broadly; as a rule, what can be done with words (asserting, demanding, expressing anger or pride or solidarity . . .) can be done without words, given the appropriate context.

1. Content and continuity

In his exploration of the place of M4BL in the black American intellectual tradition, Lebron (2017) emphasizes the continuities between past black liberatory struggles and the struggles of today. The music of Kendrick Lamar is to M4BL what the art of the Harlem Renaissance was to the cultivation of "the New Negro"; Anna Julia Cooper's and Audre Lord's struggle to place women at the center of the fight for black liberation has been taken up by Alicia Garza, Patrisse Cullors, and Opal Tometi in our own time; and so on. Harris (2019) argues, similarly, that M4BL is a response to white fear and a presumptively white understanding of humanity, themes she locates in the work of Frantz Fanon. These continuities are due in part to the fact that latter-day movements learn from and define themselves in relation to their predecessors, and in part to the fact that many of the past problems facing black people in the United States and around the world have never gone away. They are also reflected, in sometimes illuminating ways, by the specific chants and forms of protest used by M4BL.

Some popular chants at M4BL actions are listed in Table 8.1.[4] Many originate in previous anti-racist movements. For example, "No justice, no peace" appears to date to the protests over an episode of anti-black mob violence in Howard Beach, Queens, in 1986 (Zimmer 2013). Interestingly, however, many of the chants derive from earlier movements that weren't primarily focused on racial justice. Several of the chants—"This is what democracy looks like," "Whose streets?," and "Ain't no power"—date back at least to the 1999 anti-WTO protests in Seattle (*This Is What Democracy Looks Like* 2000),[5] and featured prominently in the Occupy protests of 2011. "El pueblo unido jamás será vencido" was one of the election slogans of the Chilean socialist Salvador Allende (Corvalán 2003). After Allende was killed in a CIA-backed coup, a song of that name became popular among the resistance to the authoritarian

---

[4] Many of these chants can be seen in the photographer Issa Khari's documentation of the work of NYC Shut It Down, available at https://youtu.be/V3IPQFByglM.
[5] The documentary is available at https://youtu.be/yBUZH2vCD_k.

Table 8.1 Some chants used at black lives matter protests

No justice, no peace (fuck these racist police)

If we don't get no justice, then they don't get no peace

Black Lives Matter

All lives will matter when black lives matter

El pueblo unido jamás será vencido / The people united can never be defeated

NYPD, KKK, how many kids did you kill today?

Show me what democracy looks like / This is what democracy looks like

Whose streets? / Our streets

What do we want? / Justice / When do we want it? / Now (/ And if we don't get it / Shut it down)

Shut it down

Ain't no power like the power of the people 'cause the power of the people don't stop

They say get back, we say fight back

Hey hey, ho ho, these racist cops have got to go

I can't breathe

The whole damn system is guilty as hell

Hands up, don't shoot

Chilean government. "How many kids did you kill today?" is derived from one of the more well-known chants of the Vietnam anti-war movement.

In many cases, M4BL protesters may have borrowed these chants without any special regard for these earlier groups and concerns.[6] But to the extent that it is common knowledge that these chants "belong" to movements that have fought not only racial injustice, but also economic injustice, right-wing authoritarianism, and war, their use expresses solidarity with those movements; that is, it invites listeners to see themselves and M4BL as a whole as members of a common group, participating in a shared struggle. By the same token, ironic or mocking uses of M4BL chants, such as the use of "Whose streets?" by police making arrests during one M4BL action (Edwards 2017), express disassociation from M4BL, inviting listeners to see the police as opposed to M4BL (Sperber and Wilson 2012).

---

[6] This seems especially unlikely in the case of the "pueblo" chant, however. At the very least, using a Spanish-language chant is a way of recognizing Spanish-speaking members of the movement and taking an inviting stance toward Spanish speakers beyond the movement.

If these chants express a perceived relationship between M4BL and a broad range of past social movements, they also articulate and reinforce M4BL's emphasis on institutional and structural problems. While many M4BL actions are responses to specific episodes of police violence, chants like "Shut it down" and "The whole damn system" attribute these episodes to larger forces. Of course, the chants themselves never make fully explicit what "it" or "the whole damn system" is. But if M4BL actions are also, at some level, about economic injustice, war, and right-wing authoritarianism, the system in question comes into slightly sharper focus.

When M4BL borrows the symbols and actions of past black liberatory movements in particular, it does so ecumenically. Richardson and Ragland (2018) describe the use of a broad range of features of African-American Vernacular English in protest chants and online discussion surrounding M4BL ("da" for "the," "woke" for "awake," "gon" for "gonna," zero copula), as well as references to black history and shared black cultural knowledge in the performances and clothing of prominent supporters of M4BL (Colin Kaepernick's afro, the Black Panther–style berets and leather tops in Beyoncé's 2016 Super Bowl performance). The practice of "taking a knee" or raising a fist at sports games in support of M4BL is widely compared to Tommie Smith and John Carlos's Black Power salute at the 1968 Olympics. The music associated with the movement sometimes invites a comparison to a number of genres of past protest music; consider the use of tropes from modal jazz in Kendrick Lamar's "Alright," gospel in Childish Gambino's "This Is America," and work song in Janelle Monae's "Hell You Talmbout."

Stewart (1980) describes five functions (summarized in Table 8.2) that the rhetoric of a social movement needs to perform. We have focused so far on the first two functions. "Transforming perceptions of history" is a matter of identifying a historical problem, its current manifestation, and describing what society will look like if the movement succeeds. "Transforming perceptions of society" is a matter of creating a shared understanding of the opposition and a shared understanding of the movement itself. As we've seen, the rhetorical continuities between M4BL and its predecessors both clarify how movement members might perceive themselves and how they see the historical problems to which they're responding.

But the M4BL speech that we have discussed so far, and street protests in particular, clearly serve Stewart's other three functions as well. "Prescribing

Table 8.2 Five functions of rhetoric in social movements (from Stewart 1980)

1. Transforming Perceptions of History	• Altering perceptions of the past • Altering perceptions of the present • Altering perceptions of the future
2. Transforming Perceptions of the Society	• Altering perceptions of the opposition • Altering self-perceptions
3. Prescribing Courses of Action	• Prescribing what must be done • Prescribing who must accomplish the task • Prescribing how the task must be accomplished
4. Mobilizing for Action	• Organizing and uniting the discontented • Gaining sympathy and support from opinion leaders or legitimizers • Pressuring the opposition
5. Sustaining the Social Movement	• Justifying setbacks and delays • Maintaining viability of the movement • Maintaining visibility of the movement

courses of action" is a matter of communicating what is to be done, by whom, and how. "Mobilizing for action" is a matter of motivating movement members, people in positions of power, and opponents to act on the problems the movement is devoted to. "Sustaining the movement" is a matter of overcoming failures and keeping members' and nonmembers' attention on the movement. Street protests do all three of these things. They are covered in the popular press, raising the visibility of the movement. They mobilize members and recruit the support of sympathetic spectators. We will return to Stewart's functions periodically later.

2. Challenges

Before we turn to some of the more novel features of M4BL speech, it will help to describe some of the obstacles facing the movement. M4BL coalesced around police and vigilante violence against black people, and the killing of Michael Brown in particular (Ince et al. 2017). While criminal justice and police reform are still at the center of its mission, it has since expanded its scope to a broad range of demands on the economy, democratic institutions, and the social welfare state. Taylor (2016) describes the constellation of ideological and institutional challenges confronting such a movement in our time. A partial list of these challenges would include:

- The idea that racism ended with the decline of explicitly racially discriminatory laws
- The idea that color-blindness is the racial goal of social policy and individual virtue
- The idea that racism is an individual vice, rather than a feature of social structures or institutions, and only bad if intentional
- The increased representation of black people among the US political and business elite, whose success is taken to be evidence of a "postracial" condition and the absence of structural obstacles to black flourishing
- The use of "the culture of poverty" and stereotypes of black degeneracy to explain carceral and other forms of racial inequality
- The distinction between the deserving and the undeserving poor
- The criticism of all social welfare programs as socialism
- The idea that the United States is a "city on a hill," or an international moral exemplar, which helps make some people skeptical of broad criticisms of the nation or its institutions
- High public regard for the police and widespread trust of police descriptions of their violent encounters with civilians
- The opacity and ineffectiveness of existing mechanisms for holding police accountable for misconduct
- The deep connections between mass incarceration and police brutality, on the one hand, and entrenched features of the US economy, democratic institutions, and social welfare state, on the other hand, which make it difficult to address any one of these problems without addressing all of them

Taylor's book was written during the Obama administration. Some additional challenges to M4BL have arisen since then, including a federal government less sympathetic to the cause and a news cycle often dominated by other public problems. In Stewart's taxonomy, it has grown harder to maintain the visibility of the movement.

I will add that the problems M4BL addresses include, in Young's (2000) phrase, both external and internal exclusion. Black people in the United States are more likely than whites to be externally excluded—that is, formally excluded altogether—from participating in democratic decision-making processes by, for example, felon disenfranchisement and jury selection. But they are also more likely to be internally excluded—that is, formally included in a democratic decision-making process, but in such a way that their contributions to those processes are somehow ignored or devalued. This internal exclusion is sometimes linguistic in nature, as when the testimony of Trayvon Martin's friend Rachel Jeantel at the trial of George Zimmerman was widely ridiculed, primarily because she spoke a stigmatized variety of African-American vernacular English (Rickford 2013).

3. The new language of liberation

I turn now to four characteristic communicative tools used by M4BL: the slogan and hashtag #BlackLivesMatter, videos of police violence, naming the dead, and stereotype engineering. Each of these tools helps M4BL overcome some of the challenges mentioned in the previous section. They each also have features that bear on nearby philosophical problems.

3.1. #BlackLivesMatter

M4BL crystallized around the slogan and hashtag #BlackLivesMatter. The central use of a hashtag is to categorize a social media post by its subject matter, and to allow people to discover the post by searching for posts that share that hashtag.[7] Such hashtags increase the likelihood that a post will be seen by people outside of the poster's own social network who are interested in this subject matter. When these hashtags are successful, people who see them are motivated to use them in their own posts.

For many such hashtags (#dogs, say), the existence of the subject matter in question is common knowledge, which predates the coinage of the hashtag itself. Other hashtags bring to light the existence of the subject matter, or present that subject matter to an audience under a new description. That is, prior to the widespread use of the hashtag, the audience for the hashtag was largely unaware of the phenomena that fall under the hashtag, or they didn't think of the phenomena under the description associated with the hashtag. For example, many people seeing #whitegenocide for the first time either hadn't been aware of miscegenation and the browning of the United States, or they

---

[7] I focus on the central use here. Ince et al. (2017) distinguish several uses of the hashtag #BlackLivesMatter (and some of its variants) by distinguishing the types of hashtag that co-occur with it on Twitter posts.

had never thought about those phenomena (erroneously) as genocidal. For someone who doubts the existence of the phenomena that fall under the hashtag, the range of posts sharing the hashtag can serve as more powerful evidence of their existence than any one post could.

#BlackLivesMatter is such a hashtag. It was coined in response to the acquittal of George Zimmerman in the killing of Trayvon Martin. Zimmerman was not a police officer, but it quickly came to be used to categorize posts involving police violence against black people and the failure of the justice system to hold police accountable for this violence. The hashtag also offers a sort of explanation of these phenomena—they are due to a failure on the part of police to recognize that black lives matter. Many people have long denied either that there is widespread police violence against black people, or if they have been aware of this violence, they have not thought of it as caused by a devaluation of black life. The success of #BlackLivesMatter has helped changed that, both by aggregating evidence of this violence and by giving its audience a new way of explaining it. In this way, the hashtag helps confront one of the central challenges to M4BL described earlier—widespread trust in the police and their exculpatory accounts of police violence.

#BlackLivesMatter is also a slogan, a phrase used to express solidarity and agreement with a group.[8] We can understand how slogans work by comparing them with nonslogans that are otherwise close in meaning. "Stop the Violence" was the name and slogan of a movement in the late 1980s "concerned with both counteracting [rap] music's reputation as a cause of violence and raising money to fight illiteracy and black-against-black crime" (Keepnews 1989). "The violence" referred to in the slogan is "black-against-black" violence, especially among hip-hop fans. So a nonslogan similar in meaning to "Stop the Violence" might be something like "Black people and hip-hop fans should stop hurting each other." Notice how different the slogan and its counterpart are, though: the latter is likely to sound rather conservative, if not outright racist. It would take a significant amount of scene-setting for a speaker to utter the counterpart without opening herself up to an accusation of conservatism or racism. But the "Stop the Violence" movement was closely tied to hip-hop stars known for their anti-racist politics and radical self-presentation. For that reason, uses of the slogan are unlikely to appear conservative or racist; they can express much the same attitude as uses of the

---

[8] More precisely, a slogan is a phrase used to express solidarity and agreement with a group, which is not so used merely because of its compositional linguistic meaning.

counterpart, while dodging some of the criticism the counterpart is likely to receive. In this sense, a slogan can allow someone to both express an attitude, and support that attitude with a sort of moral authority, or whatever credibility comes with membership in the group that owns the slogan.

Attention to these features of slogans can also help explain the dispute between supporters of #BlackLivesMatter and supporters of #AllLivesMatter (see Chapters 1, 6, and 7, this volume). #AllLivesMatter is also a slogan, used to express solidarity and agreement with the opponents of M4BL. But its literal nonslogan content is unobjectionable to all of the parties to the dispute. These two features of a slogan are hard to disentangle, which makes disagreement with #AllLivesMatter rather difficult. Someone who disagrees with it opens herself up to the (perhaps disingenuous) criticism that she must not value all lives. So people who disagree with #AllLivesMatter are left in the awkward, concessive position of having to explain that it's true that all lives matter, but that that's a distraction from the specific problems facing black people in the United States; or that all lives matter in a sense, but that, paradoxically, the point of stating that black lives matter is that black lives don't matter *to* the criminal justice system; or that all lives matter, but really what we're talking about is support for or opposition to a social movement. If members of M4BL want to express disagreement with their opponents, they can avoid this awkward position by focusing on the substance of that disagreement, rather than on the slogans themselves.

Of course, #BlackLivesMatter isn't the only slogan to come out of the movement. Most notably, the June 2020 uprising in response to the murders of George Floyd and Breonna Taylor saw the popularization of the slogans (and sometime hashtags) "Defund the police" and "Abolish the police." While the abolish slogan appears to be interpreted univocally by speakers and audiences (and invites comparisons with earlier movements for the abolition of prison and slavery), the defund slogan is not. Sometimes it means, roughly, "reduce police funding" and sometimes it means "eliminate funding for the police altogether."[9] This highlights an important feature of slogans—that they can be shared by groups who use them differently. In some cases, this might allow for productive solidarity between different constituencies

---

[9] It is sometimes claimed that one of these is the obvious literal meaning of the phrase, but this is false. The tokens of "defund" in a random sample from the Corpus of Contemporary American English sometimes clearly mean "reduce funding somewhat" (as in "epically defund public schools / hospitals") and sometimes clearly mean "reduce funding to zero" (as in "cut waste ... but don't dismantle or defund them completely").

within a movement. In other cases, it raises suspicions about whether some group is co-opting the phrase, or using the phrase to weaken or obscure the phrase's original meaning, or creating the appearance of solidarity where the real thing is importantly lacking. A number of city governments that violently suppressed the June 2020 uprisings also painted "#BlackLivesMatter" on major city streets (Amnesty International 2020).

3.2. Videos of police violence

Why did M4BL form when it did? Taylor (2016) points to frustration with a weak black economy under the Obama administration and the Left's rediscovery of street protest through Occupy. Another important part of the story is that only recently have large numbers of ordinary people been able to record and distribute videos of encounters with the police. Of course, antiracist protestors have been mobilized by journalistic or planned documentation of police violence in the past, from Bull Connor to Rodney King. But only in the last decade have ordinary people been equipped to make spontaneous video recordings of what goes on around us.

There are at least three things to note about these recordings. The first is that, like the use of hashtags to aggregate evidence, they function as a corrective to the testimonial injustice facing black people in their accounts of police violence (Fricker 2007). Testimonial injustice is, on Fricker's account, a systematic or persistent prejudicial credibility deficit—a failure to treat reliable speakers as reliable, based on a prejudice about some group that speaker (purportedly) belongs to. Typically, when black victims of police violence report what happens to them, they find themselves subject to such a prejudicial credibility deficit. That is, their accounts are given unreasonably low credence because of anti-black stereotypes. (I suspect that these accounts are often disbelieved not, or not just, because of an anti-black credibility deficit, but because the police's own conflicting accounts of police violence enjoy a prejudicial credibility excess. But these two hypotheses are hard to tease apart empirically in any given case.) Some people who wouldn't assign a high credence to a verbal report of police violence will believe it when they see it on video.

Second, when we think of the forms that moral discourse can take, we are likely to think of the expression of apparently belief-like moral judgments, or the expression of, so to speak, transparently moral emotions like guilt or resentment. People sharing videos of police violence in social media posts perform these speech acts in their commentary, to be sure. But the sharing of the video itself can't be understood entirely in those terms.

Suppose Josie sees her daughter Jen surreptitiously sticking her hand in the cookie jar. She says, sharply, "Jen!" Josie might be expressing anger or threatening her daughter, prosodically or through her facial expressions. But she is also letting Jen know that she is being watched, that she is the subject of her mother's moral attention.

A video of police violence works similarly. A bystander who ostensively takes out a camera and starts filming a police encounter lets the police officer know in real time that they are being recorded. To the extent that recording an officer is a communicative act, it is addressed to the officer themselves. Later, when someone shares such a video on social media, it isn't addressed to the officer, but it does let whoever sees the post know that the police are likely being scrutinized whenever they work. In both cases, part of what the videos do is let people know that they are being watched. It is hardly a new idea that surveillance is a tool of social control. Less familiar is the thought that informing someone that they are being surveilled can, on some occasions, by itself constitute a moral speech act.[10]

Lastly, videos of police violence can be helpfully compared with the staged violence of the civil rights movement. They are both varieties of what Sharp (1973) calls "political jiu-jitsu," the use of an opponent's (threats of) violence against a grievance group in order to undermine the opponent. Sharp gives a number of examples of effective political jiu-jitsu: the 1905 Bloody Sunday massacre in Russia, the killing of demonstrators in Sharpeville in apartheid South Africa in 1960, the deadly raids on temples during the Buddhist crisis in South Vietnam in 1963, French violence in the Ruhr in the 1920s, and the Qissa Khwani Bazaar massacre in Peshawar in 1930. Political jiu-jitsu can work either by changing third-party opinion, weakening the opponent's resolve, or galvanizing the grievance group. The use of political jiu-jitsu in the civil rights movement worked by each of these means. Images of angry whites throwing food at calm, seated, well-dressed young black people, of dogs and fire hoses turned on children and clergymen, heightened national

---

[10] Haidt and Kesebir (2010) define "moral systems" as "interlocking sets of values, virtues, norms, practices, identities, institutions, technologies, and evolved psychological mechanisms that work together to suppress or regulate selfishness and make cooperative social life possible." We can say that a speech act is moral, very roughly, if it is a token or instantiation of a constituent of a moral system, or an application, invocation, or enforcement of a constituent of a moral system.

and international condemnation of Jim Crow and American racism, more generally, led to defection from segregationists, and brought new people into the movement.

As Sharp notes, political jiu-jitsu works only if information about the violence in question is broadcast to the right audiences. This is one of the strengths of M4BL's use of cellphone videos—social media users don't have to rely on the press to disseminate images of police and vigilante violence.[11] There is, however, another condition on the success of political jiu-jitsu that Sharp doesn't discuss. The innocence of the victims must be evident to the audience. The political jiu-jitsu of the civil rights movement was as successful as it was in part because of the moral clarity of the violence it involved. Many of the most prominent videos of police violence depict situations with a similar moral clarity, pitting people who are (to some) visibly innocent against people who are (to some) visibly to blame. One of the reasons the death of Sandra Bland, for instance, provoked so much outrage is that the most widely shared video of her arrest shows the officer ordering her out of her car, threatening to "light her up" with a taser, pinning her down, and finally arresting her for refusing to put out a cigarette in her own car. We will return to the limits of these appeals to moral clarity later.

3.3. Naming the dead

Trayvon Martin, Michael Brown, Walter Scott, Rekia Boyd, Freddie Gray, Philando Castile, Eric Garner, Alton Sterling, Tamir Rice, Akai Gurley, Deborah Danner: these names will be familiar to many readers. They have been repeated over and over again. In particular, they are often used as stand-alone sentences or clauses, with little or no accompanying text. It is this usage that I have in mind. Sometimes an utterance will include only one such name, and sometimes a list of names. The names figure widely in the text and protest speech of M4BL members, and they are aggregated in social media posts under the hashtags #SayHerName and its variants, #SayTheirNames and #SayHisName. Janelle Monae's "Hell You Talmbout" elaborates on this theme, where each verse repeats the previous one, but names a new victim of police, vigilante, private security, or racist violence.

---

[11] Bordonaro and Willits (2018) find no month-to-month correlation between the number of police-caused deaths and the number of mentions of Black Lives Matter in newspapers from 2013 to 2016.

Sometimes, as in the Josie and Jen case earlier, moral uses of bare proper names are vocative; they refer to the utterance's addressee. Here, the speaker is informing the addressee that she is the subject of the speaker's moral attention. But names of the dead aren't addressed to their referents. Rather, they direct the addressees' moral attention toward the referent of the name. In any case, it's noteworthy that two of the characteristic communicative tools of M4BL—videos of police violence and naming the dead—both consist largely in the management of an audience's moral attention.

Unlike the tools discussed earlier, however, the use of names of the dead by social movements predates modern information technology. In her description of the emotional development of the movement to combat the AIDS crisis, Gould (2014) juxtaposes two uses of lists of names of the dead. The Names Project Memorial Quilt is a folk art project, in which each patch added to the quilt represents a new person to die from AIDS. When the quilt was shown, the name associated with each patch was read. The uniqueness of the patches and the use of each individual's name draw attention to the uniqueness and individuality of the AIDS victims themselves. The mood at these showings was solemn and funereal. They were opportunities for attendees to mourn.

In an action in 1992 organized by ACT UP, the ashes of people who had died of AIDS were delivered, in a mock funeral procession, to the White House lawn. Once there, the protesters called out the names of the dead. The mood was angry and confrontational. As Gould writes, "Held . . . the same weekend as the annual display of the Names Project Quilt, ACT UP's 'Ashes' action implicitly drew a distinction between the quilt's encouragement of grief and its own enactment of grief-inspired rage" (2014: 262).

So names of the dead can be used to express solemn sadness and to express anger. While some M4BL actions evoke a mood similar to showings of the AIDS quilt—candlelight vigils and some die-ins, for instance—the typical use of names of the dead in M4BL is more reminiscent of the Ashes action. If an expression of sadness typically recruits the care of others for the speaker herself, an expression of moral anger is typically intended to motivate others to correct some wrong or injustice of which the speaker needn't be the principal victim. #SayHerName and its variants are used to make bald, on-record demands on others, to redirect their moral attention to wrongful or unjust deaths. Like the AIDS quilt, however, the use of names of the dead in M4BL is part of a wider effort to humanize the victims (Irwin 2016). What might appear to be two mutually exclusive registers or genres of moral discourse—confrontation and humanization—can, it turns out, coincide in a single speech situation.

3.4. Stereotype engineering

Finally, I turn to a development in recent liberal and leftist discourse more generally, which may have a role to play in addressing some of the challenges facing the movement.

Here are some examples of the phenomenon I have in mind. Suppose a liberal Democrat casually asserts that the reason why black people are especially likely to be incarcerated is a deficiency in black culture, and I call her a *white supremacist*. Or suppose that I observe that black people are being displaced from a neighborhood through rising rents, and I say that *ethnic cleansing* is underway.[12]

Something interesting is happening here with the phrases "white supremacist" and "ethnic cleansing." While both of these phrases might have idiomatic, noncompositional meanings, they certainly have literal, compositional meanings. In this latter sense, at least, a white supremacist is someone who believes in the supremacy of white people, and ethnic cleansing is, roughly, the removal of an ethnic group from a location, as of a stain. But both of these phrases also have associated stereotypes. A Klan member is a typical white supremacist, and the Rwandan genocide is a typical episode of ethnic cleansing. These stereotypes likely give rise to the sorts of typicality effects psychologists have studied. For example, Klan members are likely more quickly, easily, and accurately categorized as white supremacists than others.

When I call the liberal Democrat a white supremacist, or describe an episode of gentrification as ethnic cleansing, I am applying these phrases (correctly) in their compositional sense to (for many) highly atypical objects and events. But typicality relations change over time. The more often an individual categorizes members of some kind as white supremacists or instances of ethnic cleansing, or is exposed to examples of others so categorizing members of that kind, ceteris paribus, the more typical that kind will become of white supremacists and ethnic cleansing for them.

---

[12] The use of "concentration camp" to describe migrant detention camps at the US southern border would work equally well.

These cases exemplify a form of conceptual engineering we might call *stereotype engineering*. Conceptual engineering is the task of "fixing" an existing concept (e.g., by making it explicit, changing its meaning, or operationalizing it) so that it is better suited to some job, or inventing a wholly new concept to perform a job that no existing concept performs adequately. An individual or group stereotype engineers some expression if they apply the expression using its existing literal meaning, in speech or writing, in such a way that highly atypical exemplars of the concept associated with the expression become typical, for themselves or others.

Stereotype engineering differs from other forms of conceptual engineering in some interesting ways. Philosophers studying conceptual engineering (Cappelen 2018; Chalmers forthcoming; Sterken 2019) have thought of fixing a concept or linguistic expression in terms of changing its extension or intension, or changing its meaning. That is, they have taken fixing a concept to consist in changing what it applies to in the actual world or in some possible world, or changing something like its associated mode of presentation or definition or whatever determines its extension. Whether stereotype engineering amounts to a change of meaning will depend on what meanings are, but it evidently doesn't amount to a change of extension or intension. After all, stereotype engineers apply a phrase to things that (they believe, often correctly) it already applies to; it's hard to see how applying a phrase to things that it already applies to could change what it applies to, in the actual world or in any possible world. In this way, stereotype engineering differs from familiar ways that expressions naturally change meaning, like semantic drift or semantic narrowing. Stereotype engineers don't systematically apply an expression to things that it previously didn't apply to, or applied to only metaphorically or loosely speaking, nor do they decline to apply it to things that are currently highly typical of it.

Stereotype engineering also differs from some past examples of conceptual engineering in black liberatory movements. Kwame Ture proposed that black people describe themselves as black, rather than as Negroes, "which means apathetic, lazy, stupid, and all those other things" (quoted in Stewart 1997: 516). This is not quite what "Negro" actually meant—Ture is describing the stereotypical Negro. While Ture reserved the word "Negro" to disparage black leaders he viewed as old-fashioned, he worked, rather successfully, to replace it for most purposes. By contrast, Stephen Biko proposed that the word "black" (which has a different meaning in South Africa) be used to refer to "those who hold their heads high in defiance rather than willingly surrender their souls to the white man" (quoted in Cappelen 2018: 30). Responding to negative stereotypes associated with "black," Biko keeps the word, but opts to change its meaning altogether. A stereotype engineering approach to these problems would have been different. Instead of replacing or redefining a negatively stereotyped word used to describe black people, a stereotype engineer might systematically or conspicuously apply the word to people and things that the word does, in fact, apply to, but that defy that stereotype. This is what the hashtag #BlackGirlMagic does today, more or less. By aggregating examples of black girls and women doing impressive or wonderful things, users of the hashtag are trying to change common stereotypes about black girls. It is an empirical question, which I'm not prepared to answer, what strengths or weaknesses such an approach might have.

Instances of conceptual re-engineering, if they aren't completely idle, fix some defects in a concept as it currently exists. So what conceptual defects does stereotype engineering respond to? The answer will differ from case to case. But the defects involved in the examples discussed earlier fall into two types. First, and most obviously, the stereotypes associated with "Negro," "black," and "black girl" to which Ture, Biko, and users of #BlackGirlMagic are (perhaps unconsciously) responding are *harmfully negative*.[13] It is bad for black people if the typical black person, for many thinkers, has negative traits. Stereotype engineering, in these cases, works by making positive exemplars of the concept more typical. Second, the stereotypes associated with "white supremacy," "ethnic cleansing," and "concentration camp" are, I would argue, *distractingly unrepresentative*. For many in the United States today, the forms of white supremacy and ethnic cleansing that are most practically urgent are often the most atypical. If we want to be able to quickly, easily, and accurately categorize these forms of racial injustice, we need to make them more typical. In any case, engineering that corrects distractingly unrepresentative stereotypes of racial injustice can be used to overcome the widespread belief that racial discrimination is a personal vice, or only bad if de jure.

---

[13] A stereotype might also be harmfully positive, and stereotype engineering might try to correct for that. On April 22, 2014, the official Twitter account of the New York Police Department posted: "Do you have a photo w/ a member of the NYPD? Tweet us & tag it #myNYPD. It may be featured on our Facebook." The hashtag still regularly appears in new posts, almost exclusively about police misconduct.

4. Limitations

I have focused so far on how the new language of liberation works and what makes it useful for M4BL. I will close by briefly exploring two limitations of some of these tools.

As I observed earlier, hashtags like #BlackLivesMatter both categorize social media posts thematically and broadcast that content to people who click the hashtag. So the use of a hashtag broadens the audience for a post, but also constrains it, in two ways. First, only people who actually click a hashtag are going to see the posts aggregated under it. These people are likely already at least casual supporters of M4BL. Second, the hashtag is a slogan, which is used to express agreement with a group's beliefs and attitudes. As each web user's social media feed and search results (and selective attention) are increasingly tailored to support her background political and moral beliefs, the use of a hashtag slogan in a post is likely to confine it to an echo chamber. To a lesser extent, this is a limitation of all online social movement rhetoric, and to a lesser extent still, of all social movement rhetoric period, so it should be taken with a grain of salt. And of course, as Stewart's taxonomy entails, social movements need to communicate with and among their members as well as with outsiders, so the mere fact that some post is directed only to movement sympathizers isn't a problem. It is only a problem if such communication comes at the expense of communication with the opposition, undecided third parties, and relevant decision-makers.

Lastly, I argued earlier that political jiu-jitsu works only if the violence it involves is morally clear to all, or enough, viewers—that is, if it's visible who is innocent and who is at fault. Otherwise, merely directing someone's moral attention to the scenes or facts in question won't yield the desired outcome. And again, this places two important limitations on the use of videos of police and vigilante violence in M4BL. First, political jiu-jitsu will work best with the most visibly, conventionally respectable victims—the model students and Rosa Parkses of the world. Many victims of police violence just won't fit that profile. Second, as police violence is better documented and more widely publicized, it has become clear that for a wide swath of newsreaders in the United States, police violence is simply never visibly blameworthy. This very phenomenon—that any behavior, no matter how innocuous, will be treated as an acceptable excuse for police violence and other forms of racialized violence—has become a meme in the online discourse around the Movement for Black Lives (Figure 8.1).It seems to me that this

> We can't sell CDs (Alton Sterling)
> We can't sell cigarettes (Eric Garner)
> We can't drive cars (Sandra Bland)
> We can't play in parks (Tamir Rice)
> We can't wear hoodies (Trayvon Martin)
> We can't play music (Jordan Davis)
> We can't sit in a stairwell (Akai Gurley)
> We can't play with toys in Wal-Mart (John Crawford)
> We can't be safe in police custody (Victor White)
> We can't go to the mall (McKenzie Cochran)
> We can't ask for help after an accident (Jonathan Ferrell)
> We can't be at home (Carlos Alcis)
> We can't run from robbers (Reynaldo Cuevas)
> We can't walk outside (Rekia Boyd)
> We can't ride public transportation (Oscar Grant)
> We can't drive home (Samuel Dubois)
> We can't attend our own bachelor's party (Sean Bell)
> We can't go to the store (Mike Brown)
> We can't have car trouble (Corey Jones)
> We can't sleep (Aiyana Jones)
> We can't pray (Charleston 9)
> We can't run (Walter Scott)
> We can't be afraid (Henry Bennett III)
> We can't accidentally park (Danroy DJ Henry)
> We can't comply (Philando Castile)
> Shall I continue?? smh 🤷🏾

Figure 8.1 BLM meme illustrating the tendency to excuse all people and anti-black violence.

image is a fitting place to close. While I hope to have shown that there is strategic and philosophical value in understanding how M4BL communicates, the movement speaks for itself.

References

Amnesty International (2020). *USA: The World Is Watching*. New York: Amnesty International.

Anderson, Luvell (2018). "Calling, Addressing, and Appropriation." *Bad Words*. Ed. David Sosa. Oxford: Oxford University Press: 6–28.

Bach, Kent, and Robert M. Harnish (1979). *Linguistic Communication and Speech Acts*. Cambridge, MA: MIT Press.

Bordonaro, Francesca, and Dale Willits (2018). "#Black Lives Matter? Analyzing the Effects of Police-Caused Black Deaths on Media Coverage and Public Interest in the Movement." *Journal of Criminal Justice and Law* 2 (2): 102–121.
Camp, Elizabeth (2017). "Why Metaphors Make Good Insults: Perspectives, Presupposition, and Pragmatics." *Philosophical Studies* 174 (1): 47–64.
Cappelen, Herman (2018). *Fixing Language: An Essay on Conceptual Engineering*. Oxford: Oxford University Press.
Chalmers, David (2018). "What Is Conceptual Engineering and What Should It Be?" Paper presented at The Foundations of Conceptual Engineering conference at NYU, September 14.
Corvalán, Luis (2003). *El Gobierno de Salvador Allende*. Santiago: LOM Ediciones.
Edwards, Breanna (2017). "St. Louis Police Chant 'Whose Streets? Our Streets' While Making Arrests during Continuing Protests Sunday: Report." *The Root*, September 18. https://www.theroot.com/st-louis-police-chant-whose-streets-our-streets-whil-1818503610.
Fricker, Miranda (2007). *Epistemic Injustice*. Oxford: Oxford University Press.
Gould, Deborah (2014). "The Emotion Work of Movements." *The Social Movements Reader*. 3rd ed. Eds. Jeff Goodwin and James Jasper. Chichester: Wiley: 254–265.
Haidt, Jonathan, and Selin Kesebir (2010). "Morality." *Handbook of Social Psychology*. 5th ed. Eds. Susan Fiske, Daniel Gilbert, and Gardner Lindzey. Hoboken, NJ: Wiley: 797–832.
Harris, Daniel, Daniel Fogal, and Matt Moss (Eds.) (2018). *New Work on Speech Acts*. New York: Oxford University Press.
Harris, Kimberly A. (2019). "What Does It Mean to Move for Black Lives?" *Philosophy Today* 63 (2): 275–291.
Ince, Jelani, Fabio Rojas, and Clayton Davis (2017). "The Social Media Response to Black Lives Matter: How Twitter Users Interact with Black Lives Matter through Hashtag Use." *Ethnic and Racial Studies* 40 (11): 1814–1830.
Irwin, Demetria (2016, April 28). "Families of Police Violence Victims Want You to 'Say Their Names.'" *Ebony*. https://www.ebony.com/news/say-their-names-multimedia/.
Johnson, Casey R. (Ed.) (2018). *Voicing Dissent: The Ethics and Epistemology of Making Disagreement Public*. New York: Routledge.
Keepnews, Peter (1989). "Rap Leads to Respectability and Academia for KRS-One." *New York Times*, November 17. https://www.nytimes.com/1989/11/17/arts/pop-jazz-rap-leads-to-respectability-and-academia-for-krs-one.html.
Langton, Rae (2018). "Blocking as Counter-Speech." In Harris, Fogal, and Moss (2018).
Langton, Rae, Sally Haslanger, and Luvell Anderson (2012). "Language and Race." *The Routledge Companion to Philosophy of Language*. Eds. Gillian Russell and Delia Graff Fara. New York: Routledge: 753–767.
Lebron, Chris (2017). *The Making of Black Lives Matter: A Brief History of an Idea*. New York: Oxford University Press.
McKinney, Rachel (2016). "Extracted Speech." *Social Theory and Practice* 42 (2): 258–284.
McKinney, Rachel (2018). "Emancipatory Political Dissent in Practice: Insights from Social Theory." In Johnson (2018).
Millikan, Ruth (2005). "Proper Function and Convention in Speech Acts." In *Language: A Biological Model*. Oxford: Oxford University Press: 139–165.
Morris, Charles E., and Stephen H. Browne (Eds.) (2013). *Readings on the Rhetoric of Social Protest*. 3rd ed. State College, PA: Strata.

Olasov, Ian (2016). "Offensive Political Dog Whistles: You Know Them When You Hear Them. Or Do You?" *Vox.* https://www.vox.com/the-big-idea/2016/11/7/13549154/dog-whistles-campaign-racism.

Richardson, Elaine, and Alice Ragland (2018). "#StayWoke: The Language and Literacies of the #BlackLivesMatter Movement." *Community Literacy Journal* 12 (2): 27–56.

Rickford, John (2013). "Rachel Jeantel's Language in the Zimmerman Trial." *Language Log.* https://languagelog.ldc.upenn.edu/nll/?p=5161.

Rini, Regina (2016). "Are Microaggressions Your Fault?" Paper presented at Brooklyn Public Philosophers, September 22, 2016.

Saul, Jennifer (2018). "Dogwhistles, Political Manipulation and the Philosophy of Language." In Harris, Fogal, and Moss (2018).

Sharp, Gene (1973). *The Politics of Nonviolent Action, Part Three: The Dynamics of Nonviolent Action.* Boston: Porter Sargent.

Simpson, Robert (2016). "Un-Ringing the Bell: McGowan on Oppressive Speech and the Asymmetric Pliability of Conversations." *Australasian Journal of Philosophy* 91 (3): 555–575.

Sperber, Daniel, and Deirdre Wilson (2012). "Explaining Irony." In *Meaning and Relevance.* Cambridge: Cambridge University Press: 123–146.

Sterken, Rachel (2019). "Linguistic Intervention and Transformative Communicative Disruptions." *Conceptual Ethics and Conceptual Engineering.* Eds. Alexis Burgess, Herman Cappelen, and David Plunkett. Oxford: Oxford University Press: 417–435.

Stewart, Charles (1980). "A Functional Approach to the Rhetoric of Social Movements." In Morris and Browne (2013).

Stewart, Charles (1997). "The Evolution of a Revolution: Stokely Carmichael and the Rhetoric of Black Power." In Morris and Browne (2013).

Taylor, Keeanga-Yamahtta (2016). *From #BlackLivesMatter to Black Liberation.* Chicago: Haymarket.

Taylor, Keeanga-Yamahtta (2019). "Five Years Later, Do Black Lives Matter?" *Jacobin*, September 30. https://www.jacobinmag.com/2019/09/black-lives-matter-laquan-mcdonald-mike-brown-eric-garner.

This Is What Democracy Looks Like (2000). Youtube. USA: Big Noise Films.

Tirrell, Lynne (2012). "Genocidal Language Games." *Speech and Harm: Controversies Over Free Speech.* Eds. Ishani Maitra and Mary K. McGowan. Oxford: Oxford University Press: 174–221.

Tirrell, Lynne (2018). "Toxic Speech: Inoculations and Antidotes." *Southern Journal of Philosophy* 56 (1): 116–144.

Young, Iris Marion (2000). *Inclusion and Democracy.* Oxford: Oxford University Press.

Zimmer, Ben (2013). "No Justice, No Peace." *Language Log.* https://languagelog.ldc.upenn.edu/nll/?p=5249.

PART IV
THE M4BL, ANTI-BLACK RACISM, AND PUNISHMENT

9
Can Capital Punishment Survive If Black Lives Matter?

Michael Cholbi and Alex Madva

The Black Lives Matter protests, and the broader Movement for Black Lives they inspired, came to rapid prominence in no small part because their signature cause—police shootings of unarmed or unthreatening Black Americans—is perversely telegenic and (for most Americans) jarring. The grainy web videos depicting confrontations between police and Black citizens, nearly always ending with a Black citizen crumpled over, brought attention to a phenomenon that had previously received sporadic attention outside Black communities.

However, other causes advocated by the Movement are more familiar and (at least in the context of American judicial and legal history) prosaic. For instance, the Movement's platform calls for the abolition of capital punishment on the grounds that the death penalty in the United States is a "racist practice" that "devalues Black lives" (Movement for Black Lives 2016).[1] In decrying capital punishment as a "racist practice," the Movement echoes a body of empirical studies dating back to the 1940s (Myrdal 1944), suggesting racial discrimination in the administration of the death penalty in the United States. More specifically, these studies indicate both that Black American capital defendants are more likely to be subject to execution than defendants of other races and that those who murder Black Americans are less likely to be subject to execution than are those who murder members of other races. The question of whether such apparent discrimination legally impugns the death penalty has a long legal history in the United States, and in general, while the courts have occasionally expressed worries about such discrimination, jurists have taken such evidence to warrant reform of capital

---

[1] We first explored philosophical questions based on the Movement's claims about the death penalty in Cholbi and Madva (2018). See also Cholbi (2006).

Michael Cholbi and Alex Madva, *Can Capital Punishment Survive If Black Lives Matter?* In: *The Movement for Black Lives*. Edited by: Brandon Hogan, Michael Cholbi, Alex Madva, and Benjamin S. Yost, Oxford University Press. © Oxford University Press 2021. DOI: 10.1093/oso/9780197507773.003.0010

punishment practices but not its outright abolition. In calling for abolition, the Movement thus invites us to see the death penalty as one among many fronts in a "war against Black people" and "Black communities" in the United States (Movement for Black Lives 2016).

Our purpose here is to defend the Movement's call for death penalty abolition on grounds that (we expect) those sympathetic to the Movement's diagnosis of the current state of racial justice in the United State will find congenial. We do so first by providing a sketch of recent American judiciary history surrounding race and capital punishment, a sketch that reveals how the forms of bias essential for understanding how racial discrimination in the American capital punishment regime occurs do not fit within the picture of racial bias advanced by the courts. The racial discrimination at issue, we argue, flows in significant part from *implicit* biases concerning race, criminality, and violence. That implicit biases play such a role explains both why recent capital sentencing reforms have been largely unsuccessful in diminishing such discrimination and why further procedural reforms aimed at reducing such discrimination should also be met with skepticism. We then turn to the case for abolition as a response to this persistent discrimination. Defenders of capital punishment have not fully appreciated that such discrimination grounds a complaint on the part not only of those Black Americans who interact with the criminal justice system as capital defendants or as murder victims but also on the part of Black Americans *as a class* who have not been accorded equal status under the law. The magnitude of this latter complaint, we argue, along with the intractability of this discrimination, makes abolition a compelling remedy. The time for abolition of the death penalty has therefore arrived, as it is the most efficacious and most just response to the realities surrounding race and capital punishment in the United States.[2]

* * *

In 1972, the US Supreme Court vacated the death sentences of three Black American men, William Furman, Lucius Jackson, and Elmer Branch. In each

---

[2] In claiming that capital punishment practice in the United States have failed to accord Black Americans equal legal status, we acknowledge that a range of other practices (such as extra-judicial lynchings, police brutality, drug laws imposing harsher sentences for substances used to a greater degree in Black communities, etc.) have contributed to the denigration of Black Americans' equal status as well. See James (2000) and Muhammad (2010).

case, the applicable state laws did not provide juries with unambiguous criteria by which to determine whether a defendant should be sentenced to die. In a 5–4 vote, the Court ruled in the appellants' favor, their *per curium* opinion holding that the state statutes under which the defendants were convicted were unconstitutional, and so the "carrying out of the death penalty in these cases constitute cruel and unusual punishment in violation of the Eighth and Fourteenth Amendments" (*Furman* 1972: 240). This language is puzzling on its face. The Eighth Amendment seems to impose a substantive limitation on the kinds of punishment to which criminals may be subject, to wit, that those punishments not be cruel or unusual. The post-Reconstruction Fourteenth Amendment, in contrast, is concerned with legal equality, demanding that states not deny citizens the equal protection of their laws. How then could a death sentence in these cases violate *both* such Amendments by virtue of being "cruel and unusual"? There was little unanimity in the rationales provided by the concurring justices. (The decision itself reached an astonishing 80,000 words in total.) Justices Brennan and Marshall advanced recognizably Eighth Amendment arguments, asserting that death was by its nature cruel and unusual, a sanction at odds with "human dignity" (*Furman* 1972: 291) and "shocking" to the "conscience and sense of justice" of the average citizen (1972: 365). (One dissenting justice, Blackmun, expressed similar sentiments: "I yield to no one in the depth of my distaste, antipathy, and, indeed, abhorrence, for the death penalty, with all its aspects of physical distress and fear and of moral judgment exercised by finite minds" [1972: 405].)

What, then, of the defendants' Fourteenth Amendment complaint? Their attorneys had offered evidence that non-White defendants received the death penalty more often than Whites. Such statutes thus seemed to permit racial discrimination to influence capital sentencing, such that Black Americans did not have the same legal protection or status as other defendants. Several of the justices accepted such empirical findings, and they were clearly unnerved by the prospect that capital punishment gave "room for the play of such prejudices" against "the poor and the despised," as Douglas put it (*Furman* 1972: 255). Strangely, though, it was not concerns about racial bias that primarily moved the justices. Rather, the justices emphasized that the capital punishment statutes then in existence resulted in "unusual" punishments because they provided judges and juries too much discretion in deciding which defendants are sentenced to die. Douglas decried the "uncontrolled discretion of judges or judges" in the determination whether defendants committing these crimes should die or be imprisoned. Under these laws, no standards govern the selection of the penalty. People live or die, dependent on the whim of one man or of 12. (1972: 253)

Justice Stewart denied that racial discrimination had been proven in these cases, but nonetheless concluded that death was "wantonly" and "freakishly imposed," with no more rhyme or reason than lightning strikes (1972: 310). Justice White similarly complained that "there is no meaningful basis for distinguishing the few cases in which it [death] is imposed from the many cases in which it is not" (1972: 313).

Thus, despite the race-based arguments advanced by the defendants, and despite the justices' evident dismay at the apparent racial disproportionality in capital sentencing, racial discrimination turned out to play a rather marginal role in the justices' reasoning. Their central concern was instead that the laws gave decision makers too much latitude in deciding who to sentence to die and so provided no rational basis for the allocation of the most severe punishment utilized in our legal system. This emphasis on the "freakish" or "arbitrary" imposition of the death penalty governed subsequent efforts at reforms. The *Furman* ruling resulted in a four-year moratorium on the death penalty in the United States, during which time states crafted new capital punishment statutes and sentencing guidelines. New state statutes and sentencing guidelines required that both aggravating and mitigating factors be taken into account in capital sentencing; capital trials be bifurcated into guilt and penalty phases; capital cases be subject to automatic appeal; and states conduct proportionality reviews, in which a state appellate court considers whether a given capital sentence aligns with, or is instead disproportionate to, other sentences issued in the state's capital cases. In a series of cases beginning with *Gregg v. Georgia* in 1976, the Supreme Court concluded that such state statutes satisfied the procedural criteria put forth in Furman: that capital sentencing be guided by objective criteria but still responsive to judge and jury determinations of particular defendants' record, character, and capital crime (i.e., the death penalty could not be automatically imposed on those convicted of a particular class of crimes). American capital punishment jurisprudence thus entered a period of "guided discretion," wherein the death penalty was permissible so long as the discretion exercised by judges or juries was (as the *Furman* ruling mandated) "suitably directed and limited so as to minimize the risk of wholly arbitrary and capricious action."

Neither the new state sentencing guidelines nor the language of "guided discretion" explicitly mentioned racial discrimination. Yet given the concerns about racial discrimination expressed by the justices in *Furman*, one might expect the Court to be sympathetic to defendants claiming that their own death sentences were shaped by racial biases that, for whatever reason, the post-*Furman* reforms were not able to identify or mitigate. *McCleskey v. Kemp* (1987) tested this hypothesis. Warren McCleskey, a Black American man, was convicted of the murder of White Atlanta police officer Frank Schlatt. The jury sentenced him to die because of two aggravating circumstances: that the murder occurred during the commission of an armed robbery and his victim was a police officer engaged in performing his official duties. As in *Furman*, McCleskey's attorneys invoked the Fourteenth Amendment requirement of equal protection and cited studies indicating "racially disproportionate impact" in the imposition of capital punishment in Georgia. The most prominent of these studies was conducted by David Baldus, whose examination of 2,500 murder cases in Georgia found that those convicted of killing a White victim were 4.3 times as likely to receive the death penalty than those whose victims were from other racial groups (Baldus et al. 1983). The Court ruled against McCleskey. An equal protection finding, the Court concluded, required more than evidence of "racially disproportionate impact," for sentencing disparities of the sort highlighted in Baldus's study are "an inevitable part of our criminal justice system." McCleskey had instead to "prove" either that "the decisionmakers in *his* case acted with discriminatory purpose" or that the state legislature had "enacted or maintained the death penalty statute *because* of an anticipated racially discriminatory effect." McCleskey lacked such evidence. He was executed in 1991.

As a number of critics of the *McCleskey* decision observed, the ruling sets a nearly impossible bar for claims of unconstitutional racial discrimination in sentencing. Societal opposition to overt racism, as well as the fact that many law enforcement or judicial decisions that could be influenced by race are not open to public scrutiny, makes it almost certain that "smoking gun" evidence of overt or intentional racial discrimination on the part of lawmakers, prosecutors, or law enforcement officials will not be uncovered. As Michelle Alexander, author of *The New Jim Crow*, has concluded:

> *McCleskey v. Kemp* has immunized the criminal justice system from judicial scrutiny for racial bias. It has made it virtually impossible to challenge any aspect, criminal justice process, for racial bias in the absence of proof

of intentional discrimination, conscious, deliberate bias. . . . Evidence of conscious intentional bias is almost impossible to come by in the absence of some kind of admission. (Alexander 2010)

Given the standard set by *McCleskey*, it is not surprising that capital defendants have had virtually no success in advancing claims of racial discrimination subsequently (aside from claims relating to the selection of jurors on the basis of race (see *Batson* 1986, *Miller-El* 2005, and Snyder 2008)). This is so despite the mounting evidence that patterns of racial discrimination of the sort found in Baldus's study continue to this day. Since 2000, empirical studies of nine states have found that Black American defendants are more likely to face a death penalty prosecution or to be sentenced to death than defendants of other races, while empirical studies of fourteen states and the armed forces have found an even stronger effect on capital sentencing based on victims' race, concluding that those who kill White people are more likely to be sentenced to die than those who kill members of other racial and ethnic groups (Cholbi and Madva 2018: 521–522). These two effects also appear to interact, so that cases like McCleskey's "involving black defendants and white victims are treated more punitively than cases with all other defendant/ victim racial combinations" (Baldus and Woodworth 2003: 241).

* * *

Can a case be made for the Movement for Black Lives' call for abolition on the basis of such evidence, even in the absence of proof that lawmakers, law enforcement officials, juries, and so on purposefully or intentionally discriminate against Black American defendants or victims in the capital punishment process? There is, we contend, conceptual space between purposeful discrimination and mere randomness or unpredictability, a space occupied by implicit bias. Before mapping this space, we stress that our claim is *not* that implicit bias alone explains the racial injustices of capital punishment. Implicit bias is just one factor among many. For example, some evidence suggests that due to tax cuts, local police departments have been increasingly pressured to devote greater resources to (i.e., *overpolice*) revenue-generating practices such as asset seizures and fines in Black American communities, which has forced them to devote fewer resources to (i.e., *underpolice*) preventing and solving violent crimes in those same communities (Goldstein et al. 2018). Such structural considerations are incredibly important. And we, of course, do not rule out the potential role of explicit bias in the devaluing and dehumanizing of Black lives (implicit and explicit forms of racial bias are, we believe, complexly intertwined; see Madva 2019). Consider a recent study examining mock jurors' reactions to a case inspired by the shooting of Keith Scott in Charlotte in 2016 (Cooley et al. 2018). Researchers found that jurors' *explicit* racial prejudices negatively correlated with their willingness to attribute responsibility and guilt to an officer who fatally shot a Black (but not White) victim. Researchers also found that racial bias led jurors to perceive that the officer was in a "dangerous" or "threatening" situation when the victim was Black (but not White), and to deny that the officer's own racial biases could have been a factor in his decision-making.

In what follows, however, we focus on implicit bias because, as we try to show, it poses unique constraints on which remedies will feasibly address the racial injustices at issue.

Cases like *McCleskey* unfolded at a time when overt endorsements of racial animosity were in decline yet broader patterns of racial discrimination persisted. Clearly, racism had not just vanished. Social psychologists thus began to develop a number of tools for detecting bias in contexts where individuals were either unable or unwilling to admit that they endorsed problematic racial stereotypes. Several decades on, it is clear that most Americans, including many African-Americans, carry these implicit racial biases.[3] Some of the most pernicious biases directly pertain to criminal justice, and an expanding body of research speaks to the specific role these biases play—consciously or unconsciously—in the perceptions, emotions, and decisions of eyewitnesses, police, prosecutors, judges, and juries (Behrman and Davey 2001; Nosek et al. 2007; Ogletree et al. 2012; Smith and Cohen 2012; Correll et al. 2014; Glaser 2014; Spence et al. 2016). Moreover, while these biases surely exacerbate discrimination throughout the criminal justice system, they appear especially salient in capital sentencing contexts (Lynch and Haney 2011; Hunt 2015).

For example, Whites tend to be less sensitive to the pain experienced by Black people, which suggests that Black defendants, and the families of Black victims, can expect that prosecutors, judges, and juries will be less moved by their capacity to suffer (Trawalter et al. 2016). In this vein, a field study

---

[3] For a review of "meaningful life outcomes" predicted by implicit attitudes, see Blair et al. (2015). For discussion of implicit bias measures in light of recent empirical criticisms, see Brownstein et al. (2019, 2020).

found that jurors were less likely to report that the love, grief, and loss experienced by a victim's family played an important role in their decision-making when victims were Black than when White (Karp and Warshaw 2006). This insensitivity to Black suffering is in turn likely explained by the tendencies to see Black people in some contexts as subhuman and primitive (Goff et al. 2008) and in other contexts as physically "superhuman" (Levinson 2007).

This dual tendency, toward the dehumanization and "superhumanization" of Black bodies, also helps to explain why Black people are likely to be perceived as more threatening and less amenable to rehabilitation. When defendants are Black, mock jurors are more likely to falsely remember "aggressive" details of a crime (Levinson 2007), and more likely to think that the conviction remains appropriate despite the use of inadmissible evidence (Johnson et al. 1995; Hodson et al. 2005).[4] Some studies tie these discriminatory patterns directly to implicit biases, some of which pose general problems for criminal justice, such as the automatic association of Black faces with words like "guilty" (Levinson et al. 2010; Levinson and Young 2010), while others introduce specific problems for capital decision-making, such as the automatic association of Black people with words like "expendable" and "worthless" (Levinson et al. 2014). This latter association was found to be especially prominent among mock jurors who were willing to convict regardless of a potential death sentence, and even predicted these individuals' decisions to sentence a Black defendant to death rather than life in prison.[5] The implicit devaluation of Black defendants and victims in capital contexts may also illuminate why, when victims are White, defendants who look more stereotypically Black are also more likely to receive a death sentence (Eberhardt et al. 2006).

In fact, one study (Glaser et al. 2015) found that Black and White defendants were equally likely to be convicted (67.7 percent and 66.7 percent, respectively) by mock jurors when life without parole was the maximum possible sentence, yet, when a death sentence was possible, conviction rates

---

[4] In fact, participants in Johnson et al. (1995) falsely believed that they were *less* influenced by the inadmissible evidence when defendants were Black. For further studies on juror bias, see Cohn et al. (2009) and Young et al. (2014).

[5] Researchers also found that the refusal to sentence someone to death led to the exclusion of non-White jurors, and that the death qualification process therefore exacerbated the impact of racial bias on capital sentencing. Notably, their participant sample was drawn from six of the most active death penalty states: Alabama, Arizona, California, Florida, Oklahoma, and Texas. Moreover, "those who are more likely to be allowed to serve on death penalty cases are not only more likely to harbor racially prejudiced attitudes, but also are more likely to favor the conviction of innocent defendants over letting guilty ones go free" (Young 2004); cf. Peffley and Hurwitz (2002).

for White defendants fell (55.1 percent) even as conviction rates for Black Americans *rose* (80 percent). In other words, the sheer possibility of capital punishment may be a self-igniting engine of discrimination, over and above the more familiar influences of racial bias on decisions in other spheres. That capital punishment affords unique opportunities for bias to manifest is further supported by the finding that White support for the death penalty *increases* after White people learn about racial disparities in capital sentencing (Peffley and Hurwitz 2007; cf. Hetey and Eberhardt 2014).

We hypothesize that all the aforementioned implicit racial stereotypes and prejudices—the tacit devaluation of Black life, the insensitivity to Black pain and loss, and the impulses to see Black people as either superhuman threats or subhuman beings—make crimes committed by Black defendants (or against White victims) *appear* particularly heinous.

This research also makes it clear why existing reforms have largely failed to reduce racial discrimination in capital sentencing and why the prospects for future reforms short of abolition are similarly grim. Take, for example, Matthew Kramer's proposal (2011: 245) that the death penalty be applied only in the most extreme, "defilingly evil" cases. Ordinarily, racial bias is indeed more likely to tip the scales in more ambiguous cases,[6] which at first glance suggests that reserving the death penalty for the most morally *un*ambiguous cases could bypass bias. But the evidence we just reviewed suggests that the ordinary rules do not apply in capital contexts: implicit biases make the murders committed by African-Americans *seem unambiguously grave*, while the crimes committed against them seem decidedly less so. As a result, implementing proposals like Kramer's could well result in a disproportionate number of murders by Black Americans or murders of non-Black Americans to be classified as "defilingly evil" and so eligible for the death penalty.

Even if judges and jurors could somehow evade the influence of racial bias, and consistently recommended a death sentence only in extreme cases, this would still fail to address the insidious operations of bias prior to sentencing. Consider two examples. First, bias may affect the resources that detectives and prosecutors devote to gathering evidence, such that the evidence comes to seem more damning when victims are White. One study

---

[6] For example, mock jurors' implicit biases led them to interpret ambiguous evidence as more damning when the defendant is dark-skinned than when light-skinned. See Levinson et al. (2010) and Levinson and Young (2010).

in Louisiana thus found that prosecutor case files were significantly thicker when victims were White women, and thinnest when victims were Black, which in turn correlated with severer sentences for those convicted of killing White people and women (Pierce et al. 2014). Implicit bias can, therefore, play a role in *disambiguating* cases. Second, consider the role of bias in voir dire. While most potential jurors explicitly report being unbiased, one study found that professional attorneys were nevertheless able to pick up on potential jurors' unstated racial biases, and keep or remove them from the pool partly on this basis (Morrison et al. 2016). These decisions can, however, invariably be rationalized by appeal to ostensibly nonracial reasons (Sommers and Norton 2007). The operations of bias in this context are likely to persist unless attorneys are denied the right to strike jurors altogether. Both of these examples thus reveal the special challenges posed by implicit bias insofar as it is especially resilient in the face of attempted reforms, such as more precise sentencing guidelines or the requirement to consider both aggravating and mitigating factors. One of the most effective strategies for reducing the effects of bias is anonymization, the concealment of markers of racial identity during key decision-making moments. But anonymization is clearly not a viable option in these settings.[7] Nor should we be optimistic that bias could be circumvented with seemingly more objective standards for use of the death penalty, such as having murdered multiple persons or mandatory use of the death penalty for all first-degree murders.[8] Such standards would still leave many opportunities for racial bias to influence who is convicted of murder, such as in the evidence-gathering and charging stages of the criminal justice process.

Postconviction procedures such as mandatory appeals of all capital sentences have also been introduced as checks against arbitrariness in capital decisions. While such procedures may in principle be capable of reducing the total number of unjust death sentences, they may simultaneously introduce additional ways for racial bias to shape outcomes, insofar as sentence relief becomes more likely for White than Black defendants (Petrie and Coverdill 2010).

We believe that it is therefore established to a high degree of probability that structural unfairness pervades the criminal justice system such that

---

[7] Though anonymization can be utilized in determining whether to charge individuals with crimes at all. See Williams (2019) for discussion of San Francisco's efforts to employ this strategy.

[8] Our coeditor Benjamin Yost suggested such a strategy. See also Cholbi and Madva (2018) and the *PEA Soup* blog discussion by Kelly et al. (2018).

Black Americans are discriminated against in cases in which capital punishment is a possible outcome, and that this discrimination is due in significant measure to implicit racial bias. Even if intentional or purposeful discrimination plays a minute role in such discrimination, this situation nevertheless cries out for reform. Failure to implement reform amounts to a reckless lack of concern for Black Americans' lives and liberties. Yet it is equally clear that mere procedural reforms are grossly insufficient for rooting out the systemic racial injustices in the capital punishment regime. Instead, given the evidence we have briefly reviewed here, it may very well be that abolishing the death penalty is itself one among several key steps necessary for reducing racial disparities in criminal justice more broadly.

* * *

The death penalty could be abolished in the United States de jure, through its legal prohibition, or de facto, through states retaining the death penalty in their sentencing statutes but effectively suspending its use. We contend that such abolition is the most reasonable reform in light of the role that implicit bias plays in generating the racial discrimination at issue. As noted earlier, that implicit bias plays a prominent role in generating these discriminatory patterns casts serious doubt on whether procedural reforms could ever be adequate to diminish or eliminate these patterns.

Any defensible reform must diminish or eliminate such discrimination. Abolition of capital punishment, we propose, is the only reform likely to be both effective and minimally just. Again, procedural reforms would likely be ineffective. As we have indicated, the bias at issue intercedes at multiple points in the processes that can lead to capital sentences: in investigative practices, in prosecutorial decisions, in courtroom behaviors, in jury selection, in sentencing, and so on. Law and legal institutions can, of course, be better or worse at filtering out different biases. In this case, however, there are grounds for skepticism that procedural reforms will do much to ferret out the bias in question. In addition, any move to tighten the standards for capital sentences will run the risk of diminishing the discretion of actors within these institutions, discretion that allows for cases to be adjudicated on the basis of specific facts about crimes, defendants' histories, and so on.

No doubt enthusiasts for capital punishment will view our proposal as morally costly: If the death penalty is abolished, then presumably those guilty of the most serious crimes (murder predominantly) would be sentenced to the next most severe punishment (in all likelihood, life imprisonment without possibility of parole). If death is the only deserved punishment for such crimes, then abolition would result in many criminals not getting what they deserve. For some defenders of capital punishment, such as Ernest van den Haag, racial discrimination in capital charging, trials, sentencing, and so on can never be a sufficiently serious moral cause to outweigh this loss. Van den Haag remarks:

> If and when discrimination occurs it should be corrected. Not, however, by letting the guilty blacks escape the death penalty because guilty whites do, but by making sure that the guilty white offenders suffer it as the guilty blacks do. Discrimination must be abolished by abolishing discrimination—not by abolishing penalties. However, even if . . . this cannot be done, I do not see any good reason to let any guilty murderer escape his penalty. It does happen in the administration of criminal justice that one person gets away with murder and another is executed. Yet the fact that one gets away with it is no reason to let another one escape. (van den Haag and Conrad 1983: 223)

Admittedly, we have not suggested here that death is in principle an unjust penalty for certain very severe crimes such as murder. Indeed, we have granted as much for the sake of argument. We allow the possibility that a community with a very different racial history than that found in the United States could implement the death penalty in a nondiscriminatory fashion, and on the assumption that the death penalty is in principle a just punishment, that would not be a morally objectionable outcome. Yet we do not share van den Haag's insistence that discrimination may only be rightfully addressed by abolishing discrimination without abolishing penalties. That racial discrimination in the US capital punishment regime is traceable in part to implicit bias suggests that in this instance at least we may be unable to "abolish" discrimination. Moreover, even if death is a just punishment for certain severe crimes, that it is *uniquely* just as a punishment for such crimes is a stronger and more dubious claim. There is no obvious basis for assuming a one-to-one correspondence between a crime with a specific moral gravity and a punishment of proportional severity (that, e.g., only death and not life incarceration without parole is a just punishment for murder). We doubt that the geometry of desert is so precise or that our judgments about that geometry should be uncritically relied upon. If desert should govern how we punish, then certainly it can be unjust not to subject those guilty of egregious crimes to severe punishments. But we should not overlook that life imprisonment is itself an extremely serious punishment, involving a wide range of physical and mental suffering as well as wholesale deprivations of liberty and opportunity. (Indeed, considerations like these lead some in the Movement for Black Lives to advocate the abolition of punishment altogether. Addressing their broader concerns about the criminal justice system is beyond the scope of this chapter, but see Davis [2003] and Yost, Chapter 19, this volume.) The gap, then, between the severity of death and the severity of life imprisonment is narrower than it appears. Abolition of the death penalty would result in the effective commutations of a few thousand prisoners currently on death row to life sentences (NAACP Legal Defense and Education Fund 2016), as well as resulting in about forty additional life sentences (rather than executions) per year (Death Penalty Information Center 2017). Given the small numbers of offenders involved and the small gap in severity between execution and life imprisonment, the moral costs of abolishing capital punishment that vex van den Haag are more modest than they appear at first glance.

* * *

A final consideration in favor of abolition is this: van den Haag (and many others) assumes that the only reasons we might have to favor abolition out of concern for racial discrimination are those flowing from the unjust treatment of Black American defendants or Black American murder victims. This overlooks, however, that racial discrimination in capital charging and sentencing is not only an injustice to those particular Black Americans that engage with the US capital sentencing regime. As the Movement's platform states, such discrimination also represents a political wrong done to Black Americans as a class.

To see why, return again to the issue of police shootings of Black American suspects. The most obvious victims of such wrongful shootings are those injured or killed by police in such incidents (as well as their families, friends, communities, etc.). But the pattern of such shootings also has moral consequences that extend beyond the shootings themselves. Parents of Black American children often feel compelled to have "the talk" with their children, dispensing advice about how to engage with police officers so as to prevent themselves being subjected to police harassment or violence (Pittman 2017). That parents feel the need to dispense such advice is an indication that police shootings establish a different relationship between Black Americans and law enforcement than is found between law enforcement and other racial or ethnic groups. For Black Americans, that relationship is more materially fraught, posing a greater risk of harassment or violence. But that relationship is also morally fraught. For Black Americans have good reason to believe that law enforcement does not accord them the same respect or status as other citizens enjoy. The mistreatment found in police shootings thus extends beyond those Black Americans who are criminal suspects or who are directly mistreated by police. Rather, *each and every* Black American, insofar as she can expect a greater probability of such mistreatment should she encounter the police as a suspect, is not accorded the same respect or status as other citizens, even if such encounters never in fact occur. The majority of Black Americans will never be criminal suspects or have a confrontation with police, yet they know where they stand with respect to their treatment by police, namely, that police are more likely not to show the same restraint they show toward citizens of other races.

Police shootings, therefore, alter the moral nature of the relationship between Black Americans and law enforcement; to wit, such relationships embody a lack of equal respect or ascription of equal status to Black Americans. This is an injustice separate from, and arguably far greater in scope, than the injustices done to particular victims of police victims. There is a parallel injustice that arises with respect to racial discrimination related to capital crimes. Particular Black Americans suffer *retributive* injustices in the US capital punishment regime when they are sentenced to die in part due to their race or when those that murder Black Americans avoid the death penalty because of their victims' Black race. But Black Americans as a class also suffer *distributive* injustice under that regime. More specifically, Black Americans do not receive either the equal protection of, or equal status under, the law. They do not enjoy equal status under the law because they face an increased likelihood of suffering a greater cost than others would due to factors (i.e., race) unrelated to objective desert. A fair system of justice would not effectively threaten greater sanctions, all other things being equal, for Black Americans who murder than it threatens toward members of other racial groups. This unfairness is one to which all Black Americans, not merely Black American murder suspects, face. At the same time, Black Americans do not enjoy equal protection of the law under a capital sentencing regime that threatens greater sanctions, all other things being equal, for those who murder non-Black Americans than for those who murder Black Americans.

Again, this unfairness is one to which all Black Americans, not merely Black American murder victims or their families, face.

On our analysis, then, the Black American community is mistreated by the American capital punishment regime because that regime makes it the case that two crucial political goods the legal system is responsible for "distributing" are unjustly distributed on the basis of race. Black American murder defendants are not extended the same legal status as other defendants; they are presumed less innocent than defendants of other racial groups. Black American victims of murder are not extended the same legal protection as victims of other races; their killers are presumed more innocent than those who kill members of other racial groups. The injustices wrought by racial bias in American capital sentencing extend beyond the specific retributive wrongs done to Black American murder suspects or murder victims. The injustices thus extend to the Black American community as a whole, because the capital sentencing regime generates normative realities in which Black Americans are not treated as equals (much as the injustice of police shootings extends beyond the particular shooting victims to the Black American community as a whole).

That there is an additional distributive injustice at issue here strengthens the case for abolition as the most defensible reform in light of racial discrimination in capital cases. Contra van den Haag and others, there is an additional "good reason" to abolish the death penalty independent of retributive considerations concerning which offenders receive it and which do not. That abolition would help to place thirty-nine million Black Americans on more equal footing with other Americans as far as the respect and status the criminal justice system accords them is a powerful reason in its favor. Only abolition, we contend, would do this, and it would come at a moral cost (foregoing executions) that appears modest in comparison.

* * *

Much of American jurisprudence, as well as academic argumentation surrounding race and capital punishment, has therefore been mistaken about the *sources* of racial discrimination in the American capital punishment regime. That implicit racial bias, instead of overt acts of discrimination, is a key source of such discrimination implies that abolition is likely to be the only adequate remedy for such discrimination. The Movement for Black Lives' call for death penalty abolition because it wrongs Black American communities highlights how the best *rationale* for abolition has also not been appreciated. That such discrimination constitutes a wrong not simply to Black Americans who engage with the capital punishment regime either as defendants or as murder victims but also to Black Americans as a class insofar as they are not accorded equal respect under, or the equal status of, the law implies that abolition is a remedy for a wrong of noticeably greater magnitude than extant discussions of such matters have recognized. Together, these two factors ground a stronger case for the abolition of capital punishment on the grounds of comparative justice than has been heretofore been elucidated.

References

Alexander, Michelle (2010). Interview. *Bill Moyers' Journal.* http://www.pbs.org/moyers/journal/04022010/transcript1.html.

Baldus, David C., Charles Pulaski, and George Woodworth (1983). "Comparative Review of Death Sentences: An Empirical Study of the Georgia Experience." *Journal of Criminal Law and Criminology* 72: 661–753.

Baldus, David C., and George Woodworth (2003). "Race Discrimination in the Administration of the Death Penalty: An Overview of the Empirical Evidence with Special Emphasis on the Post-1990 Research." *Criminal Law Bulletin* 39: 194–226.

Batson v. Kentucky, 476 U.S. 79 (1986).

Behrman, Bruce W., and Sherrie L. Davey (2001). "Eyewitness Identification in Actual Criminal Cases: An Archival Analysis." *Law and Human Behavior* 25: 475–491.

Blair, Irene V., Nilanjan Dasgupta, and Jack Glaser (2015). "Implicit Attitudes." *APA Handbook of Personality and Social Psychology, Volume 1: Attitudes and Social Cognition.* Eds. Marco R. Mikulincer, Phillip R. Shaver, Eugene Borgida, and John A. Bargh. Washington, DC: American Psychological Association: 665–691.

Brownstein, Michael, Alex Madva, and Bertram Gawronski (2019). "What Do Implicit Measures Measure?" *Wiley Interdisciplinary Reviews: Cognitive Science* 10 (5): 1–13. https://doi.org/10-1002/wcs.1501.

Brownstein, Michael, Alex Madva, and Bertram Gawronski (2020). "Understanding Implicit Bias: Putting the Criticism into Perspective." *Pacific Philosophical Quarterly* 101 (2): 276–307. https://doi.org/10.1111/papq.12302.

Cholbi, Michael (2006). "Race, Capital Punishment, and the Cost of Murder." *Philosophical Studies* 127 (2): 255–282.

Cholbi, Michael, and Alex Madva (2018). "Black Lives Matter and the Call for Death Penalty Abolition." *Ethics* 128 (3): 517–544.

Cohn, Ellen S., Donald Bucolo, Misha Pride, and Samuel R. Sommers (2009). "Reducing White Juror Bias: The Role of Race Salience and Racial Attitudes." *Journal of Applied Social Psychology* 39 (8): 1953–1973.

Cooley, Erin, Ryan Lei, Jazmin Brown-Iannuzzi, and Taylor Ellerkamp (2018). "Personal Prejudice, Other Guilt: Explicit Prejudice Toward Black People Predicts Guilty Verdicts for White Officers Who Kill Black Men." *Personality and Social Psychology Bulletin* 45 (5): 754–766.

Correll, Joshua, Sean M. Hudson, Steffanie Guillermo, and Debbie S. Ma (2014). "The Police Officer's Dilemma: A Decade of Research on Racial Bias in the Decision to Shoot." *Social and Personality Psychology Compass* 8 (5): 201–213.

Davis, Angela (2003). *Are Prisons Obsolete?* New York: Seven Stories Press.

Death Penalty Information Center (2017). *Fact Sheet*, March 20. http://www.deathpenaltyinfo.org/documents/FactSheet.pdf.

Eberhardt, Jennifer L, Paul G. Davies, Valerie J. Purdie-Vaughns, and Sheri Lynn Johnson (2006). "Looking Deathworthy: Perceived Stereotypicality of Black Defendants Predicts Capital-sentencing Outcomes." *Psychological Science* 17 (5): 383–386.

Furman vs. Georgia. 408 U.S. 238 (1972).

Glaser, Jack (2014). *Suspect Race: Causes and Consequences of Racial Profiling.* New York: Oxford University Press.

Glaser, Jack, Karin D. Martin, and Kimberly B. Kahn (2015). "Possibility of Death Sentence Has Divergent Effect on Verdicts for Black and White Defendants." *Law and Human Behavior* 39 (6): 539–546.

Goff, Phillip Atiba, Jennifer L. Eberhardt, Melissa J. Williams, and Matthew Christian Jackson (2008). "Not Yet Human: Implicit Knowledge, Historical Dehumanization, and Contemporary Consequences." *Journal of Personality and Social Psychology* 94 (2): 292–306.

Goldstein, Rebecca, Michael W. Sances, and Hye Young You (2018). "Exploitative Revenues, Law Enforcement, and the Quality of Government Service." *Urban Affairs Review* 56 (1): 5–31.

Gregg v. Georgia. 428 U.S. 153 (1976).

Hetey, Rebecca C., and Jennifer L. Eberhardt (2014). "Racial Disparities in Incarceration Increase Acceptance of Punitive Policies." *Psychological Science* 25 (10): 1949–1954.

Hodson, Gordon, Hugh Hooper, John F. Dovidio, and Samuel L. Gaertner (2005). "Aversive Racism in Britain: The Use of Inadmissible Evidence in Legal Decisions." *European Journal of Social Psychology* 35 (4): 437–448.

Hunt, Jennifer S. (2015). "Race, Ethnicity, and Culture in Jury Decision Making." *Annual Review of Law and Social Science* 11: 269–288.

James, Joy (2000). "The Dysfunctional and the Disappearing: Democracy, Race and Imprisonment." *Social Identities* 6 (4): 483–492.

Johnson, James D., Erik Whitestone, Lee Anderson Jackson, and Leslie Gatto (1995). "Justice is Still Not Colorblind: Differential Facial Effects of Exposure to Inadmissible Evidence." *Personality and Social Psychology Bulletin* 21 (9): 893–898.

Karp, David R., and Jarrett B. Warshaw (2006). "Their Day in Court: The Role of Murder Victims' Families in Capital Juror Decision Making." *Wounds That Do Not Bind: Victim-based Perspectives on the Death Penalty*. Eds. James R. Acker Jr. and David R. Karp. Durham, NC: Carolina Academic Press: 275–295.

Kelly, Erin, Michael Cholbi, Alex Madva, Deirdre Golash, Benjamin Yost, Victor Tadros, Michael Davis, and Fritz Allhoff (2018). "Ethics Discussion at PEA Soup: Michael Cholbi and Alex Madva's, 'Black Lives Matter and the Call for Death Penalty Abolition,' with a Critical Précis by Erin Kelly." *PEA Soup* blog. http://peasoup.us/2018/04/ethics-discussion-at-pea-soup-michael-cholbi-and-alex-madvas-black-lives-matter-and-the-call-for-death-penalty-abolition-with-a-critical-precis-by-erin-kelly/.

Kramer, Matthew (2011). *Ethics of Capital Punishment*. Oxford: Oxford University Press.

Levinson, Justin D. (2007). "Forgotten Racial Equality: Implicit Bias, Decisionmaking, and Misremembering." *Duke Law Journal* 57: 345–424.

Levinson, Justin D., Huajian Cai, and Danielle Young (2010). "Guilty by Implicit Racial Bias: The Guilty/Not Guilty Implicit Association Test." *Ohio State Journal of Criminal Law* 8: 187–208.

Levinson, Justin D., Robert J. Smith, and Danielle M. Young (2014). "Devaluing Death: An Empirical Study of Implicit Racial Bias on Jury-eligible Citizens in Six Death Penalty States." *N.Y.U. Law Review* 89 (2): 513–581.

Levinson, Justin D., and Danielle Young (2010). "Different Shades of Bias: Skin Tone, Implicit Racial Bias, and Judgments of Ambiguous Evidence." *West Virginia Law Review* 112: 307–350.

Lynch, Mona, and Craig Haney (2011). "Looking across the Empathic Divide: Racialized Decision Making on the Capital Jury." *Michigan State Law Review* 2011: 573–607.

Madva, Alex (2019). "Social Psychology, Phenomenology, and the Indeterminate Content of Unreflective Racial Bias." *Race as Phenomena: Between Phenomenology and Philosophy of Race*. Ed. Emily S. Lee. Lanham, MD: Rowman & Littlefield: 87–106.

McCleskey v. Kemp, 481 U.S. 279 (1987).

Miller-El v. Dretke, 545 U.S. 231 (2005).

Morrison, Mike, Amanda DeVaul-Fetters, and Bertram Gawronski (2016). "Stacking the Jury: Legal Professionals Peremptory Challenges Reflect Jurors' Levels of Implicit Race Bias." *Personality and Social Psychology Bulletin* 42 (8): 1129–1141.

The Movement for Black Lives (2016). *End the War on Black People*. https://web.archive.org/web/20170204012642/https://policy.m4bl.org/end-war-on-black-people/.

Muhammad, Khalil (2010). *The Condemnation of Blackness: Race, Crime, and the Making of Modern Urban America*. Cambridge, MA: Harvard University Press.

Myrdal, Gunnar (1944). *An American Dilemma: The Negro Problem and Modern Democracy*. New York: Harper.

NAACP Legal Defense and Educational Fund (2016). "Death Row U.S.A. Summer 2016." July 1, 2016. http://www.naacpldf.org/files/publications/DRUSA_Summer_2016.pdf.

Nosek, Brian A., Frederick L. Smyth, Jeffrey J. Hansen, Thierry Devos, Nicole M. Lindner, Kate A. Ranganath, Colin Tucker Smith, Kristina R. Olson, Dolly Chugh, Anthony G. Greenwald, and Mahzarin R. Banaji (2007). "Pervasiveness and Correlates of Implicit Attitudes and Stereotypes." *European Review of Social Psychology* 18 (1): 36–88.

Ogletree, Charles, Robert J. Smith, and Joanna Wald (2012). "Coloring Punishment: Implicit Social Cognition and Criminal Justice." *Implicit Racial Bias across the Law*. Eds. Justin D. Levinson and Robert J. Smith. Cambridge: Cambridge University Press: 45–60.

Peffley, Mark, and Jon Hurwitz (2002). "The Racial Components of 'Race-neutral' Crime Policy Attitudes." *Political Psychology* 23 (1): 59–75.

Peffley, Mark, and Jon Hurwitz (2007). "Persuasion and Resistance: Race and the Death Penalty in America." *American Journal of Political Science* 51 (4): 996–1012.

Petrie, Michelle A., and James E. Coverdill (2010). "Who Lives and Dies on Death Row? Race, Ethnicity, and Post-sentence Outcomes in Texas." *Social Problems* 57: 630–652.

Phillips, Scott (2008). "Racial Disparities in the Capital of Capital Punishment." *Houston Law Review* 45: 807–840.

Pierce, Glenn L., Michael L. Radelet, Chad Posick, and Tim Lyman (2014). "Race and the Construction of Evidence in Homicide Cases." *American Journal of Criminal Justice* 39: 771–786.

Pittman, Taylor (2017). "Inside the Heartbreaking Talk Black Parents Must Have with Their Kids." *Huffington Post*, November 4, 2016. http://www.huffingtonpost.com/entry/inside-the-heartbreaking-talk-black-parents-must-have-with-their-kids_us_581ca092e4b0d9ce6fbb465b

Smith, Robert J., and G. Ben Cohen (2012). "Choosing Life or Death (Implicitly)." *Implicit Racial Bias across the Law*. Eds. Justin D. Levinson and Robert J. Smith. Cambridge: Cambridge University Press: 229–243.

Snyder v. Louisiana, 552 U.S. 472 (2008).

Sommers, Samuel R., and Michael I. Norton (2007). "Race-based Judgments, Race-neutral Justifications: Experimental Examination of Peremptory Use and the Batson Challenge Procedure." *Law and Human Behavior* 31 (3): 261–273.

Spencer, Katherine B., Amanda K. Charbonneau, and Jack Glaser (2016). "Implicit Bias and Policing." *Social and Personality Psychology Compass* 10 (1): 50–63.

Trawalter, Sophie, Kelly M. Hoffman, and Adam Waytz (2016). "Correction: Racial Bias in Perceptions of Others' Pain." *PLOS ONE* 11, e0152334. https://doi.org/10.1371/journal.pone.0152334.

Van den Haag, Ernest, and John Phillips Conrad (1983). *The Death Penalty: A Debate*. New York: Springer.

Waytz, Adam, Kelly M. Hoffman, and Sophie Trawalter (2015). "A Superhumanization Bias in Whites' Perceptions of Blacks." *Social Psychological and Personality Science* 6 (3): 352–359.

Williams, Timothy (2019). "Black People Are Charged at a Higher Rate Than Whites. What If Prosecutors Didn't Know Their Race?" *The New York Times*, June 12. https://www.nytimes.com/2019/06/12/us/prosecutor-race-blind-charging.html.

Young, Danielle M., Justin D. Levinson, and Scott Sinnett (2014). "Innocent until Primed: Mock Jurors' Racially Biased Response to the Presumption of Innocence." *PLOS ONE* 9, e92365. https://doi.org/10.1371/journal.pone.0092365.

Young, Robert L. (2004). "Guilty until Proven Innocent: Conviction Orientation, Racial Attitudes, and Support for Capital Punishment." *Deviant Behavior* 25 (2): 151–167.

10
Sentencing Leniency for Black Offenders[*]

Benjamin S. Yost

1. The decarceration dilemma

The Movement for Black Lives calls for an end to policing and punishment "as we know them."[1] This exhortation responds to disparate exercises of the law's coercive power: black communities are subject to a virtual occupation by militarized police, black children are more likely than white children to be funneled into the school-to-prison pipeline, and black people are punished more frequently and more harshly for the same offences. The American criminal justice system thus reinforces the social injustices already inflicted upon many black communities, piling additional wrongs on top of preexisting structural deprivations and exacerbating the inequalities that contribute to differential punishment. To end punishment as we know is to embrace a policy of decarceration, of reducing both the intensity and scope of policing and imprisonment—decriminalizing drugs, removing police officers from schools, banning solitary confinement, eliminating cash bail, and so on—along with an effort to address social problems by redirecting human and economic capital into educational, housing, and vocational opportunities for disadvantaged communities.

This package of aspirations is transformative rather than incrementalist or reformist, and it will not be realized any time soon.[2] In the meantime, those who condemn the disproportionate enforcement of the criminal law are confronted with a difficult philosophical and practical dilemma. As M4BL's "Vision" recognizes, the perniciousness of contemporary penal practices renders unjust and immoral the imposition of custodial sanctions on black

---

[*] I want to thank Michael Cholbi, Alex Madva, John Lemos, and Brian Talbot for helpful feedback on this chapter.

[1] See https://m4bl.org/policy-platforms/end-jails-prisons-detention/.
[2] Though a few goals, like ending cash bail and drug decriminalization, are gaining surprising political traction.

offenders.[3] Respecting the value of black lives and communities thus seems to require the suspension of criminal penalties levied upon them. However, if legal authorities were to stop punishing violent offenses in particular, they would leave unprotected those individuals and communities who are, thanks to their marginalized status, most vulnerable to crime. (This is due to the intraracial nature of much criminal activity.[4]) In other words, failing to punish also seems to devalue black lives. I'll call this the *decarceration dilemma*.

The dilemma is potent enough that at least two leading philosophers of punishment, R. A. Duff and Victor Tadros, fall prey to it. Both contend that legal officials in unjust societies lack the moral standing necessary for condemning wrongdoers, and they conclude that in unjust societies punishment is illegitimate. Duff and Tadros get hung up on the second horn of the dilemma: in racially oppressive societies such as our own, legal officials would, by Duff and Tadros's lights, lack the authority to sanction lawbreakers with harsh treatment, and serious violations of rights would need to go unpunished, with all the consequences that entails for disadvantaged communities.[5]

The most successful attempts to resolve the decarceration dilemma can be found in the work of Tommie Shelby and Christopher Lewis. Lewis endorses the connection between punishment and condemnation found in the exemplified by Duff and Tadros (and expressivist penal theories more broadly), but he maintains that disadvantaged offenders' blameworthiness is *reduced* by their disadvantaged position, not evacuated altogether. Shelby takes a different route, severing the conceptual connection between punishment and condemnation and arguing that unjust societies bereft of the license to blame retain the right to punish grievous violations of natural rights. Both keep the wholesale abolition of punishment off the table and accommodate the considerations adduced in the M4BL's call for decarceration by urging that black lawbreakers be granted leniency in sentencing on account of their social disadvantages.

---

[3] A roughly similar claim could be made for Latinos and poor whites, though the situation is not as dire.

[4] Sixty-three percent of violent offences committed against black victims have black perpetrators. (Fifty-seven percent of violent offences against white victims have white perpetrators.) See https://www.bjs.gov/content/pub/pdf/rhovo1215.pdf.

[5] Duff does address this issue, though his discussion is fairly opaque (2001: 200). Tadros offers a careful and sympathetic analysis of the dilemma, but he does not endeavor to resolve it (2009: 393, 410–413).

My goal in this chapter is to offer another way out of the dilemma—a *procedural* rather than a substantive one. My proposal does not concern itself with how the law should respond to (putatively) reduced moral blameworthiness on the part of black offenders in the context of acute social deprivation. Instead, I focus on how the criminal justice system should address the procedural defects pervading its treatment of black offenders, constructing a plea for leniency out of procedural considerations. I begin with a sketch of Shelby and Lewis's respective resolutions of the decarceration dilemma and then note their strengths and weaknesses. My procedural proposal relies on what I call the principle of expanded asymmetry, which holds that, all things being equal, it is better to underpunish than overpunish. After briefly defending the principle, I highlight a crucial caveat. Expanded asymmetry obtains only under conditions of uncertainty. I clarify the notion of uncertainty at issue and show that virtually all trials of black offenders meet the uncertainty condition. Sentencing authorities are thus obliged to treat black offenders leniently. I conclude by remarking on the advantages of a proceduralist approach.

2. Some solutions to the dilemma

2.1. Confining the authority to punish

Shelby resolves the decarceration dilemma by insisting that while states blighted by racism lack authority both to punish lesser offenses and to condemn lawbreaking of any sort, they may still sanction crimes that constitute serious rights violations.[6] This enables him to promote leniency in a way that is responsive both to disadvantaged offenders and disadvantaged victims. Shelby's innovation pivots on a distinction between two types of legitimacy: justifiable-enforcement legitimacy and right-to-be-obeyed legitimacy (2016: 229 ff.). Possession of the first grants the state license to punish *mala in se* offenses that violate basic rights. Citizens must comply with these laws not because they have any obligation toward the state, but because they have a natural duty to refrain from seriously unjust acts. The second involves the right to be obeyed and the associated right to punish offenses that fall outside

---

[6] Shelby casts this dilemma in slightly different terms (2016: 247–248).

the class of acts that violate natural duties. Here the state may enforce compliance with its properly issued commands, simply as commands.

Both types of authority allow the use of punitive sanctions, but the permissions have different sources, and these sources determine the kinds of activities that may be punished. Both permit penalties for *mala in se* offenses constituted by serious rights violations. But only just states are within their rights to punish *mala prohibita* offenses, or actions that are wrong solely because they are prohibited (e.g., selling alcohol to a twenty-year-old). That is, only just states may punish disobedience to law itself. This license is predicated on what is commonly called legitimate authority. For Shelby, just states possess legitimate legal authority because they secure to a sufficient degree equal rights and liberties and a fair distribution of the benefits and burdens of social cooperation. Citizens of such states have a correlative duty to comply with the law's commands. This duty stems from the equitable distribution of benefits citizens enjoy as members of a political community governed by fair principles, as well as the reciprocity each owes to her fellows who follow the laws at occasional cost to their private interests (Shelby 2016: 230, 232). In just states, punishment is authorized partly because it strengthens citizens' resolve to meet their obligations through the sanctioning of lawbreakers for free-riding (Shelby 2016: 232). This forward-looking consideration has a backward-looking complement: punishment rightly condemns the offender's willful defiance of her obligations toward other citizens.

Because citizens of unjust states have no duty to obey legal orders, thanks to insufficient levels of equality and reciprocity, they do not merit condemnation for disobedience and may not be punished on account of it. Unjust states may, however, threaten and mete out hard treatment for lawbreaking when the criminal activities in question violate the basic rights of others. In these cases, the legitimacy of punishment is based in natural duties of justice, which grant individuals and states permission to intervene, with force if necessary, to prevent severe harms to others (Shelby 2016: 233). And so in the United States, federal, state, and local jurisdictions retain the authorization to punish serious offenses, though citizens have no duty to obey the law, and authorities have no right to punish minor crimes or *mala prohibita* offenses.

In short, Shelby escapes the decarceration dilemma by eschewing Duff and Tadros's emphasis on blame and moral standing. Shelby gives weight to social inequality by maintaining that the unjustly disadvantaged have no duty to comply with the criminal law as such. They cannot be blamed for violating it, and their defiance of the legal order incurs no negative desert.

By stripping an unjust state of its license to punish blacks for nonviolent property offences, drug offences, and low-level violent offences, Shelby's proposal ameliorates the problem of unequal punishment.[7] Yet by decoupling the standing to condemn from the authority to punish, Shelby can allow that unjust states possess the right to sanction those criminal deeds that the state has a natural duty to prevent. Indeed, such states must employ coercion to protect black communities against serious rights violations.

2.2. Reducing blameworthiness

Christopher Lewis happily joins Tadros and Duff in tying justifiable blame to the authority to punish. And he agrees that blame is justified only to the extent that sentencing authorities possess the appropriate moral standing. But he asserts that legitimate punishment is subject to a second, epistemic condition: sentencers must have good evidence of blameworthy attitudes on the part of the accused (Lewis 2016: 154). In the case of disadvantaged offenders, this condition is less likely to be met, and so we have less reason to blame disadvantaged lawbreakers than we have to blame advantaged ones. He concludes that the former must be punished more leniently than the latter.

To get a clearer view of Lewis's proposal, let's look closer at what he means by justified blame. Blame is justified only when it is warranted by justified beliefs, that is, when we have good evidence of blameworthy motivations (2016: 159). It is harder for sentencers to justifiably blame disadvantaged lawbreakers than advantaged ones, Lewis asserts, because the disadvantaged have stronger incentives to commit crime than the advantaged. "The disadvantaged" refers primarily to the black urban poor, who have the narrowest access to wealth, labor markets, education, and cultural capital (Lewis 2016: 162–163), though it also encompasses any sufficiently disadvantaged group.

Lewis bases his epistemic claim on an analysis of differences in criminal incentives. Owing to their deprivation, disadvantaged offenders have relatively weighty reasons to commit crimes to acquire basic social goods or to augment their ability to live a life they have reason to value; Lewis accepts

---

[7] Echoing M4BL's call for decarceration, Shelby adds that unjust states are obliged to gain full authority by remedying injustice. Accordingly, they may not deny former offenders the benefits of citizenship (voting rights, housing assistance, etc.), and they must work to abolish poverty, inequality, and ghetto conditions (2016: 250–251).

both metrics for measuring the strength of an incentive. Because the advantaged already have ample access to basic social goods and the ability to live a valuable life, advantaged malefactors have weaker reasons to privilege their interests over those of others. The offences of the disadvantaged involve less selfishness, insofar as the interests involved are more significant (Lewis 2016: 165). Lewis introduces us to a high school dropout named Arthur; he is a janitor at a community center whose poverty forces him to live with his grandmother. Lewis compares Arthur to Brandon, a wealthy student at an elite private college with a well-paying job waiting in the wings. Arthur sells drugs to better his economic circumstances, while Brandon does so for the thrill of it. The former, Lewis asserts, acts on more vital interests than the latter (2016: 166). (Lewis views most crimes as having an economic payoff: statistically speaking, people with steady jobs are less prone to criminal activity than the unemployed or tenuously employed, and to him this suggests that poor offenders commit crimes for pecuniary reasons rather than purely malicious ones.)

Lewis concludes that we have flimsier evidence of morally blameworthy behavior on the part of disadvantaged offenders (2016: 167 ff.). Even though legal institutions have no foolproof mechanism for discerning the strength and content of a particular offender's motives, there is a strong likelihood that each member of the class of disadvantaged lawbreakers acts on less objectionable motives than the class of advantaged offenders. There is thus good reason to think that a disadvantaged offender's attitude toward her criminal act is less blameworthy.

The practical consequences of Lewis's view appear to be far-reaching, though he declines to get into specifics (2016: 179). Thanks to the tight connection between punishment and condemnation, courts' inability to blame disadvantaged offenders to the same degree as advantaged offenders means that they will not be able to sanction them as severely as they otherwise could. At the very least, it seems that for *any* crime type, disadvantaged offenders may not be punished to the same level of severity as other offenders. Lewis's call for leniency is thus more general than Shelby's. Although Lewis would have disadvantaged violent felons punished less harshly than Shelby would, they would still be punished. Lewis thus sidesteps the two horns of the decarceration dilemma: black offenders are punished more fairly, but enough to protect black communities against rights violations.

2.3. A brief assessment

My main complaint with Shelby's program is that it does not adequately handle the normative consequences of racism on criminal procedures. Shelby recognizes that in the United States, the chance of a fair trial is slim to none, owing to entrenched racial inequality. But this means that *no* punishment is legitimate (2016: 247). Shelby's conclusion unfortunately reanimates the decarceration dilemma, insofar as it recommends the immediate abolition of punishment. We thus require a more nuanced approach to procedural injustice that ameliorates the wrongs visited upon on black offenders while retaining the possibility of sanctioning egregious rights violations.

Lewis's emphasis on the epistemic conditions of justifiable ascription of blame takes a step in this direction, but only a small one (2016: 159). While Lewis is right that disadvantaged offenders' incentives are particularly vulnerable to sentencers' misapprehension, black offenders face many hurdles that white offenders do not. As I discuss later, black offenders are more likely to receive punitive plea bargains, to be charged with mandatory minimums, to fall on the wrong end of judges' sentencing discretion, and so on. The ways in which black offenders are unfairly treated—even unfairly treated with respect to assessments of their desert—are numerous and varied. Lewis's call for leniency simply does not do justice to the specific legal-institutional disadvantages faced by black communities. To be fair, Lewis is not interested in offering such an account, but it remains the case that racial disparities in conviction and sentencing demand a response.

Lewis's view suffers from a second shortcoming, one which afflicts most arguments that foreground the notion of blame and desert. Given the tight connection between attributions of moral blameworthiness and moral responsibility, assertions of the diminished blameworthiness of black offenders risk portraying them as less than fully responsible for their misdeeds.[8] And this can suggest that black offenders possess a diminished level of moral agency compared to whites, a morally disrespectful consequence that constitutes a partial denial of black agency and personhood. As one critic puts it, we should forswear any proposed mitigation of social inequality that "deprive[s] already deprived citizens of yet another support for their dignity and self-worth" (Morse 2000: 154). It might even be said that the implication

---

[8] Lewis responds to this concern by prying apart blame and wrongdoing (2016: 178–179). For Tadros's response, see 2009: 393.

of diminished responsibility generates a second dilemma for those sensitive to racial inequalities in punishment: either black offenders are punished excessively severely, or they are afforded leniency purchased at the price of disrespect.

3. A procedural alternative

Fortunately, there is a way around these difficulties. My aim is to show that claims about moral standing or blameworthiness are not the only grounds for granting leniency to black offenders. We discover another reason by examining the procedural values of the legal systems of (purportedly) liberal, democratic societies. My procedural program develops an ameliorative view of punishment through an analysis of norms governing the calibration of sentencing under conditions of uncertainty, conditions which obtain in the United States in virtue of racial inequalities. This approach addresses the wrongs associated with procedural injustice while dodging the decarceration dilemma and its progeny. I call the principle central to my approach the *principle of expanded asymmetry*.

> **Expanded asymmetry (EA):** It is better to underpunish P by n units for crime c than to overpunish P by n units.

Expanded asymmetry is a modified version of the *asymmetry principle*. In its canonical form, the asymmetry principle holds that it is worse to punish an innocent person for crime c than it is to let someone guilty of c-ing go free. The principle finds its most famous expression in William Blackstone's pronouncement that "the law holds it better that ten guilty persons escape, than that one innocent party suffer." The asymmetry principle is commonly held to govern criminal procedure. Many scholars contend that it underlies the "beyond a reasonable doubt" standard of criminal conviction pervasive in Anglophone legal systems (Dworkin 1985: 89; Reiman and Van den Haag 1990: 240; Halvorsen 2004; Alexander and Ferzan 2009: 322; Duus-Otterström 2013; Tomlin 2013), as well as the legal presumption of innocence. The same rationale appears to underlie the rule of lenity, a principle of statutory interpretation dictating that any ambiguities or opacities in a criminal statue be read in favor of the accused. The prosecutorial burdens imposed by these norms reflect the view that legal procedures should favor lowering the risk of punishing the innocent even when doing so increases the risk of the guilty going free. If, for example, courts employed the less stringent "preponderance of the evidence" standard—"more probable than not," or .51 on the certainty scale—for establishing elements of the offense, convictions would be secured more easily, capturing more of the guilty, but at the cost of raking in more of the innocent. Asymmetry thus seems to express the normative judgment that it is worse to overpunish an offender than it is to underpunish her, which just is expanded asymmetry.

At the same time, the significance of EA to my argument means that a more robust vindication is needed. A less controversial principle anchors my defense.

> **Minimal invasion principle (MIP):** When faced with alternative means of achieving a (legitimate) political or legal aim, and when one alternative is clearly less invasive than the other, authorities must choose the less invasive means.[9]

MIP is a bedrock liberal principle. Let's call liberal states those in which officials must justify their interference in, or domination over, citizens' lives. Liberals of all stripes—libertarian, neo-republican, or egalitarian—will consider the associated demands to be quite stringent. When fundamental rights are at stake, the burden of justification will be close to insurmountable. Liberal political morality thus contains a second-order principle mandating minimal invasion of citizens' liberties. Owing to liberty's overriding importance, a state cannot justify infringing on citizens' freedom any more than is needed. When abrogations of freedom are necessary due to a compelling and legitimate state interest, authorities must choose the least invasive means of infringing thereupon; if two methods suffice to achieve the state's purpose, only the least invasive is permissibly pursued. Given the freedom-hindering nature of coercion, MIP side-constrains all aspects of the state's coercive activity, including policing, trials, and legislative deliberation regarding criminalization and sentencing.[10]

---

[9] I borrow this moniker from Hugo Adam Bedau (2002), although my characterization of the principle differs slightly from his.

[10] MIP need not be understood as mandating that states seek out the absolute least invasive means for achieving their ends, a construal that would likely place unworkable burdens on policymaking. MIP can be formulated more modestly, such that that it forbids only those actions or policies which are known to be more invasive than the alternatives; this is just how I presented it earlier.

It is MIP that generates EA's uncertainty condition. If an offender's guilt is undeniable, and if sentencers are justifiably confident that the selected sanction is appropriate to her desert bases, there are no alternatives for MIP to regulate. There is just one proportionate punishment. Only when there is a real choice between sanctions of differing severity—that is, when the choice between penalties of differing severity is marked by uncertainty—can we posit equally legitimate alternative sanctions.

Before resuming my vindication of EA, I want to flesh out the notion of uncertainty. Let's begin with what is opposed to it, certainty. One type of certainty is psychological or subjective. Subjective certainty belongs to a sentencer who is unswervingly convinced of her judgment; in epistemological terms, a sentencer is subjectively certain that P is guilty of c when she has a very high credence in P's guilt. A second type is epistemic certainty, which obtains when there is strong evidence supporting a sentencer's assessment of the accused. *Uncertainty*, to put it glibly, is weaker than certainty. A sentencer is beset by psychological uncertainty when she is not entirely confident that P is guilty of c, and her belief that P is guilty of c is epistemically uncertain when there are good reasons to doubt its truth. Now, the standard of certainty employed by a criminal justice system cannot be too stringent, otherwise no accused would ever be convicted. Absolute certainty is too high a bar: it is hard enough to be absolutely certain that I have hands, much less that a money launderer deserves n days of confinement. It is natural to ask where to locate the boundary between certainty and uncertainty. I don't have strong views on this matter, and nothing in what follows depends on getting it just right. So I will simply stipulate that certainty is somewhere between .85 and 1 on a scale where 1 is absolutely certain. That is, the threshold between uncertainty and certainty is, in the psychological sense, a .85 level of confidence, and, in the epistemic sense, an 85 percent likelihood that the belief is true.

Where the number falls within the range is going to depend partly on the legal context. When it comes to criminal *conviction*, the process of determining whether the accused is guilty as charged, the official line in the United States is that jurors must find proof beyond a reasonable doubt. This is meant to be a very high bar. In keeping with the putative stringency of the standard, scholars who venture to quantify it put it in the vicinity of .95. When it comes to the *sentencing* phase of a criminal trial, where the task is to identify the punishment appropriate to a convicted wrongdoer's offense, judges are typically granted discretion to choose from among the penalties contained within a statutorily prescribed range. At the same time, they are frequently prohibited from stepping outside the range, even when they are convinced that the statutorily mandated sentence is unjust. In practice, then, the law does not hold sentencing to anything like the beyond a reasonable doubt standard. In principle, however, both consequentialist and retributivist theorists will insist on a relatively high level of psychological and epistemic certainty regarding the appropriateness of the selected sanction, as they are loath to punish too little or too much.[11] Although I'm open to the claim that the threshold for sentencing should be lower than conviction, I will again stipulate that in the sentencing phase, the floor for certainty is a confidence level somewhere around .85 and, epistemically speaking, a likelihood that the punishment fits the crime around .85. Again, this should be understood as a rough estimate, and a revisable one.

Let's now move to the argument for EA. I'll start with the principle of symmetry, which is favored by opponents of asymmetry.[12]

1. The wrong of overpunishing P by n units for c = the wrong of underpunishing P by n units for c.

Now for MIP.

2. When faced with alternative means of achieving a legitimate political or legal aim, and when one alternative is clearly less invasive than the other, authorities must choose the less invasive means.
3. Underpunishing P by n units is less invasive than overpunishing P by n units.
4. Overpunishing P by n units violates MIP.

From (1) and (4) an intermediate conclusion can be drawn:

5. Overpunishing P by n units is wrong and also a violation of MIP.

---

[11] The uncertainty at issue in this chapter is uncertainty regarding what I call the "appropriateness of the selected sanction." Relevant here are doubts about whether a crime of severity s deserves n days of incarceration. But my primary concern is with misgivings about sentencers' ability to *know* what a defendant deserves, owing to bias on the part of legal officials, procedural irregularities, prosecutorial overreach, and the like.

[12] I know of no philosopher who argues that underpunishment is worse than overpunishment. Theorists of punishment who believe that underpunishing or failing to punish an offender wrongs the victim might be inclined to develop such an argument, but they have not done so. For more on the view in question, see Hampton (1998).

The fifth premise is a key step in the argument. The basic idea is that overpunishment encompasses two wrongs, the violation of MIP and the wrong of disproportionate punishment. The latter wrong, which can be found in the first premise, is the wrong of punishing an offender more harshly than is warranted by her offence. For example, it is disproportionate to punish petty larceny with life in prison (*pace* the US Supreme Court). The fifth premise leads to EA.

6. The cumulative wrongness of overpunishing P by n units for c > the cumulative wrongness of underpunishing P by n units for c.
7. It is better to underpunish P by n units than to overpunish by n units. (EA)

4. Uncertainty

The present argument for leniency in the sentencing of black offenders hinges on the idea that EA applies to most instances of said punishment. So I need to show that the punishment of black offenders is shot through with uncertainty. To prosecute this task, I must distinguish first-order uncertainty from what I call higher-order uncertainty. First-order uncertainty is uncertainty about the adequacy of the reasons underlying the conviction or sentencing of a particular defendant; here uncertainty is based on facts pertaining to his crime or features of his criminal proceeding. If you question whether an accused murderer should be convicted on the basis of eye-witness testimony alone, in the absence of corroborating evidence or plausible motive, it is likely because you think his case is marred by first-order uncertainty. (There are also moral species of first-order uncertainty.) Though many criminal trials feature such uncertainty, regardless of the race of the accused, I'll set this issue aside.

Higher-order uncertainty is constituted by our inability to distinguish—at the time of sentencing—between cases in which first-order uncertainty is present and those in which it is not. While first-order uncertainty is characterized by Rumsfeldian known unknowns, higher-order uncertainty involves unknown unknowns. Criminal trials feature higher-order uncertainty when it is difficult for participants and observers either to conclude that jurors and judges' findings are correct or to identify precisely where their mistakes lie. When higher-order uncertainty obtains, judges' and juries' beliefs about an offender and his sentencing can be rationally justified on the basis of the facts presented at trial and their sound reasoning about those facts, but false all the same. In the case of higher-order uncertainty, the truth of the verdict is potentially undermined by a fact of which sentencers are unaware, and whose possibility has not been broached at trial. Higher-order uncertainty is the product of what epistemologists call uneliminated error possibilities. Uneliminated error possibilities are just what they sound like, namely, potential grounds for error that have not been satisfactorily ruled out. Not just any uneliminated error possibility will generate higher-order uncertainty, because some lack legal salience. A juror need not worry that an evil genius is manipulating her mental states so that she is assured of the accused's guilt, because this uneliminated, and ineliminable, error possibility is irrelevant within the pragmatic context of the criminal justice system. We don't have to hammer out a precise standard to see that some possibilities of error *are* relevant. For me the most important possibility is that of overpunishment (i.e., punishing an offender in excess of her desert). The threat of overpunishment is relevant in light of the legal ideal of proportionate sentencing, along with the liberal values just mentioned. Of course, in the present context the overpunishment of black people is particularly worrisome. This, too, is salient, insofar as it is linked to various forms of racial bias, and the demonstration of bias in some cases provides grounds for relief under the Equal Protection Clause of the Fourteenth Amendment or the impartial jury protections of the Sixth Amendment.

4.1. *Establishing higher-order uncertainty*

As we shall see, higher-order uncertainty can be introduced at any stage of the criminal proceeding, from arrest through sentencing. To establish the higher-order uncertainty needed for my argument to go through, I'll begin with sentencing. Data show that black offenders are more severely punished for the same crimes as white offenders. A recent report by the United States Sentencing Commission that controls for age, education, and most importantly, criminal history, establishes that in federal courts, black men are sentenced to terms 19 percent longer than white men who commit the same crime (Commission 2016). The main factor here is judges' propensity to go easy on white men. White male offenders are 21 percent more likely to receive downward variances from federal sentencing ranges than black male offenders. And when black male offenders are granted leniency, their sentences are still 17 percent longer than those of whites. When we confine ourselves to sanctions falling within the specified range, black male offenders are sentenced to terms of imprisonment 8 percent longer than white offenders.[13] An independent multiagency study that followed offenders through the federal court system from arrest to sentencing and controlled for similar variables found that black men received sentences 13 percent longer than white men (Rehavi and Starr 2014: 1323). (Again, these discrepancies exist *all else being equal*.) Prosecutorial charging decisions explain up to half of this disparity. Prosecutors charge black people with crimes carrying mandatory minimum sentences far more frequently than whites; the former face a 65 percent higher likelihood of being slapped with mandatory minimums (Rehavi and Starr 2014: 1323). Charging decisions have outsized impact in plea bargaining, which is used to dispose of 97 percent of federal criminal cases (and close to that rate in state jurisdictions that report such statistics).[14] Not surprisingly, blacks are also more likely than whites to receive custodial plea deals, even when controlling for criminal record and crime severity.[15]

Things are usually no better at the state level. For example, in Florida the *Sarasota Herald-Tribune* recently conducted a comprehensive analysis of sentencing by county. Florida uses a guided sentencing system, where offenders are given points based on the circumstances of the arrest, seriousness of the crime, and prior criminal history. In theory, offenders with the same points should receive the same sentences for the same crimes; the Florida legislature introduced this mechanism precisely in order to standardize counties' divergent sentencing practices. But reality bears little resemblance to the ideal. In 60 percent of all felony cases, black offenders serve a longer sentence than whites for crimes with the same characteristics; 68 percent of blacks are treated more harshly for the most severe felonies (Salman et al. 2016). In Manatee County, whites convicted of felony drug possession are given an average of five months behind bars, while blacks with identical charges and records are sent away for more than a year. In Okaloosa County,

---

[13] Women of all races are sentenced more leniently than men. Data on female offenders are too variable to supply any meaningful conclusions about variances between black, Hispanic, and white women.
[14] https://www.nytimes.com/2011/09/26/us/tough-sentences-help-prosecutors-push-for-plea-bargains.html.
[15] https://slate.com/news-and-politics/2015/08/racial-disparities-in-the-criminal-justice-system-eight-charts-illustrating-how-its-stacked-against-blacks.html.

judges sentence white offenders to nearly five months for battery and blacks to almost a year. In Flagler County, judges put black armed robbers behind bars for nearly three times as long as whites (Salman et al. 2016). It should be noted that these results very likely underestimate the extent of sentencing disparities, as the *Herald-Tribune*'s analysis used the points assigned to establish a baseline. But points are tallied up by prosecutors, whose charging biases have been demonstrated at the federal level. Overcharging black offenders implies "overpointing" them, and we have no reason to think that state prosecutors are less likely to overcharge or overpoint than their federal counterparts. If we adjusted the Florida data to account for overpointing, the overpunishment of black offenders would probably prove to be even more egregious.

These studies do not demonstrate that black malefactors are sentenced too harshly in some idealized sense, that is, with respect to a sentence that is exactly proportionate to their desert. To render a verdict here, we would need, at the very least, a schedule of crimes and punishments that is, in some ideal moral sense, ordinally and cardinally proportionate. Such a scheme is likely impossible to come by (see, e.g., Shafer-Landau 2000). Recognizing this predicament, some prominent penal theorists construe proportionality as partly a matter of convention (Von Hirsch 1992). And if the standard is the *conventionally* proportionate punishment, the claim that black offenders as a class are sentenced too harshly for their crimes is easy to maintain, so long as we use the severity of white offenders' penalties as a proxy for the conventionally appropriate punishment. Accordingly, even if we grant that some black offenders are punished appropriately, there is a good possibility that any particular black offender will be unjustly sentenced.

My estimate is supported by the fact that we ought to *expect* the overpunishment of black Americans, given the opportunities for discretion built into the criminal justice system combined with the existence of implicit and explicit bias. Implicit bias, according to a number of researchers, pervades the criminal justice system (Kang et al. 2012: 1129–1131; Brownstein 2015: 7).[16] This body of work suggests that police offers judge black juveniles to be more culpable for their wrongdoings than white juveniles of the same age (Goff et al. 2014). Tests with mock jurors show that they more readily construe ambiguous evidence as inculpatory when it is associated with black suspects. A majority of white judges and a minority of

---

[16] For more on this, see Cholbi and Madva, Chapter 9, this volume.

black judges appear to display biases favoring whites and disfavoring blacks (Ghandnoosh 2014: 14–16).[17] The same researchers contend that implicit bias predicts behavior in unwelcome ways.

If the reader finds implicit bias research too controversial, the research on explicit attitudes also does the job, on the assumption that explicit attitudes predict behavior. A recent study analyzed the correlation between punitive attitudes toward sentencing (which were measured by strong support for capital punishment, three-strikes laws, and punishing juveniles as adults) and standard racial attitude indicators, including anti-black stereotypes, negative intergroup affect toward black people, and racial resentment. It found that the presence of anti-black attitudes was correlated with a punitive disposition toward penal policy in both black and white subjects, though the correlation was much stronger in whites (Bobo and Thompson 2010: 339). More specifically, it found that racial resentment predicts punitive attitudes, regardless of age or education level. It also ruled out alternative explanations based on conservative social values, individualistic worldviews, fear of crime, and victimization levels.

The impact of bias on the disparate treatment of black Americans is facilitated by the copious discretion enjoyed by legal officials at every step of the criminal process. For example, police officers choose which cars to pull over for minor infractions, which neighborhoods to subject to broken windows policing, and so on. Prosecutors decide whether to bring charges and which charges (or overcharges) to bring. Judges have leeway in setting bail, jury selection, trial procedure, postconviction sentencing, and postconviction appeals. Because legal authorities' discretionary powers give free reign to bias, we have good reason to believe that sentencing disparities are caused, at least in part, by explicit or implicit negative racial attitudes, rather than some other mysterious factor that would make black offenders' commission of c more serious than that of whites.[18]

Accordingly, in any proceeding involving a black defendant, there is a good possibility that she will be unjustly sentenced, even though it will be difficult to establish whether her sentence tracks desert or is excessively severe. For example, it will be almost impossible to distinguish between cases where a sentencer is rightly confident in her assessment and cases where her

---

[17] The existence and import of implicit bias are controversial topics. For a good overview of some criticisms of implicit bias research as well as vigorous replies, see Brownstein, Madva et al. (2019).

[18] Bias is not the only plausible explanation. Structural inequalities, including lack of access to quality legal representation, doubtlessly have their own effect.

confidence is misplaced owing to some form of racial bias (e.g., she deems a juvenile more culpable than he is on account of his being black). Sometimes egregious instances of overpunishment, racially motivated or otherwise, will be detectable and remediable on appeal. But very few offenders are availed of this opportunity, and plea bargains, which are used to dispose of approximately 97 percent of criminal proceedings, are essentially unreviewable. Furthermore, there clearly is no political will for disbursing the massive amount of resources required for a sufficiently comprehensive review process. So if we take the average sentence handed down to white offenders for crime c as the conventionally proportionate punishment, we have reason to think that black offenders are sentenced too severely, and we are hard-pressed to sort those upward departures that are warranted by the circumstances from those that are not. The associated possibilities of error constitute higher-order uncertainty. Given EA, black offenders must be treated leniently at sentencing.

4.2. Some remarks on policy

The practical prescriptions enabled by my proceduralist approach can be relatively fine-grained. For example, we might require leniency only in regard to those crime types for which there is some evidence of racial dissimilarities in frequency or severity. Here we could employ one of two starting points, which differ in where they allocate the burden of proof and what they count as evidence of racial disparities. The first, which is friendlier to black offenders, would stipulate that, unless there is strong evidence to the contrary, when c is committed by blacks, it is no more serious than when committed by whites. Accordingly, racial disparities in the punishment of c will by themselves be taken to establish higher-order uncertainty sufficient for leniency. Leniency will thus be in order for all black offenders who commit c. The more prosecution-friendly approach would assume that racial disparities in punishment of c reflect patterns of aggravating factors augmenting the average severity of black criminal acts. Here we would assert higher-order uncertainty sufficient for leniency only in those cases where there is independent evidence (such as that offered in section 4.1) that sentencing falls more heavily on black people.[19]

[19] Unfortunately, neither of these options addresses the serious problems intrinsic to plea bargaining.

One might, however, wonder why I describe this as a call for *leniency*. Admittedly, my argument focuses on proportionate sentencing, where proportionality is cashed out in terms of the sentences imposed on white offenders, and so I could be characterized as merely insisting that like cases be treated alike.[20] If leniency is taken to mean punishing black offenders less than proportionality demands, then I am not advocating leniency. (It's worth noting that neither Lewis nor Shelby advocates for this type of leniency either.) Rather, I'm claiming that judges should sentence black offenders less harshly than they (initially) believe they should be sentenced. This is a perfectly intelligible conception of leniency. Note that when judges sanction black offenders too harshly, they typically *think* they are treating like cases alike (unless they are consciously racist), even though they're wrong. So to tell judges to *really* treat like cases alike is to tell them to treat black offenders more leniently than they think is warranted.

4.3. Is higher-order uncertainty everywhere?

To be sure, racial bias is not the only engine of higher-order uncertainty. Laboratory misconduct, for example, is surprisingly common (see Hansen 2013; Hsu 2015). Even apparently ironclad evidence like confessions can be misleading, as false confessions, be they voluntary or coerced, are not unheard of; the Central Park Five are an infamous example. And there are numerous other candidates. This fairly obvious qualification raises a question—must *every* sentence be mitigated under expanded asymmetry? If all criminal proceedings are characterized by higher-order uncertainty, then it looks like all criminal defendants should enjoy the relief promised by EA. But a negative answer to the question can be proffered on the basis of two crucial differences between the higher-order uncertainty that flows from racial disparities and that which flows from sources like those just mentioned.

First, laboratory malfeasance and forced coercions, while not as rare as they should be, are nowhere near as common as the overpunishment of black offenders.[21] Nor, on my understanding, are they important components of

---

[20] I want to thank John Lemos for pressing me to clarify this point.
[21] To get a rough sense of the rate of laboratory misconduct in the last thirty years, see Yost (2019: 211–212). Approximately three hundred false confessions have been conclusively identified (Leo 2009), though the real rate is surely much higher.

the social and institutional structures that enable such overpunishment. So the level of higher-order uncertainty associated with the sentencing of black offenders is significantly higher than that associated with our other candidates. (In addition, though this point does not bear directly on the discussion at issue, forensic data are eminently desirable from the standpoint of penal justice. While any instrument used to increase accuracy can have the opposite effect, both laboratory evidence and the consideration of confessions are part of a collection of mechanisms aimed at shoring up confidence in a verdict. And when employed as intended, laboratory reports and statements of confession do increase a verdict's reliability.[22] But consideration of racial factors almost never has these salutary effects and instead pushes in the opposite direction, making it more probable that an offender will be treated unjustly.)

Second, there are causal connections between race and differential punishment. That an accused is black often explains why she is sanctioned more severely than she deserves, when she is so sanctioned. By contrast, the use of drug testing neither causes nor explains shoddy or doctored lab evidence. And the facts that do explain testing improprieties are external to the criminal proceeding itself; for example, Massachusetts chemist Annie Dookhan fabricated results in order to garner accolades for her speedy performance.[23]

The conclusion to be drawn is that higher-order uncertainty in trials of black Americans is particularly robust. The reasons for leniency are thus much weightier than they are in, say, proceedings which involve laboratory evidence or confessions. And so we have at least the beginnings of an argument for restricting leniency to the former.

Before concluding, I want to address any potential concerns about a third, especially pervasive, form of higher-order uncertainty, namely, that which is parasitic on the first-order difficulty of determining what any particular offender deserves. This type of higher-order uncertainty arises from the vagueness of the concepts ("malice," "future dangerousness," etc.) employed in sentencing and the consequent challenges of correctly applying them. It is plainly impossible to eliminate this uncertainty for the institutional reasons discussed in section 4.1. Maybe it can be used in an argument for generic leniency or maybe not; much will depend on the particulars. But whatever the

---

[22] I do not intend to express blanket approval of forensic data. For example, some bite mark and burn pattern analyses are based on bad science, bordering on outright superstition.

[23] See https://www.bostonglobe.com/metro/2013/02/03/chasing-renown-path-paved-with-lies/Axw3AxwmD33lRwXatSvMCL/story.html.

outcome, it poses no threat to the view on offer, as the higher-order uncertainty associated with racial disparities in punishment constitutes an additional, independent reason for leniency for black offenders.

5. Final words

I have supplied a proceduralist argument for reductions in sentencing for black offenders. It rests on claims about how legal authorities in a liberal society ought to proceed under conditions of uncertainty, rather than substantive views about culpability or blameworthiness. While I am sympathetic to Shelby and Lewis's contributions to the latter discussion, my proceduralist argument avoids the decarceration dilemmas that dog their analyses. In addition, the procedural injustices I've targeted are clearly important grounds for affording leniency, yet go unseen on a culpability-based paradigm. My proposal is in this way more responsive to concerns about fairness. Shelby leans heavily on the distinction between violent and nonviolent offenses and mandates mitigation only for the former. My view addresses the potential injustices faced by those accused of violent offenses yet disadvantaged in such a way that they cannot expect procedural fairness.[24] Lewis suggests that we ameliorate the sentences of anyone who is disadvantaged. I agree that we have class-wide evidence of the diminished blameworthiness of disadvantaged offenders, but black offenders are nevertheless more likely than disadvantaged white offenders to receive brutal plea deals, to be hit with mandatory minimums, and to receive the hard end of judges' discretionary power, and so black offenders merit special attention.

It goes without saying that ameliorating racially disproportionate punishment is an urgent task, on account of the individual and collective harms and moral wrongs it imposes, and for the social inequalities it reinforces and invigorates. A procedural approach might appear to be a pallid response to this imperative and less congenial to the transformative ideals of the Movement for Black Lives than the alternatives. So I want to conclude by noting that a procedural argument for leniency captures something significant that substantive variants do not: it highlights the moral and epistemic deformations of legal institutions in societies blighted by racial oppression.

---

[24] My approach can nevertheless countenance the prohibition on the punishment of nonviolent offenses in unjust states, if Shelby is right about this prohibition's necessity.

The substantive arguments I've canvassed hold that the criminal justice system's disproportionate treatment of disadvantaged black offenders stems from a miscalculation of offenders' desert or from ignorance about the constraints on its authority stemming from social inequality. This is true enough, but given how the legacy of racism compromises the means by which justice is distributed, it is crucial to recognize that, and how, the psychological and institutional effects of racism sabotage American legal institutions' ability to assess fairly black offenders' desert.

References

Alexander, Larry, and Kimberly Ferzan (2009). *Crime and Culpability: A Theory of Criminal Law*. New York: Cambridge University Press.

Bedau, Hugo (2002). "The Minimal Invasion Argument against the Death Penalty." *Criminal Justice Ethics* 21 (2): 3–8.

Bobo, Lawrence, and Victor Thompson (2010). "Racialized Mass Incarceration: Poverty, Prejudice, and Punishment." *Doing Race: 21 Essays for the 21st Century*. Eds. Hazel Marcus and Paula Moya. New York: W.W. Norton: 322–355.

Brownstein, Michael (2015). "Implicit Bias." *Stanford Encyclopedia of Philosophy*. http://plato.stanford.edu/archives/spr2015/entries/implicit-bias/.

Brownstein, Michael, Alex Madva, and Bertram Gawronski (2019). "Implicit Racial Bias: Putting the Criticism into Perspective." Unpublished manuscript.

Duff, Antony (2001). *Punishment, Communication, and Community*. New York: Oxford University Press.

Duus-Otterström, Göran (2013). "Why Retributivists Should Endorse Leniency in Punishment." *Law and Philosophy* 32 (4): 459–483.

Dworkin, Ronald (1985). *A Matter of Principle*. Cambridge, MA: Harvard University Press.

Ghandnoosh, Nazgol (2014). *Race and Punishment: Racial Perceptions of Crime and Support for Punitive Policies*. Washington, DC: The Sentencing Project. http://sentencingproject.org/doc/publications/rd_Race_and_Punishment.pdf.

Goff, Phillip, Matthew Jackson, Brooke Allison, Lewis DiLeone, Carmen Culotta, and Natalie DiTomasso (2014). "The End of Innocence: Consequences of Dehumanizing Black Children." *Journal of Personality and Social Psychology* 106 (4): 526–545.

Halvorsen, Vidar (2004). "Is It Better That Ten Guilty Persons Go Free Than That One Innocent Person Be Convicted?" *Criminal Justice Ethics* 23 (2): 3–13.

Hampton, Jean C. (1998). "Punishment, Feminism, and Political Identity: A Case Study in the Expressive Meaning of the Law." *Canadian Journal of Law & Jurisprudence* 11 (1): 23–46.

Hansen, Mark (2013). "Crime Labs under the Microscope after a String of Shoddy, Suspect and Fraudulent Results." *ABA Journal*, September 1, 2003. http://www.abajournal.com/magazine/article/crime_labs_under_the_microscope_after_a_string_of_shoddy_suspect_and_fraudu.

Hsu, Spencer (2015). "FBI Admits Flaws in Hair Analysis over Decades." *Washington Post*, April 18.

Kang, Jerry, Mark Bennett, Devon Carbado, Pam Casey, Nilanjana Dasgupta, David Faigman, Rachel Godsil, Anthony Greenwald, Justin Levinson, and Jennifer Mnookin (2012). "Implicit Bias in the Courtroom." *UCLA Law Review* 59: 1124–1186.

Leo, Richard A. (2009). "False Confessions: Causes, Consequences, and Implications." *Journal of the American Academy of Psychiatry and the Law Online* 37 (3): 332.

Lewis, Christopher (2016). "Inequality, Incentives, Criminality, and Blame." *Legal Theory* 22 (2): 153–180.

Morse, Stephen J. (2000). "Deprivation and Desert." *From Social Justice to Criminal Justice*. Eds. William C. Heffernan and John Kleinig. New York: Oxford University Press: 114–160.

Rehavi, M. Marit, and Sonja B. Starr (2014). "Racial Disparity in Federal Criminal Sentences." *Journal of Political Economy* 122 (6): 1320–1354.

Reiman, Jeffrey, and Ernst Van den Haag (1990). "On the Common Saying That It Is Better That Ten Guilty Persons Escape Than That One Innocent Suffer: Pro and Con." *Social Philosophy & Policy* 7 (2): 226–248.

Salman, Josh, Emily Le Coz, and Elizabeth Johnson (2016). *Florida's Broken Sentencing System*. Sarasota Herald-Tribune, December 12. http://projects.heraldtribune.com/bias/sentencing.

Shafer-Landau, Russ (2000). "Retributivism and Desert." *Pacific Philosophical Quarterly* 81 (2): 189–214.

Shelby, Tommie (2016). *Dark Ghettos: Injustice, Dissent, and Reform*. Cambridge, MA: Harvard University Press.

Tadros, Victor (2009). "Poverty and Criminal Responsibility." *Journal of Value Inquiry* 43 (3): 391–413.

Tomlin, Patrick (2013). "Extending the Golden Thread? Criminalisation and the Presumption of Innocence." *Journal of Political Philosophy* 21 (1): 44–66.

United States Sentencing Commission (2016). *Demographic Differences in Sentencing: An Update to the 2012 Booker Report*. Washington, DC: United States Sentencing Commission.

Von Hirsch, Andreas (1992). "Proportionality in the Philosophy of Punishment." *Crime and Justice* 16: 55–98.

Yost, Benjamin S. (2019). *Against Capital Punishment*. New York: Oxford University Press.

PART V
STRATEGY AND SOLIDARITY

11
The Violence of Leadership in Black Lives Matter

Dana Francisco Miranda

Since the murder of Trayvon Martin in 2012, the United States has seen the coalescing of black protestors and activists, along with their multiracial collaborators, under the banner of Movement for Black Lives (M4BL). This struggle against racialized violence, police brutality, and white supremacy has been witnessed in myriad ways, with two of its most prominent "reactions" occurring in Ferguson, Missouri, and Baltimore, Maryland, after the extrajudicial killings of Michael Brown and Freddie Gray, respectively. The aftereffects of such violence—on "communities of the violated"—have also resulted in the ascription of violence to these uprisings. In this struggle to "defend the dead" (Philip 2011: 25), the organization Black Lives Matter (BLM) has chosen to follow a "leader-full" model, which fights against cooptation and the limits of singular leaders with group-based leadership. This chapter seeks to highlight the competing notions of centralized and decentralized leadership within black liberation movements—as seen in the works of W. E. B. Du Bois, Ella Baker, and Frantz Fanon—alongside those proposed by BLM. In particular, I will explore how the organization functions not only as a historical critique of failed black leadership but also as an alternative model that violates established and misguided political norms. Using the works of Keeanga-Yamahtta Taylor, Barbara Ransby, and Patrisse Khan-Cullors, this chapter will explore forms of leadership that articulate alternative modes of accountability, service, and well-being within the struggle for black livability.

To understand the leadership model in the BLM organization, as well the broader M4BL, one first has to examine the importance of leadership in black liberation struggles. One of the most famous theories regarding black leadership and its importance was that of W. E. B. Du Bois's "Talented Tenth."

Dana Francisco Miranda, *The Violence of Leadership in Black Lives Matter* In: *The Movement for Black Lives*. Edited by: Brandon Hogan, Michael Cholbi, Alex Madva, and Benjamin S. Yost, Oxford University Press. © Oxford University Press 2021. DOI: 10.1093/oso/9780197507773.003.0012

According to the early Du Bois, exceptional leaders would need to be developed into the best of black humanity so that they would be capable of guiding the black masses, whom Du Bois believed were insufficiently educated to lead themselves. In fact, only "great" leaders are capable of uplifting nations or peoples. Thus, he argues, "Was there ever a nation on God's fair earth civilized from the bottom upward? Never; it is, ever was and ever will be from the top downward that culture filters. The Talented Tenth rises and pulls all that are worth the saving up to their vantage ground. This is the history of human progress" (Du Bois 1903: 45).[1] According to Du Bois, the racial uplift of black masses is in direct relation to the aristocratic leadership of the "Talented Tenth." However, the need for black leadership is tempered by the fact that black leaders can themselves be unworthy of the cause. Leaders, even especially talented ones, can work to the detriment of the communities they find themselves leading.

This is why, for instance, in *The Mis-Education of the Negro*, Carter G. Woodson criticizes particular forms of petty leadership. Woodson critiques black leaders who "lead" only to their benefit. Although this misleadership might be the historical result of white interference and co-optation in black communities, Woodson does not excuse it. Leadership in this regard just further solidifies the stereotype that blacks are seen as incapable of self-governing, and thus any leader that "represents" this community will do so without serving their constituents. As such, Woodson advocates abandoning leadership in favor of service. He argues: "If we can finally succeed in translating the idea of leadership into that of service, we may soon find it possible to lift the Negro to a higher level. Under leadership we have come into the ghetto; by service within the ranks we may work our way out of it" (Woodson 2017: 42).

To get a better sense of what Woodson might mean by service, consider Enrique Dussel's account in *Twenty Theses on Politics*. Dussel argues that a politics of liberation must first account for political victims. These victims cannot live relative to those who thrive within their respective political communities. The existence of victims within a political order points to the fact

---

[1] In his later life, Du Bois expanded upon this form of leadership by holding that class did not restrict the development of aristocratic talents and commitments: "my own panacea of an earlier day was a flight of class from mass through the development of the Talented Tenth; but the power of this aristocracy of talent was to lie in its knowledge and character, not in its wealth" (Du Bois 1940: 216–217).

that certain individuals or groups cannot live fully. Insofar as political systems are intentionally structured so that select individuals find their aims, ambitions, and interests routinely shortcut, if not denied, then that system can be said to produce victims. Those called toward the struggle for liberation then have a "vocation" to correct such civic disorders. As Dussel (2008: 25) states, "'Vocation' (from the Latin verb *vocare*) means 'to be called upon' to complete a mission. The one who 'calls' is the community, the *people*, and the one who is called feels 'summoned' to assume the responsibility of service." When leadership is conceived as a vocation, there is a demand that the individual is responsible and responsive to the community. Moreover, by representing the *people*, such leaders are delegated a power that is obedient and in "service" to the represented.

In this brief exposition, leadership in black struggles has been represented by the "aristocratic" guidance of elites and the direct management of self-interested misrepresentatives, as well as through acts of dedicated service. In all three, there is a conception of leadership that is directly or indirectly in relation with a group or community of "followers." In such a relationship, the leader is one who can uplift, manage, or serve. The political scientist Murray Edelman (1967: 75) argues that "Leadership . . . is not to be understood as something an individual does or does not have, at all times and places. It is always defined by a specific situation and is recognized in the response of followers to individual acts and speeches. If they respond favorably and follow, there is leadership; if they do not, there is not." What provokes a favorable or unfavorable response from groups is thus directly tied to the operational capacities of leaders. Groups may be asked to choose between an incumbent leader or an opponent, they may be asked to choose among a small number of individuals for leadership, or they may come to appoint particular leaders out of self-selection. Groups, in a sense, choose whom to follow or continue following by their results.

However, for African-Americans, the ability to choose capable leaders is complicated due to several factors. For instance, disenfranchisement, co-optation, and the assassination of leaders not only prevent chosen leaders from being efficacious but also limit the type of leaders that come to represent the interests of blacks. Maulana Karenga (2015: 28) speaks to this problem by arguing: "Black middle class leadership finds itself, then, locked into the Democratic Party, with no structural or financial ability to significantly reward or punish it to induce it into compliance with the demands of black interests." Given the predominantly two-party system in the United

States, African-American citizens have often found themselves struggling to achieve their political goals. Thus, even as these political parties have courted black voters, this did not mean these groups were able to apply any political pressure to make leaders follow through with their promises. Even the Democratic Party is not compelled in this regard. Instead, for Karenga, black leaders serve functionally as disempowered middlemen, with no viable alternatives. Thus, what is represented by this case is the fact that leadership is based in part not only on the favorable responses it provokes from followers but also upon limitations imposed by structural conditions. If groups are impeded from attaining any significant political gains and do not have the power to pressure politically either allies or enemies, then black leadership becomes merely symbolic.

This crisis in black leadership is further exasperated by the fact that there are now black leaders who have attained significant political power in the country. As Keeanga-Yamahtta Taylor (2017: 1) argues, "Today, we have more Black elected officials in the United States than at any point in American history. Yet, for the vast majority of Black people, life has changed very little. Black elected officials have largely governed in the same way as their white counterparts, reflecting all of the racism, corruption and policies favoring the wealthy seen throughout mainstream politics." The political ineptness or ineffectiveness of the black leadership class has not only caused resentment within large segments of the black population, it has also caused activists to think of alternative possibilities when it comes to leadership.

One central question then became: What if black leadership was not appointed leadership—affiliated with political parties and organizations—but rather a group-centered leadership performed by all parties within the movement, within the struggle? Within BLM, activists and participants expanded the notion of leadership from that of either "elite" guidance, direct management, or dedicated service of singular individuals to that of a decentralized, group-centered, and nonviolent model. Influenced by black feminism, the leader-full model practiced by BLM not only serves as a critique against black political elites but more importantly provides an alternative vision of liberation. Within the organization, leadership and wellness are cultivated so that all members can develop their capacities to be both politically free and free from trauma.

1. The importance of decentralized leadership

This practice is first and foremost seen in the words and deeds of the founders of the BLM Global Network. These women—Alicia Garza, Patrisse Khan-Cullors, and Opal Tometi—not only worked to bring attention to racial and gendered inequalities through their created hashtag but also consistently worked with and led organizations to fight for the rights of the violated.[2] For instance, Garza directs Special Projects for the National Domestic Workers Alliance (NDWA), Khan-Cullors is a board member for the Ella Baker Center for Human Rights, and Tometi is the Executive Director at Black Alliance for Just Immigration (BAJI). In the early days of BLM, the leadership of these three women was often erased or unacknowledged within the media. This led Garza to pen a "herstory," an informed history around the creation of Black Lives Matter as a hashtag, freedom ride, and eventual organization. More than anything, this story was meant to decry the "theft of Black Queer Women's Work" (Garza 2014: 1). After this much needed intervention, many began identifying these three women as not simply the founders of an organization but rather the leaders of an entire movement. Even in 2019, many that do not critically follow the Movement for Black Lives, the larger coalition of more than 150 organizations, are prone to depict this triumvirate as the leaders of the Black Lives Matter network. However, although these women remain dedicated to black liberation, their current roles within the organization could not be typified as that of "leaders." They are not singular individuals providing direct guidance or management of chapters or the network at large. Rather, it is the lesser-known Nikita Mitchell who serves as the Director of Organizing for the BLM Global Network (Matthews and Noor 2017: 8).

It would then seem easy, even necessary, to correct this misunderstanding. However, given the importance of decentralized leadership within BLM, such an approach would be premature. The structure of BLM is predicated on cultivating group-based leadership, the practice of being leader-full. As Jasmine Abdullah Richards, founder of the Pasadena chapter of #BlackLivesMatter, states, "This is a leader-full movement. We empower each other. If we just have one leader then that depletes that person of all their resources, their

---

[2] By violated, I mean those individuals whose public appearance and interests are deemed illegitimate and therefore a "violation" of public order. See Lewis Gordon (2012), "Of Illicit Appearance: The L.A. Riots/Rebellion as a Portent of Things to Come," *Truthout*, https://truthout.org/articles/of-illicit-appearance-the-la-riots-rebellion-as-a-portent-of-things-to-come/.

energy and everything. But if we have more than one person then, when I fall I have this person and this person on the right and left of me to pick me up and give me some of their energy" (cited in Gordon et al. 2018: 105–137). If every individual has the energy and resources to take action, then not only is there less chance for petty leadership developing, but there is a greater capacity for collective empowerment. More than anything, BLM functions to ensure that all black lives are valued and have the ability to positively enact their vision on society. In the primary policy document created by the M4BL (2016), the coalition argues that "We believe in elevating the experiences and leadership of the most marginalized Black people, including but not limited to those who are women, queer, trans, femmes, gender nonconforming, Muslim, formerly and currently incarcerated, cash poor and working class, differently-abled, undocumented, and immigrant." This elevation of those deemed marginalized, and thus vulnerable even *within* black communities, points to the ways in which a leader-full structure aims to empower all black people.

This structural approach is also seen in organizations affiliated with the larger M4BL. Umi Selah (formerly Phil Agnew) of the group Dream Defenders has worked to democratize forms of leadership as well as participation within this social movement. Selah argues that "Everyone is not an orator. Everyone is not a sign holder. Everyone can't get arrested. And so if those are the only doorways by which people see their participation being valued in the movement, then that cuts people off, a lot of people, from even trying" (Selah 2015, cited in Belton 2015: 1). If the only individuals who felt acknowledged in a black liberation movement were those typecast to certain caricatures, then such a movement would unintentionally limit which actions are affirmed and which people are seen as leaders. Selah's vision of participatory action is similar to Karenga's definition of leadership, albeit with slight modification. Karenga states that "Leadership can be defined as the self-conscious capacity to provide vision and values, and produce structures, programs and practice which satisfies human needs and aspirations and transforms persons and society in the process" (Karenga 2015: 31). The modification arises not from alterations to the qualities Karenga expresses but rather with leadership being defined as "self-conscious capacity" with no mention of how such a capacity is developed. Within a leader-full model, the focus is on cultivating and providing opportunities for leadership to manifest among everyone. Just as "every cook can govern," likewise every "follower" is free to lead (James 1992). Or in the words of the civil rights activist Diane

Nash: "Freedom, by definition, is people realizing that they are their own leaders" (cited in Khan-Cullors and bandele 2018: 196).

This attention to mass-based leadership within BLM originates in part from the tremendous influence of Ella Baker. In interviews with BLM Global Network Chapters, members continuously listed Baker as one of their "Black Liberation Idols." In fact, eleven of the chapters explicitly list Baker as an influence (Matthews and Noor 2017: 29–46). Further, the historian and political activist Barbara Ransby, as well as the sociologist Noël Cazenave, both argue that BLM's leader-full model is indebted to Baker's conception of group-centered leadership (Ransby 2018: 3; Cazenave 2018: 265). As founder of the Student Nonviolent Coordinating Committee (SNCC), Baker worked in conjuncture with other members to institute participatory democratic practices aimed at developing equal cooperation between adult and youth leaders, as the latter often found their initiative and capacities underdeveloped or suppressed in the student movement. Baker argued, "This inclination toward *group-centered leadership*, rather than toward a *leader centered group pattern of organization*, was refreshing . . . [for there] is an opportunity for adults and youth to work together and provide genuine leadership—the development of the individual to his highest potential for the benefit of the group" (Baker 1960: 4). Within SNCC, group-centered leadership encouraged the self-direction of all its members, regardless of age, while demanding that cooperation be based on equality.

Such a model contrasted directly with the gendered leadership Baker herself encountered as an organizer. Within leader-centered models, she was confronted with organizations that allowed for no public dissension with anointed leaders, and she simultaneously found her work devalued due to gender discrimination. For instance, while working with the Southern Christian Leadership Conference (SCLC), she discovered the central experience that men had with women in organizing was through the church. As such, Baker realized that in terms of leadership, "the roll [sic] of women in the southern church—and maybe all of the churches but certainly the southern churches—was that of doing the things that the minister said he wanted to have done. It was not one in which they were credited with having creativity and initiative and capacity to carry out things—to create programs and to carry them out" (Baker 1974: 51). Instead of being credited with initiative or developing her capacities, Baker and other women were reduced to a follower's role. They were thus subject to *domination*, as Iris Marion Young (2011: 31) defines it: "the structural or systemic phenomenon which exclude people from participating in determining their actions or the conditions of their actions." As a form of "leadership" that actively and systemically excluded women, leader-centered approaches too often reinscribed patterns of domination upon those they sought to empower and liberate.

Thankfully, the diminished position of a follower was "much too difficult" for Baker to assume. Similarly, BLM has found leader-centered groups "much too difficult" to accept or put into practice. Rather than trust the guidance of black elites, whose "leadership" has not alleviated the economic and racial burdens of African-Americans, BLM works instead to develop the capacities of those otherwise pigeonholed into the role of followers. Moreover, as seen in the Baltimore uprising, African-Americans were not only protesting and rioting against white police officers and politicians but also black political elites. In particular, at the time of Freddie Gray's death, Baltimore's mayor, Stephanie Rawlings-Blake, and police commissioner, Anthony Betts, were black, as were US President Barack Obama and Attorney General Eric Holder. As Keeanga-Yamahtta Taylor argues, "When a Black mayor, governing a largely Black city, aids in the mobilization of a military unit led by a Black woman to suppress a Black rebellion, we are in a new period of the Black freedom struggle" (Taylor 2016: 80). The increasing prevalence and high profile of African-American governors, mayors, prosecutors, and police officers could neither prevent the murders of Trayvon Martin, Michael Brown Jr., Freddie Gray, Sarah Bland, or Tamir Rice, nor bring justice to the dead. Even in Ferguson, criticism was directed once again toward black elites. However, this time criticism was directed toward the activists and organizational leader, Reverend Al Sharpton, who faced criticism for his attempts to silence and censure grassroots activists (Taylor 2016: 159–161). Given the apparent ineffectiveness of black political elites in securing racial justice, BLM is justified in experimenting with new patterns of organizational leadership.

Baker's group-centered leadership serves as inspiration for our contemporary leader-full model. Within the larger global network, BLM chapters are for the most part decentralized and choose their own set of local actions. As Ransby outlines, "Chapters subscribe to a set of principles, but beyond that they are given a great deal of autonomy and freedom to define their priorities, their campaigns, and even their membership" (Ransby 2018: 75). Much like the M4BL platform, a guiding principle of the chapters is to demarginalize less visible members of the black community, including women, LGBTQAI+ folks, Muslims, Indigenous people, and so on. For instance, one such guiding principle is to "make space for transgender brothers and sisters to participate and lead" (Matthews and Noor 2017: 8). Moreover, in her memoir, Patrisse Khan-Cullors lists one of her guiding principles as "We believe that all people, regardless of age, show up with the capacity to lead and learn" (Khan-Cullors and bandele 2018: 203). This commitment to developing leadership throughout chapters and across differences—so that the most marginalized are empowered—makes these organization truly leader-full.

2. The leaderless position

Yet, since BLM's inception, many have criticized the movement as leader*less* and unstructured. Some of the most critical comments were leveled at the organization as its structure was first developing. Without the coherence of guiding principles, policy positions, and organizational structure, BLM was depicted as less about black liberation and more about brand management. Expressing his doubt, the late Bruce Dixon argued that "Maybe movements nowadays are really brands, to be evoked and stoked by marketers and creators when needed. But it's hard to imagine a brand transferring the power from the wealthy to the poor. It's hard to imagine a brand being accountable to its membership, even if you could be a member of a brand" (Dixon 2015: 1). For Dixon, brand membership eschews accountability because a brand is only meant to convey membership and image. As a marketing tool, #BlackLivesMatter would be impotent in enacting the change necessary for black liberation.

The organizer Douglas Williams voiced a similar concern regarding the early days of BLM. Without clear "prescriptions," necessary to fight against white supremacy and build a movement, the organization was in danger of turning from a social movement into "a vehicle for individuals to become celebrity activists, feted by major media and nonprofits across the United States" (Williams 2015: 1). Apprehensions regarding BLM's structure and "celebrity" leadership were reduced once the platform, *A Vision for Black Lives*, was released to the greater public. However, it cannot be forgotten that the policy document in question was created through the decentralized co-operation of the constitutive organizations. No one leader created or articulated this vision. Rather, it was the collective efforts of both the M4BL Policy Table, which worked for over a year, and the gathering of the Movement for Black Lives Convening in Cleveland, Ohio, that accounted for the demands around criminalization, reparations, economic justice, community control, investments, and political power (Woodly 2017: 220; Meyerson 2016: 1).

Despite such accomplishments, BLM has still been described as a leaderless movement by detractors. In violating traditional and hierarchical models of leaderships, typically present in prior iterations of black liberation movements, BLM is seen as undermining the wider struggle for black liberation. Moreover, black radicals and racists alike decry BLM as being violent. For detractors, the destruction of property during popular uprisings and the disruption of public peace is enough to deem the entire movement as violent. Even though BLM is officially a nonviolent movement (Touré 2015: 1), this did not stop petitions from circling all the way to the White House demanding BLM be officially listed as a terrorist organization. In response, Khan-Cullors wrote of her experience: "I was called a terrorist. The members of our movement are called terrorists. We–me, Alicia Garza and Opal Tometi–the three women who founded Black Lives Matter, are called terrorists" (Khan-Cullors and bandele 2018: 8). This designation was not only unfounded given the nonviolent stance of the organization but also deeply hurtful for those who raised the issue of black life mattering as an issue of survival.

Even for those who found the charge of terrorism laughable, other criticisms of a leader-full model were based on the notion of violence. If BLM was not violent per se, it was still capable of doing violence to the cause of black liberation because it was in fact leaderless and structureless. In her influential essay, "The Tyranny of Structurelessness," the feminist Jo Freeman argues that even with so-called leaderless organizations there is structure: "Contrary to what we would like to believe, there is no such thing as a structureless group. Any group of people of whatever nature that comes together for any length of time for any purpose will inevitably structure itself in some fashion" (Freeman 2013: 232). For Freeman, the distinction between being unstructured or structured is based solely on intentions. A structured group deliberately chooses its organizational configurations. Freeman further states that "The more unstructured a movement is, the less control it has over the directions in which it develops and the political actions in which it engages. This does not mean that its ideas do not spread. Given a certain amount of interest by the media and the appropriateness of social conditions, the ideas will still be diffused widely" (Freeman 2013: 243). Hence, both structured and unstructured groups are capable of diffusing ideas. However, diffusion alone does not mean that an organization has the coordinated power to implement policies or visions. The question then becomes: Is a leader-full model structured or unstructured? According to counseling psychologists Candice Hargons et al. (2017: 878–879), "The *leader-full Black Lives Matter leadership* model prioritizes multiple actors rather than a central leading figure in its movement . . . [through valuing] spontaneity, autonomy, mutuality, affect, and networks." A decentralized structure allows local chapters to independently start direct action campaigns while still taking part in larger networks when actions are needed at a national and international level. Moreover, since action at a local level is self-determining, members continue to be empowered and impactful even if national attention around BLM falters.

Yet the question of accountability, discussed earlier by Dixon, remains. If there is no one leader in charge that can be held answerable for the successes and failures of the organization, then a leader-full model seems to make no one accountable. For instance, the co-founder of BLM-Sacramento, Tanya Faison, was accused of abusive and manipulative behavior which caused three years of turmoil and membership turnover. Who is responsible for this poor leadership? According to twenty-nine current and former members, including co-founder Sonia Lewis, "Tanya has refused to accept any responsibility for her actions or behavior. Instead, she has chosen to criticize and vilify people expressing concerns or dissent and to lay blame upon individuals who left the chapter over her irresponsible and authoritarian leadership" (Sullivan and Clift 2019: 1). For a leader-full model all members are in a sense responsible for the organization. It would seem that all members are thereby implicated by poor leadership. Fortunately, this means that even co-founders are directly accountable to the members themselves. A leader-full model allows every member to be capable of directing action within independent campaigns as well as leading the direction of their chapter. There thus seem to be internal mechanisms for all leaders to be held accountable. However, BLM has also had to deal with external critiques from organizations involved in the larger M4BL.

Many Ferguson activists as well as the organization, Mass Action for Black Liberation, have claimed that the leader-full model has been used to usurp the power of local movements and plunder their resources. This charge is especially serious given that the latter organizations took part in the national convening for *A Vision for Black Lives*. With respect to the Ferguson uprising, Ransby (2018: 174) has noted:

That some St. Louis activists do not embrace the Black Lives Matter moniker, arguing that the Ferguson uprising was not organized by the founders of #BLM and that "Black Lives Matter" was not the only chant on the streets during the rebellion. There have also been critiques about the ways in which the media's focus on #BLM and its three founders has lessened the emphasis on the leaders of the street protests in Ferguson.

The dispute articulated by activists in Ferguson and St. Louis does not derive only from differences in strategies and tactics but is also fundamentally a matter concerning which organizations and individuals ought to receive credit for actions undertaken at the grassroots level. The activist Johnetta Elzie is particularly critical of BLM and its founders. For even though the BLM co-founders decentralized their roles within the organization and worked to amplify, rather than co-opt, the work being done in Ferguson, the media still described the Ferguson Uprising as part of the BLM movement (Khan-Cullors and bandele 2018: 220; Khan-Cullors 2016: 1). Elzie found this disingenuous in part because the greater St. Louis area has no official BLM chapter. Dissatisfaction with BLM was so great in 2016 that Alicia Garza and Opal Tometi had to cancel a speaking event at Webster University in St. Louis. In her official statement, Garza stated that the duo cancelled their keynote "due to threats and online attacks on our organization and us as individuals from local activists with whom we have made an effort to have meaningful dialogue" (Garza 2016, cited in Cobb 2016: 38).

For many, the leader-full model has still created recognizable "leaders" who are accredited with the larger movement. Yet has the *model* created these leaders? Or have recognizable leaders emerged *despite* the model? Freeman argues that part of the ire felt by local organizations who find themselves overshadowed by such "stars" is due in part to the press and public presuming that BLM speaks for the entire movement. For a leader-full model this is troublesome to correct since it is not the movement itself that selects its spokesperson, but rather the press. Thus, the distinctions between the BLM organization, the M4BL coalition, and the larger black liberation movement become lost to the public. This is due, in part, as Freeman (2013: 238) argues, because "The press will continue to look to 'stars' as spokeswomen as long as it has no official alternatives to go to for authoritative statements from the movement." Since the public is conditioned to look for spokespeople, a leader-full model will struggle to contend with who actually can speak for the organization or movement in its entirety. However, leader-centered models are often thought to be better equipped to handle this issue given their focus on singular individuals and centralized structures.

This issue is further highlighted in the case of the independent organization, Mass Action for Black Liberation. Originally named Black Lives Matter: Cincinnati (BLMC), the organization decided to change its name to divorce itself completely from the work being doing by the BLM Global Network. In a statement released on their website, MABL (2018: 1) stated: "BLMC has never been a chapter of that organization or a partisan of its politics because, even at the onset of us establishing our name as BLMC, we recognized that our idea of the type of movement necessary to win black liberation was at odds with that national body and its directives." Although MABL did not want to "surrender" the name "Black Lives Matter" to those they felt were at odds with the movement for black liberation, they still found a name change necessary. It must be noted that in their statement, MABL failed to mention any attribution of #BlackLivesMatter to Garza, Khan-Cullors, and Tometi. Instead, much of the disagreement was not over who gets to claim the aforementioned title, but rather who is allowed to represent and benefit from the struggle for black liberation. This organization subsequently found that the public deification of BLM had allowed the national network to capitalize off "high-end speaking engagements and donations" while nameless individuals affected locally continued to struggle. The organization (2018: 1) further argues that "BLM is a small fraction in a larger pie of the Black liberation movement, nationally. There are many organizations and individuals doing work with no affiliation to BLM and with many different names. All the powerful sacrifices of autonomous families and groupings around the country are continuously attributed to works of BLM." Due to the outsized public attention received by BLM, other organizations have found that instead of having their initiative awarded they have instead been disempowered. The leader-full model would thus seem to suffer from the violence of hypervisibility insofar as its decentralized structure allows for the easy incorporation of organizations, even those nonaffiliated with BLM.

3. Violence and well-being for the violated

As seen in the last section, the leader-full model of organization has not been able to eliminate violence completely from its practices. Fortunately, outside of being chapter based and member led, BLM has also coupled decentralized leadership with a notion of well-being heavily influenced by black feminism. This is especially promising because the model incorporates wellness as part of the practice of getting free. BLM is conscious of the ways that organizations can practice violence on those already violated. Thus, as an institution, BLM seeks to model a space where all black lives matter. This is particularly important given that social movements all too often do not make space for activists and participants to heal within the organization. Often those who are the most traumatized or "toxic" are removed or find themselves unwelcomed. BLM has decided instead to rehumanize those who are capable of leadership. As Khan-Cullors states: "We are envisioning and creating a new movement culture in which we care for the humanity of the people we're fighting for *and with*. Recognizing that we are working with—and many of us are, ourselves—some of the most traumatized people in the United States, the BLM network has health and wellness directors dedicated to ending toxicity in our own organizations" (Khan-Cullors and bandele 2018: 251). This dedication is laudable because it signals that in order to be leader-full one must not only empower individuals; one must also work to heal them. Khan-Cullors further argues, "We don't take emotional responses or the idea of trauma very seriously in American culture, and so part our work is to try and explain why taking trauma seriously is so important to saving humanity, and how the journey in getting to freedom is just as important as freedom. We can't be engaging in the kind of behavior that traumatizes others because we're traumatized" (Khan-Cullors 2018, cited in Nicholas 2018: 1). For BLM, black liberation can only be achieved through processes that are healing.

This sentiment has also been institutionalized in the Black Lives Matter Healing Justice Working Group, which allows BLM chapters to develop network-wide healing campaigns and interventions. Importantly, this working group is focused on linking wellness with black liberation. In a toolkit available to all chapters, as well as the public, the working group (Black Lives Matter 2017: 8) states emphatically: "State violence and systems of oppression traumatize us and our communities, and make it simultaneously impossible for us to fully heal. We have the inherent right to access healing and be free of institutions and systems that explicitly harm and undermine our capacity to live with our full humanity, connection and purpose." The question of how to rehumanize institutions that have devalued black life is an important component of the leader-full model because in order to empower one another, one must also be able to care collectively for the trauma that individuals bring to the movement. In order to be leader-full, one must "collectively enter into an embodied, restorative and transformative practice towards Black liberation" (Black Lives Matter 2017: 8).

This desire for restorative liberation is directly in line with the work of queer and black feminists on leadership and liberation. In particular, the Combahee River Collective influenced BLM's conception of a decentralized leadership that emphasizes that the "means" of achieving liberation are just as important as liberation itself. The Collective (1979: 218) argued that:

> In the practice of our politics we do not believe that the end always justifies the means. Many reactionary and destructive acts have been done in the name of achieving "correct" political goals. As feminists we do not want to mess over people in the name of politics. We believe in collective process and a nonhierarchical distribution of power within our own group and in our vision of a revolutionary society.

In contrast to those who argue that care and healing are secondary to the work of social change, the Combahee River Collective and BLM believe that liberation cannot be justified if one's practice of politics is essentially traumatizing.[3] A leader-full model thus advocates for organizing on the basis of shared responsibility and accountability for the collective well-being of a group. Such an approach can be described as "collective care." Rushdia Mehreen and David Gray-Donald (2018: 1) argue that "Collective care refers to seeing members' well-being—particularly their emotional health—as a shared responsibility of the group rather than the lone task of an individual. It means that a group commits to addressing interlocking oppressions and reasons for deteriorating well-being within the group while also combatting oppression in society at large." The reason that collective care is integral to BLM's leader-full model is because decentralization can only be horizontally accessible if it develops the capacity of every individual. Thus, just as Baker's group-centered leadership allowed for youth and women to be leaders, so, too, does BLM aim to uplift those who have been traumatized.

This model of group-centered leadership and group-centered care is particularly intriguing because it is in direct contrast with the decentralized approach held by the Afro-Martinican psychiatrist and philosopher Frantz

---

[3] For an argument that collective well-being is an "impossible burden" for social movements, see D. Camfield (2018), "We Don't Need to Be Friends to Be Comrades," *Briarpatch Magazine*, https://briarpatchmagazine.com/blog/view/we-dont-need-to-be-friends-to-be-comrades.

Fanon. With respect to leadership, Fanon maintained that leaders were often a baleful influence for political parties and the nation as a whole. In fact, Fanon held that the English word *leader* is often translated in the French as "to drive." Yet the colonized do not need a driver: "The people are no longer a herd; they do not need to be driven. If the leader drives me on, I want him to realize that at the same time I show him the way" (Fanon 1965: 184). In place of a leader-based model, Fanon argued, "The party should be decentralized in the extreme. It is the only way to bring life to regions which are dead, those regions which are not yet awakened to life" (Fanon 1965: 185). Fanon valorized the leadership qualities of the lumpenproletariat—"pimps, the hooligans, the unemployed, and the petty criminals" (Fanon 1965: 130)—and rural peasants because they least benefited from colonialism and therefore had the most revolutionary potential. However, unlike the leader-full model which eschews violence, Fanonian decentralization is inherently tied to the violence of decolonization.

During the period of African decolonization, Fanon was an active participant in the Algerian War of Independence, serving as an editor for *El Moudjahid*, the newspaper for Algerian Front de Libération Nationale (FLN), and as Ambassador to Ghana for the Provisional Algerian Government (GPRA). For Fanon, violence was central to decolonization because colonial governments maintained their power through force and would not relinquish their claim to territories without first violently suppressing calls for political independence and then, if they were not successful, violently imposing economic dependence (Fanon 1994: 88). In advocating for the end of the colonial order, Fanon held that such individuals violated colonial norms. This violation is inevitably framed as being violent even without colonized people taking up arms. Tragically, since colonial governments are wholly opposed to liberating their colonies, the colonized must use the only language that is comprehensible to their oppressors—violence. As Lewis Gordon (1995: 80) argues:

> Violence, fundamentally, is a form of taking that which has been or will not be willingly surrendered.... If the postcolonial, postracist world is to emerge, colonizers face the problem of it emerging through the resistance and eventual submission of colonizers and racists. The tragedy of the colonial and racist situation, then, is the price that has to be paid for the emergence of such a society.

The tragic price of liberating Algeria can be best seen in the chapter "Colonial War and Mental Disorders," where Fanon details the disorders produced in the decolonial struggle (Fanon 1965: 249–310). The violence needed by the colonized to liberate the country—and the violence enacted upon them by French military, torturers, and doctors—are debilitating. Even national independence cannot exorcise individuals of such violence. However, Fanon still maintains that to be liberated, the colonized must be compromised. Fanon (1965: 199) argues:

> No one can get out of the situation scot free. Everyone will be butchered or tortured; and in the framework of the independent nation everyone will go hungry and everyone will suffer in the slump. The collective struggle presupposes collective responsibility at the base and collegiate responsibility at the top. Yes; everybody will have to be compromised in the fight for the common good. No one has clean hands; there are no innocents and no onlookers. We all have dirty hands.

For colonial Algeria, violence was the "means" for liberation. Even with respect to healing, Fanon accepted violence because it was capable of directly transforming social structures. Moreover, given that racism and colonialism, under a Fanonian framework, cause the development of mental disorders, treatment had to be directed externally to the dysfunctional environment. As Fanon argues, "my objective, once [the patient's] motivations have been brought into consciousness, will be to put him in a position to choose action (or passivity) with respect to the real source of the conflict—that is, toward the social structures" (Fanon 1986: 75). Once liberated from oppressive social structures, Fanon argued that wellness and freedom could then be achievable.

Yet, for a leader-full model, the question of "dirty hands" remains opaque. According to tenets of "community care," the well-being of participants and members must be part of the process of gaining liberation. Given that individuals are already compromised and traumatized by anti-black racism and police brutality, the leader-full model aims instead for a restorative and healing liberation. In framing wellness as part of the means of gaining liberation, I believe that BLM takes a positive step in fulfilling our generational mission. But, insofar as BLM has chosen nonviolence, it remains a question whether their decentralized model of leadership will be as effective as armed struggle, even as it is, perhaps, more humanizing.

By way of conclusion, BLM's leader-full model serves as a powerful castigation against the failed leadership of black political elites, while offering an alternative model of leadership that is decentralized, group-centered, and nonviolent. Although detractors have denounced the model as being "leaderless," there is a clear structure throughout the global network, which is outlined both in its strategies and goals for black liberation. The success of BLM has unfortunately led to acrimonious relationships with activists and organizations within Ferguson and Cincinnati due to the perceived hypervisibility and stature of certain BLM-affiliated individuals within the public media. This has led to accusations that BLM has unfairly capitalized off of the struggles of local activists, leaving many feeling disempowered and bitter. However, the leader-full model has also centered healing in its decentralized structure. This focus is innovative insofar as it demands that the process to achieve liberation is one in which all members can lead and all participants can develop the collective capacity be both free and well.

References

Baker, Ella (1960). "Bigger Than a Hamburger." *The Southern Patriot* 18 (5): 4.

Baker, Ella (1974). "Oral History Interview with Ella Baker." *Southern Oral History Program Collection* (G-0007): 1–100. https://docsouth.unc.edu/sohp/G-0007/menu.html.

Camfield, David (2018). "We Don't Need to Be Friends to Be Comrades." *Briarpatch Magazine*. https://briarpatchmagazine.com/blog/view/we-dont-need-to-be-friends-to-be-comrades.

Cazenave, Noël (2018). *Killing African-Americans*. New York: Routledge.

Cobb, Jelani (2016). "The Matter of Black Lives." *The New Yorker* 14: 33–40.

Combahee River Collective (1979). "A Black Feminist Statement." *Women's Studies Quarterly* 42 (3–4): 271–280.

Dixon, Bruce (2018). "Where's the #BlackLivesMatter Critique of the Black Misleadership Class, or Obama or Hillary?" *Black Agenda Report* 1.

Du Bois, W. E. B. (1903). "The Talented Tenth." *The Negro Problem: A Series of Articles by Representative Negroes of To-day*. Ed. Booker T. Washington. New York: James Pott & Company: 31–76.

Du Bois, W. E. B. (1940). *Dusk of Dawn: An Essay Toward and Autobiography of a Race Concept*. San Diego, CA: Harcourt Brace.

Dussel, Enrique (2008). *Twenty Theses on Politics*. Durham, NC: Duke University Press.

Edelman, Murray (1967). *The Symbolic Uses of Politics*. Champaign: University of Illinois Press.

Fanon, Frantz (1965). *The Wretched of the Earth*. New York: Grove Press.

Fanon, Frantz (1986). *Black Skin, White Masks*. New York: Grove Press.

Fanon, Frantz (1994). *Toward the African Revolution*. New York: Grove Press.

Freeman, Jo (2013). "The Tyranny of Structurelessness." *Women's Studies Quarterly* 41 (3–4): 231–246.

Garza, Alicia (2014). "A Herstory of the #BlackLivesMatter Movement." *The Feminist Wire*. https://thefeministwire.com/2014/10/blacklivesmatter-2/.

Gordon, Lewis (1995). *Fanon and the Crisis of European Man*. New York: Routledge.

Gordon, Lewis (2012). "Of Illicit Appearance: The L.A. Riots/Rebellion as a Portent of Things to Come." *Truthout*. https://truthout.org/articles/of-illicit-appearance-the-la-riots-rebellion-as-a-portent-of-things-to-come/.

Gordon, Lewis, Annie Menzel, George Shulman, and Jasmine Syedullah (2018). "Afro Pessimism." *Contemporary Political Theory* 17 (1): 105–137.

Hargons, Candice, Della Mosley, Jameca Falconer, Reuben Faloughi, Anneliese Singh, Danelle Stevens-Watkins, and Kevin Cokley (2017). "Black Lives Matter: A Call to Action for Counseling Psychology Leaders." *The Counseling Psychologist* 45 (6): 873–901.

James, C. L. R. (1992). *Every Cook Can Govern: A Study of Democracy in Ancient Greece and Its Meaning for Today*. Detroit, MI: Bewick Editions.

Karenga, Maulana (2015). "The Crisis of Black Middle Class Leadership: A Critical Analysis." *The Black Scholar* 13 (6): 16–32.

Khan-Cullors, Patricia (2016). "We Didn't Start a Movement. We Started a Network." *Medium*. https://medium.com/@patrissemariecullorsbrignac/we-didn-t-start-a-movement-we-started-a-network-90f9b5717668.

Khan-Cullors, Patricia, and asha bandele (2018). *When They Call You a Terrorist: A Black Lives Matter Memoir*. New York: St. Martin's Press.

Mass Action for Black Liberation (2018). *Why Black Lives Matter: Cincinnati Is Changing Its Name*. http://blacklivescincy.com/home/2018/03/28/why-black-lives-matter-cincinnati-is-changing-its-name/.

Matthews, Shanelle, and Miski Noor (2017). "Celebrating Four Years of Organizing to Protect Black Lives." Black Lives Matter. https://blacklivesmatter.com/resources/.

Mehreen, Rushdia, and David Gray-Donald (2018). "Be Careful with Each Other." *Briarpatch Magazine*. https://briarpatchmagazine.com/articles/view/be-careful-with-each-other.

Meyerson, Collier (2016). "Black Lives Matter Did Something Huge Today." *Splinter*. https://splinternews.com/black-lives-matter-did-something-huge-today-1793860729.

The Movement for Black Lives (2016). "A Vision for Black Lives: Policy Demands for Black Power, Freedom, and Justice." https://web.archive.org/web/20170204030146/https:/policy.m4bl.org/.

Nicholas, Elizabeth (2018). "Black Lives Matter Cofounder Patrisse Khan-Cullors Is Only Getting Started." *Vice*. https://www.vice.com/en_us/article/mbpm9y/black-lives-matter-cofounder-patrisse-khan-cullors-is-only-getting-started.

Philip, M. NourbeSe (2011). *Zong!* Middletown, CT: Wesleyan University Press.

Ransby, Barbara (2018). *Making All Black Lives Matter: Reimagining Freedom in the Twenty-First Century*. Oakland: University of California Press.

Taylor, Keeanga-Yamahtta (2015). "In Baltimore and across the Country, Black Faces in High Places Haven't Helped Average Black People." *Working in These Times*. inthesetimes.com/article/17888/baltimore_riots_black_politicians.

Taylor, Keeanga-Yamahtta (2016). *From #BlackLivesMatter to Black Liberation*. Chicago: Haymarket Books.

Williams, Douglas (2015). "Black Lives Matter and the Failure to Build a Movement." *Common Dreams*. https://www.commondreams.org/views/2015/08/10/black-lives-matter-and-failure-build-movement.

Woodly, Deva (2017). "Black Lives Matter: The Politics of Race and Movement in the 21st Century." *Black Lives Have Always Mattered: A Collection of Essays, Poems, and Personal Narratives*. Ed. Abiodun Oyewole. New York: 2Leaf Press: 213–223.

Woodson, Carter G. (2017). *The Mis-Education of the Negro*. Suwanee, GA: 12th Media Services.

Young, Iris Marion (2011). *Justice and the Politics of Difference*. Princeton, NJ: Princeton University Press.

12
Speaking for, Speaking with, and Shutting up

Models of Solidarity and the Pragmatics of Truth Telling

Mark Norris Lance

When we make a claim—any claim—we do many things. Much philosophical discussion, as well as much of the focus of political attention, is devoted to the content—to what is said, to how things are represented as being—but there is more to claiming than this. In order to function as a communicative act to a particular audience, from a particular speaker, a claim must function in a multiplicity of ways. This paper first identifies a range of such "pragmatic functions" that always accompany an act of asserting. It then notes how these pragmatic functions have substantive epistemological and political implications, implications that can both create and support systematic dimensions of oppression. As academics seeking to engage and work in solidarity with the Movement for Black Lives (M4BL), these are crucial matters because whatever it is that we *say about* the M4BL, we can do real harm if we do not attend to who is speaking, to whom, with what language, and in what institutional context.

I offer a broad outline of three distinct models of solidarity engagement—that is, research, activism, organizing, material support, or other social engagement that aims for solidarity with an oppressed group that one is not a part of. Each methodological model can have advantages, and each can be the right way to engage in solidarity in a particular context, but the first two have negative pragmatic effects that must be taken into account in all situations. As a result, it is worth considering ways to employ the third model—the "shutting up" model—while maintaining some of the advantages of the first two. I conclude with a case study of a research/pedagogy/activism project—the Truth Telling Project, which grew out of organizing in response

Mark Norris Lance, *Speaking for, Speaking with, and Shutting up* In: *The Movement for Black Lives*. Edited by: Brandon Hogan, Michael Cholbi, Alex Madva, and Benjamin S. Yost, Oxford University Press. © Oxford University Press 2021.
DOI: 10.1093/oso/9780197507773.003.0013

to the murder of Mike Brown Jr. in Ferguson, Missouri—in which this mode of engagement was successfully accomplished.

In short, while much attention has been paid by philosophers of language and pundits to the difference between saying "Black lives matter!" and saying "All lives matter!" my concern is with the difference between a highly educated academic with access to desperately needed resources saying "Black lives matter!" and the same statement by one of Mike's sisters.

1. A brief scenario

By a "speech act" I mean any public communicative action that essentially involves language. So saying that this paper will appear in a book on the M4BL, asking when the book will be published, and requesting my colleagues to read it are all speech acts. Philosophers of language and linguists distinguish the pragmatic function of a speech act from its semantic content. Like all things philosophical, there is no universally agreed-upon way of drawing this distinction, much less consensus on how to understand each. But roughly, consider someone uttering each of the following:

1. The door is closed.
2. Is the door closed?
3. Close the door!

Content is what 1–3 have in common. Pragmatic function is the ways they differ.[1] In order to begin untangling some of the pragmatic functions that are relevant to the political points I want to make, let's consider a simple and politically uncharged scenario.

An expert chess player, Judit, is sitting in a crowded bar, chatting with random customers. Another expert chess player, Hikaru, notices her, comes over, and says, "Hey, that was a nice swindle you pulled off in the last round at the Gibraltar Masters!"[2]

---

[1] This is not to say that the two are completely independent or that one can, in all cases, identify a neutral content that different pragmatic types of speech acts share. Indeed, I would deny both. But this will do for the present. For one systematic way to approach pragmatic function, see Kukla and Lance (2009).

[2] Chess players will recognize that the characters in this story are based on real people: Judit Polgár, the strongest female grandmaster in history, and former top-ten player; and Hikaru Nakamura, currently one of the top five in the world. There is also a yearly tournament called The Gibraltar Masters.

What does Hikaru *do* in "saying this"? One obvious answer is that he makes a claim about the world—that Judit pulled off a nice swindle. He represents the world as being a certain way, and a great deal of philosophical discussion has focused on understanding just exactly what that is, how that dimension of his performance works. This is, however, but one dimension of the pragmatic function of this concrete social interaction between Hikaru and Judit, and not the most interesting for our purposes.[3]

First, note that Hikaru said something *to Judit*. That is, he called for Judit's attention, by recognizing her as a potential interlocutor while in the same act calling on her to recognize him discursively in his role as speaker.[4]

Second, by making this comment in this way—as opposed to "Hey, was that a swindle? Could you explain why it was good there?" or "That move you played in Gibraltar seemed like a swindle to me. I really thought it was cool, but don't understand at your level"—he presents himself as someone with expertise sufficient to warrant the presupposition of this opinion. This pragmatic function of Hikaru's speech act is not to put on the table for debate whether it was a nice swindle or to present himself as a potential student of Judit's. Rather, he states this as clear and obvious background to his effort to congratulate Judit. And doing so means that he is displaying to anyone present his assumption of the social authority needed to make such determinations of reasonableness.[5]

Third, Hikaru is recognizing a certain authority on Judit's part as well. To say that the conversational function is to presuppose that the asserted claim is uncontroversial is not to say that it is uncontroversial to everyone. He presents it as something that both he and she could see as obvious, again, as a background to the primary congratulatory function of the speech act. His hail—the first element earlier—was not merely calling on Judit as a speaker

---

All other aspects of the story are made up. I have no idea whether they are on speaking terms, for example.

[3] Throughout this paper I will be making tacit use of the framework developed in Kukla and Lance (2009). No prior knowledge of that fairly technical and systematic work is presupposed, however.
[4] This is the "vocative function" as defined in Kukla and Lance (2009).
[5] This is not to deny that Judit could appropriately demand such justification. She could say, "Oh, that really wasn't a swindle. It was a solid move. Granted Ne3 looks like a decisive reply, but it wasn't . . ." but that would clearly be to take the conversation in a way that was not anticipated in the remark, and further, it is the kind of objection that itself recognizes Hikaru as a co-equal expert on such matters. (Contrast: "Uh, who are you to be calling my moves 'swindles'?")

or a generic someone he could converse with. Rather, he interpellates[6] her as having a specific sort of social, epistemic, and linguistic competence.

Fourth, and related to this, Hikaru defines a community—a line between conversational insider and conversational outsider, both by his focus on Judit as the (sole) target of his comment, and equally with his use of technical vocabulary. Some readers have likely been annoyed at not knowing what that term "swindle" means in this context. That's actually the point. "Swindle" is a complicated notion in chess. Essentially, a swindle is a move that doesn't objectively improve your position, but invites a mistake on the part of your opponent by suggesting an "obvious" reply that in fact is bad. It is something that you do in a rather desperate situation, when you are objectively losing and need a mistake by your opponent to have a shot. A serious swindle at the club level might be simply a bad move—even an insulting move—among GMs.[7] A swindle among GMs might seem like just a good move to a club player. So precisely by speaking in a way that presupposes the obviousness of this characterization of the move, Hikaru is defining a relevant audience, a boundary of a salient category of expertise. If it isn't an obvious swindle for you, you are not invited to be a part of the conversation. Though Judit is the direct target of the speech act, another GM sitting with her could perfectly aptly respond with, say, "Yeah, that was very clever!" But a chess beginner would be intruding—not merely factually wrong, but conversationally inappropriate—to jump in with "Oh, I thought that was a winning move!" Similar insider/outsider lines are drawn by things like accent, style of speech (think of the combative argumentative style of cable news shows), assumed familiarity with abbreviations, organizations, or background facts (think of most activist meetings), many aspects of body language and tone, and so on.

Fifth, Hikaru's speech act functions to set a conversational agenda. He attempts to make it appropriate—for at least a time going forward—to talk about that move and how clever it was to employ a swindle in that context. Thus, if Judit were to turn around and reply, "This is some excellent scotch," she could only be read as challenging Hikaru's authority to set a conversational agenda, or perhaps joking.

---

[6] To interpellate someone as x is to recognize them as x in a way that plays a social role in constituting, or reconstituting them as such. By seeing you as my friend, for example—responding to you as such, greeting you as a friend, and so on—I not only acknowledge an existing social fact but help constitute it. Without a pattern of mutual uptake as friends, we simply could not be such.

[7] Grandmasters. But no one who plays serious chess ever refers to them as "grandmasters." "GM" is ubiquitous among insiders, another illustration of the current point.

It is useful to distinguish between a "*reporting* function"—where an act reports that something is the case; including reporting on a normative status—and an *invocative* function—where an act seeks to invoke or institute a new normative status. I use "invoking" as a semi-technical term here to pick out any function that contributes to bringing into existence a new normative status or social position that wasn't previously present. Thus, when the umpire says, "Play ball!" or the chair says, "I call the meeting to order," they make it the case that a new array of normative statuses (three strikes and you're out, Robert's Rules of Order) and social roles (pitcher, philosophy department representative, scheduled speaker) apply to others in the conversation. But invocations are broader than such Austinian performatives. If I make a (proper) request of you, I make it the case that you now have a reason to do the thing requested that you did not have before.[8] And there are invocative functions that are not solely up to the actions of the speaker. If I propose a new rule in the department meeting, I am attempting to invoke a new deontic status—that the rule is to be followed—but my success depends on ratification by a majority of the department.

The key point here is that the many complex invocative functions listed earlier in our little interaction between Hikaru and Judit are not external to its function as a truth claim. It is not an accident that a truth claim—any truth claim—is a claim made to someone, made by someone asserting the authority to make such a claim, made to someone who is interpellated as capable of appropriately giving uptake to the performance, made using particular vocabulary that some will understand and others will not, and which either introduces or reinforces a particular conversational topic. All that is part of what it is to make a truth claim, and it is not possible to tell anyone that the world is thus and so without performing these invocative functions at the same time.

2. Epistemic and other dimensions of normative structure

Typically, when philosophers address the normative evaluation of assertoric speech acts, they do so by asking a single narrow question: what is "the norm of assertion"? This is to ask what is the single governing norm of the form "assert that P only if N!" Further, N is assumed by most working in this literature

---

[8] For details on requests and related speech acts, see Lance and Kukla (2013).

to be a specifically epistemic norm. Thus, candidate answers include "only if one knows that P," "only if one is justified in believing that P," "only if one believes that P," and so on.[9] So, for example, a typical account might say that you can only appropriately assert, "Amadou is carrying a gun," if you are justified in believing, perhaps through perception, that Amadou is carrying a gun. While it is certainly plausible that some such condition captures one aspect of appropriate assertion, my interests are broader; and I believe yours should be as well. First, I am not concerned merely with some all-in judgment as to whether it is appropriate to perform the speech act in question, but rather with its rich and detailed normative function. This richness involves at least four distinct senses:

- It can include any domain of normativity—politeness, linguistic propriety, epistemology, morality, politics, and so on.
- Due to the variety of pragmatic functions played by a single speech act, a range of distinct normative evaluations might apply even within one broad normative dimension. Thus, a speech act might be epistemically justified in the usual sense—the speaker has adequate reasons for the claim and is in a position to competently defend it from objection—and yet function counter to other legitimate epistemic ends, say by reinforcing existing epistemic injustice in who is excluded from the conversation.[10]
- I resist the flattening of the deontic to questions of what is permissible. That two acts are both permissible, even qua assertion, does not imply that they are on a normative par. A claim can be permissible, yet rude, unhelpful, and distracting, for example.
- Finally, it is at least not easy to untangle some of the different dimensions of normative appraisal. In some cases, moral or political aspects of a speech act are relevant to its overall epistemic appraisal.[11]

---

[9] Rachel McKinnon (2015) is an exception here. She takes various pragmatic and contextual issues to influence proper assertability. I do not take anything I say here to be incompatible with her account, though my emphasis on the complex normative significance of these various invocative dimensions of pragmatics is largely orthogonal to her discussion.

[10] A number of authors have raised this general concern in different ways. See, for example, Alcoff (2010) and Fricker (2007).

[11] A number of philosophers have recently argued that nonepistemic goods are relevant to the norm of assertion, in many cases suggesting that these considerations set the contextual standard of how much evidence is enough. For the reasons listed earlier, and as will emerge in more detail later, these approaches are largely independent of my concerns.

Suppose, for example, that a white male cognitive scientist makes a claim using unnecessarily technical vocabulary at an interdisciplinary conference, directing that claim to other white male cognitive scientists, in a particular tone. A whole range of normative issues are at stake beyond the narrow question of whether he has evidence for the claim in question. Is he marginalizing psychologists, sociologists, and philosophers who have important insights on the issues at hand by use of specific terminology? Is he furthering the marginalization of women and non-white folks by choice of audience, or indeed, simply by putting himself forward as the person to say this? (Perhaps the women and non-white academics are not cognitive scientists at this conference.) Is he framing the discussion—and claiming authority as discussion-framer—by pushing this specific issue as the one that should be our topic?

Though clearly political, these ways of structuring and defining a discursive community are also epistemic. I am assuming, that is, that epistemology is—at least in some crucial regards—socially external. We justify things in research teams, by producing reproducible experiments, relying on data by socially creditable predecessors employing standard methodologies, trusting that all manner of background data has been honestly and clearly transmitted, while responding to serious objections from serious interlocutors. It is beyond the scope of the paper to defend, or even to elaborate on these points, but I take them to have been amply developed in the epistemology and philosophy of science of the last thirty years. But if these obvious forms of social embedding are essential to the production of knowledge, then any pragmatic function of a speech act that affects these is, at least in part, an epistemic function.[12]

No full epistemic evaluation of a speech act can ignore these ways of influencing and constructing epistemically relevant social conditions. And since these functions are internal to the act in question, we should not talk about the normative evaluation of the truth expressed independent of these functions.

This example brings out as well that the functions outlined in section 1 are not simply local ethical issues regarding the specific communicative interaction, but rather that they occur within the context of, and often reinforce, structural oppression and inequality. The significance of the epistemic invocative function of speech acts is political.

---

[12] I am, of course, not suggesting that these are the only senses in which epistemic status is external. These are just the ones relevant here.

In what follows, I consider cases in which the subject of our speech is an oppressed or marginalized community. Since epistemic injustice is so often a correlate of economic, racial, and other forms of oppression, our concern is with the effects of speaking about—indeed for—such marginalized communities.

3. Three models of advocacy

My central concern in this paper is with the way that academics, researchers, activists, and social service providers engage with communities that they work on behalf of, whether that work is grassroots solidarity, fundraising, political lobbying, legal advocacy, or academic analysis. It is common enough that such work is semantically problematic, by which I mean that the things said, though superficially supportive of the community in question, is politically problematic. Academics might downplay structural issues. Nongovernmental organizations (NGOs) might take the central focus away from the goals of local communities. Activists might make use of struggles for their own ends. Real as these challenges are (INCITE Collective 2017), they are not my concern here. I will assume that the speaker—let's say an academic—has optimal intentions to produce research of value to the community she studies, listens fully, follows the agenda of the community, produces well-grounded research, says nothing false, includes the important truths, and makes use of her research to the benefit of the oppressed community. Even in this case, there remain political issues involved in the production of the research. Simply by being the one to make the claims, by producing them in academic journals, by using academic language, and by speaking to other academics, we reinforce patterns of epistemic silencing and marginalization.

For the last five years, I have been involved in something called "The Truth Telling Project" (thetruthtellingproject.org). This project was started by two activist-educators from Ferguson, Missouri—Cori Bush and David Ragland—as a small education/mobilization contribution to the popular uprising around the murder of Mike Brown Jr. and the broader movement for black lives.[13] The idea of the project is to provide a forum

---

[13] It is worth emphasizing, since so many academics get this wrong, that Black Lives Matter (BLM) is a specific organization, with a national board, chapters, and so on. It is one part of the broader M4BL, but by no means equivalent to it. In particular, resistance in Ferguson has been led by

for people directly affected by police violence in black communities to tell their story—to explain the effects of this violence on their lives and on their resistance—without interference, mediation, or direction. These presentations typically take the form of "testimony" to a panel of community elders that is filmed, though many artistic forms of expression have been utilized as well. Starting with this testimony, the project has developed a range of educational materials—designed for various ages and social contexts—that are meant to serve as the entering wedge for community conversations around White Supremacy and the construction of grassroots efforts to challenge it. Neighborhood groups, schools, churches, unions, and so on can take this material and find guidance toward concrete political action, under the leadership of, and directed by the voices of those directly affected by the social injustice they aim to confront.

Why is it important to center our discussions and our political strategizing around these voices—the voices of the brothers, sisters, parents, and lovers of those who have died? The answer, I suggest, is that the fundamental issue is not a technical one of reducing the use of force by police, but one of systematic marginalization. The Ferguson community is oppressed by racism, economic exploitation, political marginalization, and epistemic dismissal. Typical discussions of the problem—led by academic experts, talking to academic and political experts, using vocabulary, speech patterns, and accents of academic elites, held in privileged locations, published in venues with limited availability, that call in those experts and exclude others—reinforce this marginalization, first in the epistemic dimension, but rippling out into political, social, economic, and other dimensions.

Crucially, this is true regardless of what is said. My point is not that outsiders know less, or are less able to articulate important truths, or have an agenda different from that of local residents. Often enough, all of that is true, of course. But my point is that *even if it isn't*, even if researchers fully understand the claims and issues at stake in what is said, have only the interests of the community at heart, make proposals that genuinely benefit occupied communities, and contribute to the realization of those proposals, the mere fact of who is speaking, in what language, and to whom has effects that can reinforce structural

---

Ferguson Frontline, a local outgrowth of community organizing and protest which is not connected to BLM nor supported by it. One dimension of showing respect to the subjects of our study is to get details like this—details that matter very deeply to the people of Ferguson—correct.

epistemic violence. (Compare with http://www.npr.org/sections/codeswitch/2015/01/29/382437460/challenging-the-whiteness-of-public-radio.)

Supposing that one is concerned to produce speech in service of an oppressed community, there are three broad models for how to do so, models I dub "speaking for," "speaking with," and "shutting up." I am not endorsing one or the other of these universally. There are clear all-in advantages, in relevant contexts, to each. But I do want to make the case that the first two always have negative invocative effects, even when they are all-in the best way to go, and that the latter is often the best option. As a result, epistemically privileged academics (politicians, journalists, social workers, funders, NGOs, activists, etc.) need to consider this option far more seriously, far more often than we do.

Speaking for: A lawyer sues an abusive absentee landlord on behalf of low-income tenants. A UN investigator brings a case before the International Court of Justice. A concerned celebrity makes a pitch for material aid for a desperate population. A foundation supports funding to treat tropical diseases. A philosopher writes a probing analysis of the psychological effects of solitary confinement. In myriad ways, people with higher status speak for those who are oppressed. And often, this speaking for is both effective and crucial. Improvements in living conditions might be mandated, war crimes halted, or millions of dollars in desperately needed aid directed to a tragedy. But each of these mechanisms also tends to reinforce many if not all of the dimensions of linguistic, political, and epistemic disempowerment highlighted earlier. When educated first-world lawyers speak to first-world judges in legalese, they reinforce existing social hierarchies. And if successful, they are very likely to reinforce a central life lesson of those they are supporting: that they need a hero to rescue them from the immediate challenges of life, that they are incapable even of understanding the details of their own oppression. Of course, this might be a morally justified trade-off, if the immediate threat is great enough and other approaches distant enough, but trade-off it quite clearly is.

A second model is *Speaking with*. Again, there are many examples. Throughout the 1990s, I was frequently asked to speak on behalf of gay rights and Palestinian liberation—by LGBTQ leaders and Palestinians. The thought was that I, as a white, middle-class, apparently straight, PhD with a great deal of public speaking experience, would have a level of credibility and would be heard in a way that someone in the group in question would not be, thereby maximizing the chance of convincing a hostile audience. (No doubt there was some truth in that view.) Early on I took to insisting, as a condition of accepting such speaking engagements, that I bring along someone from the group in question and that we speak together. I would speak with the oppressed, but not for them.[14] Often this involved running trainings in activist organizations so as to help people achieve the skills and confidence necessary to play this role—to be comfortable in front of large and possibly hostile audiences, to become familiar with a wide range of facts presentable in a form conducive to lectures and classes, to become fluent in the peculiar genre of the press interview, and so on. So unlike the case of speaking for, this strategy built capacity at the same time that it worked for immediate ends.

Here the pragmatic invocative functions are more complex than in the case of speaking for. For one, whatever social authority I had was partly transferred or shared by the act of sharing a stage. By having someone as co-presenter, they were directly interpellated as a worthy figure in the conversation, as someone deserving of engagement, as someone capable of entering into the debate in a salient and important manner. But at the same time, given the background differences of power and social position that are the whole point here, it is frustratingly difficult for such dynamics to be symmetrical. I once gave a talk with a friend—a Palestinian woman who had, up to that point, lived her entire life as a refugee, and who happens to be one of the most brilliant theorists and organizers I have met in my life, as well as someone who had finished a first graduate degree under almost unbelievably difficult circumstances and would go on to become a PhD, a published researcher, and an internationally recognized spoken-word performer, not to mention that she had lived through the events we were discussing. We gave our presentation, and my friend spoke around 70 percent of the time. Shortly after, an established figure in the Arab-American community came up to me and thanked me for speaking so eloquently and brilliantly about the situation. He then thanked me as well for bringing a Palestinian along so that I could show the world her story.

Now the fact that this person was established, older, male, and so on might suggest that these points apply only to the uptake of such performances on the part of people in positions of relative power. But while uptake is always contested and always varies across different audiences, this would be far too quick. There are many studies showing that implicit biases of various sorts

---

[14] Similar dynamics govern co-authorship, co-leadership of activist organizations and NGOs, and so on.

apply across all people.[15] It is not only men who are more likely to interpret men's words as more rational, for example.

Background social constructions of relative significance—constructions that we are all a part of and trained into in a manner that is largely unconscious—function as a filter through which the further social effects of collaborative efforts are given uptake. Our implicit biases and social habits—both those of speaker and of hearer—affect all attempts at interpellation, and it is frustratingly difficult to avoid presenting such a collaboration as a form of academic charity. The mere fact that it was I who had to insist to the organizers that I bring another speaker is evidence of existing (unjust) power and status, and the effects of this cannot easily be remedied by clever seating charts and speaker time limits.

Again, this is not to say that the trade-offs inherent in speaking with imply that it is always a bad thing all-in. In many cases, it was simply not possible to transfer these speaking opportunities to others. The relevant invitations and university funds were available only to people with establishment credentials, for example. The current social conditions were such that my standing, however undeserved, opened the door and allowed those in the marginalized position opportunities to be heard where they would not have been before. But trade-offs there are.

Which brings me to the third model: *Shutting up*. Contrast the following two speech acts. The first, I (a white professor from a major research university) will perform to you (readers who are, I assume, mostly white academics). (Despite the second half of the title of this book, the first pretty much guarantees that this is the case.) It goes like this: Michael Brown Jr., like all people, played a wide variety of roles within a complex network of social systems—familial, economic, and educational, along with various looser "street networks." His role in these many systems was marked by a wide array of social signifiers of dress, posture, tone, and so on. Uptake of these signifiers is also relative to the social context of the observer. As measured by implicit association tests, the salience of particular signifiers will differ depending on race, economic status, social role, and personal relationship with the subject. As well, the social uptake of a particular action—the police-involved shooting of a suspect after an escalating encounter—will be a function of a wide range of contextual conditions and the availability of resources, both material and human. Processes of trauma and healing as well

---

[15] See Brownstein and Saul (2016).

as developments of networks of resistance are shaped by these differential uptakes, yada yada, you get the idea.

The second is spoken with multiple voices in the form of a short documentary. In the summer of 2016, the Babble Project in conjunction with the Truth Telling Project, spent two months in Ferguson teaching local teens to use cameras, to direct, to edit, and so on. Then a group of Mike Jr.'s sisters and friends produced this short film (https://vimeo.com/178857519). (Please watch this ten-minute video. It is part of the paper. For reasons that should, by now, be obvious, summarizing it will not suffice.)

These youth give us eloquent expressions of deeply important truths about Mike Jr., of the nature of his life as seen through his relationships to those closest to him. They tell us the story of the rippling social effects of his death. They tell us of the transformation of a community into one of resistance. Anyone who wants to address the oppression of the Ferguson community needs to *hear* this—not merely in the sense of knowing that the various propositions expressed are true, but in this sense of hearing their truth, from them. To build resistance on this foundation is to build a different sort of countercommunity, one that challenges epistemic marginalization in the process of building political resistance. That is, the fact that *these girls* tell us those things, that *they* are the ones defining and presenting the narrative— again, even if someone else could assert exactly the same propositional contents with exactly the same rational grounds and with exactly the same political motives—itself plays a crucial invocative role in breaking down deeply entrenched patterns of epistemic exclusion, and thereby building the capacity for further resistance.[16,17]

The very act of asserting these truths—and audiences giving uptake to these girls as the assertors of them—positions them as the ones who we should further engage with on the issue. In this film, we see *only* the faces of young black women. The *entire* discourse is shaped by them. They set the vocabulary in terms they are comfortable with; they define the relevant topic, salient issues, and political agenda; their lives are constituted as capable of

---

[16] It is by no means clear that we should concede here that the same propositions are, or could be, asserted by the different speakers. I will not address these issues in this paper. The question of how context-independent any coherent notion of content can be is a complicated one. In what follows, I simply grant that we can, and that we can have the same evidence for the truth of the proposition. If this is all impossible, then my conclusions are strengthened.

[17] The empowering function of the process of truth telling was reported by virtually all those we handed a mic to in exit interviews and often in the testimonies themselves. Cf. thetruthtellingproject.org.

public expression, knowledge production, and participation in epistemic practices. All of these are epistemological virtues of the speech acts in question. Our collective practices of pursuing truth are, thus, improved by giving voice to these speakers rather than leaders of national NGOs—for example.

I hope it is clear that when I speak starkly of a methodology of "shutting up," I do not mean to suggest that one do nothing, simply step away from the issue and let others handle it. First, the whole goal here is to articulate models of solidarity and that implies active engagement. Second, the response to differential social power by the relatively empowered should be to use one's power in the way most useful to positive social transformation. And obviously privilege—educational, institutional, economic, and so on—is being mobilized in all sorts of ways in this example. Our collective made it possible for these voices to come to audiences around the country, made it possible for this film to be produced, and so on. But the product—that which others can watch to learn about the situation and to begin discussions on what to do—does not involve speech acts by academics or professional filmmakers. The issues of Ferguson are presented to the public and addressed by residents of Ferguson. And that is a difference that makes a difference.

The national conversation around White Supremacy needs to occur in white spaces. To aid that conversation, the Truth Telling Project built a learning platform that can be found here: www.itstimetolisten.com Take a moment to listen to the testimony of Gage Hendrix speaking about watching his mother be tortured by police. Listen to Brandon Anderson speak about how he went to his commanding officer to ask for a leave to see his life partner, dying from a police shooting as a result of misidentification and profiling, only to be told that he would be dishonorably discharged for having revealed his sexual identity. Not only the emotional but the pragmatic effects of these testimonies are not replicable by anything I can say to you. Yes, I contributed to bringing these testimonies into articulable form, but I am not a part of the pragmatics of the testifying.

After each recorded testimony—a testimony delivered by a black person, to a panel of black elders—is a range of guided questions, exercises, and supplementary materials. Anyone can make use of this material. The Truth Telling Project can send facilitators to train people in running community, living room, church, or school dialogues on these issues, but the facilitator is not the voice articulating the issue. Their role is purely to ask questions, to direct people to resources, and to facilitate conversation and organizing. The conversation is centered on the testimony of affected persons.

In this way, to the extent possible (and it is never entire, of course), we, the relatively privileged organizers and educators, *shut up*. We contributed an enormous amount to this project. We organized the meetings, provided counselors on-site, had the connections to bring prominent members of the community as well as international press, raised funds for travel, understood how to develop pedagogical materials, had the background skills to teach film-making, knew how to design websites, and had access to financial resources to make it all possible. But for all that, the resulting educational process does not center us or reinforce our position. One can, for example, work through the entire online learning platform without knowing that I exist. This, I think, is a good thing. Not the only good thing, and one that can be outweighed by others, but nonetheless an important and good thing.

It remains to be seen both how effective this small project will be, and whether a similar model will be possible in other contexts. (Quite a few groups are currently building similar truth-telling processes.) No doubt shutting up should never be the only methodology of solidarity research. As I have emphasized throughout, there are contexts in which speaking for or speaking with brings advantages that cannot be achieved in any other way. Similarly, there is no hard and clear line between any of these methodologies. There are lots of ways that we step back from our discursive involvement in a particular presentation. A longer study would contrast multiple such projects and the ways that outsiders were and were not involved. But I do believe that this project is a kind of proof of concept, and one that creative researchers/teachers/activists concerned about breaking down epistemic injustice can find ways to replicate, modify, and improve upon.

4. Concluding self-critical postscript

Essentially this has been a paper by an academic, a socially recognized expert, explaining why academic experts should often shut up, or take their voices behind the scenes. And while there is a certain pragmatic contradiction in this performance, it is one case in which I think that is justified. My goal is to convince those who study language that complex political structures are central to the norms of language no matter how narrowly we try to define those norms, and to convince socially recognized experts—academics, NGO leaders, activists, social workers, and so on—that when we advocate for oppressed groups or study them with an eye to illuminating their conditions, we should have a defeasible goal of decentering ourselves.

Since at the moment, debates on academic methodology do not treat most people as significant participants or epistemically authoritative, someone like myself has a better chance of being taken seriously in making this argument. (My comrade Pali who runs the Babble project, or Dave and Cori who started the Truth Telling Project, could have articulated all these points, but even they would be far less likely to be invited to an academic conference, or accepted for publication in an academic collection, to say nothing of, for example, a typical resident of Ferguson.)

But that doesn't change the fact that a function of me writing all this—alongside whatever effect I've achieved in forcing us to attend to these dimensions of discursive injustice—serves also to reinforce my own expertise, to reinforce the boundaries of the colloquium and professional article, to further endorse the salience of a specialized and technical mode of speech. None of that is a wholly bad thing. My claim is not that philosophy articles should be banned after the revolution, nor is the point as simple as "educated white people need to shut up on all political matters." (Indeed, I think the latter would be utterly terrible advice.) But the role of and participation in publications and colloquia, not to mention the role and power of formally educated white people, in a revolutionary—indeed, in a minimally just—society would be very different from what it is in this one, shot through as it is with class exploitation, White Supremacy, sexism, and so on.

We need to keep that in mind, take it seriously, and, at the very least, not produce accounts of language, truth telling, and the norms of assertion that serve the propagandistic function of obscuring it.[18]

References

Alcoff, Linda (2010). "Epistemic Identities." *Episteme* 7: 128–137.
Brownstein, Michael, and Jennifer Saul, eds. (2016). *Implicit Bias and Philosophy, Volumes I and II*. Oxford: Oxford University Press.
Fricker, Amanda (2007). *Epistemic Injustice: Power and the Ethics of Knowing*. Oxford: Oxford University Press.

---

[18] I want to thank Todd May, Michael Cholbi, and especially Alex Madva for helpful conversations on an earlier draft. I'd also like to thank Ruth Groff and Olúfẹ́mi O. Táíwò for comments on an early version of this paper at a workshop organized by Ruth at St. Louis University.

INCITE collective (2017). *The Revolution Will Not Be Funded: Beyond the Nonprofit Industrial Complex.* 2nd ed. Durham, NC: Duke University Press.

Kukla, Rebecca, and Mark Lance (2009). *"Yo!" and "Lo!": The Pragmatic Topography of the Space of Reasons.* Cambridge, MA: Harvard University Press.

Lance, Mark, and Rebecca Kukla (2013). "Leave the Gun, Take the Cannoli: The Pragmatic Topography of Second Personal Calls." *Ethics* 123 (3): 456–478.

McKinnon, Rachel (2015). *The Norms of Assertion: Truth, Lies, and Warrant.* New York: Palgrave.

13
Sky's the Limit

A Case Study in Envisioning Real Anti-Racist Utopias[*]

Keyvan Shafiei

> *A map of the world that does not include Utopia is not worth even glancing at, for it leaves out the one country at which Humanity is always landing. And when Humanity lands there, it looks out, and, seeing a better country, sets sail. Progress is the realization of Utopias.*
> —Oscar Wilde, "The Soul of Man under Socialism" (1891)

August 2016 marked the two-year anniversary of the police shooting of Michael Brown Jr., when the dead body of Brown, an eighteen-year-old Black teenager, was left for hours in the middle of a Ferguson street, unattended in the smoldering heat of mid-summer. But August 2016 also marked the occurrence of another significant event. Shortly after the Republican and Democratic conventions, a collective of more than fifty organizations had united to form a cross-coalitionary movement against the systemic persecution and brutalization of Black Americans. This broad coalition of organizers and organizations, known as the Movement for Black Lives (M4BL), would soon put forth a detailed platform articulating their vision for wholesale social, economic, and legal changes to the status quo—demilitarization of law enforcement, economic divestment from military expenditure, investment in free education and universal healthcare, cultural and material reparations, prison abolition, universal and automatic voter registration, and the full

---

[*] An earlier paper version of this chapter was presented at the 2019 American Philosophical Association's Pacific Division meeting in Vancouver. I thank the audiences at this event for their willingness to engage with the ideas discussed in this chapter and for their helpful feedback. And I owe special thanks to Benjamin Yost, Alex Madva, and Michael Barnes on the helpful comments that they have provided on various earlier iterations of this work.

Keyvan Shafiei, *Sky's the Limit* In: *The Movement for Black Lives.* Edited by: Brandon Hogan, Michael Cholbi, Alex Madva, and Benjamin S. Yost, Oxford University Press. © Oxford University Press 2021.
DOI: 10.1093/oso/9780197507773.003.0014

restoration of the Glass-Steagall Act (which separated commercial and investment banking activities), among other similarly ambitious demands.

In the years since, however, and especially in the aftermath of Trump's election, the viability of this platform has been submitted to extensive debate. Liberal and conservative commentators alike have criticized the platform as unrealistic and utopian. Some writers, like David French, have gone as far as calling the demands of the platform "anti-American and fundamentally Marxist" (2016). Setting these histrionics aside, the substance of such criticism merits philosophical analysis. As I interpret them, debates about the feasibility of M4BL's platform largely revolve around worries about whether political utopias should inform liberatory agendas.[1]

In this chapter, I defend the claim that utopias can, and *should*, inform our attempts to craft and effectuate successful programs of radical emancipatory change. In particular, I argue that social and political organizing, even in response to seemingly intractable issues like systemic racial injustice, has to ultimately be grounded in *real* (or *realistic*) *utopian* visions. I borrow this concept from Erik Olin Wright, in whose view "real utopias" represent "ideals grounded in the real potentials of humanity [. . .] that can inform our practical tasks of navigating a world of imperfect conditions for social change" (2010: 6).[2] Thus construed, real utopias highlight the human potential for radical change and force us to recognize that the boundaries of what is possible are structurally contestable. The analysis that I offer conjoins Wright's account with Elizabeth Anderson's recent discussion of social movements as experiments in morality. According to Anderson (2014), social movements extend moral critique beyond the domain of mere theory by offering unique experiments in living morally.

Along these lines, I argue that M4BL offers a valuable case study in how large-scale moral experiments might be carried out, especially in contexts of historical and systemic oppression. In such contexts, we must conduct our experiments by starting from informed hypotheses about how pervasive forms of injustice can be resisted, and how we can build institutions that would eliminate oppression. Employing the concept of "realistic utopias" to answer questions of *how* (i.e., through what means) we might organize for radical changes, and *what* (i.e., toward what ends) those changes might

---

[1] I use the terms "liberatory" and "emancipatory" interchangeably in this chapter.
[2] Political philosophers might also be familiar with the idea of "realistic utopias" from the work of John Rawls, especially *The Law of Peoples*. My use of the concept is not antithetical to the Rawlsian conception. Readers should feel free to draw parallels as necessary.

aim to materialize, I defend a refined conception of "utopia" as integral to movements of social change.

1. No time for gradualism

The contrast between "gradualist" or "pragmatic" perspectives on social change, on the one hand, and "radical" or "utopian" perspectives, on the other, appears in many contexts. Sometimes, this contrast is invoked in legislative debates, such as the ongoing debates surrounding passage of environmental protection policies and healthcare reforms. Sometimes, the contrast appears in historical and contemporary discussions about the pace of change, and the proper means for righting historical wrongs, such as redressing the injustices of racial oppression and the legacies thereof. And other times, the contrast appears in the spaces of movement and coalition building, like questions about what alliances will best advance the liberation of all women, and not merely the interests of privileged few. In this paper, I will not limit myself to any *one* contrast between gradualism and utopianism. Rather, I'll consider both means and ends. What role, if any, should reflection and invocation of utopian possibilities play in radical progressive activism? I define "radical activism" as social and political organizing that seeks to fundamentally disrupt and uproot the status quo. This chapter focuses on forms of activism with specifically emancipatory ambitions, and on the work of those organizers that seek to radically curtail and eliminate the influence of oppressive structures and institutions, but whose visions are often demeaned and dismissed as utopian.[3]

Consider the following example. On February 22, 2019, a group of children and young climate activists, participating in a coordinated action organized by the Sunrise Movement, took a trip to the Bay Area offices of long-term California Senator Dianne Feinstein. The demands of the Sunrise activists were straightforward; they insisted that lawmakers take bold measures in response to the heightening threat of climate change. More specifically, the group appealed to Feinstein to endorse the Green New Deal Resolution, an ambitious stimulus proposal to address environmental and economic

---

[3] See Iris Marion Young (1990) for a discussion of the multifaceted phenomenon of "oppression," and for a discussion of some possibilities for resistance to oppression and interconnected accountability, see Young (1990) and (2006).

inequality, introduced just a few weeks prior by Representative Alexandria Ocasio-Cortez and Senator Ed Markey.

The interaction soon took an awkward turn, when Feinstein admonished the Sunrise activists, ranging nine to twenty-four years old, about the impracticality of their demands and the complexities of lawmaking in Congress. In a viral video, Feinstein is seen explaining that she would never endorse the Green New Deal, because it represents a radical proposal that would fail to garner bipartisan congressional support. In fact, Feinstein condescendingly informed the Sunrise children that she knew what she was doing; that she represented the people who voted for her, unlike the young activists who could not even vote; and that if the group was so keen to witness bold changes, they should run for office in her place. In the meantime, Feinstein remarked, she would introduce a more moderate and responsible piece of legislation, which she amusingly calls "[her] own Green New Deal."[4]

This is one example, among many, of the ways in which activists are often pilloried by public figures for asking for too much, for demanding the inexpedient, and for lacking a "realistic" and "feasible" appreciation for the workings of the law and political change making. In fact, this kind of dismissive antagonism, on the part of those that operate the levers of institutional power, punctuates many important junctures in the history of the American struggle for social and political justice. In the decades leading up to the passage of the Nineteenth Amendment, for example, the leaders of the suffrage movement persistently refused to adopt an explicitly anti-racist stance for "the sake of expediency," as Susan B. Anthony once put it in private correspondence with Ida B. Wells-Barnett (Duster 1970: 249). Along similar lines, the American Civil Rights era was defined in many ways by disputes between self-acclaimed realists, on the one hand, and activists involved in the various movements for civil rights, on the other. As early as 1954 and during the Montgomery Bus Boycotts, insistence on patience and gradualist reforms had become the go-to of many (predominantly white) liberals in their refusal to support the urgent demands of Black Americans.[5]

---

[4] See Lois Beckett's reporting on this in *The Guardian*, which includes the three-or-so minute video recording of the interaction between Feinstein and the children of Sunrise. From February 23, 2019. https://www.theguardian.com/us-news/2019/feb/22/dianne-feinstein-sunrise-movement-green-new-deal.

[5] In fact, this was so commonplace that Dr. Martin Luther King Jr., among other notable figures of this era, would frequently and colorfully disparage the refusal of so-called realists and white moderates to engage with the realities of a racially unjust America, famously exclaiming that such complacency troubled him more than the violent antipathy of the Klansmen. King's

These examples are noteworthy because, in different ways and in different contexts, they allude to the same problem: progressive organizers and lawmakers are too often regarded, in the eyes of the institutionally abled and powerful, as failing to engage with the practical and as peddling unrealizable utopian visions. American political discourse remains saturated with denunciations of utopianism, where politicians and commentators routinely belittle the vision and work of progressive lawmakers and organizers.

But why, we might ask? The answer to this question, in my view, will help make sense of the general mechanics of social organizing and activism. But even more specifically, a discussion of these issues will elucidate the political and normative underpinnings of the Movement for Black Lives, whose vision, as outlined in their platform, proposes a roadmap toward justice for both "dreamers and doers" (2020).

2. Are utopias real? Could they be?

Utopia derives etymologically from "nowhere" or "no place," from the Greek *ou* "not" and *topos* "place." In part, this is why social and political theorists are often hostile to the idea of theorizing about justice in ways that could be perceived as utopian. Among some political philosophers, in particular, this antipathy (or "utopophobia," to use David Estlund's [2014] amusing expression) derives from a legitimate frustration with forms of theorizing that too often dissociate from the realities of everyday oppression. If our theories are produced from nowhere, and are detached from the realities of everyday and actual injustices, how can we hope to influence practical, progressive change making in the real world?

This is a methodological question about the point of political theorizing. As Laura Valentini (2012) notes, this question about the proper nature of political philosophy has given rise to what is now known as the debate on ideal and nonideal theory. Both ideal and nonideal theorists come in heterogenous shapes and forms, and debates between these two camps can assume different shapes and forms, too. But one point of entry into such debates concerns the issue of realism versus utopianism. Realists are those class of theorists that maintain we should develop our theories of justice in response to perceived

---

condemnation of white moderates is emphatically clear, among other places, in his "Letter from a Birmingham Jail" (1963).

facts about the world, and on the basis of what these facts tell us is feasible and achievable. Utopians, however, are often seen as eschewing such considerations, instead promoting the view that justice is a timeless value that should regulate what other values we espouse and endorse. As such, utopians maintain that justice is not merely a normative value, but rather an evaluative or regulatory one.[6]

I return to these issues in the final section of this paper. But since I shall defend utopianism here, it would seem reasonable, at least superficially speaking, to lump me in with the utopians. However, as I shall demonstrate, the kind of utopian thinking that I explore here is fundamentally realistic. To that end, I shall defend the following set of interrelated claims here: (1) utopias can be realistically defined and defended; (2) utopias should configure centrally into normative and practical deliberating about oppression and justice; and (3) these realistic visions can instrumentally guide social organizing.

Let's start with the first claim: what exactly distinguishes some vision as hopelessly utopian as opposed to, say, achievably or realistically utopian? Utopian thinking, as I interpret the notion here, refers to the desire for radically better ways of living.[7] Undoubtedly, many of us harbor this desire, but disagreements typically arise when we try to devise plans of action for actual, liberatory change. So, as we should naturally wonder: how can we be realistically utopian activists, and how can embracing utopianism realistically further our liberatory activist aims?

As I interpret activism, an activist vision is deeply grounded in considerations about what is pragmatically achievable, because activists aim to uplift and materialize the most pressing needs of oppressed persons and communities. The activist and the organizer, in this way, have to be keenly attuned to the realities of what is socially urgent and politically needed. But insofar as they are interested in effectuating radical alterations of the status quo, activists also have to preserve the utopian desire for radically better ways of living, which defines and drives the creative and demanding work of radical liberation. In this sense, the activist has no choice but to confront the social and political urgencies of the here and now, and to seek to structurally

---

[6] See Stemplowska (2008) and Valentini (2012) for a fuller discussion of this point. I construe the issue of realism here in the ways that Stemplowska and Valentini do: as concerning the question of whether or not our normative theories and principles should be devised under deeply counterfactual assumptions.
[7] I borrow this particular conception of "utopia" from Ruth Levitas. See Levitas (2013), in particular, for a discussion of this account of utopia.

eliminate the suffering that such urgencies call attention to. In the words of Dr. King, the activist has to transform this "suffering into a creative force," and to draw on the powers contained therein to bring about radically better ways of life (1960).

Along these lines, Erik Olin Wright has introduced the notion of "real utopias," arguing "that what is pragmatically possible is not fixed independently of our imaginations," but rather is beholden to the visions of change that our imaginations can conjure up (2010: 4). In this sense, real utopias offer radical departures from the existing ways of the status quo, but they are also grounded in an understanding of what is doable and feasible in the *here* and *now*. In Wright's account, in particular, the activist has to contend with limitations on what they can aspire to accomplish. That is, the activist has to acknowledge that the road to a radically alternative future is uncertain, since the effort for radical justice is beset by various "contingent concatenations of causal processes" that lie beyond one's control (Wright 2010: 70). If we are interested in the practical work of social organizing and social transformation, we have to avoid the business of peddling false promises of "hope" and "change," especially in the way of advertising overly determinate visions of what a radically progressive future might entail.

Classical Marxist theories, for example, insist that socialism is the inevitable alternative to capitalism, because capitalist modes of production are not internally sustainable in the long run. These theorists argue that more and more intense crises will disrupt the capitalist market, resulting in endemic and unmanageable instabilities when profits decline. And such instabilities will overtime exhaust the tolerance of the working class and their willingness to put up with the status quo. And thus, socialist revolution![8]

For Wright, however, these kinds of progressive road mapping, which insist on devising meticulous blueprints for the actualization of a meticulously planned future, travel on bridges that often disappoint and lead nowhere. Instead, Wright invites us to think of the project of emancipatory social change as a "voyage of exploration" (2010: 70). This voyage has to start in the belief that radical emancipatory change (i.e., utopia) is possible. As voyagers, however, we also have to be realistic and recognize that secure arrival at our desired destinations is never guaranteed. The best we may hope for, in this

---

[8] Admittedly, this is a drastic oversimplification of Marx's theory of revolutionary social transformations. Nonetheless, as Wright argues (2010: 70), Marxist theories do often rely on predictions about crisis intensification over time, which are critical aspects of their argument that capitalism is fundamentally unsustainable.

way, are developing guiding principles that tell us, as we experiment with established and new forms of organizing and movement building, whether or not we are moving in the right direction. Drawing on Wright's account, then, we can answer the questions from earlier. We are utopian activists insofar as we are committed to radical alterations of the status quo. But we are realistic insofar as we maintain epistemic humility and openness about the prospects of achieving these desired radical changes. We recognize that our commitment to radical change points to a range of possibilities for materializing such changes. Nonetheless, we acknowledge that the vagaries of the real world cannot be determinately account for, and as such, we are willing to experiment with different means toward achieving our ends.

This is why Wright conceptualizes the project of radical liberation in accordance with a theory of "structural possibility," as opposed to a theory of "dynamic trajectory" (2010: 70). Unlike the latter, which tries to predict the future according to a deterministic understanding of the dynamics of social change, especially in capitalist contexts where the status quo appears inherently contradictory and unstable, a theory of structural possibility charts the range of possibilities for radical transformation in changing contexts of social empowerment. Theorists of structural possibility conceptualize social struggle along pathways of social empowerment and as "an experimental process in which we continually test and retest the limits of possibility and try, as best as we can, to create new institutions which expand the limits themselves" (2010: 270). Real utopias, along these lines, are visions of radical emancipatory change that centrally incorporate an understanding of structural transformation as fundamentally experimental. Let me unpack this a bit further.

At their core, proposals for radical social change represent attempts at disrupting and uprooting the status quo, and for creating institutions, in the place of extant ones, that will promote the flourishing of all people. As detailed as such proposals might be, however, or as desirable as their realization might seem, it is important to recognize that their outcomes are not certain. We cannot pretend to know in advance, as classical Marxists did, that some eventuality is unavoidable; the uncertainties of the real world are simply too fickle, and we do not have the cognitive and material resources to predict the future. For Wright, however, this is not a shortcoming of radical change making, because projects of whole-sale emancipatory change cannot emphasize outcomes and eventualities at the expense of articulating the means through which these outcomes are realized and secured. If we are *actually* interested in achieving justice, we cannot sit back and stake our hopes of emancipation on the internal contradictions of oppressive institutions. Rather, the work of emancipation demands that we get down and dirty, through action and right away, and in doing so to reckon with questions about what is actionable, possible, and achievable.

Traditionally, this has been the crux of the disagreement between gradualists and radicals. The latter want immediate and large-scale change, whereas the former insist on slow-paced reforms from within. The notion of "realistic utopias" fundamentally embraces this tension, insofar as it recommends that we neither abandon the desire for radical improvement nor deny that barriers stand in the way of fulfilling such a desire. As such, realistic utopias place philosophical and practical emphasis on the need for action orientation and moral experimentation, insofar as it is only through action that we can experiment with and contest the limits of what is possible.

3. Experiments in morality

One of the clearest and most influential recent defenses of moral experimentation is given by Elizabeth Anderson. Anderson puts forth a pragmatist conception of morality, where moral disagreements are not typically resolved on the basis of pure reflective thought alone, but on the basis of "practical action in the world" (2014: 5). For pragmatists, morality is fundamentally action oriented, insofar as the difficulties of moral decision-making are salient only from within the normative practices that we engage in.[9] As such, when we deliberate about moral issues, pragmatists claim that we have to do so with a clear understanding of the uncertainties and difficulties that define real-life moral experiences. For this reason, pragmatists argue that the point of morality is to develop constructive methods and experiments for navigating moral quandaries that arise in action, and for determining how moral theorizing can be continually improved to address new challenges. Put somewhat differently, pragmatism, as a moral orientation, will not offer us principles that "apply in all possible worlds" (Anderson 2014: 5). Rather, it emphasizes the need for devising contextually reliable methods of regulating interpersonal action, and for questioning the practical applicability of moral norms

---

[9] I am referring to practices here in the ways that Anderson does; in the very thin sense, if you will, of ordinary action and activity.

when conflicts arise. For pragmatists, in other words, the basic function of morality is to adjudicate conflicting moral claims as these arise in everyday contexts of shared living.

From this point of view, the Golden Rule and the Categorical Imperative are not higher-order moral principles that apply universally, irrespective of actual practice. Rather, they are heuristics which may or may not be useful for coordinating joint action and for navigating different sorts of moral claim making. When disagreements arise, pragmatists argue that we have to engage in joint reflection about whether these heuristics help us adjudicate conflict. This kind of reflection has to take place internally, within the context of our practices, not from some external, idealized point of view.

But perhaps pragmatists are too optimistic. After all, the world of practical and moral decision-making, to colloquially quote the kids, is messy AF! Take into consideration, for example, the sheer interconnected complexity of the various networks in which we are individually and collectively situated, and the ways in which moral disputes can implicate large numbers of persons within such networks, thus extending the scope of our interpersonal interactions beyond simple dyadic examples. To further complicate matters, also consider such disputes arising in contexts of large-scale and systemic injustices. How could we hope for action-oriented moral reflection when ongoing and entrenched injustices have skewed the scales of power in favor of the privileged and the powerful? In such circumstances, to whom do we appeal in calling for unbiased moral deliberation, as we seek to disrupt oppressively established norms and ways of life?

Recognizing such concerns, Anderson's analysis is fundamentally oriented toward the role that social movements play in enacting *collective* practices of moral contestation. In her view, social movements are the most reliable tools for large-scale moral contestation, negotiation, redress, and progress. People in powerful positions are often insulated from the claims of those over whom they wield power. Those with power and privilege "rarely have the characteristic experiences through which they would learn that what they are doing to social inferiors is wrong" (2014: 8). Moreover, the powerful often confuse their political authority with moral authority, and use the former to enforce an exacting morality on their social inferiors. When the oppressed try to challenge such forms of confused authority from below, the powerful interpret their dissent and disapproval as moral and political insurrection, and often resort to violent means to neutralize this perceived disorder.

In such cases, then, what are needed are social and moral forms of organizing that can achieve at least the following: (1) forcefully convey to the powerful the needs of the powerless; (2) articulate what is needed for change and procure opportunities for moral critique and accountability; and (3) offer the powerless the resources for establishing their own moral worth. Consider how M4BL seeks to fulfill these desiderata of successful social organizing, in the opening lines of M4BL's platform:

> In recent years we have taken to the streets, launched massive campaigns, and impacted elections, but our elected leaders have failed to address the legitimate demands of our Movement. We can no longer wait.
>
> In response to the sustained and increasingly visible violence against Black communities in the U.S. and globally, a collective of more than 50 organizations representing thousands of Black people from across the country have come together with renewed energy and purpose to articulate a common vision and agenda. We are a collective that centers and is rooted in Black communities, but we recognize we have a shared struggle with all oppressed people; collective liberation will be a product of all of our work. (M4BL 2016)

In Anderson's terms, organizers for racial justice believe that their legitimate demands have gone unattended. Patience is no longer feasible, as systemic forms of violence continue to destroy Black lives and tear Black communities apart. Thus, the urgency of the moment calls for the formation of a large-scale and coordinated movement, in the effort to impress on the powerful the need for immediate structural change. After all, structural moral progress demands practices of coordinated contestation. And movements with expansive networks of membership offer the resources for such forms of coordination, insofar as they provide the opportunity to organize around shared principles, on the basis of which oppressed persons and allies can attempt a disruption of business as usual. In sum, then, this is why social movements are fundamental to Anderson's pragmatist account of morality. Such movements offer the opportunity for disrupting the status quo, and for experimenting with suitable alternatives and engaging in collective reflection about what works morally and what doesn't.

And this is exactly where we can link up Anderson's analysis of social movements with the earlier discussion of realistic utopias. Social movements offer avenues for fulfilling the collective desire for radically better ways of life.

They do this through representing the most effectual forms of contentious politics, insofar as they offer both the imaginative and the material resources for experimenting with visions of radically different, and possibly better, worlds. As such, Anderson calls social movements "experiments in living," which are fundamental to theorizing about justice, and without which ex ante moral argumentation will always remain an unreliable tool of moral change and progress—and especially of large-scale and systemic forms of moral progress.

But if social movements, at their core, are experiments in living morally, then there is no reason why such forms of experimentation should not start from hypotheses that encapsulate visions of realistic utopias. In fact, one could say *they have to* start from this place, if the aim of such organizing is to effectuate radically better alternatives in a world that will invariably impose practical barriers on the way of doing so. Recall, a realistic utopia is the vision of radically better ways of life, brought about through means that are in equal measure practical and imaginative. An experiment, in similar ways, is a theoretically and empirically informed attempt at validating some set of propositions about what works and what doesn't. Crudely speaking, this is how scientific experiments are devised and conducted. We formulate a hypothesis, conduct an experiment, and the results either confirm or disconfirm our original conjectures. And outside of methodological and practical constraints on what we can experiment with, there are no constraints on what we can and cannot experimentally do. Technically speaking, then, the sky is (more or less) the limit when it comes to formulating a hypothesis for scientific experimentation.

Along similar lines, when it comes to experiments in living morally, we tend to start our experiments from hypotheses about what will maximize the flourishing of all persons and bring about a truly just world. Presumably that is the point of moral theorizing: to figure out how to bring about a just state of affairs, and to articulate clear, practicable, and revisable guidelines for how this can be achieved. But herein lies the possibility of a happy meeting between theory and action, which can give rise to large-scale experiments of progress and justice. Outside of postulating transformative proposals lacking in concretely graspable details—and lacking, even more importantly, in guiding principles that could lead visions of emancipatory change to their actualization—there are no constraints on what we can experiment with through politics of movement building and social contention.

In this vein, M4BL represents a valuable case study in experimenting with realistic utopias.

4. The case study of M4BL

M4BL's platform is far-reaching and extremely detailed; it is organized around six central planks of criminal justice, reparations, investment and divestment, economic justice, community control, and political power. The platform offers a detailed and rigorous defense of each of its demands. At the same time, however, the ambitiousness of the platform is controversial. In large part, this is because the platform does not offer only a litany of policy proposals, engaging merely with the political practicalities of realizing its vision. While it offers a vision of what can be achieved on the basis of extant legislation, it also calls for experiments in envisioning grand-scale anti-racist utopias. The architects of the platform make this point maximally clear in the statement of their mission. As they put it:

> We recognize that not all of our collective needs and visions can be translated into policy, but we understand that policy change is one of many tactics necessary to move us towards the world we envision. The links throughout the document provide the stepping-stones and roadmaps of how to get there. We have come together now because we believe it is time to forge a new covenant. We are dreamers and doers and this platform is meant to articulate some of our vision. (M4BL 2016)

As I see it, two core insights of this chapter's arguments can be identified in just this statement—specifically regarding the ways in which realistic utopias can structure experiments in living morally.

First, the organizers emphasize envisioning a radically different world, as manifested in both real and imaginative disruption and resistance. Each plank of the platform offers a series of detailed proposals modeled after extant pieces of legislation. These include proposals for fairly practicable measures, like retroactive forgiveness of student loans, guaranteed minimum income, universal healthcare, and paid parental leave, but also more radical demands, such as the demilitarization of law enforcement and prison abolition. In so doing, the architects of the movement are explicitly overstepping the boundaries of what we typically deem feasible. They are dreaming of grand narratives of justice, which, in the view of some members of both the public and the political establishment, represent instances of thoroughgoing utopianism. Reallocating large sums of money, for example, from policing and incarceration to free education and healthcare will strike many as highly impracticable. Just imagine how those same people would react if, on top of such demands, we also asked for the closing of American jails, prisons, and juvenile and immigration detention facilities.

Interestingly, however, proposals for constitutionally amended rights to free education and healthcare have already been introduced through ballot initiatives in some states; and they have been met with moderate to high levels of electoral enthusiasm. Even in deeply red states like Mississippi, such proposals are moderately popular among the voters. In 2015, for example, 48 percent of Mississippi's electorate voted to change the state's constitution to ensure funding for free public schools. The initiative fell short of garnering majority electoral support, but there are good reasons to believe that the same piece of legislation would today pass a threshold of majority voter support. In like fashion, on the issue of criminal justice reform, in 2018 the American Civil Liberties Union's Campaign for Smart Justice unveiled the Smart Justice 50-State Blueprints, a comprehensive and state-by-state plan for how states can fundamentally overhaul their criminal justice system and cut prison population by half. This program also benefits from far-reaching public enthusiasm.

Around the same time in 2018, voters in Suffolk County in Massachusetts elected the progressive, pro-poor, anti-incarceration Rachel Rollins as their next District Attorney. Rollins has named an external committee to review police-involved fatal shootings, instead of entrusting such forms of oversight to prosecutors, many of whom work with police officers and are often loath to indict law enforcement representatives. And as of late 2019, at least two of the leading Democratic presidential candidates have promised to retroactively cancel trillions of dollars of student debt, not to mention introduce aggressive legislation for free education and universal healthcare. Just a few years back, all of this would have been anathema in mainstream American political discourse.

What brought about this swift change in popular and political opinion? It is very plausible that expansive social organizing, continued movement building, and tireless consciousness raising all played a role. People rallied on the streets in large numbers; conversations took place that we had not listened to before; and many of us realized that the precarities of our existing ways of life called for experiments with ideas that were once deemed utopian and radical. And all of this resulted, in part, from the emphasis that M4BL and other organizations placed on these much-needed forms of social and political experimentation.[10]

And this brings me to my last point. M4BL's platform deliberately qualifies the vision as partially formed one, which only articulates "some of [the] vision." The platform is not intended as a be-all-and-end-all blueprint for the realization of radically transformative objectives. Rather, the platform is offered as an experiment in transformative politics, which draws on the available resources of the present, but also calls for strategizing about new forms of organizing and activism that move us beyond the constraints of what is presently feasible. As such, the M4BL platform attempts, as Anderson recommends, to strategize about how to engage effectively in moral experimentation through social organizing and movement building:

> We are dreamers and doers and this platform is meant to articulate some of our vision. The links throughout the document provide the stepping-stones and roadmaps of how to get there. (M4BL 2016)

The platform envisions a society that fundamentally values and refuses to denigrate Black humanity; a society that acknowledges its past wrongs and seeks to actively redress them; and a society of social, political, and legal harmony, where equality is the order of the day, not the exception. As such, we cannot repeat the same routine ways of doing things. How we achieve change, however, is not obvious. First, the proponents of the status quo will push back. Second, the world is unpredictable, and we cannot foresee all the vagaries of worldly practice. Thus, we need boldly defined commitments, but we also have to improvise and experiment as we seek to systemically and structurally enact these commitments. In many places, as the M4BL platform emphasizes, such experiments are already ongoing. Large-scale social movements, then, have to incorporate fundamentally such experiments into their own vision of social empowerment and political organizing.

---

[10] I recognize that this is a partially empirical claim, which has to be substantiated by quantitative and scientific studies into the nature of consciousness raising in the ways that I am suggesting here. For an example of this kind of work, see Freelon et al. (2016). In the view of these authors, one way through which movements like M4BL are good at shifting conversation at the level of mainstream is through mobilizing in large numbers and efficaciously on social media.

For this reason, and those that I have summarily elaborated earlier, M4BL and its platform offer an invaluable case study in envisioning real anti-racist utopias, and for materializing such utopias on the basis of a fundamental commitments to experimentation, in practice and action, with what morally works and what does not.

5. Objections and conclusion

In recent years, political philosophers have begun to question long-standing methodological approaches to questions concerning the nature of justice. More specifically, many theorists have begun to question the role that political theorizing can and should play in guiding various forms of action in the real world. These debates around the proper relationship between theory and action have given rise to a "methodological turn" in the field of political philosophy—away from highly abstract and ideal forms of theorizing about justice, and toward approaches that are ostensibly relevant to real-world politics. As you may recall, earlier I suggested that the origin of this methodological turn can be found in ongoing debates about ideal versus nonideal approaches to justice, and the respective merits and demerits of these approaches. A detailed discussion of the convoluted nature of this debate is beyond the scope of this paper. But let me briefly discuss some of the way in which we can profitably distinguish ideal from nonideal theory.

Among other features, a theory can be plausibly described as ideal if it helps itself to assumption of full compliance—the presumption that the people to whom the theory applies will invariably do what the theory asks of them. Naturally, critics of ideal theory charge that this is an idealization, insofar as people in the real world are far more complicated and should not be expected to always comply with what is requested of them. As some authors have noted, however, full compliance may be neither sufficient nor necessary to distinguish some theory as ideal. Colin Farrelly, for example, has recently (2007) made just this point, arguing that instead of full compliance, we regard inappropriate insensitivity to facts as the defining feature of ideal theory. In Farrelly's view, this kind of fact insensitivity involves idealization, and all forms of idealizing fundamentally rely on assumptions about the nature of reality that are false.[11] Assuming full compliance is one example of

---

[11] Farrelly's distinction, as Zofia Stemplowska (2008) points out, relies on a distinction that was introduced by Onora O'Neill (1987) between abstraction and idealization. Abstracting is a way of

such forms of idealizing, but not necessarily the only kind that ideal theorists may be committed to.[12] For Farrelly, in any case, what distinguishes many forms of ideal theorizing as ideal, including the views of moderate ideal theorists like Rawls, is a robust form of insensitivity to the circumstances of the real world.

For nonideal theorists, however, we cannot design our normative theories independently of such realities; rather we have to take real-world limitations and constraints into the design of our normative principles. In the view of these theorists, such as Charles Mills (2005) most notably, this is where ideal theory will always and invariably come up short. Ideal theorists primarily devise their principles of justice independently of the status quo, and at the expense of prioritizing that which is counterfactually desirable. But our theories of justice have to be *both* attuned to the realities of the status quo and propose counterfactual visions of a desirable world, or else their recommendations will be irrelevant. And in some cases, in fact (sorry!), their recommendations might even further entrench the very injustices that they ultimately seek to uproot and alter.

This brings us to a potential objection to my view. If ideal theory entails theorizing about justice in ways that are foundationally insensitive to extant circumstances of the world and, moreover, is the kind of theorizing whose recommendations are seldom achievable, could it be the case that I have here committed ideal theory? After all, I have argued that utopias should play an important part in getting experiments of emancipatory change off the ground and in ensuring their successes. But, as you also might recall, utopias are definitionally places from nowhere. Along these lines, a potential criticism of my view might emphasize that utopias are fundamentally idealized visions of a desirable world. And if we are incorporating such idealized visions into our conceptions of a better world, and doing so at an important level of normative analysis, are we not proposing theories that are founded on false assumptions about the nature of reality? This is the essence of Mills's critique of ideal theory, where he argues that ideal theory cannot substantively engage with the normative problems of our world, because it is

---

zooming out from the granular complexities of some problem without assuming any falsehoods. Idealizing, however, refers to the kind of theorizing that makes false assumptions.

[12] As Farrelly puts it, liberal theorists that function at the level of ideal theory might adopt, in place of full compliance, "cost blind" approaches to rights, or overly narrow conceptions of human misfortune (2007: 844–848).

founded on false assumptions about the nature of persons and the world. Is it possible that my account similarly lacks normative seriousness?

In responding to this valuable criticism, I propose that we go back to Mills and look at how he disambiguates what "ideal" can mean for normative theorizing. First, there is the sense of "ideal" that applies to all of moral theorizing, insofar as moral theory is ultimately a normative endeavor concerned with issues of evaluative and prescriptive significance. This is the sense *of ideal-as-normative* that Mills claims is both unavoidable and theoretically innocuous in moral theorizing, because it fundamentally grounds the enterprise of normative analysis. However, there is a further sense of "ideal," which Mills refers to as *ideal-as-idealized-model*, and subsequently contrasts with *ideal-as-descriptive-model*. The latter, in the view that Mills develops, tells us accurately how a system *actually* works, whereas the former tells us how the system *should* work. For example, in producing a descriptively ideal model of how our political institutions presently work, we have to acknowledge that they work largely to the benefit of the rich and powerful few. Of course, this is not how these institutions *should* operate; they should instead work to the fair benefit of all. As such, we can posit these democratic ambitions as articulable principles to which we should conform our actions to make the world better. To develop and defend principles of how the world ought to be structured around egalitarian ideals is not, even on Mills's own account, in and of itself ideologically worrisome.

In Mills's view, however, much of ideal theorizing has long been analytically stuck in *only* the discussion of such issues—that is, ideal theorists persistently abstract away from the workings of actual institutions of social and political life, as they currently are set up, to focus instead and exclusively on how we *should* guide our actions and ourselves to make the world an ideally just place. In doing so, Mills contends, ideal theory goes to extreme lengths to develop idealized social ontologies of persons, unrealistic epistemologies of belief and knowledge formation, strict compliance theories of ideal ethical conduct, and impossible-to-navigate maps of political action and interaction. In this ideal theoretical cosmos, ultimately, all we have to do is identify the right ideals, and graft these ideals onto idealized ontological, epistemological, and ethical commitments, and justice will supposedly ensue.

But, as Mills forcefully argues, this is a deeply bizarre way to approach the project of achieving justice. The central plank of Mills's critique of ideal theory is that such theories ideologically obscure the ways in which the actual institutions and structures of everyday life are set up to perpetuate the oppression of marginalized groups:

> Almost by definition, it follows from the focus of ideal theory that little or nothing will be said on actual historic oppression and its legacy in the present, or current ongoing oppression, though these may be gestured at in a vague or promissory way [. . .] Correspondingly, the ways in which systematic oppression is likely to shape the basic social institutions (as well as the humans in those institutions) will not be part of the theory's concern. (2005: 168–169)

In other words, ideal theory is fundamentally an inadequate way of theorizing about matters of justice, because it neglects to engage critically with the historical and ongoing realities of oppression, marginalization, subordination, violence, exploitation, and wholesale disenfranchisement.

Does any of this apply to my view? The answer, as I hope to have demonstrated in this chapter, is no. My account of realistic utopias is grounded in the specific need for *urgently* tackling everyday injustices. The realities of injustice and oppression take center stage in utopian theorizing about the ways in which the status quo can be challenged and dismantled. In a similar vein, the activists and organizers, on whose work I have drawn, are not merely articulating idealized visions of what the world ought to look like. Rather, activist work is spurred and driven by the recognition that something has to be done here and now. The urgencies of our situation are too grave for gradualist and incremental solutions, and the same holds for counterfactually unrealistic proposals.

For example, the M4BL platform aims to "intervene in the current political climate and assert a clear vision, particularly of those that claim to be our allies, of the world that we want them to help us create" (2020). M4BL is explicitly organized around the need for responding to such forms of suffering, and for supporting the work of those that are seriously and practically committed to uprooting the structures that inflict and perpetuate such suffering. And at the heart of the movement's vision, very importantly, lies the recognition that business as usual, in the actual real world, can no longer be tolerated, especially as large numbers of people continue to suffer preventable injustices. This recognition informs their realistic utopianism, which proposes to address oppression and its consequences through detailed platforms whose visions, if there is political will and collective willingness, are viably achievable.

References

Anderson, Elizabeth (2014). *Social Movements, Experiments in Living, and Moral Progress: Case Studies from Britain's Abolition of Slavery*. https://kuscholarworks.ku.edu/bitstream/handle/1808/14787/Anderson_Social_Movements.pdf.

Duster, Alfreda M. (ed.) (1970). *Crusade for Justice: The Autobiography of Ida B. Wells*. Chicago: University of Chicago Press.

Estlund, David (2014). "Utopophobia." *Philosophy & Public Affairs* 42 (2): 113–134.

Farrelly, Colin (2007). "Justice in Ideal Theory: A Refutation." *Political Studies* 55 (4): 844–864.

Freelon, Deen, Charlton McIlwain, and Meredith Clark (2018). "Quantifying the Power and Consequences of Social Media Protest." *New Media & Society* 20 (3): 990–1011.

French, David (2016). "Black Lives Matter Keeps Getting More Radical—Will the Media Care?" https://www.nationalreview.com/2016/08/black-lives-matter-media-left-radical/.

King Jr., Martin Luther (1960). *Suffering and Faith*. https://kinginstitute.stanford.edu/king-papers/documents/suffering-and-faith.

King Jr., Martin Luther (1963). *Letter from a Birmingham Jail*. https://www.africa.upenn.edu/Articles_Gen/Letter_Birmingham.html.

Levitas, Ruth (2013). *Utopia as Method: The Imaginary Reconstitution of Society*. New York: Palgrave MacMillan.

Mills, Charles W. (2005). "'Ideal Theory' as Ideology." *Hypatia* 20 (3): 165–184.

The Movement for Black Lives (2016). *Platform*. https://web.archive.org/web/20170205032409/https://policy.m4bl.org/platform/.

The Movement for Black Lives (2020). *Preamble*. https://m4bl.org/policy-platforms/the-preamble/.

O'Neill, Onora (1987). "Abstraction, Idealization and Ideology in Ethics." *Moral Philosophy and Contemporary Problems*. Ed. J. D. G. Evans. Royal Institute of Philosophy Supplements (22): 55–69.

Rawls, John (1999). *The Law of Peoples*. Cambridge, MA: Harvard University Press.

Stemplowska, Zofia (2008). "What's Ideal about Ideal Theory?" *Social Theory and Practice* 34 (3): 319–340.

Valentini, Laura (2012). "Ideal vs. Non-Ideal Theory: A Conceptual Map." *Philosophy Compass* 7 (9): 654–664.

Wilde, Oscar (1891). *The Soul of Man under Socialism*. https://www.marxists.org/reference/archive/wilde-oscar/soul-man/

Wright, Erik Olin (2010). *Envisioning Real Utopias*. London: Verso.

Young, Iris Marion (1990). *Justice and the Politics of Difference*. Princeton, NJ: Princeton University Press.

Young, Iris Marion (2006). "Responsibility and Global Justice: A Social Connection Model." *Social Philosophy and Policy* 23 (1): 102–130.

Index

For the benefit of digital users, indexed terms that span two pages (e.g., 52–53) may, on occasion, appear on only one of those pages.

Tables are indicated by *t* following the page number.

African-American Vernacular English, 180
All lives matter. *See* slogans
Anderson, Elizabeth, 148–51, 155, 288–91
apartheid, 119–22
authority
   collective, 149–50
   hate speech and, 151–53
   legal authority to punish, 219, 220–22
   moral, 139–40, 145, 147, 148–53, 154–56, 184–85, 289
   political, 289
   social, 265–67, 269, 273

Baker, Ella, 243, 249–51, 257
Baldus, David, 203, 204
Baldwin, James, 43–44
belief, 39–48, 55
Bell, Derrick, 31–32
Black boys, 59–60, 73–79
Black Lives Matter (organization), 1, 2–4, 6, 10, 18–33, 35–36, 55, 56–57, 59, 60–64, 68–69, 71, 133–34, 139, 145, 162, 167–68, 169, 172–73, 187–88, 199, 243–44, 246, 247–60, 270–71
   marketing/branding, 63–65
   platform, 93–94, 105, 110, 211
Black Lives Matter (slogan). *See* slogans
#BlackLivesMatter, 184
Black men, 59–61, 68, 69–70, 71, 72–75, 76–78, 80, 82–84
Black power, 163–64, 166–67, 169, 170
Black women, 68–69, 74–75
Boxill, Bernard, 103, 147, 153
Brown Jr., Michael, 61–62, 65, 181, 280–81

capital punishment
   abolition of, 209–14
   empirical research on, 199–200, 201, 203, 204–8
   history of jurisprudence, 200–4
   implicit bias and, 200, 204–5
capitalism, 35, 36–37, 38, 51–52, 55, 64
   racial (*see* racial capitalism)
Castile, Philando, 68–69
Cavell, Stanley, 21–23
chants, used by Movement for Black Lives, 178–80, 179*t*
civil rights, 15–16
Civil Rights Act of 1964, 116–17, 125, 126–27, 128–29, 131–32
   civil rights movement, 15–16, 48, 61–62, 63–64, 80–81, 116–17, 144, 150, 161, 187–88, 283
class (socio economic), 61, 63–65
collective care (community care), 257–58, 259
colonialism, 95, 98, 105
Combahee River Collective, 257
comparative justice, 211–14
conversational background (common ground), 142–43, 265–66, 269
Crenshaw, Kimberlé, 70–73

death penalty. *See* capital punishment
decarceration, 218, 219, 220–22, 223, 224, 225, 237
decentralization, 61–62, 247–53, 254, 257–58, 260, 293
demagoguery, 141, 143–44, 156
Democratic Party (US), 63, 66–67

distributive justice, 95, 107–9, 149–50, 212–13, 221
domination, 249–50
Du Bois, W.E.B, 49, 50–51, 143, 144, 147, 243–44
Dussel, Enrique, 244–45

Eighth Amendment to the United States Constitution, 200–2
empowerment, 106
Engels, Friedrich, 37, 41, 45–47, 55
equal status, 8, 17, 25, 44–45, 103, 141–42, 154–55, 161, 169, 200–1, 203, 212–14
equality, 11, 31, 52–53, 96–97, 122–23, 133, 140, 161, 221, 249, 294
    civic, 146
    legal, 146–47, 169, 200–1, 203, 212–14

false consciousness, 36–48, 50–53, 54, 55
Fanon, Frantz, 178, 243, 257–59
Ferguson, MO, 15, 61–62, 64, 65–66, 69, 154, 243, 250, 253–54, 260, 263–64, 270–71, 275, 276, 278, 280–81
Floyd, George, 67–79, 93
Fourteenth Amendment to the United States Constitution, 200–1
Freeman, Jo, 252–53, 254–55

Garza, Alicia, 1, 15, 18–24, 30, 32, 59, 61–63, 70–71, 73, 80–81, 167–69, 178, 247, 252, 254, 255
gender discrimination, 77–78

Hampton, Fred, 62
harm, 96–101
hashtags, 183–84, 191–92, 193
hate speech, 151–53
historical materialism, 41
human rights, 118

ideal theory, 284–85, 295–98
ideology, 35, 36, 37, 38–39, 41, 45, 51–52
    racist ideology, 44–45, 48, 50, 53, 54, 55
implicit bias, 200, 204–8, 232–33, 273–75
inequality, 5–6, 20–21, 76–77, 118–19, 122, 130–31, 144, 149–50, 164, 182, 221–22, 224–25, 237–38, 269, 283
    See also equality

injustice
    epistemic, 186, 271–72
    structural, 118, 204–5, 269
intersectionality, 67–68, 70–71
    intersectional invisibility, 76–78

Jim Crow, 122–24
justice, 291
    distributive (see distributive justice)
    procedural (see procedural justice)
    restorative (see reparations)
    retributive (see retributive justice)
    transitional (see transitional justice)

Khan-Cullors, Patrisse, 9–10, 15, 19, 61–63, 139, 147, 178, 243, 247, 250–51, 252, 255–56
King Jr., Martin Luther, 48–49, 52–53, 62, 105–6, 161, 166–67
Kramer, Matthew, 207

leader-full (leaderless), 176–77, 243, 246, 247–49, 250–55, 256–57, 259–60
Lebron, Christopher, 61–62, 178
Lewis, Christopher, 222–23, 224–25
liberation, 7–8, 35, 53–54, 83–84, 129–30, 177, 193, 244–45, 259–60, 272–73, 281, 285–86, 287, 290
    Black liberation, 2, 9–10, 11, 63–64, 66–67, 71, 93–94, 105–6, 176–77, 243–44, 247–49, 252, 255–57
    class liberation, 71
    liberatory and emancipatory agendas, 281, 285
Locke, John, 102–3
lynching, 123, 131–33

Mandela, Nelson, 121, 125–26
Martin, Mike W., 168
Martin, Trayvon, 61–62
Marx, Karl, 35, 36–37, 39, 41–42, 55
Marxism, 63
Mass Action for Black Liberation, 255
Mills, Charles, 293–98
moral experiments, 281–82, 286–92, 293–95, 296–97
Movement for Black Lives (platform), 1, 5, 7–8, 93–94, 105, 106, 110–12, 113,

116, 145, 176, 177, 193–94, 199–200, 204–5, 210–11, 213–14, 237–38, 247, 250–52, 263, 264, 270–71, 280–81, 284

Nigeria, 93
non-ideal theory, 284–85, 295, 296
nonviolence (nonviolent model), 252, 259–60
norms of assertion, 267–70

police/policing, 2, 4–5, 56–57, 59–84, 93–94, 125–27, 133, 145, 146, 161–63, 164, 167, 170, 179–80, 181, 182, 184, 185–86, 188–92, 193–94, 199, 203, 204–5, 211–13, 218, 232–33, 243, 250, 259, 271, 274–75, 276, 280–81
    police violence, 1, 7–8, 60–62, 65, 69, 70, 71–74, 76–77, 80–81, 173–74, 177, 183, 188–90, 193–94, 199, 270–71
political jiu-jitsu, 187–88, 193–94
pragmatics, 139–59, 263–79
prejudice, 162, 166–67, 186, 201, 204–7, 233
procedural justice, 225, 237–38
propaganda, 37, 45–46, 120–21, 141–48, 156
    positive, 140, 143–48
protest, 2, 6–8, 15–17, 27–28, 56, 59–60, 63–64, 65, 68–69, 93, 119–20, 125, 127–28, 131, 133, 144–56, 165–71, 178–79, 180–81, 186, 199, 243, 250, 254, 270–71
    protest language, 1, 180, 188
provocation, 153–56
punishment
    leniency in, 219–20, 234–35

racial capitalism, 35, 36, 44–45, 50–51
racial discrimination, 8, 103, 105, 117, 122–23, 128, 131–33, 182, 192, 199–200, 201–5, 206–7, 208–11, 212–14, 230–32, 236, 249–50
racial prejudice. *See* prejudice
racism, 35, 36–37, 38, 39–40, 43–46, 48, 50, 53–54, 55, 56
Ransby, Barbara, 2, 61–62, 243, 249, 250–51, 253–54
rape of Black people, 59–61, 74–75

reasonableness in public discourse, 141–42, 143–44, 156
reparations, 96–101, 132–33
    constructive view of, 95, 107, 108–12
Republic of New Afrika, 95, 109–10
retributive justice, 212–13
Russell, Tory, 65–66

second-personal calls, 149–51
self-determination, 94, 95, 105, 106–7
Shelby, Tommie, 46, 220–22, 224
slavery/trans-Atlantic slave trade, 94–95, 99–100
slogans, 6–7, 35–36, 53, 56–57, 62–63, 146–47, 152–53, 161, 162, 165–74
    All lives matter (also ALM), 6–7, 20, 22, 146–47, 156, 161–65, 166–68, 170–71, 173, 185, 264
    Black lives matter (also BLM), 6–7, 18–33, 35–36, 53–54, 62–63, 139–40, 145–46, 147, 156, 160–74, 177, 182–83, 264
social movements, 7–8, 10–11, 37, 61–62, 95, 105, 116–17, 125–28, 144, 148–53, 156, 165–71, 180, 181–83, 185–86, 187–88, 189, 193, 243, 246, 248–49, 251–56, 281–82, 283, 286–87, 289, 290–91, 292–94
solidarity engagement, 263–79
South Africa, 119–22, 125–26, 129–31
speech acts, 264, 267–70
Stanley, Jason, 140–45, 146, 149, 153, 156, 176n.1
stereotypes, 37, 50, 53, 68–70, 82, 119–20, 142, 182, 186, 190, 191–92, 205, 207, 233, 244
    engineering, 193–94
structural injustice. *See* injustice

Taifa, Nkechi, 106, 109–10
Taylor, Keeanga-Yamahtta, 2, 243, 246, 250
Taylor, Paul C., 166
Tometi, Opal, 61–62, 247, 252, 254, 255
transitional justice, 116, 128–34
Truth and Reconciliation Commission of South Africa, 129–31
Truth Telling Project, 270–77

utopia, 281, 282, 284–88, 292–94, 295, 296–97
  realistic utopia, 281–82, 285, 288, 290–92, 298

violence, 68–69, 70–71
  decolonization, 257–59
  naming dead victims, 190–92
  state violence, 93, 243, 256–57

well-being, 255–60

white Americans, 64, 68–69
white supremacy, 119, 122–23, 165, 190
Wittgenstein, Ludwig, 21–23
Woodson, Carter G., 244–45
Wright, Eric Olin, 286–88
Wright, Richard, 123–24

Young, Iris Marion, 249–50

Zimmerman, George, 15, 17

Printed and bound by CPI Group (UK) Ltd, Croydon, CR0 4YY